Advanced Graphics in C:
Programming and Techniques

D1568324

Nelson Johnson

Osborne **McGraw-Hill**
Berkeley, California

Osborne **McGraw-Hill**
2600 Tenth Street
Berkeley, California 94710
U.S.A.

For information on translations and book distributors outside
of the U.S.A., please write to Osborne **McGraw-Hill** at the
above address.

A complete list of trademarks appears on page 661.

Advanced Graphics in C: Programming and Techniques

Copyright © 1987 by McGraw-Hill, Inc. All rights reserved.
Printed in the United States of America. Except as permitted
under the Copyright Act of 1976, no part of this publication may
be reproduced or distributed in any form or by any means, or
stored in a database or retrieval system, without the prior written permission of the publisher, with the exception that the
program listings may be entered, stored, and executed in a
computer system, but they may not be reproduced for publication.

7 8 9 10 11 12 DOC/DOC 9 9 8 7 6 5 4 3 2 1 0

ISBN 0-07-881257-7

Jeffrey Pepper, Acquisitions Editor
Herbert Schildt, Technical Reviewer
Fran Haselsteiner, Project Editor
Nancy Leahong, Text Design

This book is dedicated to my wife, Shelley. She is gifted with common sense, warmth, tolerance, kindness, and rare intelligence. Thanks also to my son, Stefan, who gave up a lot of our shared time. Without their loving help this book might never have been written.

You gotta know when to code 'em, know when to modem, know
when to load 'em up, know when to run.
You don't count your money when you're sittin' at the keyboard.
There'll be plenty time for countin' when the program's done.

—Anonymous

Contents

Introduction   xi

1   Graphics Programming   1

Principles of Successful Graphics Programming
The Top-Down Philosophy
Misconceptions About Top-Down Programming
Graphics Programming Tips
Graphic Coding Style

2   Graphics Software Design   15

Setting Display Modes and Pages
Enhanced Graphics Modes on the EGA
Using Debug to Draw Lines
Beginning to Use C for Graphics
Parts of a Graphics Program in C
Structure Flow Diagrams
Memory Models
Other Display Buffers

3   GRAPHIQ: A Prototypical Application   47

GRAPHIQ Program Description
Supported Devices
Database Design
GRAPHIQ File Structure
Limitations of GRAPHIQ
Suggestions for Improving GRAPHIQ

4   Graphics Algorithms   63

Coordinate Systems
Drawing Elements
Line Algorithm
Circle Algorithm
Drawing Arcs
Fill Algorithm
Crosshatching
Dithering
Clipping
Shape Tables
Using Algorithms to Generate C Code

5   Transformations   125

Objects
Rotation
Translation
Scaling
Combined Transformations
Projection
General Notes for Coding Transformation Functions

6   Edit Mode   147

Functions Used in Editing
Menus and Commands Used in Editing
Drawing a Point
Drawing Lines
Drawing Circles and Arcs
Drawing Boxes
Filling Boxes
Complex Fills
Lines, Circles, Boxes, and Fills in Combination
Using a Brush
Copying
Editing Orchestration

7   **Text Mode**   213

The ASCII Character Set
Stroke Fonts

8   **Printing and Plotting**   245

Printing Drawings
Plotting Drawings
Orchestrating Printing and Plotting Functions

9   **Menu Design**   283

Creating Menus
Selecting from Menus
Fast Menu-Display Techniques
Keyboard Interaction

10   **Locators**   321

Locator Design
Coding Locators

11   **Parallel and Serial Interfacing**   341

Parallel Ports
Serial Ports

12   **Maintenance Modes**   387

Functions in Context
Program Startup and Termination
Files for Drawings and Commands

13   **Graphics Documentation**   417

Graphics Task Differentiation
Graphics Programs for Your Own Use
Graphics Programs for Individual Clients
Graphics Programs for the Mass Market
Graphics Icons and Words

14 **Using the Compiler** **433**

The Microsoft C Compiler
The Graphics Toolkit

15 **Linking the Toolkit** **453**

Creating a Library
Using the Linker

A **GRAPHIQ Source Code Listing** **471**

How to Use the GRAPHIQ Source Code
GRAPHIQ Source Code
GRAPHIQ Headers

B **GRAPHIQ Command Syntax** **613**

General Functional Description

C **Optimizing Using Assembler** **623**

D **Making Commands Accessible** **637**

E **Television Graphics** **639**

Using a Video Camera
The Transfer Algorithm
Raster Output to Disk
Raster Input from Disk
The TRANSFER.C Program
Other Sources of Information

Index **662**

Acknowledgments

A book is the product of experience, and experience is never gained in a vacuum. The efforts of a host of people go into the education of an author. The author owes much to those who have been kind enough to provide that education.

I owe a great deal to Bryan Higgins, a superior programmer, who helped me understand 8086 assembler and opened my eyes to the C language. More directly, he provided me with an incredible text editor, EMAX, that was used to write this book. The sophisticated buffering and fast editing characteristics of EMAX made possible the rapid development of GRAPHIQ. I would also like to acknowledge the friendship and support of Emil Flock, of Computer Handholding, who suggested that I might be able to write a book on graphics in C language. Without the kind guidance of Tony Crispino and Jim Gordon, of Number Cruncher Microsystems, I would probably still be working in one big subdirectory. They gave me an understanding of the dynamics of DOS. Until Liz Fisher and Jeff Pepper of

Osborne/McGraw-Hill helped me understand the editing process I didn't fully realize how valuable and necessary professional editing can be.

The origin of much of my work over the last 12 years can be credited to Lou and Genevieve Katz, who, at Columbia University, decided that architectural students could and should know something about computers. Their foresight and imagination guided this student to graphics programming and the creation of the MicroCAD software.

—Nelson L. Johnson
January 22, 1987

Introduction

Years ago, computer graphics were considered unnecessary, impractical, or too expensive. Not so today. Hardware and software are beginning to be fast enough and powerful enough to make graphics not only feasible but essential. The emergence of desktop publishing integrates graphics with text in modern computing. Soon database applications will routinely include images as well as text.

The kinds of tasks we use computers to perform are changing. At one time computers were used primarily for accounting, but now they are used for everything you can imagine. Analytical software depends on graphics to reveal everything from flaws in metals to weather patterns to the properties of geologic formations. Graphics systems are used in graphic arts, medical, scientific, robotics, security, and quality control applications. Drafting, business planning, and design applications are flourishing.

This book is designed to give you the general concepts you need to program graphics in C. The source code for a practical graphics system called GRAPHIQ, written specifically for this book, follows in Appendix A. Each of the program's functions is explained individually. Together they provide a **toolkit** of functions that help you program for graphics on the IBM Enhanced Graphics Adapter (EGA) and the AT&T Image Capture Board (ICB). Toolkits are particularly valuable for an open-ended language like C. They add an ever-expanding functional richness to the language.

This book also contains many techniques that will increase your understanding of the complex field of graphics software development. Algorithms used in graphics programming, graphics editing, hard-copy creation, user access, and communications, as well as the design of effective documentation, are covered in detail. When appropriate, these areas are related to specific functions in GRAPHIQ.

In addition to detailed graphics functions, you will find useful tools needed for sophisticated graphics programming and production. These include general-purpose functions that support serial and parallel input/output, pop-up menus, and graphics text. A complete graphics text font is provided in source form. *Advanced Graphics in C* also includes interfacing techniques for many devices, including printers, plotters, digitizers, and mice.

Appendix A presents all the functions of GRAPHIQ as one integrated program. Because most of the functions and tools presented in this book are used in GRAPHIQ, by studying this program you can learn how they can be made to work together. GRAPHIQ also demonstrates how graphics programming is intimately involved with the entire computer system. Even if you are not primarily interested in graphics programming, you will find useful information in this book.

The approach taken was intended to be generous, open, and sharing, rather than protective. It is hoped that presenting a graphics program from the inside out, in source code form, will cause many of the mysteries of graphics programming to disappear.

HOW MUCH DO YOU KNOW ABOUT C?

If you are just starting to program in C, you may find some of this book hard to understand. It is not intended to teach fundamentals. It is, rather, intended for the intermediate- to advanced-level C programmer who wants to know how to program for graphics.

If you are just beginning, however, this book may prove useful to you. By studying the complete program written in C language, GRAPHIQ, you may learn a great deal. As your knowledge of C increases, you will be able to understand how the functions presented here are constructed, as well as how to modify them when writing your own graphics programs.

HOW TO USE THIS BOOK

The information in this book is presented in two ways. You can read detailed explanations in the chapters, or you can read complete source code listings in the appendixes.

The first two chapters deal with graphics programming from a stylistic and conceptual point of view. You will find in these chapters some general rules for programming in C and for designing graphics software.

Chapter 3 introduces the GRAPHIQ program itself. This chapter explains the purpose behind GRAPHIQ and describes the program's general features.

Chapters 4 and 5 describe algorithms used in graphics programming. You will find algorithms for changing the colors of pixels, drawing lines, drawing circles, filling areas, and many other functions that are routinely used in graphics programming.

Chapters 6 and 7 discuss graphics editing (where most of the drawing actually takes place) and the creation of text. Chapter 7 describes how graphics text fonts can be created and stored.

Chapter 8 describes how graphics hardware and software can be used to create hard copy. You will see how to send graphics information to printers and plotters.

Chapters 9 and 10 are concerned with the way the computer system communicates with the user. Pop-up menus and locator crosshairs are described in detail. You will see how to move graphics and text quickly onto and off of the display surface.

Chapters 11 and 12 deal with the use of your computer's hardware for communication with the outside world. Detailed information is provided regarding serial and parallel ports. You will see how to save drawings on a floppy disk or hard disk and create command files to run your system by remote control, as it were.

Chapter 13 discusses the all-important but too often overlooked subject of documentation. The use of icons and commands as communication tools is discussed.

Chapters 14 and 15 show you how to use the Microsoft C compiler and linker. General techniques for compiling and linking are covered. In addition, the specific requirements for compiling and linking GRAPHIQ are presented.

The appendixes contain the complete source code listing for GRAPHIQ, including a command summary and helpful hints on using your C compiler to help you program in assembler. The new field of video programming is discussed, including some useful routines you can use with the ICB to transfer images between it and the EGA.

If you wish to use the functions in this book on hardware other than the IBM PC with an EGA, you can do so with relative ease. Because the toolkit in this book is provided in source code form, you will be able to make the necessary changes.

New standards are emerging daily. In graphics, "standards" are so profuse they can hardly be called standards at all. Because there is no current consensus as to which standard hardware and software to use, it is impossible to provide and maintain complete compatibility across all devices.

The toolkit source code that was developed as part of this book is available to you on disk, including an executable copy of GRAPHIQ and a library of object modules. If you are interested in ordering a copy, please use the coupon that follows, or send $21.95 (California residents add 6 1/2% sales tax) to

Imagimedia Technologies
P.O. Box 210308
San Francisco, California 94121-0308

Advanced Graphics in C
Disk Offer

The functions and programs described in this book are
available on a 5-1/4 inch IBM PC disk in PC-DOS format. If
you wish to receive this disk send your check or money order
in the amount of $21.95 (which includes shipping and
handling) to:

Imagimedia Technologies, Inc.
PO Box 210308
San Francisco, CA 94121-0308

(California residents add 6-1/2 percent sales tax)

Name _____
              (please print or type)

Address _____

City _____ State _____ Zip _____

Telephone number _____

Amount enclosed _____ US dollars

1

Graphics Programming

Programming can be accomplished by intuition or by plan. The best method for approaching a programming project is to apply your intuition under control of a well-conceived structure. Graphics programs tend to be more complex than non-graphics programs. For this reason they can be harder to create, harder to standardize, and harder to use. By beginning with a clear concept in mind, however, you will go a long way toward minimizing the confusion graphics software can generate.

In this book you will find detailed information about programming for graphics in the C language. Because this book is oriented toward intermediate to advanced C programmers, many terms are assumed to be understood without the need for elaborate definition. No attempt will be made to educate you in the fundamentals of the C language, except as they pertain to intermediate and advanced graphics concepts. If, for example, you wish a clear definition of what "function," "offset," or "argument" means, you should consult your favorite text on the C language.

PRINCIPLES OF SUCCESSFUL GRAPHICS PROGRAMMING

The principles of successful graphics programming are not fundamentally different from the principles of successful programming in general. Systems that are based strictly on text benefit from the fact that the C language, like the program product, is used in text form. Graphics applications are different. You will be using code in the form of text to draw points, lines, and other graphical constructions that are not text. Because of the confusion this can create, you will need to emphasize structure in your code even more than you would if your product's output were limited to text.

Be Persistent   The first principle of successful programming is persistence. If you are interested in what you are doing, it will not be hard to muster the passion to stick to the task. Graphics problems are less obvious than problems involving only text. It can take longer and be more frustrating to debug graphics programs.

Structure Your Programs   The second principle of successful programming is the wise use of **structure.** The computer program is built from the general to the specific. Like a building, it begins with a simple concept that is expressed in greater and greater detail until you are able to walk around within a real structure of concrete, wood, or steel.

Of course, a building could have been built in many ways. You might have a pile of wood in your backyard and nail something together using scraps from this and parts from that, improvising as you go along. The result might be a structure built from the "bottom up" and might be expected to look that way. It would stand a good chance of being unsafe as well, because no thought was given to how the lower part of the building would support the upper part. In short, it would have been *built* but not *designed*.

Design is the process of bringing something into being through the use of a plan, of marking out or defining something. The German concept of "Das Ein," meaning "therein-ness," expresses another nuance of design. In designing something you ask yourself what it wants to be.

Divide and Conquer   The third principle of successful programming is to "divide and conquer." In the fourteenth century William of Ockham, a British scholastic philosopher, when he wasn't trying to turn lead into gold formulated a principle that has come to be known as "Occam's Razor." (The spelling has been corrupted over the years.) According to Occam's Razor, any problem can be divided into parts in such a way that by solving all of the parts separately you will solve the entire problem. The design of the C language is basically driven by this concept. In C you are encouraged to break your program down into a collection of more-or-less isolated functions that are designed and tested separately. This feature is fundamental to the implementation of the **top-down** approach to programming.

THE TOP-DOWN PHILOSOPHY

The programs in this book are designed with the philosophy of top-down programming in mind. The top-down approach works well for graphics because it helps organize very abstract, nonverbal concepts.

Experience has shown that, like buildings, programs designed from the top down are much more successful and safer than those designed the other way around or those not designed at all. The philosophy of top-down programming helps the programmer think of the overall design purpose of a piece of software rather than hoping that an assembly of miscellaneous functions (a kludge) will turn out to be useful for something.

The Problem Statement

The top-down approach begins with a statement of the problem to be solved. For example, a problem in graphics might involve the need to see a graph of stock highs, lows, and closing prices for a given month. You might have a disk that contains the price data and need to convert these numbers into a chart that shows price as a vertical distance and time as a horizontal distance.

In this example you can see that the statement of need — the problem statement — contains the input and output requirements for the program. Input will be from a file of stock prices and dates. Output will be to a display "surface" that can show a graphical representation of stock prices over time.

You need not know what that surface will be. It could be a computer display, a piece of paper, a slide, or almost anything on which graphics can be presented, but it isn't necessary to know its final form this early in the design process. What goes on between input and output is the substance of the application.

Know the Goals You Wish to Achieve

It is impossible to know how to begin the design of an application without knowing the goals you wish to achieve. A well-designed program is like an onion. At its outermost layer, you can see the entire program. As you strip off layers, you descend into its depths by a hierarchy of paths, and you ascend back to the surface by that same hierarchy. To evolve such a hierarchy, you must clearly define your goals.

The statement of a problem contains within it the solution to the problem. You can see that this is true in your daily life. To solve a problem you need only concentrate on gaining an accurate understanding of everything about the problem. In doing so you inevitably come up with goals. If you keep the goals you wish to achieve clearly in mind throughout the design process, your applications will be clean and appropriate.

MISCONCEPTIONS ABOUT TOP-DOWN PROGRAMMING

Over the years some misconceptions about the use of top-down, structured programming have developed. Two of the most common of these are discussed here.

Begin-End Orientation

One misconception involving the top-down approach is that the programmer should not be concerned with the end product in the early stages of design, the theory being that the end will naturally evolve out of the process of "becoming."

The correct implementation of the top-down philosophy is to think of the program as a hierarchy of nested functions. The outermost functions must contain the beginning and the ending of the program. To the outermost shell of functions is added the depth of detail that provides the substance of the application. The top-down process refers to the top and bottom of such depth, rather than to the beginning and ending of the program.

Top-Down Always

Another misconception regarding top-down programming is the assumption that everything is always done from the top down. In reality, the *design* of the application is done from the top to the bottom. The building (or coding) of the application is often done from the bottom up.

When the structure of a building is designed, it is always designed from the top down, as any structural engineer will attest. Obviously, the lower levels support the upper ones. The weight of the roof will contribute to the floor below, and the combined weights of the roof and floor below will contribute to the weight supported by the floor below that. When the building is built, however, it would be an expensive task indeed to begin construction with the roof under most circumstances. Similarly, the actual coding of an application often involves the construction of low-level input and output routines that dictate restrictions that must be placed on what can successfully be used as output.

GRAPHICS PROGRAMMING TIPS

In reading this book and using graphics functions, you may want to consider some techniques that have proven to be helpful over the years. Every programmer has his or her preferences in terms of programming tricks. These are a few that you may find useful.

Be Aware of Two Arithmetic Worlds

The concept of a **world** is important in graphics and has a special meaning. People often refer to the "outside world" or the "world view," using the word "world" to refer to any state or sphere of existence. In this book there are many worlds. When real numbers are used, for example, it means that part of the program is in a "world of reals." By using the world concept to your advantage, you will be able to keep in mind the principles that govern the separate parts of a graphics program at different times.

It is useful to keep in mind two kinds of arithmetic worlds. One of these is the world of **counts,** and the other is the world of **offsets.** A value in the world of offsets is *always* one integer less than a value in the world of counts! When you declare variables or count items, you use the world of counts. When you are trying to locate something in a file or in a string, you are in the world of offsets. For each number you intend to use in your program, it helps to ask yourself, "Is this a count, or is it an offset?"

For example, the width of a display may be 640 pixels. The display width is invariably a count, not an offset. You begin at offset 0 and end at offset 639. This seems obvious, but you can easily get confused in graphics programming unless you clearly separate these two types of number references.

Manipulate Memory Directly

There are two fundamentally different ways of putting pixels (points of light) on the display surface: through the BIOS (Basic Input/Output System) or by changing the graphics memory directly. Graphics programs need all the speed they can get.

Because going through the BIOS involves the extra step of generating an interrupt and is additionally slowed by decisions made in the BIOS that determine which adapter is in use, you should avoid the use of BIOS calls unless you cannot predict what display adapter will be used. The faster and preferable way is to use direct access to display RAM (random-access memory).

Because you are already experienced in C programming, it is assumed you know what RAM is, what the BIOS is, and how to generate an interrupt. If you don't, become familiar with these terms before reading further. There are many excellent texts on the fundamentals of C, assembler, and computer system architecture that you can consult.

Optimize Your C Code Using Assembler

Use your favorite techniques to optimize your C code at the assembler level. You can always generate an assembler listing and go through it, looking for ways to accomplish the same thing more quickly. This takes time, of course, but in graphics it can mean the difference between a slow program and a fast one. Graphics programs involve lots of operations repeated many times. If such operations are not optimized, the aggregate effect is a slow-running program. Concentrate on such functions as point() and block pixel moves in your optimization efforts.

Although this is a book on graphics programming in the C language, you will find that a knowledge of your machine's instruction set will make you a better programmer. In Appendix C, for the advanced reader, there are descriptions of the processes you might use to optimize your code using 8086 assembler.

Consider Compatibility Carefully

When the first IBM personal computers were introduced, many companies came out with products that were "almost compatible" with it. Today many of those vendors are out of business. The ones who decided early to be 100% compatible with IBM often survived.

When you design graphics systems, you will encounter many compatibility problems if you are not careful in your selection of display devices. It does not make sense to write software for hardware that no one will use.

Think of Programs as Commands

Your software may have fancy menus, but do not overlook the value of creating graphics commands that can be used from the DOS command level. The DOS and UNIX operating systems are designed to permit operations such as piping and redirection to chain commands together in complex ways. Don't isolate your graphics program from the operating system. Use the environment to make system-known parameters available. Read about piping, redirection of standard I/O, and the environment in your DOS manual if you are not familiar with these concepts.

Keep It Simple

Graphics programs have a tendency to get very complicated very fast. You should make a major effort to keep from going overboard in the use of color, pop-up menus, and other tricks that can obscure the usefulness of your software.

Use a Fast Screen-Write

Instead of using printf(), use sprintf() and pass a string pointer to a function that writes characters to the screen. This gives you as much control as you want over color and speed. For example, you might normally do the following to create a command prompt:

```
printf("Default filename: %s", filename);
```

Instead, use the following technique:

```
sprintf(buffer, "Default filename: %s", filename);
write__screen(buffer, x, y, RED, BLUE);
```

With this method, you will have control of the location of the prompt as well as its foreground and background colors. When you wish to write a simple string, omit sprintf() and pass the string pointer directly to write__screen(), your fast screen-writer function. Because printf(), sprintf(), and fprintf() require a lot of overhead, they tend to slow the process down.

Use Normalized Device Coordinates

Each display device you use will have its own width and height. If you wish to use more than one device in your graphics application (for example, a plotter and CRT display), you will need to use an NDC (normalized device coordinate) system.

With NDCs your program is separate from its drivers. You will have a driver for each display device. When you send the coordinates of a point out to the device, they will be in NDC units. When the device receives coordinates they will have been converted by the driver into actual device coordinates.

Your coordinate system might, for example, begin with 0,0 at the lower left corner and extend to 32,767 along both the x and y axes. All work in the system would be done using a range of values from 0 through 32,767 NDC units. When a selected device received coordinates expressed in these units, it would convert them to the units required for its own display resolution. For example, an EGA (Enhanced Graphics Adapter) would convert from a count of 32,768 units horizontally to a count of 640 units. Vertically it would convert from a count of 32,768 units to a count of 200 units.

Of course, to keep circles from turning into ellipses and squares from becoming rectangles, the device drivers must multiply the NDCs by scaling factors. Each device driver thus contains standard factors to convert from the 1:1 aspect ratio of NDC units to the ratio needed to work with its display surface.

Firmware

Use the **firmware** supplied on board any display adapter, plotter, or printer. It was put there to help you use the device efficiently. A well-designed device will have useful firmware built into it. Because firmware is coded in ROM (read-only memory), it is much faster than any RAM-based code would be. You can save yourself many headaches by simply using utilities that are already there, rather than reinventing the wheel.

GRAPHIC CODING STYLE

This book assumes certain stylistic conventions for coding. Although your style is your own, you will be better able to read the code contained herein if you know some of the assumptions that underly the coding style used in this book.

Appearance and Clarity

The way your code appears on the display has a lot to do with how easily you, and others, will be able to read it later on, when the project you are now working on is a thing of the past and you need to go back and modify it. Style, as opposed to substance, involves the *appearance* and *clarity* of your code. C is capable of such variety in usage that it is very easy to generate totally opaque code. As an example of the extremes in opacity, see Function 1-1, Beauty and the Beast.

Both examples of code express the same thing, but it is obvious which one can be read by a human being. Although extreme, the functions show how clarity and style can influence readability. Variable names clearly convey the use of each variable. The "beast" has no style at all but follows all the rules of C. The appearance of your code means a lot.

It is important to expand your understanding of the concept of *graphics* beyond thinking of it only as "pictures." Your use of style in coding is graphic in itself. Graphics embraces all aspects of the positioning of lighter areas against darker areas. In graphics one talks of lines and masses, of colors, of areas, and of forms. The text of a C program is certainly a written and logical expression, but it is also a grouping of masses of characters. The creative grouping of masses is a graphical process.

White Space

Made of space characters, line feeds, and tabs, white space should be used creatively and used often, especially between functions within the same file. White space is graphical in nature, and the use of indentation graphically shows how a purely logical hierarchy is controlled.

■ FUNCTION 1-1

Beauty and the Beast

```
BEAUTY:

main()
{
unsigned int albatross, marlin, whale;
char sea_string[81];
double stars_in_sky, fish_in_sea;

while(stars_in_sky > fish_in_sea)
    {
    save_whales(&albatross, &marlin, &whale);
    which_greater(&stars_in_sky, &fish_in_sea,
                 sea_string);
    }

printf("%s", sea_string);

}


THE BEAST:

main() { unsigned int albatross, marlin, whale;
char sea_string[81]; double stars_in_sky, fish_in_sea;
while(stars_in_sky > fish_in_sea) { save_whales(&albatross,
&marlin, &whale); which_greater(&stars_in_sky, &fish_in_sea,
sea_string); } printf("%s", sea_string); }
```

Variable Names

Use names for your variables that make their meanings clear. When the use of a variable changes, change its name accordingly.

Above all, don't be lazy. Develop your own style and use it consistently. No style is universally accepted. Some programmers like to indent everything one tab stop and then nest from there. Others like to put the left curly brace at the end of the initial argument rather than below it. As long as your code is readable by those who need to read it, the style is appropriate.

2

Graphics
Software Design

Structured programming for graphics involves the wise use of memory for storing graphics information. When you draw lines and other objects with a computer, you are actually manipulating the computer's memory. This has advantages and disadvantages compared with drawing on paper. The technique of drawing with a computer is by no means obvious, and it can be very constrained and unforgiving, yet if you master it you will be able to convert raw data into meaningful charts much more rapidly than by using manual methods. You will find graphics programming to be much different from drawing.

This chapter is an introduction to graphics memory management, the single most important aspect of graphics programming. Much of your effort in programming will be directed toward the use of your computer's memory as an output device. As you will see in this chapter, you change the colors of dots on the display surface by changing the contents of memory.

Although graphics programs use external devices, such as printers and plotters, to display graphics elements to the user, most often a program will be writing to and reading from a display buffer in memory. This is not the only use your programs will make of memory. There are many hidden structures that manage information both on and off the display.

SETTING DISPLAY MODES AND PAGES

Before getting into the details of display memory, you must be able to set display modes. The Enhanced Graphics Adapter (EGA) is capable of supporting several types of display, including simple color displays, IBM's Enhanced Color Display, the IBM Monochrome Display, and numerous clones of these devices. It is a very versatile product.

The EGA uses modes to govern its overall performance, depending on the display hardware you are using and the settings of switches. There is some ambiguity surrounding the use of the word "mode" in this book and in computer terminology in general. If you keep in mind that modes, globals, and system states are terms that define information that is known to the system (whether software or firmware) as a *whole,* you won't have difficulty understanding modes.

In order to enable the EGA to support a variety of devices, four completely new modes have been created in addition to those that were available on IBM's original Color/Graphics Adapter (CGA). The CGA supports modes 0 through 7. The four new modes, 13 through 16, enable graphics with enhancements including 16 colors (from a palette of 64), 640 by 350 resolution, and graphics on the Monochrome Display.

Table 2-1 shows the modes available with the EGA. Note that modes 8, 9, and 10 are omitted because they are not used by

the EGA. They are used by the IBM PC*jr*. If you are using a
PC*jr*, the functions in this book will still be useful if you make a
few modifications in accordance with your PC*jr* documentation. Modes 11 and 12 are used for the loading of text fonts. All
the other modes from 0 through 16 are available for your use,
depending on the availability of the necessary hardware.

```
EGA Mode
 | Text or Graphic
 |   | Display connected (Color, Enhanced or Mono)
 |   |   | Pages
 |   |   |   | Colors
 |   |   |   |   | Resolution (horiz x vert)
 |   |   |   |   |     | Characters (horiz x vert)
 |   |   |   |   |     |     | Cell (horiz x vert)
 |   |   |   |   |     |     |     |
```

EGA Mode	Text or Graphic	Display connected	Pages	Colors	Resolution (horiz x vert)	Characters (horiz x vert)	Cell (horiz x vert)	
0	T	C	8	16	320 x 200	40 x 25	8 x 8	64K
1	T	E	8	16/64	320 x 350	40 x 25	8 x 14	64K
2	T	C	8	16	640 x 200	80 x 25	8 x 8	64K
3	T	E	8	16/64	640 x 350	80 x 25	8 x 14	64K
4,5	G	C,E	1	4	320 x 200	40 x 25	8 x 8	64K
6	G	C,E	1	2	640 x 200	80 x 25	8 x 14	64K
7	T	M	8	4	720 x 350	80 x 25	9 x 14	64K
13	G	C,E	2 4 8	16	320 x 200	40 x 25	8 x 8	64K 128K 256K
14	G	C,E	1 2 4	16	640 x 200	80 x 25	8 x 8	64K 128K 256K
15	G	M	1 2	4	640 x 350	80 x 25	8 x 14	64K 128K
16	G	E	1/2 1 2	4/64 16/64 16/64	640 x 350	80 x 25	8 x 14	64K 128K 256K

Sources for data: IBM Technical Reference, PC Magazine

TABLE 2-1.   Modes of Operation for the EGA

If the switches aren't set properly, some modes will not be accessible, so be sure you have paid attention to the instructions in the EGA installation guide regarding the proper settings for the four switches at the back of the adapter.

The mode chosen for use in this book is mode 14, which gives 16 fixed colors and a resolution of 640 by 200 pixels. If you wish to support other modes, you should not find it difficult to change a few constants. An attempt has been made to consolidate constants such as the display width, height, and mode in a central location so that these changes will be easier to make. Because the time required to support several modes would have detracted from the more important graphics programming concepts in this book, the customization of functions for different modes is left to you. Likewise, the discussion of details regarding the EGA is left to other texts. To avoid digression from the complex graphics concepts in this book, the EGA is used as a convenient, readily available tool for demonstration—nothing more.

Compatibility

If your major concern is compatibility, use the functions in this book that use the EGA BIOS. The BIOS is contained on the EGA itself and contains some general-purpose, although slower, routines that automatically compensate for the modes you have set. If you are programming for speed, however, which most users seem to prefer, use the functions that directly address the hardware through the display controller.

In order to make your graphics functions compatible across the greatest variety of devices, you should keep, as a matter of style and structure, the following four elements in mind:

1. Keep the starting address of the display buffer in a global variable.

2. You must know the physical location of the starting address on the display surface. For example, on the EGA it is the upper left corner; on the ICB it is the lower left corner.

3. The display resolution will determine how many pixels, and hence how many display records, will correspond with horizontal and vertical distances on the display surface.

4. The format of bits in the color record for each pixel will determine your color-map structure.

Setting the Display Mode

You can write a simple program that will change modes from the DOS command line. The DOS MODE command does this, but it is limited to the modes supported by the CGA and the Monochrome Display Adapter. As a first exercise in graphics programming, transcribe and compile the program shown as Function 2-1, MODEGA.C.

MODEGA.C uses the EGA BIOS, which is located in ROM on the EGA board, to set any mode supported by the EGA. The EGA mode is a predefined status that is set in memory on the EGA and that governs its overall functioning.

MODEGA accepts the number of the desired mode as the first argument on the command line. For example, mode 6 can be set by entering the following command:

```
E:>modega 6
```

After you enter the command, the desired mode will be set immediately. If it is successful, you will see the screen change to its desired appearance; if it is not successful, the command will have no effect. This lack of error messages is necessary so that you can use this command from software that permits you to

■ FUNCTION 2-1

MODEGA.C

```
/* MODEGA.C sets ega mode */

#include <stdio.h>
#include <dos.h>

union REGS regs;

main(argc, argv)
int argc;
char *argv[];
{

if (argc == 2)
    modeset(atoi(argv[1]));

if (argc != 2)
    printf("EGA Mode is %d", modeget());
}


modeset(mode)
int mode;
{

regs.h.al = mode;
regs.h.ah = 0;
int86(0x10, &regs, &regs);
}


modeget()
{

regs.h.al = 0;
regs.h.ah = 0x0f;
int86(0x10, &regs, &regs);
return(regs.h.al);
}
```

execute DOS commands. If you pass the argument, nothing will be printed to the screen that might upset the operation of the parent process.

   If you enter the command without an argument, MODEGA

will display the number of the prevailing mode at the time the command was entered. For example, enter the following:

E:>modega

The command line will end up looking like this if the current mode is 6:

E:>modega
EGA Mode is 6
E:>__

MODEGA.C contains a function called modeset( ), which becomes the first function in a toolkit you will find useful in working with your EGA. If you study the code, you will see how it works.

Setting the Display Page

The second program you may find useful is one called PAGEGA.C, the listing for which is to be found in Function 2-2. PAGEGA will enable you to select **pages** on the EGA. A page is the amount of RAM that constitutes the display buffer required for a given mode. The number of pages available depends both on the amount of RAM on the adapter and on the mode selected. Since each mode has different requirements, the sizes of display buffers vary, and the total RAM allotted can be divided accordingly into pages. See Table 2-1 for the number of pages of memory available in each mode for a given amount of RAM on the EGA.

You can select the page (from 0 to 7) by running PAGEGA in the same way you ran MODEGA, except that the argument on the command line will be the page number and not the desired mode. The contents of the page you selected will appear imme-

■ FUNCTION 2-2

PAGEGA.C

```
/* PAGEGA.C sets ega page */

#include <stdio.h>
#include <dos.h>

union REGS regs;


main(argc, argv)
int argc;
char *argv[];
{
int page;

if (argc == 2)
     page = pageset(atoi(argv[1]));

if (argc != 2 || page == -1)
     printf("EGA Page is %d", pageget());
}


pageset(page)
int page;
{

if (page < 0 || page > 7) return(-1);

regs.h.al = page;
regs.h.ah = 5;
int86(0x10, &regs, &regs);

return(page);
}


pageget()

{

regs.h.al = 0;
regs.h.ah = 0x0f;
int86(0x10, &regs, &regs);
return(regs.h.bh);
}
```

diately on your display. Fast page swapping can be used to great advantage in speeding up your graphics applications.

ENHANCED GRAPHICS
MODES ON THE EGA

A good reason to start with graphics in mode 6 on the EGA is that this is the least complicated mode you can use. There are only two colors to worry about, BLACK (0) and WHITE (1). Display memory starts at segment B800 (hex) and ends at an offset (640 * 200) / 8 − 1 bytes away, at B800:3E7F. The mapping of pixels onto bits is very straightforward. Each byte of display memory corresponds with exactly eight pixels, one for each bit. The bits and pixels correspond in memory with their positions on the display surface. Figure 2-1 shows the bit mapping for a typical byte in the EGA display buffer. Mode 6 is the shallow end of the graphics pool.

Remember, mode 6 is being used for illustration purposes only. The EGA is capable of much more, including higher resolution and up to 16 colors from a palette of 64. The general principles involved in drawing lines are the same as those used in drawing other graphics figures. Instead of using the direct approach, however, the EGA differs from the CGA in its use of a **graphics controller.**

```
Bit position:              7 6 5 4   3 2 1 0
Left to right pixel map:   1 1 1 1   1 1 1 1
Corresponding hexadecimal: F         F
```

FIGURE 2-1.   Bit mapping for a byte in mode 6 on the EGA

The EGA Graphics
Controller

The graphics controller is a chip that was especially designed by IBM to go between the programmer and display RAM. Instead of changing RAM directly, you must first send out an index number to the graphics controller index register (port 0x3CE). This number selects a function on the controller. You will see this process in action in the functions described in this book. If you wish to understand the secrets of the display controller, study the functions used to draw points and lines.

If you change the EGA mode to 14 and then try to change display memory without using the display controller, you will find that it doesn't work. The display RAM is hidden from you. In color modes on the EGA, each pixel is represented by *four* bits (a nibble), as illustrated in Figure 2-2. On the CGA portion of the EGA (that is, modes 0 through 6), these four bits are mapped directly into RAM and can be changed using direct memory access. In modes 13 through 16, however, the display controller must be used to change colors.

In enhanced modes 13 through 16, the EGA uses more than the IRGB (intensity, red, green, and blue) four-bit color specification. Color lookup tables contain not four-bit but six-bit values for the colors, in a format called rgbRGB. There are six combinations, each with two states, or two to the sixth possible colors.

```
Bit positions:      7 6 5 4  3 2 1 0
Colors on or off:   I R G B  I R G B

I = Intensity  R = Red   G = Green   B = Blue
```

FIGURE 2-2.   *Red, green, blue, and intensity bits on the EGA*

This means that 64 colors can be stored in the tables, and that instead of selecting 16 colors directly, the IRGB code selects from 16 of the 64.

This book is not devoted to the EGA but to graphics programming in C, and so you will need to look elsewhere for more detail than this regarding the specific design of the EGA. IBM produces a technical specification for the EGA that you may find helpful. There have also been several articles written about it. One in particular, "Graphic Enhancement" by Thomas V. Hoffmann, appeared in *PC Tech Journal* in April 1985. You will find many techniques for programming the EGA embedded in the functions presented in this book.If you study those functions, the operations of the EGA should become very clear.

USING DEBUG
TO DRAW LINES

To begin to understand how to make lines appear on a display, you need to grapple with the relationship between binary numbers stored in memory and the appearance these numbers create on your computer's display. You may already have a vague sense that somehow you "draw" lines by using numbers, but the precise behavior of binary numbers when converted into dots of light has to be seen to be understood.

You can use an EGA in one of modes 4 through 6 to explore how your computer's memory relates to graphics on your computer's display. A CGA will also work for this. The technique about to be described will work with both the EGA and the CGA in mode 6, giving you a 640-by-200 display resolution and two colors, black and white. Your adapter should be connected to a color display, not a monochrome one.

With minor tweaking these techniques can be used on devices other than the EGA, as well as in other modes on the EGA itself.

A simple way to gain immediate access to a display buffer is to use DEBUG.COM, a program supplied with DOS. If you are even moderately experienced as a programmer, you probably already know how to use DEBUG. If you do not, take some time to get acquainted with it before trying the exercises in this book.

If you haven't compiled MODEGA.C, do so now, and use it to set the adapter to mode 6.

Horizontal Lines Using DEBUG

The following exercise is not meant to teach a practical way to draw lines. It is simply a handy means of illustrating the relationship that exists between the computer's memory and the appearance of the display. In all of your graphics work you will use techniques that are similar to the ones you will use here. The only difference is that in your later programming you will be using a C compiler to generate code rather than entering data directly using DEBUG.

The illustration in Figure 2-3 shows a session in DEBUG that illustrates how you can draw white lines on a black surface using mode 6. You can copy it starting from the command line, if you wish, and see the process in action on your own computer. Be careful to copy it exactly, though.

First, a bit of explanation, just to make sure you didn't miss a step. The DEBUG "e" command is used to enter values into consecutive bytes in memory beginning at the segment:offset address shown at the left. The command e b800:0f00 ff, for example, means to put the value ff (hex) in a byte storage location offset 0f00 (hex) from the segment b800 (hex). If you are unfamiliar with the segment:offset form of notation, you can learn about it from books on 8086 assembler, many of which can be found on the shelves of your local bookstore.

The result of the entry of the values "ff ff ff ff," and so on is a solid line, shown in the figure as the first of the four horizontal lines created by this process. By changing the values you enter into storage locations, each time advancing the offset by 50 (hex), you can generate a variety of line types: dotted, dashed — literally anything as long as it is horizontal!

Vertical Lines
Using DEBUG

You now know what happens in mode 6 when you draw horizontal lines. What about vertical lines? Remember, each horizontal resolution line is 640 bits long in mode 6. If eight bits are contained in each byte, you can expect that each scan line will begin at an additional offset of 80 bytes (50 hex); hence, vertical rows of pixels can be generated by selecting the horizontal offset

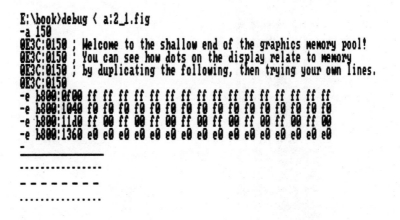

FIGURE 2-3.   Horizontal lines drawn using DEBUG

distance modulo 8, adding this to the display base address, and then adding the number of dots in the vertical line times 50 (hex). Figure 2-4 will help to illustrate this process for you.

DEBUG's Obvious Limitations

There is no practical advantage whatsoever in using DEBUG to draw lines, as you probably have discovered. Using DEBUG to draw lines is only valuable as an illustration of the process of drawing points and lines by changing values at memory addresses in a display buffer.

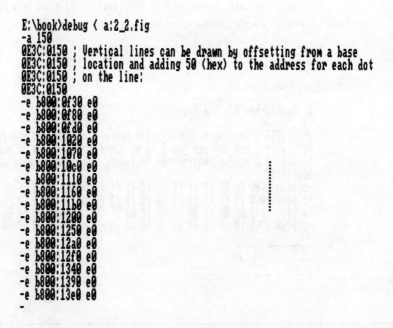

```
E:\book>debug < a:2_2.fig
-a 150
0E3C:0150 ; Vertical lines can be drawn by offsetting from a base
0E3C:0150 ; location and adding 50 (hex) to the address for each dot
0E3C:0150 ; on the line:
0E3C:0150
-e b800:0f30 e0
-e b800:0f80 e0
-e b800:0fd0 e0
-e b800:1020 e0
-e b800:1070 e0
-e b800:10c0 e0
-e b800:1110 e0
-e b800:1160 e0
-e b800:11b0 e0
-e b800:1200 e0
-e b800:1250 e0
-e b800:12a0 e0
-e b800:12f0 e0
-e b800:1340 e0
-e b800:1390 e0
-e b800:13e0 e0
-
```

FIGURE 2-4.   Vertical line drawn using DEBUG

DEBUG is limited, obviously, because you can't *graphically* draw lines in the same way you would using a pencil. To make the memory-management aspect of graphics software transparent to the user, a great deal needs to be done. It is essential to master software techniques that put numbers into the display buffer under control of a **locator** device.

Locators are devices that transfer the spatial location of a point into numbers that your software stores in memory. A simple locator you are probably familiar with is the ubiquitous mouse. A mouse is held in the hand and moved across a tablet or other surface. As the mouse moves, it sends information to the computer regarding the direction of movement. This information is usually in the form of letter codes, such as U (up), D (down), L (left), or R (right). Your software receives these codes and adds or subtracts numbers accordingly from the x or y coordinates contained in memory. At certain times these coordinates are used to read a block of numbers into display RAM, which results in the appearance of locator crosshairs of some form. This method is much easier than using DEBUG to change those numbers.

BEGINNING TO USE
C FOR GRAPHICS

The simplest thing you can do in graphics programming is to change the color of a specified pixel. This is usually called drawing a point, and you can write a simple C function to do it.

The easiest way to draw a point, although not the fastest way, is to use the EGA firmware contained on the adapter itself. Later on you will see how to draw points faster, but you will need more knowledge to do this. Let's get started using C to program for graphics.

Two Ways to Draw
a Point Using C

You can write C programs with lots of globally defined variables, or you can write them with few globals and lots of arguments that are passed on the stack. It is assumed that you are experienced enough in C programming to know what globals, arguments, and the stack are.

No matter how experienced you are, you will find it tempting to use globals to avoid the effort of tracing variables from function to function. In graphics you must be very careful with the use of globals because very complex events can change global variables without your being aware it is happening. Points and other graphics elements can be drawn either by using isolated functions or by using functions that receive information from globally defined externals.

Function 2-3, POINT.C, is an illustration of the design of a typical isolated function to draw a point with no use of external references to global variables. Compare it with Function 2-4, POINTG.C, which contains a function that depends entirely on globally known variables defined externally.

The functions point() and pointg() represent two extremes of function types between which you will forever be vacillating. There is nothing inherently problematic about either function; each might have its use. The decision as to when to use one approach or the other is a matter of judgment.

A Command to Draw
a Point from DOS

Consider the simple program in Function 2-5, DRAWPT.C. It creates a command called DRAWPT, which can be used to draw a point on your EGA display at any time from DOS, given four arguments. It will accept only four arguments, no more, no less.

■ FUNCTION 2-3

POINT.C

```
/* POINT.C reads or writes a dot at x,y in given color */

#include <dos.h>

point(x, y, read_write, color)
int x, y, read_write, *color;
{
union REGS regs;

regs.x.dx = y;                /* set row number */
regs.x.cx = x;                /* column number */
regs.h.ah = read_write;       /* 12 READPT, 13 WRITEPT */
regs.h.al = *color;           /* color of the dot (0 - F) */
int86(0x10, &regs, &regs);    /* invoke int10h */
*color = regs.h.al;
}
```

■ FUNCTION 2-4

POINTG.C

```
/* POINTG.C reads or writes a dot at x,y in
** globally-defined color */

#include <dos.h>

pointg()
{
extern int x, y;
extern union REGS regs;
extern int read_write;
extern int color;

regs.x.dx = y;                /* set row number */
regs.x.cx = x;                /* column number */
regs.h.ah = read_write;       /* 12 READPT, 13 WRITEPT */
regs.h.al = color;            /* color of the dot (0 - F) */
int86(0x10, &regs, &regs);    /* invoke int10h */
color = regs.h.al;
}
```

■ FUNCTION 2-5

DRAWPT.C

```
/* DRAWPT.C draws a point on the display surface */
/* Usage:  drawpt x y color */
/* Example: drawpt 320 100 1
**    draws a point at the center of the display. */

#define WRITEPT 13

main(argc, argv)
int argc;
char *argv[];
{
int x, y, read_write, color;

if (argc != 4) return;

x = atoi(argv[1]);
y = atoi(argv[2]);
read_write = WRITEPT;
color = atoi(argv[3]);
color = (color < 15) ? color : 15;
color = (color >= 0) ? color : 0;
point(x, y, read_write, &color);
}
```

It screens those arguments for validity before drawing the point. This isn't a practical application, but it illustrates the most primitive graphics program you could imagine.

If you successfully compile and link the program in Function 2-5, you will be able to place points on the screen anywhere in any mode supported by the BIOS. Later in this book, you will see how to draw points and lines faster, without using the BIOS. Experiment with various modes and pages to get a feel for the range of the EGA, and then go on to begin making structured use of these new tools.

PARTS OF A GRAPHICS PROGRAM IN C

Graphics programming involves, perhaps more than non-graphics programming, a great deal of memory management. You should use structures and unions creatively in declaring memory for use in your graphics programs. This will help you to keep track of information that, in graphics programming, is often not easily comprehended.

Like non-graphics programs in C, graphics programs have headers, definitions, declarations, and other structural elements. Although it is impossible to present a thorough review of all aspects of C programming, each of these parts will be discussed as it pertains to the graphics programming process.

Headers

The body of your C code is important, but much of the power of your program will come from intelligently designed data structures. One of the earliest considerations in your design should be the design of data formats. As an example of how a typical graphics header is developed, Function 2-6, DISPLAY.H, shows the EGA mode 6 mapping of bits onto a byte in memory.

Notice that the typedef declaration creates two new types, which can be used in any part of the program where display.h is included. You merely need to use #include <display.h> at the top of your file to make use of the new keywords "bits" and "bytes."

If you wish to examine the contents of the entire color specification byte, you can use it like this:

```
color_byte = display.all.pixels;
```

■ FUNCTION 2-6

DISPLAY.H

```
/* DISPLAY.H  header contains display structures */

typedef unsigned char byte;
typedef unsigned char bits;

#define EGAMODE 6          /* could initialize these */
#define EGASEG 0xB800      /* as variables from a file! */


union DISPLAY
     {
     struct
          {
          byte pixels;
          }all;

     struct
          {

          bits bit0        : 1;      /* bit 0 */
          bits bit1        : 1;      /* bit 1 */
          bits bit2        : 1;      /* bit 2 */
          bits bit3        : 1;      /* bit 3 */
          bits bit4        : 1;      /* bit 4 */
          bits bit5        : 1;      /* bit 5 */
          bits bit6        : 1;      /* bit 6 */
          bits bit7        : 1;      /* bit 7 */

          } bit;
     };
```

Use of Headers   The small function shown in Function 2-7, SHOW—BYT.C, takes the position values of the first pixels at the upper left-hand corner of the display by reading the first nibble in the display buffer, starting at B800:0000 (hex), which is the start of the buffer used with EGA mode 6.

■ FUNCTION 2-7

SHOW—BYT.C

```
/* SHOW_BYT.C shows pixels in first byte of display buffer.
*/

#include <display.h>
#include <memory.h>
#include <dos.h>

union DISPLAY display;


main()
{
byte intensity, red, green, blue;
byte entire_byte;
int srcseg, srcoff, destseg, destoff;
unsigned nbytes;
struct SREGS segregs;
unsigned int cs, ds, es, ss;


/* read the values of the current registers */
segread(&segregs);

/* move a single byte into entire_byte */
nbytes = 1;
srcseg = 0xB800;
srcoff = 0x0000;
destseg = segregs.ds;
destoff = (int)&entire_byte;
movedata(srcseg, srcoff, destseg, destoff, nbytes);

display.all.pixels = entire_byte;

/* print the results on the display */
printf("\ndot 7 6 5 4 3 2 1 0");
printf("\n    %d %d %d %d %d %d %d %d",
    display.bit.bit7,
    display.bit.bit6,
    display.bit.bit5,
    display.bit.bit4,
    display.bit.bit3,
    display.bit.bit2,
    display.bit.bit1,
    display.bit.bit0);

}
```

Reading a single byte using this method is hardly worth the effort, but by using movedata() to read entire lines or even the entire buffer, you can do a lot of work with a minimum of equipment. This sample program isn't meant to do any real work, just to help illustrate one way in which to deal with the contents of your EGA buffer.

Color is mapped onto each position in the buffer in a more complex way, involving the use of index registers. Later in this book you will see how the ICB (Image Capture Board) display can be mapped onto the EGA buffer in full color.

Bitfields

The transition from version 2 to version 3 of Microsoft C introduced a new ordering of bitfields, reversing the bit ordering within the field. Bits are assigned from lowest to highest position in the integral value. When you are working with integers, where two bytes are combined, this means that the actual positions of the bytes will be reversed, as is usual when the 8086 stores integral values in memory. You probably know that the memory image of, for example, the number 0xff00 is actually stored in memory as 00 ff.

The low-order byte is always stored first, meaning that the reference to the field in a graphics display buffer will sometimes surprise you. The bitfield will map out into two bytes when the type of the field is integer, not char. The result will be extremely confusing if you don't use structures containing bitfields or if you look directly at display memory values.

As an example of how this reversal can cause confusion, consider the following number:

```
Bit position:  F E D C  B A 9 8  7 6 5 4  3 2 1 0
Binary:        1 0 0 1  1 0 1 0  0 1 1 1  0 1 0 1
Hexadecimal:   9        A        7        5
```

Bits in an unsigned integer bitfield would be mapped from lowest to highest in the *value* of the integer, but when the integer is stored in memory its lowest and highest bytes would be reversed:

```
Bit position:  7 6 5 4  3 2 1 0  F E D C  B A 9 8
Binary:        0 1 1 1  0 1 0 1  1 0 0 1  1 0 1 0
Hexadecimal:   7        5        9        A
```

Understanding the preceding explanation will save you hours of confusion when you write an integral value longer than a byte into the display buffer, only to find later that the byte is not where you expected it to be. This is why the structures in DISPLAY.H are made byte rather than unsigned int.

Declarations

In C you have a choice of several types of integral object and several types of real object. In general, on a 16-bit processor such as the 8086, 16-bit integers are processed very efficiently with or without the active participation of the 8087 coprocessor. If you express graphics variables as integers (type int), you will be using the fastest method.

If floating-point reals are involved, an 8087 coprocessor should be considered mandatory. Floats are important whenever you wish to obtain accuracy in a database, as is the case in programs that perform financial analysis.

Two general rules regarding the placement of declarations are to avoid global variables, for the reason that it is difficult to track values changed globally, and to avoid local variables passed as arguments because of the time involved in pushing and popping variables to service a stack. There is obviously some ambiguity here, which calls for lots of good judgment.

Definitions

It is generally better to define numbers mnemonically in a header than to use actual number values in your program. The following is a definition of a mnemonic for a number:

```
#define WIDTH 640
```

It is much clearer to use the "WIDTH" mnemonic in your program to distinguish it from other instances of the number 640, thus avoiding confusion. An added benefit is that you can change your entire system's display width by changing one number.

Define macros, especially where passing arguments to a function would slow things down. It is assumed that you know what a macro is. If not, consult the Microsoft C manual. A typical macro definition might be

```
#define OUTVAL(a, b) { outp(BASE, a); outp(OFFSET, b); }
```

Structures and Unions

Structures and unions are very powerful tools for graphics applications. You can use them to take apart and put together all kinds of complex data structures. It is easy to forget they are there and start fielding strings numerically.

Dynamic Memory Allocation Using Malloc

Use malloc() and calloc() to allocate buffers and deallocate them when not in use. This practice will keep you from running out of data space and help to avoid stack overflow. Graphics programs tend to use large buffers intensively.

STRUCTURE FLOW DIAGRAMS

For simple programs flow diagrams are optional, but for any complete graphic system such a diagram is very helpful. Use whatever method works for you to generate your flowchart. The purpose behind a flow diagram is to help you visualize the overall functioning of the program, not to conform to a predetermined stylistic convention.

The flow diagram shown in Figure 2-5 was created for a typical graphics program. The diagram depicts several "worlds." These are the world of control, the world of reals, and the world of display.

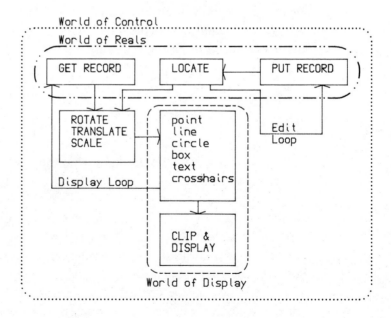

FIGURE 2-5. A structure flow diagram

World of Control

The world of control surrounds the entire system and implies that a person is exercising control options to modify the functioning of the program. Outside of the world of control is the world we all live in, the "real" world, which should not be confused with the world of reals.

World of Reals

The world of reals is a world in which floating-point real numbers contain a record of locator positions and attributes that explain what those positions mean. The world of reals is contained within the world of control. When any number enters the world of reals, it is converted to a floating-point *real number*. Whenever a number leaves the world of reals it is converted into an *int* — a signed 16-bit integer value.

World of Display

The world of display is contained within the world of control and is separate from the world of reals. Only signed 16-bit integer values are allowed in the world of display. When a number enters the world of display it is assumed to be already of type int. Numbers are used within the world of display to represent locator positions and attributes on the display surface. Possible attributes are pen color, line style, and layer, but many other attributes can be created. The locator can refer to the center of a circle, the beginning of an arc, the location of a fill, or the corners of a rectangle, among other things.

Editing

Editing is accomplished in the world of control. When you edit you can revise the location or attribute of any locator record in the picture database, or you can add records to the database. Editing involves finding, inserting, appending, and deleting records.

Locating

Locating is done in the world of reals. The locator crosshairs are moved by adding or subtracting real values along the horizontal axis (x axis) and/or vertical axis (y axis). A global or group-global rotation angle, translation offset, and scale factor can be applied to the locator using floating-point real numbers. If applied, the angle and offset will change the apparent locator position.

When the display is generated while editing or when reading from a file, the same interpretations are used to convert from the world of reals and attributes to a display representation. Each attribute uses its own generator in the world of reals to create a display list for the display surface.

Remember, the display surface can be a computer CRT, a printer, a plotter, or any other device that has a driver. The locator can be any locating device, such as a mouse, a digitizer, or a light pen.

You can use any function in the system, subject to the world it is in. Worlds are outside the concept of flow. Flow in a program is from function to function. The world the function is in governs the kinds of numbers that are used, the global scale factor, the pen colors, and possibly many other aspects of the system.

MEMORY MODELS

Memory models are options the compiler manufacturer gives the programmer. They represent assumptions that the programmer instructs the compiler to use in allocating memory for the data, the stack, and the executable code. In version 3 of Microsoft C, there are three built-in memory models, but you can also create your own. Version 4 of Microsoft C expands the options further. If you are not familiar with memory models, it pays to study your Microsoft C manual.

The Small Model

The Small memory model is efficient for most programs you will write because it permits up to 64K for the program and another 64K for your data and stack. In the Small model, the segment contained in CS is used for code and the segment in DS for data. Because a 16-bit code pointer is used, code is accessed quickly. Jumps that are far (changing the CS register) are not required. Data is also near (within 64K), allowing fast access.

The Medium Model

Graphics programs can get much larger than 64K, and so you may need to use the Medium memory model for them. A slight reduction in speed is evident when you switch to the Medium model because your code now uses far calls more often. In the Medium memory model, your program code can use the entire addressable range of the machine, but your working data and stack still occupy only 64K. This isn't a problem, because you can always use the Ze compile option to enable the FAR keyword to access data in segments other than DS when you wish to. You can use the Medium model to compile any C function in this book.

The Large Model

Why not use the Large memory model? For most purposes you can swap data into and out of the 64K you have available with the Medium model and take advantage of the fast processing you can do when your data pointers are word sized. Access to data in the Large model is by a LONG pointer, involving use of a changing DS register. This is noticeably slower and should be avoided, particularly in graphics applications. The range of data you can access is by no means limited when you use the Medium model, because the movedata() and other memory-management functions allow you access to data in segments other than DS. In other words, it is all right to use FAR pointers when you have to, but when you don't have to they can slow everything down.

OTHER DISPLAY BUFFERS

The EGA is by no means the only graphics option you have at your disposal, although it is perhaps the most likely to become a standard. Display buffers are sold in a variety of types and sizes. Many different methods are used to manipulate the contents of display buffers. The cost of such buffers to a Personal Computer (PC) user is becoming lower and lower as time goes by.

Today's marketplace offers so much that it is possible to cover only a few options here.

The Professional Graphics Adapter

Beyond the EGA in display color capability is IBM's Professional Graphics Adapter (PGA), which has up to 256-color capability and display resolution of 640 by 480. The rules for this device are similar to those for the EGA except that, as you might expect, a 256-color code requires more storage.

The PGA can be used for any high-quality graphics purpose. It is obviously more expensive than the EGA and requires a more costly analog display. This book was written using the EGA as an example because more people are likely to use the EGA, for reasons of economy. Most of the functions in this book can be modified to run on the PGA very easily.

Television

Television imaging and graphics on PCs is becoming not only feasible but affordable. It is a shame that 16-color graphics preceded affordable digital television hardware, because many of us devoted our budgets to graphics equipment that is woefully inadequate when compared to the capabilities of the new hardware.

The Video Display Adapter

AT&T's TrueVision line of products is a level above the PGA in color display capability. At the lowest level the Video Display Adapter (VDA and VDAD) enables 256 colors to be displayed simultaneously on a 256-by-200—resolution display surface. The buffer is capable of holding data for 256-by-256 resolution, but not all of it can be displayed at once.

The Image Capture Board

The next step up — the Image Capture Board (ICB) — permits the display of 32,768 colors simultaneously on a 256-by-200– pixel display surface. This product also gives you a 256-by-256 buffer, part of which is not displayed. The spare display area can be used to store parts of images and scroll the display.

The ICB is a very affordable product with potentially very wide appeal. Remember, if you have a television set you already have the necessary display device.

The AT&T color graphics products are extremely powerful and are oriented toward television-quality images. They are capable of capturing images from a home-quality television camera into a display buffer, where the images can be manipulated. The organization of display memory on the AT&T display adapters is very straightforward. As an example, notice in Figure 2-6 the locations of the red, green, blue, and overlay bits in the word assigned to each pixel on the ICB.

```
                       High byte        Low byte
Bit position:     7 6 5 4 3 2 1 0   7 6 5 4 3 2 1 0
Colors:           O R R R R G G     G G G B B B B B

O = Overlay   R = Red   G = Green   B = Blue
```

FIGURE 2-6.   Red, green, blue, and overlay bits on the ICB

The overlay bit determines whether a given dot is to be "live" or "static." If live, the dot will be whatever color is coming in from the video source on that scan cycle. If static, the color of the bit comes from the display buffer. This means that each pixel on the display can be either live or static, depending on the setting of this bit. This permits the superimposition of titles onto live video, as might be done to display a title for a videotape presentation.

The TARGA Boards

The AT&T TARGA boards include the TARGA 8, TARGA 16, and TARGA 32. The TARGA 16 permits 32,768 colors to be displayed simultaneously on a 512 by 400 displayable color surface!

TV Hard Copy

Some of the images used in this book were captured onto an ICB and then transferred onto an Epson dot-matrix printer or into an EGA display buffer. Appendix E illustrates some techniques for doing this and discusses how you can use these techniques in preparing graphics icons and other fascinating graphical applications. The process used, called "dithering," is the basis for digital hard-copy devices.

You may not own a PGA or an ICB. It doesn't matter. You can still learn about the buffering of display information. In the future you will find that television-quality images will be much more common in personal computing.

3

GRAPHIQ:
A Prototypical
Application

To illustrate the graphics capabilities that you can achieve with C, it is necessary to write a good many graphics functions. The program GRAPHIQ, given in Appendix A, was invented especially for this book in order to illustrate how graphics functions fit into a typical application. You may wish to use the functions in this book, or you may choose to develop your own. The purpose of this chapter is to give an overview of the functions of GRAPHIQ.

You have used prototypical systems before. As a child you may have used coloring books or paint-by-numbers sets. Other prototypical products you might remember are Tinkertoys, Erector sets, and even toy trains. Adults use prototypes, too. You can buy books containing prototypical house plans. Why not use a prototype to construct a computer program?

The advantage of a book of house plans is that you can quickly select the overall design of your house and suggest a few changes to the contractor. The design process is reduced to something that is quick and easy to understand. If it suits your purposes, the prototypical solution speeds you on the way to getting just what you want. GRAPHIQ, like the book of house plans, gives you a catalog of functions to put together. Like a set of Tinkertoys, GRAPHIQ can be put together quickly in many different combinations.

The functions used in GRAPHIQ are very powerful in themselves. You will be able to see how to draw lines quickly by writing directly to the display buffer. You will see how menus can be created and managed. GRAPHIQ shows how toolkit functions can fit together. It is up to you to be creative and use your toolkit to improve GRAPHIQ or create software that is completely different.

GRAPHIQ PROGRAM DESCRIPTION

GRAPHIQ is a simple graphics program that enables you to draw lines, circles, and arcs and to fill areas with color in mode 14 on the EGA. You can also write text in a simple font, save the display on disk media, and retrieve a display from a file. The display can be dumped to a dot-matrix printer for hard copy.

GRAPHIQ works from a command language and uses pop-up menus, direct command entry, or command entry from a file as input. The locator device used is a readily available mouse.

A vector list with attributes is maintained for each drawing, enabling the user to replay the drawing at any scale or rotation angle. A plotter can be used to draw from the display list, although no specific plotter drivers are included. It is up to you to customize for any particular plotter language.

Some drivers are described but not coded in this book because they are too complicated to debug within a feasible time frame. Where time allows, GRAPHIQ will be expanded to include as many well-coded drivers as possible, but the task of interfacing to specific devices will be left to the reader. The complete prototype GRAPHIQ program in source code form can be found in Appendix A.

SUPPORTED DEVICES

GRAPHIQ supports two display devices, one for editing and one for hard copy. One locator device is supported, and one storage device is available.

The Locator Device

The locator is an ordinary mouse. The brand of mouse is insignificant. You will need to know only what input characters define left, right, up, and down incremental movement, and what input characters identify the press of a button.

The Editing Display Device

The editing display consists of the IBM EGA operating in mode 14. You can use this mode with an inexpensive RGB monitor, or you can attach the IBM Enhanced Display. If you wish to gain the highest resolution and the most color options, you can modify GRAPHIQ to work in mode 16, but you should have 256K of RAM on the EGA, and you must use the Enhanced Display.

The Hard-Copy Display Device

The hard-copy device is an Epson MX100 printer. You can also use the Epson FX100, MX80, FX80, or any of the compatibles. If you have a laser printer, you can, with some effort, modify GRAPHIQ to work with it. Other dot-matrix and ink-jet printers can also be used with some modification. A plotter interface is described, but the implementation is left to you.

The Storage Device

The storage device is a common floppy drive or hard disk. Curiously, the computer industry has been forced to standardize disk input/output to the extent that any drive that works with DOS will work with GRAPHIQ. Why have graphics devices not been similarly standardized?

DATABASE DESIGN

The single most important and varied part of the design of a graphics system is the design of the database. Although the process of display is important, it is fairly uniform from application to application. What really makes an application unique is how it contains information.

A database must be designed to serve a purpose, however abstract. Do you want to import numbers from a spreadsheet? If so, you need a database designed to contain those numbers. Do you want to do three-dimensional graphics? If so, you need a database that can store three numbers per record. Do you want to process television pictures and store them? If so, you need a format that can hold all the information that goes into a television image.

Vectors and Rasters

A **vector** is a single number (a scalar), a pair of numbers (two dimensions), a trio of numbers (three dimensions), or any other grouping of numbers that expresses the location of a point in space in accordance with a coordinate system.

A **raster** is an organized grid of positions that may be occupied by graphical information. The display surface of the EGA is a perfect example of a raster.

You need to decide whether your database will be vector or raster based. In a vector-based system, the data is stored as a series of numbers of some given precision. The list of numbers represents the coordinates of points on a plane or in space, along with information that specifies what those points mean.

In a raster-based system, the image is made up of only the information that was contained in the display buffer itself. There is no display list in the raster-based system, and there is usually no need for transformations to data on the way onto and off of the display surface.

Most business and scientific systems use vectors instead of rasters to store data because vectors are so much more flexible.

Screen Dumps

Even in a vector-based system, raster graphics are not necessarily excluded. A **screen dump** is often used to save the display buffer for later use in a slide show. Screen dumps can also be used to store the contents of a display temporarily when the user wishes to view a help menu. The raster can be rapidly restored to the display without the need to regenerate an entire vector list. There is another method, by the way, called **page swapping** that can be used when your display buffer has multiple pages in a given mode (as is the case with many modes on the EGA). Remember that a page is the amount of memory needed to store a screen or display (see Table 2-1). Page swapping is the practice of changing the part of graphics memory that is visible on the display.

GRAPHIQ FILE STRUCTURE

Files are used to store records of the locations of graphics objects, such as lines, circles, arcs, rectangles, and text. As with files used in non-graphics applications, graphics files may be structured in two general ways. They may be sequential or random.

Sequential Files

Sequential file structures are used typically in word processing systems where a record delimiter determines the location of the end of a record. In a word processor a typical record would be a line of text, and a typical delimiter would be a line-feed character.

The record size in a sequential file structure is variable, not fixed. Because of this it is impossible to compute the location of a given record by using a fixed record length. The file must be read from beginning to end in order to get to the record in the file you wish to change.

Avoid the use of sequential file structures in graphics; they severely limit your access to a given record. You must read all records in sequence from the beginning of the file each time you wish to change a line or group of lines.

The file access method used in GRAPHIQ is not sequential but is exclusively random access.

Random-Access Files

A random-access or fixed-record file structure uses the record length to distinguish one record from another. Because of this the offset of a given record can always be found by multiplying the desired record number by the record length.

Sample File Structure

The header in Function 3-1, FILE.H, shows a typical file structure that permits the use of several types of record and a fixed record length. It will be used in modified form in GRAPHIQ.

You can do a lot with this record layout; it is extremely flexible. Of course, it is only an example of what can be done, and you can and should expand on it. This header defines a high-precision graphics system that should be able to satisfy the needs of business and scientific users alike. Much more can be added to it, such as object hierarchies, three-dimensional aspects, surface modeling, additional geometric primitives, and more. You can even include properties for use in robotics.

Unions in File Headers   Notice that unions are used in Function 3-1. A union in C language accommodates overlapping structures. It is used to redefine data fields.

One of the rules regarding unions is that the largest structure in the union governs the minimum size of all other structures in the union. Padding through the use of space characters is used to make up the difference between the size of the largest structure and that of the smaller ones.

A 64-byte record is specified in one of GRAPHIQ's structures, and all other structures are kept smaller than this size.

■ FUNCTION 3-1

FILE.H

```
/* FILE.H contains record structures */

#define HEADER 0
#define POINT 1
#define LINE 2
#define CIRCLE 3
#define ARC 4
#define BOX 5
#define FILL 6
#define TEXT 7
#define LOC 1
#define STRG 2
#define ATTRLEN 2
#define TEXTLEN 62
#define RECLEN ATTRLEN + TEXTLEN
#define FILENAME 12


struct ATTRIBUTE
     {
     union
          {
          char attr;
          char subattr;
          } parts;

     union
          {
          unsigned attrib;
          } whole;
     };


struct ELEMENT
     {
     unsigned attrib;      /* master attribute */

     union
          {
          struct
               {
               char filename[FILENAME+1];
               long date;
               long time;

               long records;
               } header;
```

■ FUNCTION 3-1 (continued)

FILE.H

```
struct
    {
    double x;
    double y;
    char color;
    char layer;
    } point;

struct
    {
    double x1;
    double y1;
    double x2;
    double y2;
    char color;
    char linestyle;
    char layer;
    } line;

struct
    {
    double x_center;
    double y_center;
    double radius;
    char color;
    char linestyle;
    char layer;
    } circle;

struct
    {
    double x_center;
    double y_center;
    double x_start;
    double y_start;
    double x_end;
    double y_end;
    char color;
    char linestyle;
    char layer;
    } arc;

struct
    {
    double x1;
    double y1;
```

■ FUNCTION 3-1 (continued)

FILE.H

```
        double x2;
        double y2;
        char color;
        char linestyle;
        char layer;
        } box;
struct
    {
    double x1;
    double y1;
    double x2;
    double y2;
    char color;
    char linestyle;
    char layer;
    } fill;

/* length of text string plus 5 determines
** maximum record length */

struct
    {
    union
        {
        struct
            {
            double x_origin;
            double y_origin;
            double rotation;
            int height;
            int width;
            char font;
            char color;
            char linestyle;
            char layer;
            } loc;

        struct
            {
            /* governs record size */
                char string[TEXTLEN];
                } strg;
            } t_attr;
        } text;
    } attr;  /* end of attr union */
}; /* end of ELEMENT struct */
```

These 64 bytes have been chosen to be the length of the largest text string plus the length of the general attributes section. Within your program you will use the sizeof() operator to determine the size of this structure, so if you change it or any part of it you will not have to dissect the entire program.

Two-Dimensional Attributes   The database defined by Function 3-1 has a two-dimensional attribute to conserve space and increase the speed of access. The attribute (attr) and its subattribute (subattr) control the use of single records or groups of records. It works like this: the first attribute controls the second. If the first attribute permits the use of a second, or at least if the second attribute is nonzero, additional records are made available to expand the master attribute. This way, if the record does not require a subattribute, only 64 bytes are read. If the record does require additional fields, however, as many as are necessary can be read.

The two-dimensional attribute system is particularly good for text because it makes strings of unlimited length possible. Each time a subattribute after a text attribute is set to STRG (as defined at the top of FILE.H), an additional line of TEXTLEN characters is made available. Word processing can be included in graphics applications using this method. Object attributes can be extended without limit and without the use of complex naming conventions.

Desktop Publishing   The structure shown in Function 3-1 works well for desktop publishing because it merges the capabilities of a word processor with those of a high-precision graphics tool. When you work with laser printers and even more sophisticated graphics output devices, you can use the preceding structure almost as is to store your data.

Use of Variables   The attr and subattr variables in Function 3-1 deserve some explanation. They are grouped together so that attr ends up in the low byte and subattr ends up in the high byte of a 16-bit word. This means that when this field is treated as an integer, the low byte will govern. To ensure that the subattr is 0 when it is not needed, the program treats attr as an int and the high-order byte is automatically made 0 for values up to and including +127, the highest positive value that can be returned by type char.

The ATTRIBUTE structure breaks the master attribute down into two parts, so that when the master attribute is used without subattributes, it automatically sets the subattr member of the structure to 0. When subattributes are used, however, the ATTRIBUTE structure can be used to set both the master attribute and its subattribute.

File Access Method

Function 3-2, ACCESS.C, shows a typical means of retrieving a line of text from the structure. Although this seems complicated at first, it enables high-speed access to a high-precision database.

You will find that this all becomes clearer as the design of your graphics application progresses. And remember that this structure is only a suggested method. Experiment with different formats to find the one that works best for your application. Make a habit of experimenting.

This structure is about as advanced in concept as graphics applications usually get, so spend some time trying to understand how it works. You will see that it can be extremely powerful and fast because it carries along very little excess baggage. No matter how fast your hardware is, an awkward database design will slow you down.

■ FUNCTION 3-2

ACCESS.C

```
/* ACCESS.C shows how to access a text record */

#include <file.h>

struct ATTRIBUTE attribute;
struct ELEMENT element;

/* code fragment */

do    {
    fread(&element, sizeof(char),
            sizeof(element), draw_stream);

    attribute.whole.attrib = element.attrib;

    if (attribute.parts.attr == TEXT)
        {
        /* get location of string */
        if (attribute.parts.subattr == LOC)
            get_loc(&element);
        /* otherwise display string itself */
        else if (attribute.parts.subattr == STRG)
            get_text(&element);
        else {
            print_err(TEXT, STRG);
            break;
            }
        }
    }
    while (attribute.parts.attr == TEXT &&
            !feof(draw_stream));
```

LIMITATIONS OF GRAPHIQ

Admittedly, GRAPHIQ has its limitations. Graphics systems these days are very powerful indeed, and you can expect much more in the future. One reason to be interested in computer graphics is that the field is full of variety and very broad. Word processing applications are many, but there is a limit to how many different ways you can play with characters on a display. With graphics you can make use of incredible depths of color, texture, shading, solids modeling, and more.

SUGGESTIONS FOR IMPROVING GRAPHIQ

Many things can be done to improve GRAPHIQ. You could add an ellipse generator, perhaps by modifying the circle function. You could add three-dimensional modeling capabilities with hidden-line removal. You could add surface modeling, enhanced color palettes, high-speed array processing, dynamic dimensioning, multiple character fonts, Bezier splines, polynomial curve generators, circles by three points . . . the list goes on. A few of these possibilities are discussed next.

Ellipse Generator

An ellipse generator could be added by increasing the information provided to the circle generator. Whereas a circle has a diameter, an ellipse has a major axis and a minor axis. Therefore, you would need to install a routine to identify the location of the horizontal axis of the ellipse (relative to its rotation), the vertical axis, and the locations of the maxima and minima on these axes.

Three-Dimensional Modeling

Three-dimensional modeling is a more difficult undertaking. You would need to modify the database to contain an additional field for the z scalar. Rotation, translation, and scaling would all be influenced by this and would become more complex. You might need to use, instead of the **pointer list** database design shown in this book, a **nodal-connectivity** database. Whereas a pointer list is literally a list of coordinates read successively, a nodal-connectivity database consists of *two* lists: one for the **nodes,** or coordinates, and one to identify which nodes are connected together. You will probably wish to install some sort of hidden-line-removal algorithm that works. Be forewarned that because of the great variety of possible line and surface combinations it is very easy to fool even the most advanced hidden-line-removal algorithm. You are likely to meet with much frustration in this area.

Surface Modeling

If you wish to use a simple method of surface modeling, you may want to use a **point-priority** technique. This method depends on a rich color palette but works unambiguously and is to be greatly preferred over the hidden-line-removal algorithm. Stated simply, this technique involves sorting points in space by their distance from the observer and plotting those points on the perspective plane starting with the farthest from the observer and progressing to the nearest. Naturally, the nearer points will overwrite the farther points, and the result will be a solid-appearing object.

Business and Scientific Graphics

Business and scientific graphics often require graphs and charts. You could create an interface that would transport output from popular spreadsheet programs to create custom graphs for specific projects. This would require modification of the program to include a translator function for each data format you might wish to use.

Admittedly, GRAPHIQ won't perform like off-the-shelf software. But it has the advantage that you can see how it works, and you can extend it to suit your needs.

4

Graphics Algorithms

The fundamental graphics elements used in GRAPHIQ are points, lines, curves, and fills. Although there are many ways in which these fundamental elements can be made more elaborate, almost everything you wish to do in graphics can be done using them. But a word of caution: A little knowedge is a dangerous thing. Never use functions without knowing how they work. The algorithms in this chapter will provide a theoretical basis for your graphics programming.

All of the functions you will use in graphics are derived from carefully designed algorithms. Feel free to create your own or to modify the algorithms you find in books like this. There is always a way to improve the state of the art. By understanding how these algorithms work, you will be able to understand how the functions in the toolkit that appears later in this book were developed. You will also be better equipped to extend those functions for your own purposes.

COORDINATE SYSTEMS

In computer graphics your primary concern is with locating points on a display surface. To specify the location of a point, you need to use a coordinate system. The coordinates of a point are numbers (otherwise known as scalars) that define the location of a point with reference to an origin. The coordinate system is usually one of two types, rectangular or polar.

Rectangular Coordinates

A **rectangular coordinate system** consists of horizontal and vertical axes that are at right angles to each other. The coordinates themselves are equally spaced units in both x (horizontal) and y (vertical) directions. The origin of such a system is at 0,0. Negative values can also be used.

A rectangular coordinate system, otherwise known as the Cartesian coordinate system, is used in digital graphics systems because it adapts well to a raster display surface. Digital systems are usually raster based, meaning that memory is mapped onto the display as a series of horizontal lines placed one above the other. Values in memory are binary, with bits (on or off states) controlling pixel states on the display. Colors of pixels are discrete; each pixel is either one fixed color or another, rather than having smooth color transitions as you would see, for example, if you mixed paint to paint a house. Figure 4-1 shows an example of a rectangular coordinate system.

Polar Coordinates

A **polar coordinate system** is sometimes used in graphics, but is less valuable than a rectangular coordinate system in mapping pixels onto the display. A polar coordinate system is defined by angles and distances rather than by scalar values. In a polar coordinate system, the location of a point is defined by the angular deflection of a line. The endpoints of the line are the

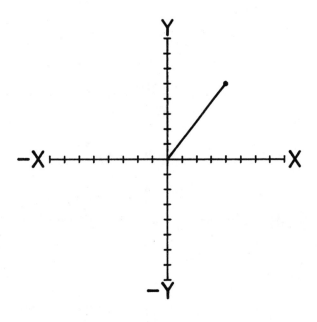

FIGURE 4-1.   A rectangular coordinate system

origin of the system and the location of the point. In a polar system, coordinates are represented by *theta* and *rho,* Greek symbols that stand for the angle (theta) and radius (rho), or length, of the line. See Figure 4-2 for an example of a polar coordinate system.

Polar coordinates are sometimes provided in graphics software as an option for engineers. In surveying applications it is useful to know both the Cartesian and polar coordinates of a station.

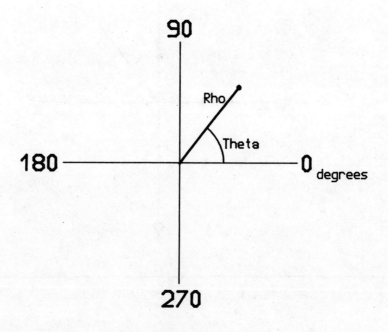

FIGURE 4-2.   A polar coordinate system

In designing systems for engineering use, keep in mind also the measuring conventions that might prevail. Although your software uses no actual dimensional units internally, you must be concerned about the process of translating display coordinates to dimensions that are absolute in the real world. It is perhaps ideal to base your real-world coordinates on the metric system and then translate from metric to feet and inches as required.

DRAWING ELEMENTS

In order to represent graphics in a coordinate system, you use various elements such as points, lines, curves, circles, and other fundamental graphics primitives. Because of differences between the analog world we live in and the digital world of the computer, some very special processes are used when drawing with a computer.

Points

In analytic geometry, a point has no dimensions, no size. It represents only a location in a coordinate system. In graphics systems, points are represented by their numerical coordinates. In a two-dimensional system, a point can be represented by two coordinates. In a three-dimensional system, a point can be represented by three coordinates. More than three dimensions are also possible; there can be an n-dimensional system in which n coordinates are used to represent each point.

Technically, a point has no algorithm. It has only a location. In a two-dimensional coordinate system, the location of a point is contained in two scalar numbers, usually denoted as x and y.

The x dimension is plotted horizontally, with positive values to the right. The y dimension is plotted vertically, with positive values extending upward.

There are many algorithms that enable you to produce lines, curves, and fills using the coordinates of points. This chapter presents a few algorithms that you will find useful and which you can extend for your own purposes. Each algorithm is described to give you a basic understanding of how it works.

There is no way to draw a single point as a separate object in GRAPHIQ. There are only lines. You may think this is strange, but there is a very good reason for it. If you adhere to the strictest definition of a point as a location and nothing more, it stands to reason that points are invisible. If you want to draw a pixel, therefore, you need to use an object that is defined, such as a filled area or a line. It turns out that defining points in this way automatically solves many problems in your software. Think of points as lines with minimum length.

The functions that draw points actually change the colors of pixels on the display surface. In this sense, but only in this sense, they draw points. In terms of the algorithms in this chapter, points have no dimensions.

Locations

You will find that thinking of points as dimensionless locations automatically solves many problems in graphics programming. Algorithms designed to work with lines tend to be difficult to construct if line endpoints are construed as parts of the lines themselves. If endpoints can be treated differently, or even ignored, problems that would have been extremely difficult to solve often become much simpler. Later in this chapter you will see how this concept is implemented in the fill algorithm to avoid confusion in the pen status.

Pixels

The word **pixel** comes from the words "picture element." A pixel is not a point. Pixels exist at all times, only their colors change. They inhabit the display surface, covering it uniformly in rows. Pixels have coordinates, just like points, which is why we often make the mistake of thinking that they are points. A point-drawing function does not draw the point itself; it actually selects the pixel nearest to the point. Thinking about pixels as distinct from points helps to clarify the difference between information in the world of real numbers and information in the world of the display.

Looking at a digital display surface is similar to looking through a glass that has a gridded pattern of lenses on its surface. Such a glass, when placed near a picture, breaks the picture up into a checkerboard of colors. Depending on the sizes of the many lenses, the pattern will be fine or coarse, easy or hard to recognize, full or empty of meaning. Pixels portray the real world in this way. They give you only an approximate view of the world.

Lines

You probably remember that a line is defined in geometry as the shortest distance between two points. This is the Euclidean definition. Lines in themselves are one-dimensional; that is, they have length but no other dimension.

Lines are the lowest order of graphics object that have any dimensionality and can be said to exist in graphics. When a line is drawn, it is drawn as a series of pixels that are computed to be close to it. The point-drawing function is used to turn the pixels on or off. Think of lines in two ways. First, a line exists in the world of real numbers. Second, a line is represented on the display surface as the pixels that are close to it. There is really no line on the display. The only place the line really exists is in the database.

Curves

Curves are an extremely general class in geometry, including circles, ellipses, arcs, and the plots of many other types of equations. For the purposes of graphics programming, curves are best defined as sets of points that do not constitute straight lines.

Like lines, curves are used to compute the locations of pixels that are near them. The curve is revealed on the display surface by pixels that are all of the same color. The curve does not exist on the display, only in the database.

Fills

A fill is an area of color, whether uniform or nonuniform, bounded by lines or curves. Fills are accomplished in many different ways, depending on how the database is designed. They can be **floods,** in which pixels in the desired region are all set to a specified color, or they can be accomplished by crosshatching a region using lines spaced at a certain crosshatching interval. Fills can also be done with gradients generated by equations. A shadow can be computed by projecting lines from a light source, with the pixels in the fill area changed accordingly. Depending on the sophistication of your hardware and software, fills can be no more than one of a few colors, or no less than realistic simulations of materials from the real world. The high cost of hardware for doing complex fills is coming down, so you will soon be able to do many new things.

LINE ALGORITHM

Because a point exists only as the expression of its location, points are never actually plotted on a display surface. This might seem confusing or contradictory, but there is a very good reason for this rule. A pixel, which is the smallest unit of information on the display, *must* have physical dimensions in a digital system. It is either on or off. It can't be "almost" there, "almost" on, "almost" off, "almost" red, or "almost" blue. Points that are represented on the display surface are actually one-pixel fills by this definition. You can also think of points as one-pixel lines. To draw a point on the display surface, you must at least draw a line. It is important to emphasize this property of points because much confusion can result from thinking of points as having dimensions.

Lines are made up of points. More accurately, they are expressed by pixels that are close to the line. How do you know which pixels are close to a line and which aren't? You use an algorithm.

As an experienced computer programmer you may already know that an **algorithm** is the expression of a series of operations. Algorithms are traditionally used to represent ways of solving problems using computers, as opposed to using strictly mathematical methods. Graphics elements have mathematical expressions in analytic geometry, but graphics algorithms are often quite different from these expressions.

The key to understanding graphics algorithms lies in a comparison between the analog and digital worlds. A pen in your hand can draw a straight line using a straightedge. This is an analog line. It varies smoothly from beginning to end. To draw that same line using a digital system, it must be plotted as the pixels that lie nearest to the analog line. The algorithm that selects those pixels, given the coordinates of the endpoints of the line, uses a "rasterization" process.

Rasters

Rasters are not smooth. They are made up of discrete pixels, each of which has dimensions. Depending on how large each pixel is, a line drawn on a raster will be more or less broken into steps, or **aliased.** Aliasing occurs (not only in graphics) when analog numbers are converted to their nearest digital counterparts. The concept of rasterization is similar to rounding in mathematics, but rasterization refers to the effects of rounding on groups of numbers rather than single numbers. In Figure 4-3 a grid is shown that represents a display surface. On that grid an analog line is drawn from the center of one pixel to the center of another. Figure 4-4 shows how the line-drawing algorithm used in this book determines which pixels best represent the line of Figure 4-3.

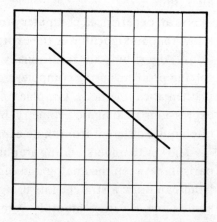

FIGURE 4-3.   An analog line drawn on a pixel grid

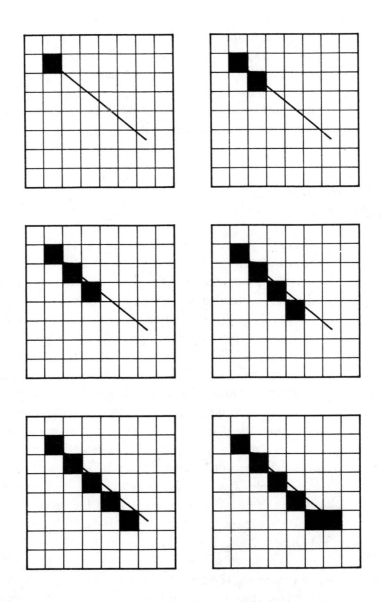

FIGURE 4-4.   Pixels selected by line-drawing algorithm

You can animate "flip-art" figures like Figure 4-4 by using a camera and slide projector. If you make a slide of each grid and project the slides quickly in sequence, you will get the same effect you would see on the computer display. Using the tools in this book, you could create "slides" in the computer's memory and put your slide show on the computer.

Bresenham's Algorithm

The most popular algorithm for drawing lines is called Bresenham's algorithm. It converts the equation of a line into an iterative process of comparing test values over the horizontal distance subtended by the line. The values are incremented and tested repeatedly. Each time a new value of x or y increases to make a new pixel possible, the pixel is plotted. The test increments are derived, before the line is drawn, from the slope of the line and the differentials of its horizontal and vertical components. The code for Bresenham's algorithm is given in Function 4-1. Read through it carefully. This is not compilable C code but a pseudocode that uses natural language to make the algorithm easier to understand. Later in this book you will see how the algorithm is translated into a C function.

A table of values can be evolved for each step in the algorithm. Table 4-1 shows values for a line drawn from (2,7) to (7,3). Compare the values in the table with the line shown in Figure 4-3 and Figure 4-4. Figure 4-4 shows the sequence of steps the algorithm goes through as it draws the line. Trace these values through each step in the algorithm. After performing this exercise, the mysteries of Bresenham's algorithm should unfold for you.

■ FUNCTION 4-1

Line Algorithm

```
Pseudocode for Bresenham's line-drawing algorithm.

Given a line from x1, y1 to x2, y2...

dx is the difference between the x components of endpoints
dy is the difference between the y components of endpoints
ix is the absolute value of dx
iy is the absolute value of dy
inc is the larger of dx, dy

plotx is x1
ploty is y1 (the beginning of the line)
x starts at 0
y starts at 0

plot a pixel at plotx, ploty

for all increments i from 0 through inc
      increment x using ix
      increment y using iy
      plot is false

      if x is greater than inc
            plot is true
            decrement x using inc
            increment plotx if dx is positive,
                  decrement plotx if dx is negative

      if y is greater than inc
            plot is true
            decrement y using inc
            increment ploty if dy is positive,
                  decrement ploty if dy is negative

      if plot is true, plot a pixel at plotx, ploty

      increment i.
```

dx = 5, dy = -4, ix = 5, iy = 4, inc = 5

i	x	y	plotx	ploty	plot
	2	7	2	7	T
0	5	4	2	7	F
1	10	8	3	6	T
2	10	7	4	5	T
3	10	6	5	4	T
4	10	5	6	4	T
5	10	4	7	3	T

TABLE 4-1. Test Values for the Line-Drawing Algorithm

Line Style

To enhance the line-drawing function, you could make it capable of drawing not only solid lines but lines in various patterns, or styles. To do this you need to pass an additional argument to the line-drawing algorithm. The usual practice is to use an unsigned integer that contains a bit pattern that is duplicated repeatedly along the line. This is simple to do. The passed integer is tested in each of its bit positions in rotation. Whereas for a solid line the plot variable in the pseudocode is set to TRUE, for a patterned line the condition of the current bit in the rotating test of the integer is used to set the plot variable. If the bit is on, and it is permitted to plot the pixel, the plot variable is set to TRUE; otherwise, it remains FALSE.

Line Width

The width of a line can be varied by replotting the line at several offsets. This requires an additional function that calls the line function. In a sense, the width of the line is equivalent to a filled rectangle. You could implement the algorithm this way, but using a fill algorithm could slow the line-drawing process. A better way is to draw lines next to one another, separated by one pixel at a time. You can easily determine the pixel-to-pixel distance for various rotational positions of the line by using the cosine of the slope of the line. This variation of the line-drawing technique is much more complicated to implement than the line-style variation.

A particularly troublesome aspect of line width is how you handle the endpoints of wide lines when they meet. If the ends are rectangular, they will look like pieces of tape that have been poorly matched at the ends. If they are rounded, they will match up better, but your corners will not be sharp. Very complex techniques have been evolved to deal with the meeting of lines. You will need to decide, depending on how much time and money you have at your disposal, how much you are willing to spend to address the ways in which wide lines meet. You will probably want to provide a collection of options from which the user can select.

Antialiasing

The process of **antialiasing** a line is used to reduce the "stepped" or "staircased" appearance of the line. Techniques for antialiasing depend on having a rich palette of color or a gray scale. On displays with relatively low resolution, the aliasing effect is extremely distracting. As resolution is increased, however, the effect is much less pronounced. Acceptable displays, from an antialiasing standpoint, begin at a resolution of about 640 horizontal by 480 vertical, the resolution of IBM's PGA. To achieve true state-of-the-art alias reduction relying only on resolution, you need at least a 1024-by-1024—pixel display.

For lower spatial resolution and a greater number of colors, the effects of aliasing can be reduced by computing the amount of pixel area that is subtended by the line as it passes through the pixels that lie on top of it. If only a small portion of the pixel is cut by the line, the color intensity of the pixel is reduced proportionately. In this way pixels that are not a part of the major portion of the line are given less emphasis, making the line appear smoother.

Another way to antialias a line is to add pixels into the jagged edges and have their color intensities taper off. This method results in a smooth line, but the line also appears to be wider.

By combining these two techniques, lines can be made to appear very smooth indeed. The computational requirements are great, however, and personal computers are not equipped to handle such advanced antialiasing methods without the addition of expensive array processor hardware. Even then the performance can be slow. For the purposes of this book, it is sufficient to know about antialiasing, but it will be difficult to demonstrate.

CIRCLE ALGORITHM

You can make circles by plotting lines as chords. A **chord** is a line segment with its endpoints on the perimeter of the circle. Under certain circumstances this may be desirable, for example, when you need to work with circles in a three-dimensional system. However, circles generated by chords tend to appear less than smooth unless the number of chords is greater than 36, allowing at least 10 degrees per chord. As the display resolution increases, the chords should be made more numerous. It is common practice to give the user control over the number of chords in order to control the smooth appearance of the circle.

Another problem is that the amount of computation required to generate circles as chords reduces the speed of drawing. To speed things up you need to use an algorithm that is like the line-drawing algorithm. In simple two-dimensional systems, however, you can take advantage of another of Bresenham's tricks.

Bresenham's Circle Algorithm

Like a line, a circle can be generated by adding and subtracting cumulative values. Figure 4-5 shows an analog circle drawn through pixels on a grid. Figure 4-6 shows the result of applying a rasterizing algorithm to the same circle. The sequence of nine grids shows the selection of pixels in animated form.

In Figure 4-7 you can see the final result, after the octant generated in Figure 4-6 has been reflected eight times. The process is similar to the way in which images are mirrored inside a kaleidoscope.

The pseudocode for drawing a circle can be found in Function 4-2. As with the line-drawing algorithm in Function 4-1, the code cannot be compiled. The location of each pixel is derived from the value of d, which varies depending on x, y, and some constants. Elsewhere in this book the algorithm is expressed as a function in C, and you will see that the expression must take certain other factors into consideration. First of all,

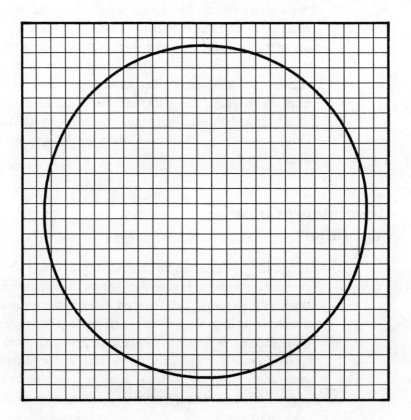

FIGURE 4-5.   A circle centered on a pixel grid

the pseudocode demonstrates only the first octant of the circle, from 90 degrees through 45 degrees. In order to generate the other seven octants, you must use a symmetry function. In addition, displays are unequal in their aspect ratios, and so a circle will sometimes appear as an ellipse. A correction ratio must be included in the algorithm to give the user control over the appearance of the finished circle.

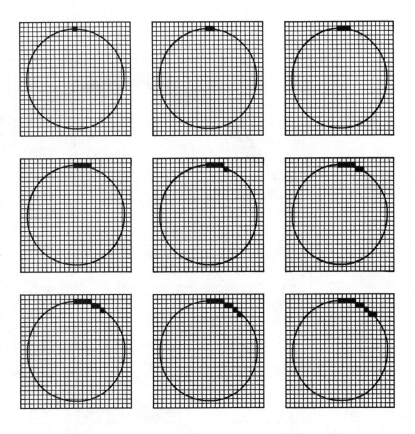

FIGURE 4-6. Pixels selected by circle-drawing algorithm

Origin Transfer

The circle described here is assumed to be drawn centered on the origin of a rectangular coordinate system. In order for it to be drawn anywhere else, it must be capable of being offset in the x and y directions. This, too, is accomplished in the actual implementation of the algorithm as a function.

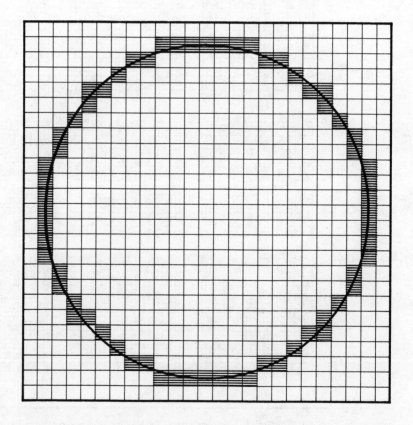

FIGURE 4-7. Pixels after being reflected 8 times around the circle

■ FUNCTION 4-2

Circle Algorithm

```
Pseudocode for Bresenham's circle-drawing algorithm.
Only one-eighth of the circle is produced by this algorithm.
You need to reflect it eight times to make the circle.

Given radius y...

d is 3, less two times y

while x is less than y
     plot a pixel at x, y
     if d is less than 0, increment d using 4 times x, plus 6
          otherwise, increment d using 4 times (x less y),
               plus 10, decrement y
     increment x

if x equals y, plot a pixel at x, y.
```

Circle Style

As with line styles, circles can be drawn with various patterns. The technique is similar to that used for lines. In the circle-drawing algorithm shown, each pixel is tested against a rotating byte or word, with the bits in the pattern represented in the test word determining whether or not the pixel near the circle's circumference will be drawn.

Circle Width

The circle's line width can be increased by drawing circles first inside, one pixel distant, and then outside, one pixel distant, around the generating circle. As with line width, the circle function is called from within another function that determines the width and draws the additional circles required.

DRAWING ARCS

You could use the same approach for drawing arcs as for drawing circles, but you would encounter some problems. Arcs, being portions of circles, need to be drawn through *subtended angles*. The angle subtended by the arc is the angle through which a radius would need to rotate to generate the arc.

Directionality

The problems begin when you realize that arcs need to be drawn from starting points and must end at ending points. They must be drawn according to rules having to do with directionality. You can draw arcs clockwise or counterclockwise from a starting location. A circle can be defined in many different ways, but it usually does not matter where on its circumference you begin and end.

With arcs it is often better to use a chord-drawing technique rather than a faster pixel-oriented method. Bresenham's algorithm will not be as fast as using chords to draw arcs. Because of the octant method used in Bresenham's algorithm, it is extremely complicated to select octants needed to construct an arc. In the last analysis, except for extremely simple systems, it is better to draw circles and arcs using a chording technique even if you need to sacrifice some speed to do it. Using the numeric coprocessor, you can make liberal use of trigonomic functions, otherwise known as **transcendentals,** to compute the endpoints of chords that are then drawn as lines.

Three-Point Circle

A circle or arc can be defined by locating its center and indicating a radius. You can also define a circle by specifying the locations of three points on the circle's circumference. Such a function is valuable in engineering applications because the center of an arc or circle may not be known. If you have three points and need to fit an arc to them, Function 4-3, CENTER.C, will derive the location of the center of the circular arc and its radius.

Study Function 4-3 carefully; it incorporates techniques that are very valuable in converting concepts from analytic geometry to C code. You will encounter simultaneous equations often in your graphics work.

The function works like this: Three simultaneous equations are solved using the equation of a circle, since the three points lying on the circumference must satisfy the following circle equation:

r = sqrt(sq(x) + sq(y))

This equation is centered on the origin. An intermediate set of variables that correspond with the coefficients of terms in the circle equation is used to contain the results of subtracting the equation for the second point from the equation for the first, and the equation for the third point from the equation for the second. These intermediate variables are in turn solved simultaneously to derive the coordinates of the center of the circle. These coordinates are then plugged back into the circle equation along with the coordinates of one of the three original points. The result is the radius.

The technique illustrated in Function 4-3 can be used to great advantage whenever simultaneous equations need to be solved. Typical problems requiring simultaneous equations are line intersections, interpolation, and perpendiculars. If you

■ FUNCTION 4-3

CENTER.C

```
/* CENTER.C derives the coordinates of the center of a
** circle and its radius from the coordinates of three
** points on the circle's circumference. */

#include <math.h>

center(x, y, xc, yc, r)
double x[], y[], *xc, *yc, *r;
{
double x2[2], xh[2], y2[2], yk[2];
double x2y2[2], xnyn, ykn;

x2[0] = x[0]*x[0] - x[1]*x[1];
xh[0] = 2.0 * x[0] - 2.0 * x[1];
y2[0] = y[0]*y[0] - y[1]*y[1];
yk[0] = 2.0 * y[0] - 2.0 * y[1];

x2[1] = x[1]*x[1] - x[2]*x[2];
xh[1] = 2.0 * x[1] - 2.0 * x[2];
y2[1] = y[1]*y[1] - y[2]*y[2];
yk[1] = 2.0 * y[1] - 2.0 * y[2];

x2y2[0] = x2[0] + y2[0];
x2y2[1] = x2[1] + y2[1];

xnyn = x2y2[0];
ykn = yk[0];

x2y2[0] *= xh[1];
yk[0] *= xh[1];

x2y2[1] *= xh[0];
yk[1] *= xh[0];

*yc = (x2y2[0] - x2y2[1]) / (yk[0] - yk[1]);
*xc = (xnyn - *yc * ykn) / xh[0];

x[0] -= *xc;
y[0] -= *yc;

*r = sqrt(x[0]*x[0] + y[0]*y[0]);
}
```

master the straightforward method of the center( ) function, you
will be able to forge ahead into the realms of analytic geometry
required for sophisticated computer graphics systems.

FILL ALGORITHM

Although the ability to draw lines and curves satisfies most of
the requirements for line drawings, you will often wish to fill
areas with color. You can do this in several ways, depending on
the accuracy, speed, and flexibility you need. One method that
works well is presented here.

Filling

Fill algorithms are used to change the colors of pixels that lie
within specified regions. This may seem at first to be intuitively
simple, but computers, as you must know by now, are not
intuitive. Whereas a human being can easily perceive the *inside*
and the *outside* of an outlined area, the computer must use a
hit-or-miss method. The algorithms used *know* only about the
colors of pixels in one small area, usually the single pixel being
addressed at any given time.

Simple fill algorithms start at a pixel identified by the user to
be inside a region and test the colors of the rows of pixels above,
row by row, and then the rows below. Usually, the **boundary** that
defines the region consists of pixels that are all of a given color.
When it encounters a pixel of that color, the algorithm goes on
to the next row. Boundaries are, in general, lines or curves that
define the outer extents of regions. Boundaries can be defined by
pixel color, or they can be defined by a line list.

Floods

A **flood** is a rapid area fill. Although this term is vaguely defined in the computer industry, a flood is distinguished from a fill by speed and lack of user control. The problem with floods is that they are confused by incursion of the boundary into the region. Figure 4-8 shows such an incursion of the boundary and what happens when the simple flood algorithm is used. Note that a part of the region is missed. It is extremely difficult to construct a flood algorithm that will work for all boundary conditions.

Of course, computers don't *know* anything. They are very good at sorting numbers, though. If you take advantage of sorting, you will have the key to giving the computer a kind of *knowledge* about groups of lines.

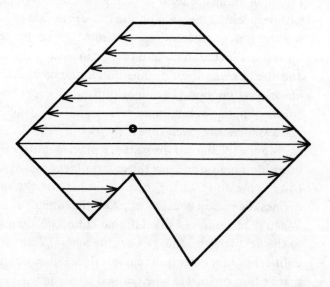

FIGURE 4-8.   A simple flood algorithm misses incursions

Identifying an Object   If you give a set of lines an identity as an **object,** you will solve the single most important problem in the fill algorithm. You can give an object its identity simply by giving it a name in the database.

Locating the Object   You locate the object by identifying at least one pixel on it. Once this is done, you activate a function that regenerates the drawing from the database until the identified pixel is displayed. At this time, the display process stops. The object that is being displayed has a name that can be used to identify the set of lines, circle, rectangle, or other object for use in the fill algorithm.

Simplifying Floods   One way to solve the problem of floods is to rely on object definition and a line database. Once you identify the object, its boundaries are known. You can test for intersections, sort, and use other techniques to deal comprehensively with recursions, inclusions (holes), and other such phenomena.

The algorithm used in this book for "fast fills" will be the simple technique described in pseudocode in Function 4-4. To use the algorithm, you identify one pixel on the boundary that outlines the region you wish to fill and choose a color for the fill. It is assumed that the object that contains this pixel can be found.

The algorithm reads the line list for the object. A special point-drawing function is used that, instead of drawing a point, records the location of the point in a coordinate list. Each such point is, by definition, an intersection of the line with the horizontal raster.

After the list is finished, it is sorted by ascending values of x in y. After the sort the algorithm starts with the largest y value and plots lines using an alternating "pen-up, pen-down" technique until it reaches the lowest y value.

■ **FUNCTION 4-4**

Fill Algorithm

```
Fast fill algorithm based on a vector list.

Given the beginning and ending vector numbers in the list...

find the greatest and least y values in the list

use line algorithm to plot line, store pixel coordinates in
list without plotting

sort the list into ascending values of x

plot the sorted list from greatest to least y value, alternating
pen-up and pen-down for each x value in a given raster line.
```

Each raster line starts with the pen up at the leftmost line intersection (remember, the list has been sorted by ascending values of x in y) and draws pixels until it reaches the next line intersection. If the line intersection is the last one on the raster, the algorithm raises the pen and goes on to the next lower raster. If, however, the line intersection is not the last one on the raster, the pen is raised until the next intersection. The "pen" in the case of a CRT display is imaginary. In the case of a plotter, of course, it is real. In each case the pen is conceptually the same thing.

Incursions

The fill algorithm depends on a unique property of the topography of regions with incursions. The number of times a continuous boundary of a region is crossed by a line will always be *even.* You can test this by studying Figure 4-9. Count the dots on any line you choose. The number will always be even as long as the boundary is continuous. The test also works for included regions.

This is not a rigorous proof. In practice you need to be concerned with maximum and minimum values. For example, the maximum values for curves ideally consist of single points. If a horizontal fill line crosses a single point, it will make the count of line crossings odd. For this reason, such maximum and minimum values must be ignored. You need to treat line end-points as special cases because they can be maximum or min-

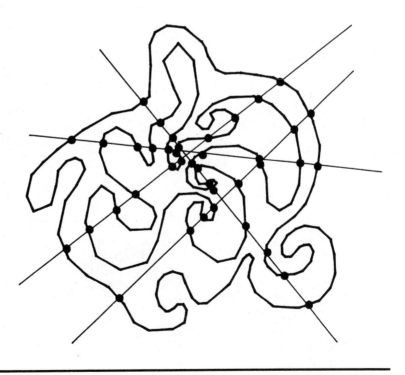

FIGURE 4-9.   Incursive boundary with included region

imum values. When a line endpoint is intersected, it must be ignored. If you are already aware that endpoints are merely records of locations and not parts of lines, you will find this easy to understand.

Figure 4-10 illustrates the fill algorithm in animated form. The grids are shown in sequence from left to right and top to bottom.

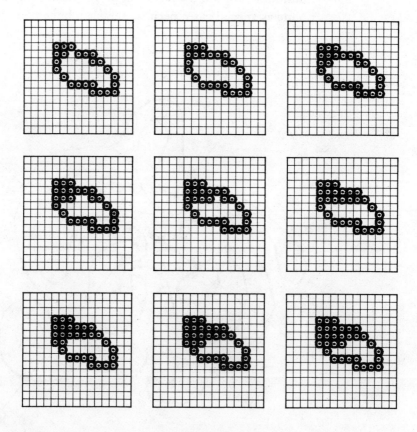

FIGURE 4-10. The pixel fill algorithm in action

Nonuniform Fills

If you wish to simulate the effects of shading on a filled area, you will need to add some sophistication to your fill algorithm. Shading, reflections, textures, and many more attributes can be assigned to fills. The amount of shading and so forth that you can do depends on how rich your color palette is and how fast and powerful your hardware is. Shading can be computed using an imaginary light source or done according to an equation that decreases color intensity by spherical, parabolic, or conic rates. In low-cost computing applications, it is usually much faster to sacrifice the precise realism of a computed light source for each pixel and use the equations of cones, spheres, or other simple geometric objects to govern the shading.

Smoothing

If you have lots of color (and money) to work with, you can add smoothing functions to your software. With the EGA this is difficult to do because the 16 colors available limit smoothing, but with the ICB you can implement smoothing functions quite effectively. Smoothing involves the use of several methods to "average" the color intensities in a defined area. You can define the area as the entire display surface, but you will usually use a brush to smooth smaller areas. Your brush can be designed to smooth according to conic, spherical, or other equations.

Brushes

In your graphics applications you will undoubtedly want to implement a paintbox capability to permit the editing of display contents. In doing so you will need to create **brushes.** A brush is an area on the display surface that can be moved under user control. The design of the area can be anything from a point to a random pattern of dots and is left to your imagination. Brushes can also have gradients that produce a nonuniform effect over the area of the brush. Such gradients can be defined by equations, usually the equations of cones or spheres.

Palettes

A brush needs a **palette,** as every artist knows. Your palettes can pop up on the display surface wherever you need them, and should contain a series of colors as well as a mixing area in which you can combine colors. You use the brush to select a color from the palette and then paint with it elsewhere on the display. Study the process a painter uses with real paint and brushes to get an idea of what is needed. Few graphics systems have been thoroughly successful in emulating the techniques actually used by artists.

CROSSHATCHING

If your graphics system uses a line database, consisting of a list of x, y coordinates, you can be very flexible in filling regions. You can selectively fill regions more predictably than with pixel-bounded methods, and discontinuities in the boundaries can be better controlled.

Function 4-5 is pseudocode for a crosshatching algorithm that was developed to do the same thing the fill algorithm does, but it uses an interval rather than confining crosshatching to the raster. To start the procedure, you provide the beginning and ending line numbers in a sequential list. The algorithm draws

■ FUNCTION 4-5

Crosshatching Algorithm

```
Crosshatching algorithm based on a vector list.

Given the beginning and ending vector numbers in the list and
the hatching interval...

find the greatest and least y values in the list

find intersections for each interval
     (start with pen up each time)
     store each intersection in a separate list

sort the list into ascending values of x

plot the sorted list from greatest to least y value, alternating
pen-up and pen-down for each hatching interval.
```

horizontal lines. Because the crosshatch elements are lines, the line style can be altered to provide additional variety in the pattern. The crosshatching algorithm computes line intersections rather than raster intersections. It does this by using the slope of the line.

The crosshatching algorithm is surprisingly simple, but it depends on some tricks that are shown in the completed C function for crosshatching elsewhere in this book. One advantage of this algorithm is that as long as boundaries are connected (they begin and end at the same point) you can have any number of "holes" in the region. The algorithm ensures that holes are skipped over.

The regions do not need to be rectangular, and the number of lines is limited only by the maximum number of lines permitted in your drawing file.

Crosshatching at
a Rotation Angle

You are not limited to horizontal lines. With a little ingenuity you could enhance the algorithm so that it accepts a rotation angle. Instead of dealing with the complicated geometry required to compute the hatching interval and intersections for rotated hatch lines, try rotating the object itself temporarily and using the horizontal hatching method. When crosshatching is finished, you merely rotate the object back to its original position, along with the crosshatching.

Line-based Versus
Point-based Systems

Crosshatching algorithms are essential for line-based systems. A distinction needs to be made between such systems and paint-box systems. Most software falls into one category or the other. The GRAPHIQ program is an attempt to combine both worlds to illustrate the range of graphics options available. In practice you will want to predict the needs of users whenever you can. If the output of the system will go to a plotter, you must concentrate on lines. Fills will then be crosshatched areas. If the output of the system is intended for television, your tools must include paintbrushes and palettes. The result will be raster based rather than line based.

DITHERING

Dithering is the process of combining adjacent pixels into groups to increase color resolution. Dithering algorithms are many and varied. They are used to expand the color resolution on systems with limited color capabilities. Where only black and white are available, dithering can produce shades of gray, otherwise known as a gray scale.

Additive Versus Subtractive Colors

Let's say that a computer display is capable of only three colors: red, green, and blue. When you add equal amounts of red, green, and blue together on the computer display, the result is white. The colors are thus said to be **additive.** Colors that are transmitted (as in a slide projector) are additive. Colors that are absorbed (as in an oil painting) are **subtractive.** Colors generated by a cathode ray tube are additive. When all colors are off, the result is black.

When you dither from a computer display where colors are additive, you must invert the color values to create a positive image on printed hard copy. The printed output is, remember, like a painting, subtractive for color.

The four-color display can show only one of the four colors at once in any given pixel position. To increase the color content of the display, you must use dithering to increase the number of pixels that, taken together, will portray a single color.

The Dithering Matrix

As an example, let's make the four-color display show 252 discrete colors. To do this, 16 pixel positions will be necessary. Six positions will be assigned to red, five to green, and five to blue. In order to make the dithered cell symmetrical (which may or may not be desired), the cell will be four pixels square. Figure 4-11 shows the dithered cell and the distribution of red, green, and blue pixels within it. The color positions and the sequences of those colors in the dithering matrix must be chosen carefully. Above all, avoid sequences that make pixels of the same color line up horizontally or vertically.

Note that the example in Figure 4-11 distributes colors symmetrically. Red is assigned one more pixel than blue or green. This is done because the red content in a picture tends to improve contrast. The effect is similar to the effect of using a red filter in photography. Because the number of available positions in this matrix is even and the number of colors is odd, one additional pixel must be allocated to one of the colors. The color might as well be red.

The sequences in which the pixels are turned on (denoted in the figure by small numbers next to the letters R, G, and B) are chosen such that the pixel farthest away from its neighbor in sequence is used. In this way neighboring pixels are never activated in sequence.

This matrix is probably the optimum for spatial and sequential distribution of pixels, given a four-by-four cell. Of course, the effective resolution of your display will be reduced by dithering. In the example the horizontal and vertical resolution of the display will be divided by 4. If the display is 640 horizontal by

R_1	G_3	G_1	R_3
B_4	G_5	R_5	B_1
B_2	R_6	B_5	B_3
R_4	G_2	G_4	R_2

FIGURE 4-11. A typical dithering matrix

200 vertical, its dithered resolution will be 160 by 50. Dithering gives you a way to trade spatial resolution for color resolution.

Dithering from a Television Source

Figure 4-12 shows a dithered picture that was created using the dithering matrix in Figure 4-11. In adjusting for a natural **aspect ratio** (the ratio of horizontal to vertical dimensions), the matrix in the example overprints a few lines, so don't try to count pixels.

FIGURE 4-12.   An image dithered using a dithering matrix

The section on television in Appendix C contains an example of a dithering algorithm for use with the EGA. An ICB was used to buffer the image, and the image was dithered onto the EGA using a much simpler matrix than the one described in Figure 4-11.

Dithering from a Coordinate List

Function 4-6 is an actual dithering algorithm written in C called, appropriately enough, DITHER. It takes its input from a list of integers with values for red, green, and blue. Note particularly that cutoff levels are necessary to translate between a range of values that is greater on input than the range can be on output. For example, where red on input can have 32 possible values, it must be reduced to 7 possible values for the dithering matrix.

If you wish to compile and use the DITHER program, you will need to supply the list of color values from some source. You could modify this dithering program to work with your choice of hardware. The program contains all the information you need to translate any color list into an image using a dithered matrix. Dithering can be used any time you need more color than your hardware provides and you are willing to sacrifice some spatial resolution.

Analysis of the DITHER Program

Let's go through DITHER in detail to see how dithering works in practice. First of all, as in any C program, you need to include headers that contain definitions, declarations, and other information for use in the program. In this case all the headers to be included are standard for Microsoft C.

■ FUNCTION 4-6

DITHER.C

```
/*   DITHER.C
 *   An example of a dithering algorithm which prints an image
 *   on a dot-matrix printer.  The source for color values is
 *   an array of words defined at a user-defined location in
 *   RAM.
 */

#include <stdio.h>
#include <memory.h>
#include <ctype.h>
#include <process.h>
#include <string.h>
#include <dos.h>
#include <math.h>

#define BLANK ' '
#define CHARSOUT 1024
#define COLORANGE 32
#define COLORLIM COLORANGE - 1


union
    {
    struct
        {
        unsigned blue : 5;
        unsigned green : 5;
        unsigned red : 5;
        unsigned overlay : 1;
        } colors;
    struct
        {
        unsigned colrs;
        } all;
} picwd;


main(argc, argv)
int argc;
char *argv[];
{
int count;
int status;
int row;
int inchar;
char *out[10];
float ln_inc2;
struct SREGS segregs;
char lines;
```

■ FUNCTION 4-6 (continued)

DITHER.C

```c
char red_array[81], green_array[81], blue_array[81];
int i, j, color_val;
FILE *curve_stream;
int contrast;

/* send out [esc_code][CHARSOUT characters][space_down] */

segread(&segregs);

if (argc < 2 || argc > 3)
    {
    printf("\nUsage: -L5, /L5 mean 5 lines per linefeed.");
    printf("\n   Use 1 to 85 lines per linefeed (5 default).");
    printf("\n       -C1, /C1 all mean contrast normal.");
    printf("\n   Use 1 (default) or 2 (high contrast).");
    printf("\nExample: DITHER /4 -1  is 4 lines per linefeed,");
    printf("\n                       normal (1) contrast.\n\n");
    }

lines = 5; contrast = 1;

for (i = 2; i <= argc; ++i)
    {
    switch (argv[i-1][0])
        {
        case '-':
        case '/':
            switch (toupper(argv[i-1][1]))
                {
                case 'L':
                    lines = includes(atoi(&argv[i-1][2]),
                            1, 85);
                    break;
                case 'C':
                    contrast = includes(atoi(&argv[i-1][2]),
                            1, 2);
                    break;
                }
            break;
        }
    }

/* default color distribution */

if (contrast == 1)
```

■ **FUNCTION 4-6** (continued)

DITHER.C

```
        {
      strcpy(red_array,   "0000011111222223333344444455555566666\n");
      strcpy(green_array, "00000111112222223333334444444455555\n");
      strcpy(blue_array,  "00000111112222223333334444444455555\n");
        }
else    {
      strcpy(red_array,   "0000000001234566666666666666666\n");
      strcpy(green_array, "00000000012345555555555555555555\n");
      strcpy(blue_array,  "00000000012345555555555555555555\n");
        }

printf("\n%s%s%s", red_array, green_array, blue_array);

for (i = 0; i <= COLORLIM; ++i) /* -1 omits '\n' processing */
    red_array[i] -= '0'; /* adjust ascii to numeric */

for (i = 0; i <= COLORLIM; ++i)
    green_array[i] -= '0';

for (i = 0; i <= COLORLIM; ++i)
    blue_array[i] -= '0';


count = 512;

reset();

fprintf(stdprn, "\x1bA%c", lines);  /* set linefeed in 72nds*/

for (row = 199; row >= 0; row -= 2)
    pr_line(row, count, red_array, green_array, blue_array,
                   segregs.ds);

fputs("\x0c", stdprn);  /* page feed */
fprintf(stdprn, "\x1bA%c", 9);  /* set for linefeed in 72nds*/

exit(0);
}

pr_line(row, count, red_array, green_array, blue_array, ds)
int row, count;
char *red_array, *green_array, *blue_array;
unsigned ds;
{
unsigned offset;
unsigned buffer[256];
int srcseg, srcoff, destseg, destoff;
```

■ **FUNCTION 4-6** (continued)

DITHER.C

```
/* prints CHARSOUT bits wide condensed */
/* room for header, pr_buff[],  */
/* and null character */
static char out_buff[4+CHARSOUT] = "\x1bL\x00\x04";

int counter, outrow;
char hibyte, lobyte;
int next_row;
int shift_val;
int i;
unsigned transfer;

if (kbhit())
    {
    fputs("\x0c", stdprn);  /* page feed */
    fprintf(stdprn, "\x1bA%c", 9);  /* set linefeed in 72nds*/
    fputs("\x1bA\x9", stdprn);  /* 9 wires per linefeed */
    getch();   /* keeps character from appearing on console */
    exit(12);  /* exit with arbitrary but unique return code */
    }

for (counter = 4; counter <= 1027; ++counter)
    out_buff[counter] = '\0';

next_row = row - 1;

for (; row >= next_row; --row)
    {
    offset = row * 0x200;

    srcseg = /* you define origin of color array */
    srcoff = offset;
    destseg = ds;
    destoff = (int)buffer;
    movedata(srcseg, srcoff, destseg, destoff, count);

    for (counter = 0; counter <= 255; ++counter)
        {
        picwd.all.colrs = buffer[counter];

        /* must use inverse, - more color means more white */
        transfer = 0xffff;

/*
** This is a good color dithering matrix to use:
** r1 g3 g1 r3
** b4 g5 r5 b1
** b2 r6 b5 b3
** r4 g2 g4 r2
*/
```

■ **FUNCTION 4-6** (continued)

DITHER.C

```
switch (red_array[picwd.colors.red])
    {
    case 0:
        break;
    case 1:
        transfer &= 0x7fff;
        break;
    case 2:
        transfer &= 0x7ffe;
        break;
    case 3:
        transfer &= 0x6ffe;
        break;
    case 4:
        transfer &= 0x6ff6;
        break;
    case 5:
        transfer &= 0x6df6;
        break;
    case 6:
        transfer &= 0x6db6;
        break;
    }

switch (green_array[picwd.colors.green])

    {
    case 0:
        break;
    case 1:
        transfer &= 0xdfff;
        break;
    case 2:
        transfer &= 0xdffb;
        break;
    case 3:
        transfer &= 0x9ffb;·
        break;
    case 4:
        transfer &= 0x9ff9;
        break;
    case 5:
        transfer &= 0x9bf9;
        break;
    }

switch (blue_array[picwd.colors.blue])
    {
    case 0:
        break;
```

■ **FUNCTION 4-6** (continued)

DITHER.C

```
        case 1:
            transfer &= 0xfeff;
            break;
        case 2:
            transfer &= 0xfe7f;
            break;
        case 3:
            transfer &= 0xfe6f;
            break;
        case 4:
            transfer &= 0xf66f;
            break;
        case 5:
            transfer &= 0xf64f;
            break;
        }

    buffer[counter] = transfer;
    }

shift_val = (row % 2) << 2; /* 4 if odd, 0 if even */

    for (counter = 0; counter <= 255; ++counter)
        {
        out_buff[(counter << 2) + 4]
            |= (char)((buffer[counter] & 0xf000)
                >> 12 - shift_val);
        out_buff[(counter << 2) + 5]
            |= (char)((buffer[counter] & 0x0f00)
                >> 8 - shift_val);
        out_buff[(counter << 2) + 6]
            |= (char)((buffer[counter] & 0x00f0)
                >> 4 - shift_val);
        out_buff[(counter << 2) + 7]
            |= (char)((buffer[counter] & 0x000f)
                << shift_val);
        }
    }

/* write the formatted array out printer port as characters */
fwrite(out_buff, 1, 4+CHARSOUT, stdprn);

fputs("\x0a", stdprn); /* send a linefeed */
}


int includes(value, low, high)
int value, low, high;
{
```

■ **FUNCTION 4-6** (continued)

DITHER.C

```
value = (value > high) ? high : value;
value = (value < low) ? low : value;
return(value);
}


reset()
{
union REGS regs;

/* reset printer in accordance with IBM Technical Reference */

regs.h.ah = 1;
regs.x.dx = 0;
int86(0x17, &regs, &regs);
}
```

Following this are some constants that define the maximum number of characters in a buffer (CHARSOUT) and the number of color levels permitted for red, green, or blue. After this, a union combines the separate red, green, blue, and overlay values in the color specification word so that they can easily be extracted from a word when retrieved from memory.

After main( ), which is provided with argc and argv arguments to take information from the command line, segread( ) reads the segment registers to find out what has been assigned for code and data. If an improper number of arguments has been passed on the command line, a "usage" message is displayed and the program is not run. If you wish to know at any time in the future how this program works, simply enter the program name with no arguments and you will get an explanation.

Lines Variable   The lines variable defines how many lines on the printer are to be printed per pass. This allows the user to control the aspect ratio of the image on hard copy.

Contrast Variable   The variable contrast allows the user to select one of two color value distributions defined in two built-in matrix sets. The strings red_array, green_array, and blue_array contain cutoff values for color levels that divide the 32 possible color levels in different proportions. This gives the user controls that are similar to those a photographer has over film contrast in a darkroom.

Color Distribution Report   The color cutoff settings are printed to show ~~which matrix set the user has chosen. Then the~~ strings are converted into numeric values by subtracting the ASCII value of the zero character. You can also use this technique to convert ASCII to integer values for your other programs.

Count Variable   The count variable is multiplied by two by shifting left one bit. It contains a count of the number of bytes across the display surface. Because display values are stored in words, and each word is two bytes, the number of bytes across the display is twice the horizontal resolution. XRES is defined as 256.

Reset Printer   Next, the printer is reset by using IBM's recommended procedure, which is incorporated in Function 4-6. It is set up for the desired number of lines per pass of the print head. The default is 5 lines. This produces an aspect ratio that is close to normal.

pr—line( ) Function   The pr—line( ) function is executed once for each scan line in the source buffer. You could use the same technique, with some modifications, to dump the EGA display to the printer. If you want to modify the program, remember that the dither pattern receives its color values from two states per red, green, and blue, rather than six. Why not write a program to dither colors from the EGA to the Epson printer? This is done in the GRAPHIQ program listed in Appendix A.

CLIPPING

When you change the colors of pixels on the display, you may wish to limit the area in which this can occur. You might want to define a portion of the display where colors can be changed, leaving the rest of the display unchanged. Areas you define for such purposes are called **windows.** To define a window, all you need to furnish are the locations of two diagonally opposite corners.

Clipping Windows

The display as a whole could be said to be within a clipping window defined by its outermost extremities. In practice, however, it is usually faster to reject those values sent to your point-drawing function that fall outside the display boundaries than to use a clipping function for each line, circle, rectangle, or other object. Clipping usually involves several tests, which take time. If your point-drawing function makes a quick test and ignores values that are off the display surface, there is no need for a clipping function for the unwindowed display.

One of the compelling reasons to have source code for all the software you use (if possible) is that you can modify programs at any level. If you can change the way pixels are drawn at the source level, you can implement techniques that would ordinarily not be available to you. It can be frustrating, for example, to work with a high-level language that has built-in commands for drawing lines, circles, and other primitives. If you can't change the way those entities are drawn, you have no control over the software you are creating or using. The several point-drawing functions you will find in this book attest to the need for more than one way to implement any type of function. This is particularly important for functions that involve the use of clipping.

A Clipping Algorithm

When you wish to employ windowing in your displays, you should make use of a clipping algorithm like the one shown in Function 4-7 and illustrated in Figure 4-13. The clipping window is defined by the values XMIN, XMAX, YMIN, and YMAX. These are usually presented as arguments to the function, but they can be made global or constant if you wish to save some time and avoid popping them off the stack. This depends on how flexible you wish your function to be.

As you can see from the clipping window shown in Figure 4-13, there are many possible situations in which a candidate line might be presented to the algorithm. The entire line could be either within the window or outside it. The line might start outside the window and enter it, or it might start inside and exit. The line might start and end outside the window but intersect it. In all, the problem seems perplexing because there are so many different possibilities.

■ FUNCTION 4-7

Clipping Algorithm

Generalized rectangular clipping algorithm for windows.

Given a line defined by endpoints x1, y1, x2, y2, XMAX, XMIN,
YMAX, YMIN find new values if the clipping window is
intersected...

if both x1, y1 and x2, y2 are outside the window and in the
same sector, return NOPLOT

if both x1, y1 and x2, y2 are within the window, return PLOT

if x2 is less than x1, subtract x1 and x2 from XMIN
    subtract XMAX from XMIN, x was flipped

if y2 is less than y1, subtract y1 and y2 from YMIN
    subtract YMAX from YMIN, y was flipped

compute slope of line as (y2 - y1) / (x2 - x1), being sure to
treat infinity when x2 = x1

if x1 is less than XMIN, increase y1 by slope * (XMIN - x1)
    x1 = XMIN

if y1 is less than YMIN, increase x1 by (YMIN - y1) / slope
    y1 = YMIN

if x1 is greater than XMAX or y1 is greater than YMAX the
start of the line is outside the display, return NOPLOT

if the line is now entirely on the display, return PLOT

if y2 is greater than YMAX, reduce x2 by (y2 - YMAX) / slope
    y2 = YMAX

if x2 is greater than XMAX, reduce y2 by slope * (x2 - XMAX)
    x2 = XMAX

if x was flipped on entry, flip back again

if y was flipped on entry, flip back again

return PLOT.

As usual, however, it is possible to eliminate the obvious conditions first and then proceed to normalize as much of the problem as you can. It turns out that you can simplify the problem by converting all lines to lines having a positive slope and then reversing the procedure after your tests have been made and intersections have been computed. Imagine the line to be on a transparent sheet of plastic. You can reverse the sheet by flipping it right over left or top over bottom. As long as you flip it back again the same way before you are through, the same operations can be performed on the flipped (normalized) image that could be performed on the raw image, but with considerably less effort.

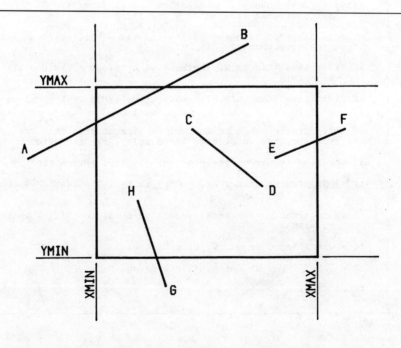

FIGURE 4-13. *Examples of lines requiring clipping*

The Cohen-Sutherland Algorithm   The clipping algorithm presented in this book is a variation of the Cohen-Sutherland algorithm. The algorithm makes use of several interesting techniques. It is designed to make the easiest decisions first. For example, the first test simply involves finding out if the coordinates are all greater than or less than the maximum and minimum extents of the display. The next test involves greater-than-or-equal-to testing and so if the easiest test was flunked, this one will determine whether the line falls entirely within the window.

Having failed both the "outside window" and "inside window" tests, the line endpoint coordinates are normalized, that is, their signs are changed as required to make the slope of the line positive. This reduces the problem to one of solving only for values that are less than or greater than the window minima and maxima.

In essence, if the beginning of this line with positive slope is below the window, to the left of it, or both, it will be truncated. If the ending of this line is above the window, to the right of it, or both, it will be truncated. To truncate, the slope of the line is multiplied or divided as required, and the result is added to or subtracted from the endpoint coordinates to determine the new clipped coordinates.

After the clipping process has been completed, the line endpoint coordinates are flipped back again, if required, and a normal return is then made. The contents pointed to by the arguments to the function are now the clipped coordinates.

The Clipping Algorithm in Action

Figure 4-14 shows the clipping algorithm in action for a worst-case example. The line drawn from (x1, y1) to (x2, y2) in Figure 4-14a must first be reflected around the y axis to make x2 temporarily greater than y2. The result of this is shown in Figure

4-14*b*. Because y1 is greater than x2, the line must then be flipped around the x axis, as shown in Figure 4-14*c*. After the line has been made to conform to the orientation required for the rest of the algorithm, it is first truncated to the minimum x value of the window, as in Figure 4-14*d*. The line is then, in Figure 4-14*e*, truncated to the minimum y value. In Figure 4-14*f* the line is further truncated to the maximum y value, and finally, in Figure 4-14*g*, it is truncated to the maximum x value. After the line has been clipped in its standard orientation, it is flipped around y again (Figure 4-14*h*) and then flipped around x (Figure 4-14*i*) to restore it to the orientation it was in when it entered the algorithm. The only difference is that now no values on the line exceed the window boundaries.

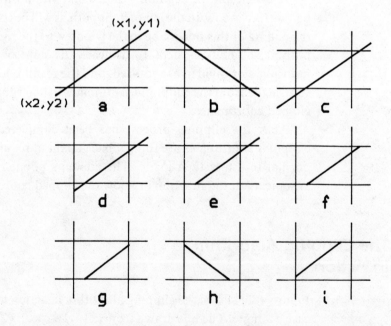

FIGURE 4-14. The clipping algorithm in action

The function calling the clipping algorithm must know whether or not it is all right to attempt to plot the line. The clipping algorithm returns TRUE if plotting is permitted. If no plotting is necessary because the line lies outside the window, the algorithm returns FALSE.

The Numeric Coprocessor Used in Clipping

Clipping can be accomplished in many different ways. You can speed the process by avoiding the use of nonintegers, for example, when calculating the slope. If you use a numeric coprocessor, double-precision variables shouldn't slow the process down. Make sure, for any use you make of the 8087 coprocessor, that you have set the proper compiler options. If you do not enable the coprocessor, the compiler will substitute a coprocessor simulator from its library.

EGA and Software Clipping

Even though the EGA has no on-board clipping or line-drawing capabilities, its real virtue is that it is very standardized on IBM equipment and is likely to be found in offices and homes around the world. Since the introduction of IBM's PC AT, the EGA has essentially replaced the CGA. In addition, new hardware seems to be designed with the EGA or a compatible adapter built in. More expensive hardware often has the utilities you need to draw lines, circles, arcs, and more. The disadvantage of such hardware, aside from its price, is that you cannot predict how widely it will be used.

SHAPE TABLES

Some graphics objects are not generated by algorithms. Such objects might be the characters of the alphabet, icons, or other graphics entities. Since these symbols are not generated by algorithms they must be stored and communicated in other ways.

One way to communicate this type of object is through a shape table. A **shape table** is an array of shape matrices that specifies nodal points that can be connected together by lines. Each matrix within the shape table defines a graphics element. The shape table is read by the system as though from the system's line database, except that positions in the table are offset to the display surface relative to an origin for the shape.

Rotating, Translating, and Scaling Shapes

The information contained in a shape table can be rotated, translated, and scaled. A typical graphics character set, if contained in a shape table, can be rotated, translated, and scaled as well. Figure 4-15 shows a typical cell representing the letter "m" in a shape table. The resolution of this cell is lower than is typical for actual graphics systems. Common practice is to make the cell resolution fit into a byte specification. This enables the coordinates of cell elements to be very compact. Because an object of type char occupies one byte, it is capable of storing, in its unsigned form, a number as large as 255. Thus, two bytes could store the coordinates of a point in a 256-by-256 matrix. If used in unsigned form, the coordinates of a point in a 512-by-512 matrix could be expressed.

Pitch

Notice that the cell in Figure 4-15 is used right up to its edges. If the character in the cell were placed side by side with other characters that were also defined this way, the resulting string of characters would be hard to read. The spacing of characters (their pitch) must be included when the character cells are read out onto the display surface. In simple systems you could include the separation between characters in the character cell itself. Most ROM character generators do this. The disadvantage to this is that pitch becomes harder to control when it is included in the character cell. You must then compensate for the additional space in computing the width of the character or its position.

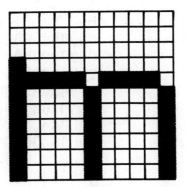

FIGURE 4-15.   A character shape on a shape cell matrix

Cell Specification for Shape Tables The cell specification for shape tables varies from system to system. In a simple system it could consist of a character array with each bit either on or off, as in Figure 4-16. It could also consist of an array of coordinates, as in Figure 4-17. The way a cell is specified depends on what is fastest and best for a specific implementation. If shapes have few lines, the coordinate array may be best. If shapes are permanent, or if you want to be able to design them as parts of headers, the character array might be better.

Shape Matrix

The shape table in Figure 4-16 takes up a lot of space in RAM, but it has the advantage that, while programming, you can easily create and change shapes. The technique also works for,

```
char *table_m[] = {
"00000000000",
"00000000000",
"00000000000",
"10000000000",
"11111011110",
"10000100001",
"10000100001",
"10000100001",
"10000100001",
"10000100001",
"10000100001"};
```

FIGURE 4-16. A character shape cell as it might be coded

and is perhaps better suited to, bit-mapped symbols that are not composed of lines. In such a use, each cell directly represents pixel patterns on the display at a fixed scale.

Shape Coordinate List

Figure 4-17 is a list of coordinate pairs that specify all the information required to represent the symbol in Figures 4-15 and 4-16. Each element in the list is composed of four character values. The first two represent the starting point of a line (stroke), and the second two represent the stroke's ending point. The line list thus represents the specification of a stroke character. A **stroke** character is one that is drawn on the display using line strokes rather than being created by dots. In this case ASCII representations are used, but the actual byte value can be used for higher resolution. For example, instead of each position in the list element being a number from 0 through A, each position could be a char value from 0 through 255.

```
0007
0646
5055
6696
A0A5
```

FIGURE 4-17.   A character shape coordinate list

Graphics characters and shapes are much different from ROM-generated characters. They are never drawn as quickly on the display, but they have the advantage that they can be drawn at any size or angle, and can even be distorted, skewed, shrunk, or expanded in any direction. You can use one character in many different ways, thus expanding the appearance of the characters in the character set.

Fonts

A character font in a graphics system can consist of any conceivable font you might find in the real world. Your system can enable different fonts by reading them from external files on demand. The usual practice is to maintain one default font that is optimal for most uses and then make space for one or more alternate fonts, which can be loaded when the user wants them.

Designing your own fonts can be a difficult process. If you think of the time designers of type have spent to originate new fonts for printing over the centuries, you will appreciate that your own efforts will be miniscule compared with the wealth of fonts already available. You can, if you find fonts that are in the public domain, trace them and use them commercially. Be aware, however, that type fonts are often copyrighted and that to use them commercially you must obtain permission from the designer.

String Objects

The process of drawing shapes from tables is similar to the process used for other drawing tasks in your graphics system. Your database should contain definitions for any unique object, such as a line, line group, circle, or string of text. When a string object is found in your database, you must let the system know that the contents of the string are to be generated from a specific shape table.

Each character in the string will refer to its shape definition. Depending on the prevailing text rotation, translation, and scaling parameters in effect, the character shape will be drawn on the display surface in different ways.

Adding Primitives to Shape Tables

Your shape tables can be much more elaborate than simple line lists. You can use fills, line styles, circles, arcs, and any other primitives that you have assigned codes in the shape table specification. Remember, a shape table is really nothing more than a miniature, abbreviated version of the drawing database. If you keep this in mind, you can make shape tables perform all the tasks your system can perform.

USING ALGORITHMS TO GENERATE C CODE

The algorithms presented in this chapter form a basis for the specific functions developed later in this book. If you design your algorithms first, as has been done here, you will solve most of the problems you would otherwise encounter during coding. The extra burden of code generation is enough to bring confusion to what are otherwise elegant concepts.

If you are interested in creating code that is efficient and clean, it pays to deal with graphics at the lowest level. Beware of generalized functions for drawing graphics primitives, especially for points and lines. There are many ways to draw points, depending on how fast you need to do it. If you do not have access to source code for drawing points and lines, you cannot possibly optimize your system's performance.

Be Careful About Assumptions

When you convert from the algorithm to the C function, be careful to check the algorithm for assumptions that need elaboration for practical use. Be particularly cautious regarding boundary conditions, where numbers exceed limiting values. Such boundaries exist, for example, where the limits of display surfaces are involved. If you fail to correct a condition where values are written into RAM beyond the limits of the display buffer, you could accidentally overwrite important DOS information or interrupt vectors.

Round-Off Problems

Problems having to do with round-off errors can be particularly vexing. Because graphics involves a great deal of rounding to get from floating-point reals to integer values, the attention you pay to rounding off numbers is important.

Remember that a number, once converted from a floating-point to an integral value, cannot be converted back again without losing information about the decimal portion. Avoid converting values that have been used for the display surface back to real numbers in the database. In other words, the flow of information is always *from* the database of real numbers *to* the display surface. If you wish to modify the database, always stay within the "world of reals," and read this world into the "world of display" to view the results. The display is merely a tool to be used to view the database, not the database itself, in a line-based system.

Keep a Line Database

Finally, even if you are creating a paint-only program, you should nevertheless keep a line database for use in efficient filling and to give flexibility for scaling and revising your pictures. Such a system might be called a "hybrid" graphics system. It bridges the gap between strictly raster-based and strictly line-based software.

5

Transformations

The word **transformation** literally means "a change of form." Computers are ideal transformers. In computer graphics you have unlimited resources for changing the appearance of an object or for changing the object itself permanently.

Transformations are required whenever you wish to change (transform) the locations of graphics elements from their original locations in space. A transformation is required when you move an object in its entirety from one location to another. A transformation is also required when you rotate all the points in an object around a central point. Changing the size of an object also involves a transformation.

For most purposes in graphics you will require only three basic transformations: rotation, translation, and scaling. All transformations are performed on objects that are identified during the editing process.

OBJECTS

In order to identify the set of entities (lines, points, and other elements) that are to be transformed, you need to incorporate into your program a method of assigning object identities. In general, an **object** is a collection of entities identified by a name or names. Many different methods can be used to identify objects.

Object Identifiers

One method of recording object identities that works well is to use a special record that contains the name of the object. This record is called an **identifier.** In addition to the name of the object, it contains the number of records that follow the identifier. In your program you could search for this identifier by name and work with the entities following it, or you could search for a particular entity by its spatial location and read backward to find the identifier. In either case the object is defined by its identifier name and is read by offsets of entities from the base address of the identifier record.

The FILE.H header in Chapter 3, Function 3-1, uses a filename string variable to store an object name. Study FILE.H to see how objects can be given identities, in this case by reference to the filenames under which such objects might be stored separately.

Managing Object Identities　Working with object identities requires sophisticated database management. Creating the object is not a problem, but changing the object can be very difficult. You need to make sure that the identifier offset record for the object is changed when you increase or decrease the number of entities in the object. One reason this can be difficult is that entity records must be inserted into the database. When you insert records into a file, the records at the point of insertion must be moved to make room for the new records. The database needs to be opened up to accommodate the inserted records. When records are removed the database must be closed up to avoid gaps.

Editing Objects

In order to identify the data to be transferred, you must create an object identity. When an object is recognized by the system, its contents can be copied to a separate file (or portion of memory) and edited there. After the object has been edited, the objects that came before it could be copied into a separate file, the edited object could be appended to this file, and finally the objects following the edited object could be appended. The newly created file could then be renamed using the old filename. This process could be made automatic.

Locator Crosshairs   When you edit an object you will need to use a locator crosshairs. This tool usually consists of a matrix of pixels in the form of a cross. You can even make the appearance of the crosshairs programmable by the user.

You use crosshairs to locate parts of objects. The program then searches through the database until it finds objects that contain the points you have located.

Once an object has been found, the editing process depends on the use of the locator to add new locations to the database or to change existing locations. You use the locator to define nearly everything you pass to the transformation functions.

Identifier Name   Another way of designating an object for editing is by reference to its identifier name. If you know the name of the object you wish to edit, this method can take much less time than letting the computer search for it.

ROTATION

A rotational transformation implies displacement of points around an origin. Each point is at a specified distance from the origin and at a specified angular deflection. After a point has been rotated, the distance remains the same, but the angular deflection is changed by the desired amount.

It is difficult to work with distances and angular deflections mathematically. In analytic geometry it is customary to use a Cartesian (rectangular) coordinate system. Trigonometric transcendental operators can be used with the rectangular coordinate system to determine new positions for points based on angular deflections.

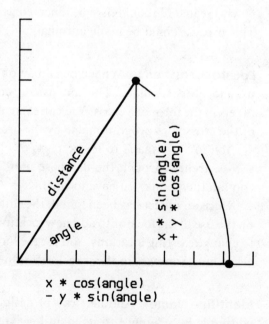

FIGURE 5-1. Rotation of a point around the origin

■ FUNCTION 5-1

ROTATE.C

```
/* ROTATE.C rotates a single point around the
** origin of a two-dimensional coordinate system.
** Angle is in radians.*/

#include <math.h>

rotate(x, y, angle)
double *x, *y, angle;
{
double x_temp = *x;

*x = x_temp * cos(angle) - *y * sin(angle);
*y = x_temp * sin(angle) + *y * cos(angle);
}
```

Rotational Parameters

Figure 5-1 shows the trigonometric relationships involved in rotating a point around the origin. The equations can be used as shown in Function 5-1, ROTATE.C. This function will rotate a point around the origin, but you will not be able to specify a center for rotation other than the origin. Of course, in your finished system you will want to be able to do this. Later in this chapter we will see how rotation, translation, and scaling can be combined into one transformation function that can be used as a filter for all coordinates on their way from the database to the display surface.

Note in particular the necessity of a temporary variable in Function 5-1. Without x_temp the value of x would be reused after it has been transformed.

Rotation State

You may wish to incorporate a rotation state capability into your system. This way you could rotate an entire drawing during the editing session. Objects in the drawing could still be rotated independently, but the rotation function used to rotate separate objects would be separate from the global rotation state you set for the edit session.

You might also create a way for the rotation state to be applied permanently to the entire drawing. This would allow you to rotate an entire drawing from horizontal to vertical, perhaps to put the drawing into a pamphlet or brochure. By combining this feature with scaling and windowing, you could give the user a great deal of control over the positions of book illustrations, for example.

Three-Dimensional Rotation

If you are interested in creating a three-dimensional system, you will want to rotate your objects in space rather than in the plane of a drawing. To do this you need to add a third parameter to the equations of Figure 5-1.

The Rotation Function   Function 5-2, ROTATE3D.C, shows a new rotational function. Note that this function, in addition to rotating a point in succession around x and then y and then z, also translates the center of rotation to the origin and back again. It does this by first subtracting the state.home[] position and then adding it back again.

The state.home[] structure is included in this function for purposes of clarity. In actual practice the state header would be placed in a master header for the system and would contain

■ FUNCTION 5-2

ROTATE3D.C

```
/* ROTATE3D.C rotates a single point around the
** origin of the three-dimensional coordinate system.
** Angles are in radians.*/

#include <math.h>

#define X 0
#define Y 1
#define Z 2
#define FNX(x, y, theta) ((x) * cos(theta) -\
                          (y) * sin(theta));
#define FNY(x, y, theta) ((x) * sin(theta) +\
                          (y) * cos(theta));

struct
    {
    double home[3];
    } state;

rotate3d(x, y, z, angle)
double *x, *y, *z, angle[];
{
double rotx, roty, rotz;
double tempx, tempy;

if (angle[X] == 0.0 && angle[Y]
    == 0.0 && angle[Z] == 0.0) return;

rotx = *x - state.home[X];
roty = *y - state.home[Y];
rotz = *z - state.home[Z];

tempy = roty;
roty = FNX(tempy,rotz,angle[X]);  /* around X axis */
rotz = FNY(tempy,rotz,angle[X]);
tempx = rotx;
rotx = FNX(tempx,rotz,angle[Y]);  /* around Y axis */
rotz = FNY(tempx,rotz,angle[Y]);
tempx = rotx;
rotx = FNX(tempx,roty,angle[Z]);  /* then around Z axis */
roty = FNY(tempx,roty,angle[Z]);

*x = rotx + state.home[X];
*y = roty + state.home[Y];
*z = rotz + state.home[Z];
}
```

global values. To avoid going through the entire computation when all rotation angles are 0, you can test these values on entry and return if they are all 0.

You can keep state information in a similar header in a two-dimensional system. The state header can contain the current position of the locator (crosshairs) in space as well as the location of the diagonal corners of a rectangle, which might be used to define a set of points to be moved. There are many other state parameters that you might want to invent.

Reversal of Compound Three-Dimensional Rotation

If you rotate an object around x and then around y and finally around z, as is done in rotate3d(), you cannot rotate it back again by using negative angles in the same order. For example, if you rotate around x 30 degrees and then 30 degrees around y and then 30 degrees around z, you will not return to the starting position by rotating around x −30 degrees and then around y −30 degrees and then around z −30 degrees.

In order to reverse the process of three-dimensional rotation, you must reverse the order of rotation as well as each rotation angle. To reverse the above rotation, you would need to rotate first −30 degrees around z, and then −30 degrees around y, and finally −30 degrees around x.

TRANSLATION

Translation is the easiest of the transformations to understand. You will need to **translate** a point whenever you want to move it to a new location. To translate a group of points, you move them along parallel lines.

■ FUNCTION 5-3

TRANSLATE.C

```
/* TRANSLATE.C translates a point by a specified offset. */

translate(x, y, offset_x, offset_y)
double *x, *y, offset_x, offset_y;
{

*x += offset_x;
*y += offset_y;
}
```

To specify translation you first locate the beginning location of one point on the object, and then you locate the ending position. The third step is to begin the move. Each point in the object is then erased from its beginning location and drawn, along with any entity information (that is, whether it is a line, circle, arc, or other entity), at the new position.

If your hardware is fast enough you can **drag** the object across the display. Dragging is accomplished by successively **undrawing** and then drawing the object again in small increments. Undrawing a pixel is different from erasing it. Undrawing means using a logical XOR that reverses the color rather than substituting another for it.

Function 5-3, TRANSLATE.C, shows a simple function that takes an offset in x and an offset in y and translates the coordinates of each point by adding the offset values. Remember, offsets can be negative as well as positive.

Three-Dimensional Translation

The problem of translating a point in three-dimensional space is not conceptually more difficult than translating one in two-dimensional space. In practice you will merely add the z axis to your translation function.

SCALING

Whereas translation is additive, scaling is multiplicative. The original coordinate values are multiplied by a scaling factor to obtain scaled coordinates. Scaling, like rotation and *unlike* translation, is always done relative to an origin. When scaling, the offsets of coordinates from the origin are multiplied by the scaling factor.

Function 5-4, SCALE.C, shows how scaling can be applied to each point. In practice you will wish to allow the user to specify a scaling factor for the entire drawing as well as to scale individual objects separately.

If the scaling factor is 1.0, no scaling will be performed. All coordinates will be multiplied by 1.0. If the scaling factor is less than 1.0, the size of the object will be reduced. If the scaling factor is greater than 1.0, the size of the object will be increased.

Axial Scaling

You can scale along axes instead of scaling in all directions. This function, also called stretching, enables you to turn squares into rectangles and circles (if they are chorded) into ellipses. Function 5-5, STRETCH.C, shows how Function 5-4 can be modified to *stretch* an object along either the x axis or y axis.

■ FUNCTION 5-4

SCALE.C

```
/* SCALE.C scales the size of an object. */


scale(x, y, offset_x, offset_y, factor)
double *x, *y, offset_x, offset_y, factor;
{
*x -= offset_x;
*y -= offset_y;

*x *= factor;
*y *= factor;

*x += offset_x;
*y += offset_y;
}
```

You could also generalize Function 5-5 to work in any given direction rather than along only a given axis. A straightforward way to do this is first to rotate the point to an easy axis (say, the x axis) and perform the stretch. After stretching you rotate the point back to its original deflection.

Three-Dimensional Scaling

Scaling in three-dimensional space is the same as scaling in two-dimensional space, except that you must include the z axis. The offset from the origin must also be in x, y, and z.

■ FUNCTION 5-5

STRETCH.C

```
/* STRETCH.C scales the size of an object along either the X
** or Y axes. */

#define X 0
#define Y 1

stretch(x, y, offset_x, offset_y, factor, axis)
double *x, *y, offset_x, offset_y, factor, axis;
int axis;
{

if (axis == Y)
    {
    *x -= offset_x;

    *x *= factor;

    *x += offset_x;

    }
else {
    *x -= offset_x;

    *x *= factor;

    *x += offset_x;
    }
}
```

Distortion

In engineering and scientific applications, you may need to analyze surfaces that are subjected to nonuniform stresses. In three-dimensional analysis, distortion must be considered as a transformational problem.

Distortion is often accomplished through the use of a parametric equation that generates point displacements. Your software, if it is oriented toward engineering or scientific applications, can be equipped with a mathematical interpreter that accepts equations to generate objects.

In a typical two-dimensional system, distortion is seldom considered. Distortion is to be found quite often, however, in three-dimensional analysis.

COMBINED TRANSFORMATIONS

Rotation, translation, and scaling can be combined into one function for most purposes. The reason you might do this would be to avoid pushing and popping the stack when each separate function is run. When double-precision arguments are passed, eight bytes must be pushed onto and popped from the stack for each argument. This takes time.

Function 5-6, XFORM.C, shows a single function that accomplishes rotation, translation, and scaling according to settings that are passed to it. You could avoid passing anything to the function but the coordinates themselves by using externals, if you wanted to make this function even faster.

Notice that translation, being additive, requires no origin. Rotation and scaling, however, are relative to an origin. Function 5-6 performs translation first and then subtracts out the offset of the point from the origin. Rotation and scaling are then performed on the point, which has been reduced to the origin. After rotation and scaling, the offset of the point is added back.

Transformation Sequence   In actual practice the sequence in which these transformations are performed might make a big difference. If translation is performed first, as in Function 5-6, the point will be in a different location than it would if translation were performed after scaling. In general, translation is

■ FUNCTION 5-6

XFORM.C

```
/* XFORM.C transforms a point's location including rotation,
** translation and scaling.  */

xform(x, y, xlate_x, xlate_y, offset_x, offset_y,
        angle, factor)
double *x, *y, xlate_x, xlate_y, offset_x, offset_y,
        angle, factor;
{
double x_temp;

*x += xlate_x;
*x += xlate_y;

xtemp = *x -= offset_x;
*y -= offset_y;

*x = x_temp * cos(angle) - *y * sin(angle);
*y = x_temp * sin(angle) + *y * cos(angle);

*x *= factor;
*y *= factor;

*x += offset_x;
*y += offset_y;
}
```

performed on database units rather than being applied to the product of scaling and rotation.

When Function 5-6 is used in an actual system, it is controlled by having the arguments that are not used set to 0. You can speed things up somewhat by using only the functions you need based on the job to be performed. If you are scaling, use the scaling function. If you are translating, use the translating function. If you are rotating, use the rotation function.

If you want to eliminate doubt about which functions are in effect, however, it is preferable to combine the rotation, translation, and scaling functions. Then you know you have changed all the system state transformations each time you make a change to the system state.

PROJECTION

A form of transformation you will need to consider for use in three-dimensional systems is **projection.** Projection is the act of transforming an object's location in space into its shadow on a projection plane. A single point can be projected onto a surface in much the same way that a point on a slide can be projected onto a wall using a slide projector.

Projection Coordinate System

It has become customary for coordinate systems used in three-dimensional graphics to be different from those used in two-dimensional graphics. This book uses a slightly unconventional approach to the specification of three-dimensional coordinates. An attempt is made to make two-dimensional and three-dimensional coordinate systems compatible.

Traditional Two-Dimensional Coordinates   In a typical two-dimensional expression, the x and y axes are used to specify location. The plans for a building might be drawn using coordinates in x and y. Because plans are drawn using this system, we will call it the **plan** view. A plan is what you see when you look down on an object from above.

Traditional Three-Dimensional Coordinates In a typical three dimensional expression, the x and y axes are used to express horizontal distance (x) and **elevation** (y). The elevation view is the vertical part of a building, for example.

The Observer Projection requires an **observer.** An observer is really just a point from which imaginary light rays are sent through points on an object to intersect a projection plane. The observer in the traditional coordinate system looks down the z axis and, therefore, down onto the plan, not horizontally ahead as real observers do.

A New Coordinate System The approach to three-dimensional coordinates taken in this book deviates from the traditional system in favor of one that reconciles the two-dimensional x,y world of the plan with a new type of three-dimensional system. In this new system, plan information is still expressed in x and y. Elevation information, however, is expressed in z. The eye of the observer looks in the positive direction along the y axis. This new system is much more natural than the traditional one. In the traditional method, you are always looking down on an object from above rather than from the side, where most real observers tend to be.

Projection of a Point

Figure 5-2 shows a single point specified in x, y, and z. It is shown in two views. One view shows its location in the x,z plane. The other view shows its location in the x,y plane. It is assumed that the x,y plane is a standard rectangular coordinate system. The z direction refers to coordinates that lie *above and below* the x,y plane. The entire three-dimensional coordinate system is capable of representing any number of points, and all such points can be projected in the manner shown here.

One additional requirement for the projection of a point is an observer who, like a person, looks directly at a projection plane. The projection plane is like a wall. It is located directly in front of the observer, such that the observer's line of vision is perpendicular to it.

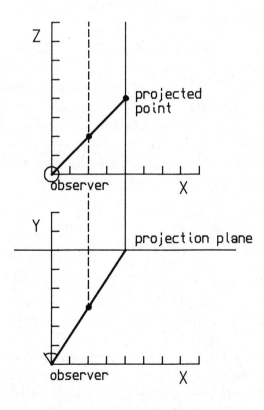

FIGURE 5-2.   Projection of a point onto a projection plane

The Observer Location   For the purpose of illustration, it is assumed that the observer's eye is located at the origin of the coordinate system (at 0,0,0). A ray is projected through the point and stops at the projection plane. You can see the ray drawn in the x,y plane at the bottom of Figure 5-2. The ray intersects the projection plane (also called the picture plane), and its horizontal position becomes the horizontal position for intersection of the ray in x,z, shown at the top of the illustration.

Computing the Projection

To compute the location of the projection on the plane, you need to use a function like the one shown in Function 5-7, PROJECTR.C. The process is simply to use the ratio of the distance between the observer and the projection plane to the point's y coordinate as a multiplier that is applied to the point's x and z coordinates. The result is a new coordinate pair (xp,zp) that represents the location of the projected point on the projection plane.

Filtering the Projection

There are many ways to make the process of projection more complex. In practice there are other things to consider, such as what happens when the function tries to project a point that is behind the observer.

A simple way to avoid the problem of projecting points that lie behind the observer is to filter them out altogether. Intuitively this seems adequate, but when you try it you will find that unless you apply the projection process to each point on a line, you will have trouble with lines that have either endpoint behind the observer.

■ **FUNCTION 5-7**

PROJECTR.C

```
/* PROJECTR.C projects a point onto a projection plane given
the X,Y,Z location of the point, the location of the
observer, and the distance from the observer to the plane of
projection. */

#define TINY 1.0E-306  /* smallest positive real number */
#define ABS(a) (((a) < 0.0) ? -(a) : (a))

projectr(x, y, z, xo, yo, zo, d, xp, zp)
double x, y, z, xo, yo, zo, d, *xp, *zp;
{
double ratio;

x -= xo;  /* bring observer to origin */
y -= yo;
z -= zo;

/* eliminates points behind observer */
y = (y < TINY) ? TINY : y;

ratio = ABS(d) / y;  /* you can eliminate ABS() if you */
                     /* guarantee d is positive */

*xp = x * ratio;
*zp = z * ratio;

*xp += xo;  /* return observer to old location */
*zp += zo;
}
```

Points by Projection   One interesting method for filtering projections and, by the way, producing more accurate perspectives, is to incorporate the projection algorithm into the point-drawing function. Although such a function can be quite efficient, it will draw points more slowly than the point-drawing function without perspective transformation. You need fast hardware to use it effectively. In Chapter 6 you will see how to draw lines using a perspective version of the pixel-drawing function.

GENERAL NOTES FOR CODING TRANSFORMATION FUNCTIONS

In order to produce clean, efficient code, you should follow some general rules for coding transformation functions. Transformations make heavy use of double-precision variables and transcendentals such as sines and cosines. The use of a math coprocessor is essential for such processing. Knowledge of MacroAssembler helps a great deal. You should at least know how the stack is used when functions are called.

Beware of Math Errors

In general, beware of divide-by-zero errors produced when values are at or near zero. This condition has been screened out in Function 5-7 by setting a threshold called TINY. TINY is the smallest positive number that can be held in a variable declared to be double precision. Study the error-trapping features of the Microsoft C Compiler for details regarding underflow, overflow, and other math errors.

Use Faster Hardware, If Possible

If speed is a problem, you may need to use faster hardware. With considerable programming effort you can adapt almost any function in this book to work on an array processor. In some equipment all the necessary functions are built in. The IBM PGC, for example, gives you access to many built-in functions for three-dimensional work.

Use Pointer Arguments

When you wish to pass more than one coordinate pair or triplet to a function, use arrays rather than individual variables. When a C function is called, it pushes any arguments onto the stack, transfers control using an interrupt, and then pops the arguments back off the stack for use. Especially with double-precision numbers (which are each eight bytes long), it is much faster to push a pointer to an array than to push the numbers themselves. For example, instead of passing the double-precision variables x, y, and z, you could pass a pointer to an array declared coords[3]. Each of the three doubles would require 8 bytes, for a total of 24 passed to the function. In a Small-model program, the pointer to coords[ ] would require only two bytes.

Use Assembler to Optimize Transformations

The examples in this book are not necessarily fully optimized. Instead, they are designed to be clearly understood. Before using these functions for any practical purpose, examine them carefully to see whether you can make them run faster. For professional applications this will mean that the C function is often only a starting point.

Graphics Are Hardware Dependent C is intended to be as hardware independent as possible, but graphics are *very* hardware dependent. The whole point of this book is to illustrate how the C language gives you a powerful programming tool that is close enough to the machine level to give your programming a boost, yet does not insulate you from what is actually happening at machine level. To really make your functions sing, you need to take it one step further and optimize in assembler. In essence, you use the C language to get you most of the way, and then you tweak where necessary to make things work right.

This does not mean that *all* your functions need to be written in assembler. The ones for which speed is not critical can bind the application together in C. The ones that require as much speed as possible can still be called just as though they were C functions, but they will have been fine-tuned using Macro-Assembler.

A lot depends on *why* you are programming graphics applications. If you are creating programs for your own use and you do not care how fast they run, the functions in this book can be used literally as is. If, however, you are creating professional software for a client or for the market, you will find that you are drawn into assembler a great deal, despite all the arguments for machine independence. The C language is great, but it has its limitations.

Universality of expression has been sought throughout history. Civilizations have risen and fallen without successfully creating a single language that everyone in the world understands. It is unlikely that the computer industry will ever achieve, even with a language as elegant as C, universal machine independence.

6

Edit Mode

Most activities in a graphics system involve editing. You will create new lines, circles, arcs, and other entities in **edit mode.** Your software will be in edit mode whenever you create or change graphics. Editing is such a central activity that most graphics systems make editing the first function the user sees when the software is run.

This chapter covers the practical aspects of making your graphics software work. Until now, for the most part, graphics have been discussed in abstract terms. You have seen how, in theory, lines, circles, and other entities are drawn. In this chapter you will encounter actual functions that can be used to draw graphics entities.

In addition, you will see how functions are bound together into a working application, which is even more important than the workings of the individual functions. Graphics programming involves the *orchestration* of functions.

FUNCTIONS USED IN EDITING

Graphics systems can be designed for many purposes. In all cases they have finite capabilities, that is, each system contains a limited set of functions that is appropriate for solving certain specific problems. The generic graphics system GRAPHIQ presented in this book is no exception.

Typical Graphics Functions

In Figure 6-1 you see a collection of functions that you might find in a limited graphics software package like GRAPHIQ. You can draw lines of various styles. You can draw a box (or rectangle) by specifying two diagonal corners. You can draw a circle or arc by specifying the center and two points on the perimeter or by specifying any three points on the perimeter. You can fill or

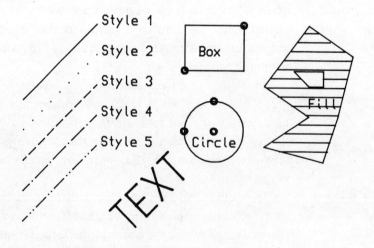

FIGURE 6-1. Some of GRAPHIQ's functions

crosshatch an arbitrary region. And you can draw text characters at various sizes and angles.

Some systems have more capabilities than those represented here, some fewer. In general, the collection in Figure 6-1 will enable you to solve most business graphics problems.

MENUS AND COMMANDS
USED IN EDITING

The careful design of menus to execute system commands can go far to reinforce the effectiveness and attractiveness of your software. Menus supply a unifying force that can be very powerful if used carefully. Editing can be easy or difficult depending on the clarity of your menus.

Programs as Frameworks
for Functions

Graphics programs can be seen as frameworks for collections of functions. Each function needs a context in which it can be executed easily and meaningfully. The program framework provides a context and method for execution for each function. Menus are the visible evidence of the application's framework.

There has been a good deal of talk about friendly software. A loose collection of disconnected functions can hardly be called friendly. Much unfriendly software is such because no clear frame of reference is established to help bind the functions together.

A kludge, the height of unfriendliness, is so named because the sound of the word evokes something that is thrown together haphazardly, like an old pair of shoes and an umbrella full of holes, with a vague hope that the assembly will keep the rain out.

The word could have been put together from an awkward combination of clumsy, crude, and sludge. You don't want to create a kludge.

Menus as Frames of Reference

The frame of reference in a program of any kind is visible to the user most readily in the form of a menu. Menus convey mental images of the system in operation. They are extremely important and, in graphics software, can and should be graphic.

In GRAPHIQ, for example, menus can be brought up at many locations. They can temporarily cover the graphics you are working on to explain how to execute a function or to make a series of options available. When they are no longer needed, the menus can disappear altogether, leaving only the display and locator crosshairs. This way menus do not clutter the display surface, and the entire display can be used for drawing.

You should establish a clear mechanism for displaying menus. By spending some time on the design of this mechanism, you will alleviate many potential headaches later on. Menus, like chapters in a book, serve a unifying purpose.

Use color with your menus to reinforce differences between them, but be careful not to overdo it. A tasteful, rational use of color can enhance your software. A careless, arbitrary use of color can detract from it.

Executing Functions by Command

Before you can construct meaningful menus, you must evolve a **command language** for your application. A command language is the body of commands that are used to invoke and pass arguments to the functions in your system. Menus are secondary, although essential, enhancements to your software. The primary organizational feature of a program is its implied or explicit command language.

Command Execution   The simplest and most flexible, but hardly the friendliest, method of command execution is to enter a command, in response to a prompt, from the keyboard. It is hard for users to remember command names and syntax, and it is difficult to interrupt a graphics-oriented activity to enter text. But commands have very definite uses and should be included as an option in any software you write.

If you consciously develop a command language along with other execution methods, the language will have a second use: execution from a file. This will automatically solve the problem of creating a macro capability. Macro languages are usually created after the fact, instead of evolving as fundamental operating languages that are expressive of the full functional capabilities of the system. Commands executed from files can be used to run the entire system by "remote control."

Single-Keystroke Commands   In addition to the command language, you could abbreviate most commands to single keystrokes. This method allows the advanced user to avoid having to enter entire commands on the command lines.

Executing Functions from Menus

There are many ways to use menus to activate functions and pass information to them. Remember, menus always activate commands; the menu is secondary to the command structure. A few simple techniques for selecting items from a menu follow.

Function Keys   Do what you can to provide the user with shortcuts. One way to do this is to enable whatever function keys are available to perform quickly what might take several steps if individual commands were used. For example, you might allow users to draw lines quickly, change colors, or change line styles by pressing various function keys. Such functions are executed repeatedly and benefit from a short form of execution.

Selection Using a Locator   To select from a menu with a locator, the user moves the locator crosshairs to the desired item and presses a button on the locator device. The button that activates the selection might be the ENTER key, so that the keyboard could be used in the absence of a mouse or digitizer. When a mouse or digitizer is used, the locator device buttons might be programmed to simulate the pressing of the ENTER key when a button on the device was activated. Selecting using a locator is a very straightforward method, but it does have its drawbacks.

   The prime disadvantage to selection by locator is that the locator must be moved away from what it was working on in order to select a function. The locator must then be moved back again to complete the selected function.

Selection by Cursor   To select a function by cursor, the user presses the arrow keys on the numeric keypad or uses a locator device to move a cursor on the menu. The cursor is usually a reverse-video area that covers the name of the function to be executed. When the ENTER key or a button on the locator device is activated, the function identified by the cursor is selected. Selection by cursor is fast and accurate because the locator device does not need to be moved far from the drawing element on which you are working.

DRAWING A POINT

The simplest graphics activity is to draw a point on a display surface. There are many ways to do this, depending on how independent, fast, or colorful you want to make your system. Graphics on your computer's display are made of points of light.

A point represented on the display surface is usually more accurately termed a pixel, or unit of picture information. It is the smallest possible unit that the graphics system can express. If you have not already done so, visit Chapter 4 for a general discussion of points and pixels in the context of analytic geometry and graphics algorithms. Drawing a pixel usually represents the lowest level of a graphics system. As such, it must also be the fastest if the entire system is to be fast.

Variations on Pixel Drawing

One of the major assertions made in this book is that there are *many* distinct types of pixel-drawing functions rather than just one. The tendency with many graphics languages is to provide only one way to draw. In graphics programming you need more control. For this reason, you will find in this book alternate ways to draw fast pixels, slow pixels, pixels on and off the display, pixels used in groups, pixels drawn using the BIOS, and pixels drawn using the EGA graphics controller. In the three-dimensional world, touched upon briefly in this book, you will even find pixels drawn in perspective. If you grasp the importance of having a variety of methods for drawing pixels, you will understand how to do extremely advanced things with graphics that are impossible using high-level graphics languages.

Drawing Pixels Using the EGA Graphics Controller

The fastest method of changing the colors of specific pixels, using the EGA in mode 14, is to use the graphics controller directly. The graphics controller is an intermediary between the EGA's on-board display RAM and the microprocessor. There may be some obscure way to gain access to the EGA's display RAM using the microprocessor directly, but it would be foolish to try to do so. The EGA firmware keeps its own records of its status, which removes the burden of doing so from the user. To attempt to bypass the EGA firmware, aside from being difficult, would disturb the accuracy of the EGA's on-board system.

Use Firmware Tools   Instead of trying to defeat the integrity of the EGA hardware, it is best to use its built-in tools efficiently. The graphics controller gives you access to individual bytes in the EGA display buffer without interfering with the screen-refresh cycle. On the other hand, it makes block moves of data (as would be done using movedata( )) into the display buffer impossible. As such, it is a compromise that, taken as a whole, improves rather than diminishes overall graphics performance.

The graphics controller is a complex piece of firmware that is not readily understood by many programmers due to the absence of clear documentation. Using it you can perform Boolean operations on pixel colors and achieve many startling effects, but the effort required to do so is Herculean.

The General Pixel Drawing Function

Function 6-1, POINTF.C, is the most important method for drawing pixels to be found in this book. It is central to most functions that put pixels on the display. Because this function is so important, it will be discussed in detail.

■ FUNCTION 6-1

POINTF.C

```
/* POINTF.C is a function to draw a point on the EGA display.
** This function assumes you are using Mode 14.
** It is faster than using the BIOS INT10h method. */

#define TRUE 0xFF
#define ENABLE 0x0F
#define INDEXREG 0x3CE
#define VALREG 0x3CF
#define OUTINDEX(index, val)   {outp(INDEXREG, index);\
                                outp(VALREG, val);}
#define EGABASE 0xA0000000L
#define WIDTH 80L
#define XMAX 639
#define YMAX 199
#define XMIN 0
#define YMIN 0

pointf(x, y, color, orxor)
int x, y, color, orxor;
{
unsigned char mask = 0x80, exist_color;
char far *base;

/* If coordinates are off display, abort. */

if (x < XMIN || x > XMAX || y < YMIN || y > YMAX) return;

base = (char far *)(EGABASE
                    + ((long)y * WIDTH + ((long)x / 8L)));

mask >>= x % 8;

exist_color = *base; /* read existing color to EGA register */

OUTINDEX(0, color);   /* set new color*/
OUTINDEX(1, ENABLE);  /* enable write */
OUTINDEX(3, orxor);   /* XOR = 0x18, OR = 0x10, AND = 0x08 */
OUTINDEX(8, mask);    /* set mask */

*base &= TRUE;         /* force a write to the EGA */

/* To gain additional speed you can omit this in
** pointf(), but make sure the function calling
** resets the controller before trying to exit to DOS. */

OUTINDEX(0,0);         /* reset register */
OUTINDEX(1,0);         /* reset ENABLE */
OUTINDEX(3,0);         /* reset logic and bit rotation */
OUTINDEX(8,TRUE);      /* reset bit mask */
}
```

The function shown here includes definitions to avoid the need to refer to isolated headers elsewhere. In actual practice the definitions in this function could be put into a general header and included. The definitions in Function 6-1 deserve some explanation.

INDEXREG The INDEXREG definition refers to the index register on the EGA graphics controller chip. To gain access to any of the functions of the graphics controller, you first need to output the function's number to the index register port. INDEXREG contains the address of the graphics controller's index register (which is a port).

VALREG The function number for the desired function on the EGA graphics controller chip is also sent to another port, identified by the VALREG definition. INDEXREG and VALREG are always used in combination.

OUTINDEX(index, val) The macro OUTINDEX( ) contains the actual outp( ), or output, statements that supply the necessary information to the INDEXREG and VALREG registers in sequence. The index number and the function number (val) desired are passed through this macro.

A macro is used to send output values because macros do not involve the use of interrupts or the stack, as do functions. If you are not familiar with this concept, please study the use of macros in your favorite text on the C language. The macro, along with its arguments, is literally substituted into the source code by the compiler's preprocessor. Think of macros as being shorter ways of inserting groups of statements directly into your source code.

EGABASE The EGA display buffer for advanced modes 13 through 16 begins at segment 0xA000. The far keyword is used, and so the address is expressed as a long value. You will gain access to the display buffer by using offsets from EGABASE.

WIDTH   The WIDTH of the display is 640 pixels, but the addressing is done using bytes. This permits each byte to change the colors of eight pixels. The display width in *bytes* is 640 divided by 8, or 80 bytes.

Display Extremities   The extreme values in the x and y directions on the display surface are represented by XMIN, YMIN, XMAX, and YMAX. These are offset rather than count values. See Chapter 1 for an explanation of the difference between offsets and counts used in graphics.

POINTF.C Explained   Function 6-1 is passed four integer arguments. It receives the offsets of x and y from XMIN and YMIN as the coordinates of a pixel on the display. The color of the pixel (values from GRAPHIQ's screen.h are used) is passed as an argument. In addition, pointf( ) receives the orxor argument, which specifies how the color will interact with the current color of the pixel.

In addition to the arguments passed to pointf( ), some local stack variables are declared. A mask of type unsigned char is used to determine which bit in the byte in the display buffer will be changed. A dummy variable, exist __ color, is used to effect a read from the display buffer (more on this later). A far pointer *base is declared that refers to the base address of the EGA display buffer.

The first thing the pointf( ) function does is to filter out pixels that would fall beyond the edges of the display surface. The following expression is used to do this:

```
if (x < XMIN || x > XMAX || y < YMIN || y > YMAX) return;
```

If x is less than XMIN or x is greater than XMAX or y is less than YMIN or y is greater than YMAX, the rest of the function is not executed and control is returned to the caller. In practice you could create another form of pointf( ) that did not require this step if you were to change pixels from a caller that had already filtered out pixels that were not within the bounds of the display surface. Don't think of pointf( ) as an end in itself; it can be taken apart and used in several different ways.

After Function 6-1 has filtered out illegal pixel locations, it goes on to establish the address of the byte that contains the desired pixel. Figure 6-2 illustrates how the offset of such a byte is derived.

The display surface has a WIDTH and HEIGHT. Its width corresponds with the definition given earlier. Its HEIGHT is a count of 200 lines. The origin of the EGA buffer is at the upper left-hand corner, and so the upper left-hand corner of the dis-

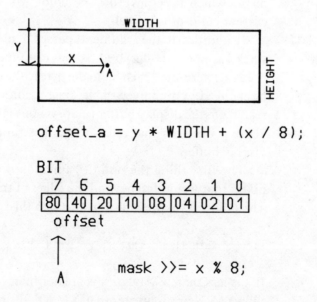

FIGURE 6-2.   *Access to a single pixel record in the EGA buffer*

play is at coordinate 0,0. The following expression will determine the offset of the desired byte, given the offsets of the pixel:

offset__a = y * WIDTH + (x / 8);

The pointf( ) function uses the above method of deriving the
offset of a byte in the display buffer to increase the base address
pointer. The FAR keyword option must be implemented to
enable this offset to be identified as a far pointer value. Notice
that the offset, when used as a far pointer, must be cast as type
long:

```
base = (char far *)(EGABASE
            + ((long)y * WIDTH + ((long)x / 8L)));
```

To derive the offset of the pixel within the byte just located, you
need to use the % (modulus) operator. This operator gives you
the *remainder* after integer division. In this case the remainder
after dividing the x coordinate by eight corresponds with the
offset of the bit (which controls the desired pixel) within the
byte. The following expression uses the mask (which was initialized to be 0x80, or binary 10000000) to rotate through the offset
obtained using the modulus operator:

mask >>= x % 8;

Figure 6-3 illustrates the effect of rotating the mask byte from
offset 0 through offset 7, as though the mask were used to plot
pixels for values of x from 0 through 7. Notice that if x has a
value of 8, the offset is 0. Study the way the modulus operator
works if this is not clear to you.

Causing the Read   To cause the display controller to read all
of the bit planes on the EGA into its internal registers, you need
to cause a read into a dummy variable at the address of the byte

containing the pixel bit. This is hard to understand because you are not really reading information in the computer's RAM, which is accessible to the computer's microprocessor! Instead, the display controller intercepts the data and uses it to load its own registers. In other words, the value read into the dummy variable does not contain graphics information. You cause the read by reading the contents of the byte pointed to by the recently derived base location:

exist—color = *base;

You cause the read to happen because you want the display controller to contain the status of all of the bits in the existing display byte. If you do not read the byte as just described, you will later write arbitrary bits in the same byte as the bit you *really* wanted to change.

hex	binary
80	10000000
40	01000000
20	00100000
10	00010000
08	00001000
04	00000100
02	00000010
01	00000001

FIGURE 6-3. Hex numbers and corresponding bit offsets

You can actually use your computer's RAM (if available) at the same location as the EGA's RAM for nongraphics information or for a copy of one of the bit planes. If you do this, be careful not to enable the graphics controller if you do not want to change the display.

Enabling the Controller   To activate the display controller so that it changes the display, you must **enable** it. Enabling the controller makes it responsive to reads and writes in the display buffer address range. Normally the display controller is kept disabled until it is used. This prevents the arbitrary or intentional use of addresses in the range of the EGA buffer from changing the display contents. You enable the display controller by the following series of operations:

```
OUTINDEX(0, color);   /* set new color*/
OUTINDEX(1, ENABLE);  /* enable write */
OUTINDEX(3, orxor);   /* XOR = 0x18, OR = 0x10, AND = 0x08 */
OUTINDEX(8, mask);    /* set mask */
```

First you set the color using function 0 on the graphics controller. Then you enable the write using the ENABLE value (0x0f) just defined. Graphics controller function 3 is used to determine the logic of the combination of the new pixel with the existing pixel. Pixels, like binary numbers, can be logically ORed, XORed, or ANDed. Finally, you set the mask register to contain the mask value derived earlier.

Causing the Write   Now, with the graphics controller enabled, loaded, and configured as desired, you cause a write of an arbitrary nonzero value to the address base derived above — the same address you read earlier. This causes the display controller to write new color values into its own bit planes, at the bit set in the mask, without affecting any pixels other than the one you desired. Notice that you are also writing the nonzero dummy value into any RAM that may be accessible to your microprocessor at that address, exclusive of the RAM on the EGA board. As long as there is no RAM actually visible to the microprocessor at this location, or any RAM there is not important to you, this dummy value will do no harm.

Consider, however, that you may want to customize this pointf( ) function to keep a record of bits that are on in the EGA buffers. You could do this by substituting an expression for the write that would instead OR the mask value at this location. This is food for thought. Using this technique you could use the non-EGA RAM accessible to your microprocessor to obtain the locations of pixels that are *on,* without regard to color. Such a search would be limited to very direct RAM access, avoiding the display controller. This is complicated but could speed up any operation requiring massive reading of the buffer information.

Resetting the Controller   After the color of the pixel has been changed, you must return the graphics controller to its neutral state. If, for example, your software drew only one pixel and then tried to exit to DOS, your display would be inaccessible from the system. The following code sequence reverses the process of enabling the controller:

```
OUTINDEX(0,0);          /* reset register */
OUTINDEX(1,0);          /* reset ENABLE */
OUTINDEX(3,0);          /* reset interaction logic and bit rotation */
OUTINDEX(8,TRUE);       /* reset bit mask */
```

You do not need to do this reset, or for that matter much of the initialization, for each pixel draw. Your software will be greatly enhanced if you use custom-designed pixel-drawing functions within element-drawing functions, rather than using only one way to draw a pixel. The practice of performing only those functions that are absolutely necessary will greatly improve the performance of your software.

Drawing Points in Perspective

If you are interested in constructing graphics software with three-dimensional capability, you will need to transform points and lines using a perspective transformation like the one discussed in Chapter 5. The projectr( ) function, introduced as Function 5-7, can be used within a variation of Function 6-1. If you create a function like the one shown as Function 6-2, POINTP.C, you will be able to project lines and other geometric entities point by point onto a projection plane.

Standard Real Coordinates   Function 6-2 is quite different from the pointf( ) function. Arguments passed to it are not integers. Instead, double-precision reals are used in a standard coordinate system that has positive values of y extending upward rather than downward as on the EGA display. In addition, an observer is located by the coordinates xo, yo, and zo. The distance from the eye of the observer to an imaginary projection plane is also passed to the function. Finally, the color of the desired pixel is specified.

Projection   The projectr( ) function from Chapter 5 (Function 5-7) is used to project the point in space onto the projection plane. The variables xp and zp contain the coordinates of the point after projection. These coordinates are rounded upward and converted into integers. They are then used to generate an offset into the EGA display buffer and write a pixel of the desired color there.

Uses for Perspective Points   Drawing each pixel in perspective leads to many applications. You can use the technique to draw lines in perspective, as you will see later in this chapter. If

■ FUNCTION 6-2

POINTP.C

```
/* POINTP.C projects a point in perspective.  */


#define TRUE 0xFF
#define ENABLE 0x0F
#define INDEXREG 0x3CE
#define VALREG 0x3CF
#define OUTINDEX(index, val)   {outp(INDEXREG, index);\
                                 outp(VALREG, val);}
#define EGABASE 0xA0000000L
#define WIDTH 80L
#define XMAX 639
#define YMAX 199
#define XMIN 0
#define YMIN 0


pointp(x, y, z, xo, yo, zo, d, color)
double x, y, z, xo, yo, zo, d;
int color;
{
int xout, yout;
double xp, zp;
unsigned char mask = 0x80, exist_color;
char far *base;

projectr(x, y, z, xo, yo, zo, d, &xp, &zp);

xout = xp + 0.5;
yout = zp + 0.5;

yout = YMAX - yout; /* invert display so 0,0 is lower left */

/* If coordinates are off display, abort. */

if (xout < XMIN || xout > XMAX
      || yout < YMIN || yout > YMAX) return;

base = (char far *)(EGABASE
               + ((long)yout * WIDTH + ((long)xout / 8L)));

mask >>= xout % 8;

exist_color = *base; /* read existing color to EGA register */


OUTINDEX(0, color);  /* set new color*/
OUTINDEX(8, mask);   /* set mask */

*base &= TRUE;       /* force a write to the EGA */
}
```

you use parametric equations to express the boundaries of planes, you can generate planar surfaces in perspective. By recording the locations of pixels in a list and sorting the list after all points have been drawn, you can effect an extremely efficient and error-free form of hidden-surface removal. The method can also be used to simulate light sources, translucency, transparency, and a host of other effects limited only by the capabilities of your hardware.

DRAWING LINES

A line is a graphics element, as opposed to a pixel, which is the product of a hardware-dependent graphics function. As an element, a line is composed of numerous discrete pixel locations on the display. When you see a line on the display, remember that you are not really seeing a line but a record of pixel locations that are *close* to the line.

Lines Drawn Using Algorithms

You will recall from having read Chapter 4 that lines are drawn by using algorithms. The algorithm tells you the theory of how pixels are selected to represent a line, given its endpoints. The algorithm does *not,* however, direct the computer to draw pixels. In order to program the computer, the algorithm must be expressed in the form of compilable code.

Function 6-3, LINEF.C, is a fully coded line-drawing function that uses Bresenham's algorithm, which is discussed in Chapter 4. At this time, if you have not already done so, you may wish to go back to Chapter 4 and examine the line-drawing algorithm there.

■ FUNCTION 6-3

LINEF.C

```
/* LINEF.C is a generalized function to draw a line
** using Bresenham's Algorithm.
** Line can be XORed against background.  First point, if
** XORed would produce gaps at endpoints, so no XOR for it.
** Style mask, if 0, gives solid line.  If not 0 the style
** mask produces a bit-pattern line as desired.
*/

#define TRUE -1
#define FALSE 0
#define max(x,y)    (((x) > (y)) ? (x) : (y))
#define abs(x)        (((x) < 0) ? -(x) : (x))
#define sign(x)  ((x) > 0 ? 1 : ((x) == 0 ? 0 : (-1)))
#define ENABLE 0x0F
#define INDEXREG 0x3CE
#define VALREG 0x3CF
#define OUTINDEX(index, val)   {outp(INDEXREG, index);\
                                  outp(VALREG, val);}
#define EGABASE 0xA0000000L
#define WIDTH 80L
#define XMAX 639
#define YMAX 199
#define XMIN 0
#define YMIN 0
#define XORIT 0x80
#define ORIT  0x00


linef(x1, y1, x2, y2, color, style, orxor, first_on)
int x1, y1, x2, y2, color, orxor, first_on;
unsigned style;
{
int ix, iy, i, inc, x, y, dx, dy, plot, plotx, ploty;
unsigned style_mask;

style = (style == 0) ? 0xFFFF : style;

style_mask = style;

OUTINDEX(1, ENABLE); /* enable write */
if (orxor == XORIT)
    OUTINDEX(3, 0x18);  /* code to graphics controller */

dx = x2 - x1;
```

■ FUNCTION 6-3 (continued)

LINEF-C

```
dy = y2 - yl;
ix = abs(dx);
iy = abs(dy);
inc = max(ix, iy);

plotx = xl;
ploty = yl;
x = y = 0;

if (first_on)  /* first point can be left off if needed */
    points(plotx, ploty, color);

for (i = 0; i <= inc; ++i)
    {
    if (style_mask == 0) style_mask = style;
    x += ix;
    y += iy;
    plot = FALSE;

    if (x > inc)
        {
        plot = TRUE;
        x -= inc;
        plotx += sign(dx);
        }

    if (y > inc)
        {
        plot = TRUE;
        y -= inc;
        ploty += sign(dy);
        }

    if (plot && style_mask & 0x0001)
        points(plotx, ploty, color);

    style_mask >>= 1;
    }
OUTINDEX(0,0);        /* reset register */
OUTINDEX(1,0);        /* reset ENABLE */
if (orxor == XORIT)
    OUTINDEX(3, 0); /* reset XOR to unchanged */
OUTINDEX(8,TRUE);    /* reset bit mask */
}
```

How the Line Function Works   If you examine Function 6-3, you will see a set of definitions that are similar to those used for drawing a pixel. An exception is the definition of the following new macros that enable several types of test used in the function:

```
#define max(x,y)    (((x) > (y)) ? (x) : (y))
#define abs(x)      (((x) < 0) ? -(x) : (x))
#define sign(x)   ((x) > 0 ? 1 : ((x) == 0 ? 0 : (-1)))
```

These macros allow you to determine the maximum of two numbers, the absolute value of a number, and the sign of a number. You have probably encountered them before.

Function 6-3 itself is a general-purpose line-drawing function that will draw a line on the display surface for coordinate values ranging from $-32,768$ to $32,767$. Coordinates that lie outside the display surface are ignored, and so no clipping window need be specified for the maximum and minimum coordinate values on the display.

The linef( ) function accepts the coordinates of the beginning point of the line (x1, y1), the coordinates of the ending point of the line (x2, y2), the color of the line, the line style, the logical combination status (orxor), and a variable that determines whether or not the first point on the line will be displayed.

Beginning and Ending Coordinates   The coordinates of the beginning and ending points on the line are expressed as signed integer values. This permits the use of negative as well as positive integers. The coordinates can be any values permitted in the range of a variable of type int.

Line Color   The color of the line (often coordinated with pens on a plotter) is expressed as a variable of type int. It can be a number from 0 through 16. Mnemonics for color numbers can be found in the GRAPHIQ screen.h header, Appendix A.

Line Style   The line style is expressed as an unsigned integer value whose bit pattern will create the actual line style by rotating the pattern along the extent of the line. Examine the function to see how this is done. Line-pattern mnemonics are to be found in the generic version of GRAPHIQ, shown as source code in Appendix A.

First Point On or Off   It may seem trivial that one might be concerned about the status of the first point on a line. In practice you need control over the first point on the line when lines that share the same endpoints are drawn using the XOR setting. Recall from your study of logic that the XOR operator reverses the status of bits; it will turn a bit on if it is off and will turn it off if it is on. It does the same to color values.

If you were to draw two lines, with the second line sharing its beginning point with the endpoint of the first, the XOR process would turn the first point of the second line off again. If, however, you can specify to the line-drawing algorithm that this first point is not to be changed, you will avoid gaps in continuous line segments. The first—on argument thus turns out to be very important.

LINEF.C in Action   Function 6-3 uses incremental values in a complex orchestration of rotation to generate lines. Numeric values are rotated incrementally. An unsigned integer is rotated bitwise. The natural capabilities of the microprocessor are used to turn an analog world into a digital one.

The first expression in the linef( ) function sets the style variable to represent a solid line if style 0 is passed to the function. After this the style mask (style—mask) is initialized. It will later be rotated to determine, in conjunction with the algorithm's tests, whether a given pixel in the bit pattern will be changed.

Use of Macros   If you refer back to Function 6-1, you will see how the OUTINDEX( ) macro was used to send values to the graphics controller. You will recall that the features of the pointf( ) function that govern initialization and resetting of the display controller can be taken out of the pixel-drawing function and used in the calling function to help draw the pixels faster. In linef( ) you can see this in action. The graphics controller is enabled externally to the pixel-drawing function, and Function 6-4, POINTS.C, is used instead of pointf( ). If you examine Function 6-4, you will see that it is nearly the same as Function 6-1, except that no initialization or reset is included. Function 6-3 uses points( ) rather than pointf( ) because doing so eliminates a significant number of repetitive outp( ) calls.

As you progress through the linef( ) function, you will see how the algorithm is coded. The magic of Bresenham's algorithm is accomplished by using a very simple principle. Examine the following loop to see how the code works:

```
for (i = 0; i <= inc; ++i)
    {
    if (style_mask == 0) style_mask = style;
    x += ix;
    y += iy;
    plot = FALSE;

    if (x > inc)
        {
        plot = TRUE;
        x -= inc;
        plotx += sign(dx);
        }

    if (y > inc)
        {
        plot = TRUE;
        y -= inc;
        ploty += sign(dy);
        }

    if (plot && style_mask & 0x0001)
        points(plotx, ploty, color);

    style_mask >>= 1;
    }
```

■ FUNCTION 6-4

POINTS.C

```
/* POINTS.C is used to plot points when OUTINDEX will be used
** in the calling function to set and reset the controller.
** If set and reset can be done only once for a set of points
** it saves time for each point. */

#define TRUE 0xFF
#define ENABLE 0x0F
#define INDEXREG 0x3CE
#define VALREG 0x3CF
#define OUTINDEX(index, val)   {outp(INDEXREG, index);\
                                  outp(VALREG, val);}
#define EGABASE 0xA0000000L
#define WIDTH 80L
#define XMAX 639
#define YMAX 199
#define XMIN 0
#define YMIN 0


points(x, y, color)
int x, y, color;
{
unsigned char mask = 0x80, exist_color;
char far *base;

/* If coordinates are off display, abort. */

if (x < XMIN || x > XMAX || y < YMIN || y > YMAX) return;

base = (char far *)(EGABASE
                    + ((long)y * WIDTH + ((long)x / 8L)));

mask >>= x % 8;

exist_color = *base; /* read existing color to EGA register */

OUTINDEX(0, color);   /* set new color*/
OUTINDEX(8, mask);    /* set mask */

*base &= TRUE;        /* force a write to the EGA */

}
```

The resolution of an integer number system is limited to its smallest nonzero absolute value. In the absence of floating-point real numbers, the differentials between the endpoints in the x and y directions are used. In other words, instead of using sine and cosine values or the local slope of the line, the algorithm uses the integer slope based on the overall delta (change) in x and y. Integer values can then be added and subtracted incrementally to simulate what would happen if the noninteger slope of the line were used. In essence, the total distance subtended by the line in x and y yields exactly the same slope for the line as any portion of the line would yield. Dealing with any other portion of the line, however, would require fractional values, which are not available in an integer system.

For each increment in the loop in Function 6-3, a test is made to determine if the x or y value will set a pixel. At the same time the style mask has been rotated one bit to the right. The style mask is tested along with the test for whether the pixel can be plotted according to the algorithm. If the current right-most bit in the style mask is set and the algorithm permits the setting of a pixel, the pixel will be set. In order to repeat the rotating style mask, the following expression is used:

```
if (style_mask == 0) style_mask = style;
```

Finally, after the line is drawn, the graphics controller is reset. This enables your software to continue and exit back to DOS, if desired.

How the Line Function Is Used

In edit mode your software will display a locator crosshairs on the display surface. In order to pass arguments to the linef( ) function, you will move the locator to the beginning of the line.

You will indicate that you have moved to the beginning of the element by selecting the MOVE command from a menu, typing the MOVE command on a command line, pressing a function key, or pressing an abbreviated command key. Your software can and should allow any or all of these methods for specifying the move.

Moving   A move is like drawing without using a pen. In essence, you move the pen to a location to draw, but you do not use it yet.

Locating the Endpoint   Once the move has been recorded, you change the locator position to the position of the line endpoint. Again, you use a menu or other method to specify that the current location is a line endpoint. Once you have done this, the line is drawn using the prevailing line style, pen number, color, or other attribute.

Sample Lines   Figure 6-4 shows lines of various styles drawn using linef( ). GRAPHIQ was used to transfer the display buffer to an Epson printer.

Lines in Perspective

Lines can be drawn in perspective in many ways. The simplest way is to compute perspective projections for the endpoints only. This works well for lines within the observer's 60-degree cone of vision, but for lines that extend far outside the cone you will perceive considerable distortion.

Cone of Vision   If you have not had much experience with drawing in perspective, you will not know what a **cone of vision** is. It is simply an imaginary cone of rays that project from the observer's eye toward the projection plane. All such rays are at an angle of 60 degrees from the line of sight of the observer. It turns out that straight lines in perspective also appear to be straight in the plot as long as their endpoints lie within the cone of vision.

Outside the cone of vision, lines plot as curves, yet from the observer's position they appear to be straight. If you want to learn more about this phenomenon, study a text on perspective drawing, of which there are many. For the purposes of this book, you should study the problem by coding Functions 6-2 and 6-5. When you plot lines using these functions you will see that for extreme cases of projection they will plot as curves. It is only

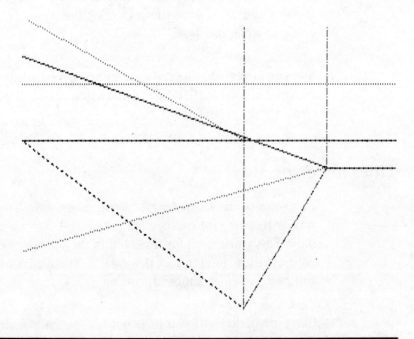

FIGURE 6-4.   Lines of various styles drawn using linef( )

when you place your eye at the identical position as the observer relative to the projection plane that projected lines will appear to be straight.

Lines in Space   Function 6-5, LINEP.C, plots a line using the pointp( ) function (introduced in Function 6-2) and the coordinates of the line's endpoints in space. To do this, a third dimension needs to be added to Bresenham's algorithm. For an explanation of Bresenham's algorithm working in two dimensions, see Chapter 4. Compare it with the line-drawing technique shown in Function 6-5. Also compare the technique used in Function 6-3 with that used in Function 6-5. To extend Bresenham's algorithm into spatial rather than planar applications is really not very difficult.

Three-Dimensional Line Drawing at Work   The algorithm works by dividing up three-dimensional space into a cube made up of tiny unit cubes with a user-defined resolution. This is, in effect, a rasterized three-dimensional space, much like the raster of the display surface. The linep( ) function does to this imaginary raster almost the same thing that Bresenham's algorithm does to the planar display raster. An additional consideration needs to be made, however. Whereas Bresenham's algorithm works with integer values for an integer raster, the linep( ) function will show different distances between pixels depending on the distance of a line segment from the observer. To control this the user can supply a cell value, which can be less than 1.0. The cell can be made small enough so that the line appears to be continuous for a given plot. The smaller the cell, the more computationally intensive the drawing of the line will be, and the longer it will take to draw the line. On the other hand, large values of cell will *reduce* computation time and can be used for fast test plots.

■ FUNCTION 6-5

LINEP.C

```
/* LINEP.C plots a line in 3-space and projects it, point by
point, onto a projection plane.  */

#define TRUE -1
#define FALSE 0
#define max(x,y)    (((x) > (y)) ? (x) : (y))
#define abs(x)       (((x) < 0.0) ? -(x) : (x))
#define sign(x)  ((x) > 0.0 ? 1 : ((x) == 0 ? 0 : (-1)))
#define ENABLE 0x0F
#define INDEXREG 0x3CE
#define VALREG 0x3CF
#define OUTINDEX(index, val)  {outp(INDEXREG, index);\
                                outp(VALREG, val);}
#define EGABASE 0xA0000000L
#define WIDTH 80L
#define XMAX 639
#define YMAX 199
#define XMIN 0
#define YMIN 0


linep(x, y, z, xo, yo, zo, d, cell)
double x[], y[], z[], xo, yo, zo, d, cell;
{
double i2, ix, iy, iz, incl, inc2, xt, yt, zt;
double dx, dy, dz, plotx, ploty, plotz;
int plot;

/* cell is physical dimension of single raster cell */
cell = (cell <= 0.0) ? 1.0 : cell;

OUTINDEX(1, ENABLE); /* enable write */

dx = x[1] - x[0];
dy = y[1] - y[0];
dz = z[1] - z[0];
ix = abs(dx) / cell;
iy = abs(dy) / cell;
iz = abs(dz) / cell;
incl = max(ix, iy);
inc2 = max(ix, iz);

plotx = x[0];
ploty = y[0];
```

■ FUNCTION 6-5 (continued)

LINEP.C

```
plotz = z[0];

xt = yt = zt = 0.0;

pointp(plotx, ploty, plotz, xo, yo, zo, d, color);

for (i2 = 0.0; i2 <= inc2; i2 += cell)
    {
    xt += ix;
    yt += iy;
    zt += iz;
    plot = FALSE;

    if (xt > inc2)
        {
        plot = TRUE;
        xt -= inc2;
        plotx += sign(dx);
        }

    if (yt > incl)
        {
        plot = TRUE;
        yt -= incl;
        ploty += sign(dy);
        }

    if (zt > inc2)
        {
        plot = TRUE;
        zt -= inc2;
        plotz += sign(dz);
        }

    if (plot)
        pointp(plotx, ploty, plotz, xo, yo, zo, d, color);
    }
OUTINDEX(0,0);      /* reset register */
OUTINDEX(1,0);      /* reset ENABLE */
OUTINDEX(8,TRUE);   /* reset bit mask */
}
```

LINEP.C, to be effective, needs the fastest hardware you can find. Since the arguments passed to it are double precision, it would be well to optimize this function in assembler using pointers even more extensively than they are used in the C expression. The numeric coprocessor is absolutely essential if the function is to move faster than a snail's pace. Still, if you use this function, the wait may be worth the effort. Its output is optically correct.

Perspective Lines Are Slower   If you code the linep( ) function and test it, you will find that it is a bit slower than the unadorned linef( ) function, but not unacceptably so. If you compile it with the numeric coprocessor option, it works surprisingly well. In action you will be pleased to see that it treats foreground values differently than background values. It is even possible to modulate the thickness of the line as it approaches the observer. To do this you will need to modify the function yourself, as the scope of this book does not permit a discussion of this detail. Lines drawn from the distance toward the observer start slowly and then zoom toward the observer. The effect created by drawing lines in perspective using this technique will add excitement to your software.

DRAWING CIRCLES
AND ARCS

Whereas lines are drawn using one method, circles can be drawn using several different methods. Two completely different methods for drawing circles will be covered here.

The most common method, Bresenham's circle, is often used in simple graphics systems because it is fast and easy to use. It has one serious drawback, however. You can use it to draw only whole circles, not parts of circles. If you try to adapt it to treat arcs, you will make it much more complicated and much slower.

The second method for drawing circles and arcs is more general. It treats the circle as a continuous series of line segments, or chords. The radius of the circle is used to trace its perimeter at equal angular increments (which can be varied), and the line-drawing function linef( ) is used to draw lines from point to point.

Bresenham's Circle

Bresenham's circle-drawing algorithm was presented in Chapter 4. Read the discussion there to understand how this algorithm generates circles, and then examine the C code in Function 6-6, CIRCLE.C.

Function 6-6 is a general-purpose circle-drawing function that will work very well as long as full circles are required. In principle, it computes only the first **octant,** or eighth part, of the circle. The other seven octants are drawn by reflecting the first octant using the symmetry( ) function.

Because the eight octants are generated using symmetry, it is extremely difficult to generalize this function to work with parts of circles. To do so you would need to filter out pixels in any parts of the circle you did not want to see. Doing this would be computationally intensive and, hence, impractical.

The arguments to circle( ) are the coordinates of the center, the radius, the aspect ratio, and the desired color. All of this is fairly straightforward. Only the aspect ratio needs some explanation.

Compensating for Aspect   An **aspect ratio** in graphics governs the ratio of horizontal to vertical size. In general, the theoretical aspect ratio used with the EGA is four horizontal units to three vertical ones. In practice an actual monitor may or may not produce a display that conforms to this aspect ratio.

■ **FUNCTION 6-6**

CIRCLE.C

```c
/* CIRCLE.C is a generalized function to draw a circle
** using Bresenham's Octant method.  Note that an aspect
** ratio is accommodated and that it expands the horizontal
** pixel from one dot to several as required to fill in when
** the aspect ratio is greater than 1.0. */

#define TRUE 0xFF
#define ENABLE 0x0F
#define INDEXREG 0x3CE
#define VALREG 0x3CF
#define OUTINDEX(index, val)    {outp(INDEXREG, index);\
                                 outp(VALREG, val);}
#define EGABASE 0xA0000000L
#define WIDTH 80L
#define XMAX 639
#define YMAX 199
#define XMIN 0
#define YMIN 0

double ratio;

circle(xc, yc, radius, aspect, color)
int xc, yc, radius, color;
double aspect;
{
int x, y, d;
unsigned char mask, exist_color;
char far *base;

ratio = aspect + 0.5;

y = radius;
d = 3 - 2 * radius;

OUTINDEX(1, ENABLE); /* enable write */

for (x = 0; x < y;)
    {
    symmetry(x, y, xc, yc, color);

    if (d < 0)
        d += 4 * x + 6;
    else {
        d += 4 * (x - y) + 10;
```

■ **FUNCTION 6-6** (continued)

CIRCLE.C

```
        --y;
        }
    ++x;
    }

if (x = y) symmetry(x, y, xc, yc, color);

OUTINDEX(0,0);       /* reset register */
OUTINDEX(1,0);       /* reset ENABLE */
OUTINDEX(8,TRUE);    /* reset bit mask */
}



symmetry(x, y, xc, yc, color)
int x, y, xc, yc, color;
{
int x_start, x_end, x_out;
int y_start, y_end, y_out;

x_start = x * ratio;
x_end = (x + 1) * ratio;
y_start = y * ratio;
y_end = (y + 1) * ratio;

for (x_out = x_start; x_out < x_end; ++x_out)
    {
    points(x_out+xc, y+yc, color);
    points(x_out+xc, -y+yc, color);
    points(-x_out+xc, -y+yc, color);
    points(-x_out+xc, y+yc, color);
    }

for (y_out = y_start; y_out < y_end; ++y_out)
    {
    points(y_out+xc, x+yc, color);
    points(y_out+xc, -x+yc, color);
    points(-y_out+xc, -x+yc, color);
    points(-y_out+xc, x+yc, color);
    }

}
```

Add to this the fact that the horizontal resolution of the EGA is 640 units, whereas the vertical resolution is 200 units. If you were to measure this on an actual display, the distance from pixel to pixel horizontally would be approximately 0.37 millimeters horizontally and 0.85 millimeters vertically. Clearly, if a circle were drawn on such a grid, treating the grid as though there were equal distances between pixels, the horizontal radial distance would be less than the vertical, and the circle would appear to be an ellipse.

To compensate for horizontal and vertical differences in actual resolution, an aspect ratio is used. In the case of Function 6-6, the aspect ratio is multiplied by the horizontal coordinate, and pixels are added in as required to fill any gaps. You can see how this is done in detail by studying Function 6-6.

The symmetry( ) function does the work of normalizing the aspect ratio of the circle. The ratio double-precision variable is multiplied by the derived x coordinate of a candidate point. Another point at a unit distance away is also calculated. Then the distance between the two points x—start and x—end is filled in with pixels. If the aspect ratio were 1.0, no correction would be applied and the circle would appear to be an ellipse standing on end. A ratio of 2.0 creates a circle that appears to be undistorted, but ratios of any size can be used to fine-tune the appearance of the circle.

Compensating for Center The circle algorithm works only for a circle at the origin of the coordinate system (0,0). To draw circles anywhere else, the desired location must first be subtracted out and then added back into the location of each pixel before it is drawn.

Sample Circles Figure 6-5 shows a few circles generated using circle( ). As with Figure 6-4, GRAPHIQ was used to draw the circles and print them on the Epson dot-matrix printer.

Chorded Circles

Drawing circles using chords gives the user more control over the circle than is available with the rasterization approach taken in Bresenham's circle. As was mentioned earlier, you cannot draw arcs easily using a nonchorded method.

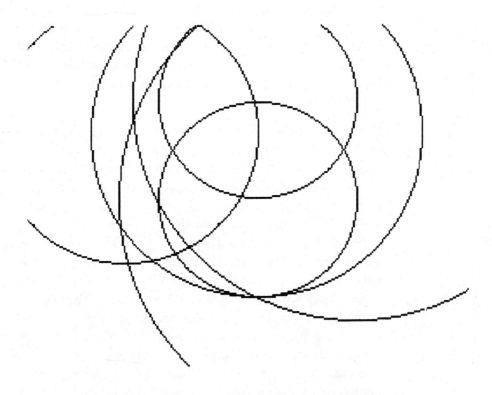

FIGURE 6-5.   Circles drawn using circle( )

Horizontal Chording   In order to draw a complete circle, you must rotate a radius through 360 degrees. You can use analytic geometry to express a circle by an equation, which in turn can be coded into an expression in C:

```
#include <math.h>
#define SQ(a) ((a) * (a))
double x, y, h, k;
x -= h;
y -= k;
r = sqrt(SQ(x) + SQ(y));
```

The coordinates of any point on the perimeter of the circle (x, y) can be directly related to the radius. The center of the circle (h, k) is simply related to the coordinates of the set of points on the circle's perimeter. The source of the equation can be found in the Pythagorean theorem, where the sides of a right triangle are related to the hypotenuse by the sum of their squares.

Parametric Form   Function 4-3 presented CENTER.C, a generalized function that enables you to derive the center of a circle from any three points on its circumference. The equation of the circle is in **parametric** form, that is, only the parameters of the x and y components are used. A parametric equation is one in which unknowns are represented by parameters, usually multipliers, that can be evaluated by their positions rather than their associations with symbolic variables. A parametric equation can be easily expressed using matrix notation, although the computer is not directly programmed using matrix algebra. The C language permits you to write parametric solutions with a clarity that is perhaps more easily grasped than matrix algebra, and so all illustrations of parametric solutions in this book are done directly in C. You can solve almost any combination of simultaneous equations using the parametric method shown in Function 4-3, for example.

Chord Endpoint List   To solve the problem of generating a circle by using its chords, a list of points must be generated by using known values to derive unknowns. The radius of the circle is assumed to be known, as is the location of its center. In order to solve for x or y the equation must be rewritten. The circle equation can be rewritten to solve for y in terms of x and r:

y = sqrt(SQ(r) − SQ(x));

You can use this expression, varying x or y incrementally, to solve for each coordinate pair. You could vary x, for example, from 0 to +r/2 by some increment and generate a list of coordinates for points on the circumference. This is essentially the same method used to generate an octant in Bresenham's circle algorithm.

Radial Chording   To chord the circle radially rather than horizontally, you must use the trigonometric relationships of the sides of the triangle, rather than their rectangular relationships. Keep in mind that the tangent of an angle is the ratio of the sine of the angle to its cosine.

   If, instead of varying x to derive y, you vary the angle of the radius incrementally, you will generate points on the perimeter that are equally spaced angularly rather than horizontally. The expressions required to do this follow:

x__new = x * cos(theta) − y * sin(theta);
y__new = x * sin(theta) + y * cos(theta);

These expressions are the same as those used in rotation transformations. See Function 6-7, CIRCLE__R.C, for a complete circle-generation function using Function 5-1 to rotate a point around the perimeter.

■ FUNCTION 6-7

CIRCLE—R.C

```
/* CIRCLE_R.C  generates a circle or arc given the location
 *  of the center and the radius, or the locations of any
 *  three points assumed to be on the perimeter.  The circle
 *  can also be specified as an inside or outside arc drawn
 *  between two points.  The angular resolution (chording) of
 *  the circle can also be specified.
 *
 *  Usage:  values of r      values of arc       action taken
 *             > 0                0               full radial circle
 *             > 0                1               interior arc
 *             > 0                2               exterior arc
 *              0                 0               full 3 point circle
 *              0                 1               interior arc
 *              0                 2               exterior arc
 */

#include <math.h>

#define TRUE -1
#define FALSE 0
#define max(x,y)    (((x) > (y)) ? (x) : (y))
#define min(x,y)    (((x) < (y)) ? (x) : (y))
#define abs(x)        (((x) < 0) ? -(x) : (x))
#define sign(x)   ((x) > 0 ? 1 : ((x) == 0 ? 0 : (-1)))
#define PI 3.141592654
#define ON TRUE
#define OFF FALSE


int circle_r(xc, yc, r, x_list, y_list, arc, increment,
          color, style, orxor)
double xc, yc, r, x_list[], y_list[], increment;
int arc, color, style, orxor;
{
int xnew, ynew;
double angle[3], angle_a, angle_b, max_angle, min_angle;
double inc_angle;
double xrot, yrot;
double local_min, local_max;
int i;


if (r != 0)  /* if radius specified, no 3 points */
    {
```

■ FUNCTION 6-7 (continued)

CIRCLE—R.C

```
        x_list[2] = x_list[1];
        y_list[2] = y_list[1];
        }

for (i = 0; i <= 2; ++i)   /* find subtended angles */
        {
        angle[i] = atan2(y_list[i], x_list[i]);
        if (sign(angle[i]) == -1)
            angle[i] += 2 * PI;
        }

if (r == 0) /* derive xc, yc and r using list */
        {
        center(x_list, y_list, &xc, &yc, &r);

        angle_a = max(angle[0], angle[1]);
        angle_b = max(angle[1], angle[2]);
        max_angle = max(angle_a, angle_b);

        angle_a = min(angle[0], angle[1]);
        if (angle_a == angle[1])
            {
            swap(x_list[0], x_list[1]);
            swap(y_list[0], y_list[1]);
            }
        angle_b = min(angle[1], angle[2]);
        if (angle_b == angle[2])
            {
            swap(x_list[1], x_list[2]);
            swap(y_list[1], y_list[2]);
            }
        min_angle = min(angle_a, angle_b);
        }
else {
        max_angle = max(angle[0], angle[1]);
        min_angle = min(angle[0], angle[1]);
        if (angle_a == angle[1])
            {
            swap(x_list[0], x_list[1]);
            swap(y_list[0], y_list[1]);
            }
        }

/* now (xlist[0], ylist[0]) has the coordinates with the
 *  smallest angle from 0 */
```

■ FUNCTION 6-7 (continued)

CIRCLE—R.C

```
/* draw circle or arc */
switch(arc)
    {
    case 0:  /* full circle */
        lastx = r - xc;
        lasty = 0;

        for (inc_angle = 0; inc_angle < 2 * PI;
                inc_angle += increment)
            {
            rotate(r - xc, 0 - yc,
                    &xrot, &yrot, inc_angle);
            linef(lastx, lasty, xrot+xc, yrot+yc,
                    color, style, orxor, OFF);
            lastx = xrot;
            lasty = yrot;
            }
        linef(lastx, lasty, r+xc, 0+yc, color,
            style, orxor, OFF);
        break;

    case 1:  /* interior arc */
        lastx = x_list[0];
        lasty = y_list[0];
        local_min = 0;
        local_max = max_angle - min_angle;
        for (inc_angle = local_min; inc_angle < local_max;
                inc_angle += increment)
            {
            rotate(x_list[0]-xc, y_list[0]-yc,
                    &xrot, &yrot, inc_angle+min_angle);
            linef(lastx, lasty, xrot+xc, yrot+yc,
                    color, style, orxor, OFF);
            lastx = xrot;
            lasty = yrot;
            }
        rotate(x_list[0]-xc, y_list[0]-yc,
                &xrot, &yrot, max_angle);
        linef(lastx, lasty, xrot+xc, yrot+yc,
                color, style, orxor, OFF);
        break;

    case 2:  /* exterior arc */
        lastx = x_list[2];
```

■ FUNCTION 6-7 (continued)

CIRCLE—R.C

```
            lasty = y_list[2];
            local_min = 0;
            local_max = max_angle - min_angle;
            for (inc_angle = local_max; inc_angle < 2 * PI;
                    inc_angle += increment)
                {
                rotate(x_list[2]-xc, y_list[2]-yc,
                        &xrot, &yrot, inc_angle+min_angle);
                linef(lastx, lasty, xrot+xc, yrot+yc,
                        color, style, orxor, OFF);
                lastx = xrot;
                lasty = yrot;
                }
            rotate(x_list[2]-xc, y_list[2]-yc,
                    &xrot, &yrot, min_angle);
            linef(lastx, lasty, xrot+xc, yrot+yc,
                        color, style, orxor, OFF);

            break;
        }
}


rotatec(xin, yin, x, y, angle)
double xin, yin, *x, *y, angle;
{

*x = xin * cos(angle) - yin * sin(angle);
*y = xin * sin(angle) + yin * cos(angle);
}


swap(x, y)
double *x, *y;
{
double t;

t = *x;
*x = *y;
*y = t;
}
```

A Versatile Circle Generator   Function 6-7 is a very versatile circle generator. Depending on how you pass arguments, it will draw a circle given its center and radius, or, if the radius is 0, it will use a list of three coordinates to find the center and radius. If the value for arc is nonzero, the function will use the coordinate list in conjunction with either the center of the circle and its radius or the two outermost points and the point between them to generate an arc between the two outermost points. If an arc rather than a circle is designated and the radius is 0, the arc will be drawn through the third point. If the radius is not 0, the function will draw either the greater or lesser arc, depending on the value of the arc variable.

Circles and arcs drawn using Function 6-7 will always be drawn counterclockwise. Interior arcs will always be drawn from the starting point to the ending point. Exterior arcs will always be drawn from the ending point to the starting point. The difference between interior and exterior arcs is one of sequence rather than size. This makes it easier for the user to understand. You can specify the circle by selecting nearly any three points. The two that are farthest away from each other on the perimeter will be the starting and ending points for the desired arc.

In order to use Function 6-7, you need to pass it a very complex argument list. This may seem difficult at first, but the reward is that one function replaces several. It can be comparatively difficult to coordinate the actions of several functions as opposed to specifying a known set of parameters for a single function. You can see a variation on Function 6-7 in action in GRAPHIQ, the complete source code for which is in Appendix A.

Additional Requirements for Circles

Function 6-7 does not solve all the possible problems you will encounter using circles. It works only for the circle or arc with a known radius or three points on its circumference.

There are boundary conditions that have not been screened out. For example, the three points you select as being on the perimeter may be nearly in a straight line. If so, the radius would be nearly infinite in length and would generate an overflow with unpredictable results unless you were to filter for this condition in your call to circle__r( ). If both the x and y values for any point's coordinates are 0, a DOMAIN error will be generated from the atan2( ) function. You will need to test for many such conditions if complex functions such as this are to be used in your software. The function shown will work for most arguments passed to it, but be aware that there is more to it than meets the eye.

Other Ways to Draw Circles   Circles can be drawn in ways other than those accommodated by Function 6-7. You might wish to draw a circle tangent to two lines. You may need a circle in perspective if you are designing a three-dimensional system. Variations on circles are helixes, sinusoidal figures, conchoids, and a host of other geometric forms. Consult your favorite text on analytic geometry for the equations required and plug them into the functions discussed in this book. You will find that once you solve the circle problem, other geometry dealing with curves will not be difficult to master.

DRAWING BOXES

Although you can draw rectangular figures by using the linef( ) function, there are times when you will find this process to be slow, especially when you need to draw numerous boxes. A function can be created that uses linef( ) to draw the sides of a box. Function 6-8, BOXX.C, accepts arguments for the coordinates of the diagonal corners of a box. It then draws the box using the prevailing line style, color, and orxor status.

In practice you will establish one of the diagonal corners of the box and then another, after which the box will be drawn. If

■ FUNCTION 6-8

BOXX.C

```
/* BOXX.C draws a box given the coordinates of two diagonal
*  corners. */

#define TRUE -1
#define FALSE 0
#define ON TRUE
#define OFF FALSE


boxx(x1, y1, x2, y2, style, color, orxor)
int x1, y1, x2, y2, color, orxor;
unsigned style;
{
int xul, yul, xlr, ylr;

xul = (x2 > x1) ? x1 : x2;
yul = (y2 > y1) ? y1 : y2;
xlr = (x2 > x1) ? x2 : x1;
ylr = (y2 > y1) ? y2 : y1;

linef(xul, yul, xlr, yul, color, style, orxor, OFF);
linef(xlr, yul, xlr, ylr, color, style, orxor, OFF);
linef(xlr, ylr, xul, ylr, color, style, orxor, OFF);
linef(xul, ylr, xul, yul, color, style, orxor, OFF);
}
```

desired, you could drag the box under control of the locator, using the XOR setting of linef( ) to alternately draw and then undraw the box.

Using Boxx( )

The operation of Function 6-8 is really very simple. It first swaps the coordinates, if necessary, so that they represent the upper left- and lower right-hand corners of the box. Then four lines are drawn to these coordinates. If the orxor argument is

TRUE, the lines are XORed against the background; if orxor is FALSE, the lines are drawn normally. If you decide to drag the sides of the box, make sure that when the lines are placed in their final positions they are drawn normally rather than XORed. Also note that the first—on variable disables the first point on the lines of the box. Because line endpoints in a rectangle always overlap, the corners of the box would disappear if they were XORed twice.

Sample Boxes Some sample boxes drawn using boxx( ) are shown in Figure 6-6. GRAPHIQ was used to draw the boxes and print them on the Epson dot-matrix printer.

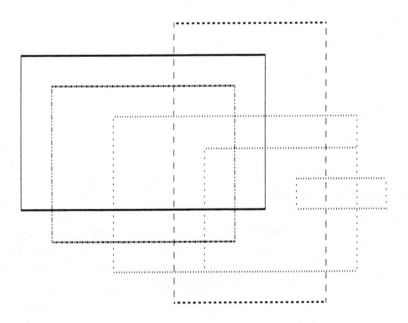

FIGURE 6-6. *Boxes of different styles drawn using boxx( )*

■ FUNCTION 6-9

FILLBOX.C

```
/* FILLBOX.C draws a box given the coordinates of two diagonal
 * corners and fills the box. */

#define TRUE -1
#define FALSE 0
#define ON TRUE
#define OFF FALSE


fillbox(x1, y1, x2, y2, style, color, orxor)
int x1, y1, x2, y2, color, orxor;
unsigned style;
{
int xul, yul, xlr, ylr;
int row;

xul = (x2 > x1) ? x1 : x2;
yul = (y2 > y1) ? y1 : y2;
xlr = (x2 > x1) ? x2 : x1;
ylr = (y2 > y1) ? y2 : y1;

for (row = yul+1; row < ylr; ++row)
    linef(xul+1, row, xlr-1, row, color, style, orxor, ON);
}
```

FILLING BOXES

Simple filled boxes are often desirable in graphics because they allow you to cover large areas with color quickly. You can create very attractive displays by superimposing simple filled areas. Function 6-9, FILLBOX.C, shows a variation of boxx( ) that, in addition to drawing a box, fills in its area with a selected color and line style.

Using fillbox( )

To use the fillbox( ) function, you must pass it the same arguments that were passed to boxx( ). You could use boxx( ) first to locate the fill area on the display and then use fillbox( ) with the same parameters to fill the box. There are many ways in which to call the fillbox( ) function. One way of doing it is to be found in the source code for GRAPHIQ in Appendix A.

Fill Avoids the Edges   Function 6-9 does not include the outline of the fill area in the fill. This is done so that you can use boxx( ) to draw an outline and then use fillbox( ) to fill the area using a different color. If you want a box to include the outline, just use the boxx( ) function and the fillbox( ) function with the same color.

Sample Fills   Figure 6-7 shows several overlapping filled areas using different line styles. Notice that you are not limited to only the styles available. You can overlap them creatively to produce any number of combinations. The method incorporated in GRAPHIQ is one way to do this. Feel free to elaborate on it. There are many ways to do such fills.

COMPLEX FILLS

In order to fill complex areas, you need to have a list of lines and use an approach similar to that described in the algorithm in Function 4-4. A line list can be recorded in the database as an object. If you construct closed boundaries from such lines so that no lines intersect or touch one another, you will be able to use the technique described in Function 6-10, COM__FILL.C.

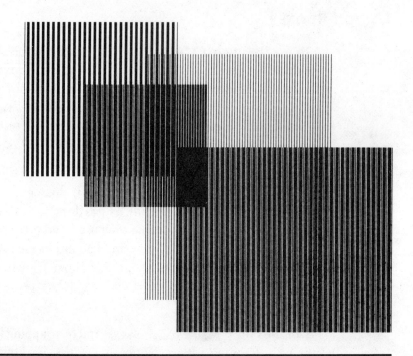

FIGURE 6-7. Overlapping filled areas drawn using fillbox( )

The rules for drawing boundaries for complex fills can be summarized as follows:

1. Boundaries must be continuous, that is, there must be no gaps between line endpoints. The last of a group of lines defining the boundary must share its endpoint with the beginning point of the first line in the group. All lines in the boundary must share endpoints.

2. Boundaries must not intersect or touch. Lines that form boundaries must be kept at least one pixel distant from one another. Boundaries may be included within other boundaries, but such included areas may not overlap or touch.

■ FUNCTION 6-10

COM—FILL.C

```
/* COM_FILL.C creates a complex fill for non-regular
 *  boundaries.  The procedure is tolerant of inclusions and
 *  incursions as long as boundaries are continuous (they
 *  connect) and do not intersect or touch each other.
 *  Lengths of arrays must be predicted carefully.
 */

#define TRUE -1
#define FALSE 0
#define ON TRUE
#define OFF FALSE
#define X 0
#define Y 1


com_fill(line_array, coord_array, length, style, color, orxor)
int line_array[][4], coord_array[][2];
unsigned length, style;
int color, orxor;
{
unsigned pointer, element = 0, sorted = FALSE, new_start = 1;

for (pointer = 0; pointer < length; ++pointer)
    line_int(line_array[pointer], coord_array, &element);

while(!sorted)   /* sort on y */
    {
    sorted = TRUE;
    for (pointer = 1; pointer < element; ++pointer)
        if (coord_array[pointer-1][Y]
            > coord_array[pointer][Y])
            {
            swap(&coord_array[pointer-1][Y],
                &coord_array[pointer][Y]);
            swap(&coord_array[pointer-1][X],
                &coord_array[pointer][X]);
            sorted = FALSE;
            }
    }

sorted = FALSE;
while(!sorted)   /* sort on x within y */
    {
    sorted = TRUE;

    for (pointer = new_start; pointer < element; ++pointer)
        if (coord_array[pointer-1][Y]
            == coord_array[pointer][Y])
            if (coord_array[pointer-1][X]
                > coord_array[pointer][X])
```

■ **FUNCTION 6-10** (continued)

COM—FILL.C

```
                        {
                        swap(&coord_array[pointer-1][Y],
                             &coord_array[pointer][Y]);
                        swap(&coord_array[pointer-1][X],
                             &coord_array[pointer][X]);
                        sorted = FALSE;
                        }
            else {
                    if (sorted == TRUE) new_start = pointer;
                    sorted = FALSE;
                    break;
                    }
        }

for (pointer = 0; pointer < element; pointer += 2)
      linef(coord_array[pointer][X],
            coord_array[pointer][Y],
            coord_array[pointer+1][X],
            coord_array[pointer+1][Y],
            color, style, orxor, ON);
}


line_int(line_array, coord_array, element)
int line_array[4], coord_array[][2], *element;
{
int ix, iy, i, inc, x, y, dx, dy, plot, plotx, ploty;

dx = line_array[2] - line_array[0];
dy = line_array[3] - line_array[1];
ix = abs(dx);
iy = abs(dy);
inc = max(ix, iy);

plotx = line_array[0];
ploty = line_array[1];
x = y = 0;

/* first pixel on line is not plotted */
/* last pixel on line is not plotted */
/* thus endpoints are not included */

for (i = 0; i < inc; ++i)
    {
    x += ix;
    y += iy;
    plot = FALSE;
```

■ FUNCTION 6-10 (continued)

COM—FILL.C

```
if (x > inc)
    {
    plot = TRUE;
    x -= inc;
    plotx += sign(dx);
    }

if (y > inc)
    {
    plot = TRUE;
    y -= inc;
    ploty += sign(dy);
    }

if (plot)
    {
    coord_array[*element][X] = plotx;
    coord_array[*element++][Y] = ploty;
    }
    }
}
```

It is important that these rules be followed exactly in using complex fills. Complex graphics functions are like prescription drugs. They can be very dangerous to your drawings unless you follow the instructions carefully.

How Complex Fills Work

The complex fill works by using sorted arrays. Computers are very good at sorting numbers. If you first find all of the intersections of the horizontal lines with the lines making up the boundary of an area and sort these by values of y and then by values of x, you can plot lines using an alternating pen-up, pen-down technique.

Complex Fills in Action

You can see the complex fill function in operation if you compare it with Function 4-4. Note particularly how arrays are sorted. The sequence of steps is as follows:

1. A list of intersections is generated by using a variation of linef( ) called line__int( ), which does not change pixel colors but instead records pixel coordinates in a coordinate list.

2. The coordinate list is sorted by values of y.

3. This list is sorted by values of x within y.

4. The sorted coordinate list is plotted. Each horizontal line begins with the pen up. As values of y remain the same, the pen is lowered, a line is drawn, the pen is raised, a line is drawn (with the pen up), the pen is lowered, and so on. When the value of y changes, the pen is (by definition) raised. As long as the rules for drawing region boundaries have been followed, the number of x intersections within y must be *even*.

Line Endpoints   There is only one other criterion that must be met for this function to work properly. If an intersection of a horizontal scan line matches the endpoint of a line being intersected, it must *not* be put into the coordinate list. This is where it helps to think of line endpoints as being theoretical but not actual. You can test whether or not the line endpoint was used as an intersection. If an endpoint is encountered, the intersection is ignored. Even though the line endpoint puts a pixel on the display, it must not contribute to the coordinate list, because it would raise the pen without lowering it again during the plot sequence. Of course, there is no actual pen to raise or lower on the computer display. Instead, only lines beginning with even-numbered coordinates are plotted.

Only an Example   Function 6-l0 is only an example of the organization of a special complex fill function. In practice you must be very careful that the size of any array whose pointer is passed to the function is large enough to contain the entire coordinate list generated by the function. Serious overflow problems could result if this condition is not met. As a potential solution to such problems, you could use disk files instead of arrays to hold the lists. This slows the process down considerably, but makes it possible to accommodate much larger lists.

The complex fill function described here has been used very successfully and represents a simple, general method for solving what has always been a difficult problem. You will find that the solution is robust and surprisingly accurate. As long as you follow the rules and there is enough space to store the coordinate lists, this function will accurately fill around included areas and handle any combination of irregular boundaries. The function works even for circles within circles within circles and any other type of nested figure.

LINES, CIRCLES, BOXES, AND FILLS IN COMBINATION

You can create many combinations of fills, boxes, lines, and circles to enhance your graphics. Figure 6-8 shows a combination of arbitrary elements thrown together to illustrate the variety available.

Practical Uses

It is fine to make abstract art using your graphics functions, but to make practical use of graphics elements you must focus on a purpose. Lines and other elements can be put to use to create charts of all kinds. Engineering and scientific uses abound.

In order to make practical use of graphics, you need to tailor your software for specific purposes too numerous to mention here. The application as a whole will provide a framework within which the functions discussed here can be effective.

The framework for your software can emphasize free-form graphics design, or it can mechanistically produce charts from data in files. The range of options in between these extremes is great, but all the uses you make of the functions in this chapter will share the fundamental principles discussed here.

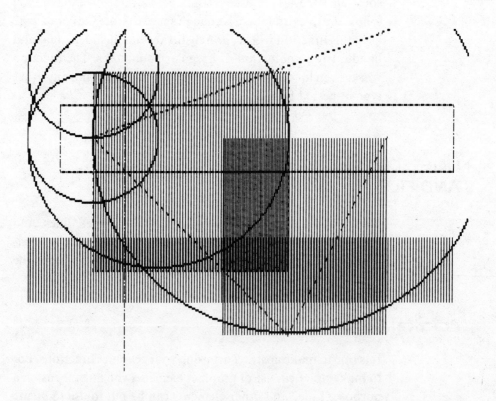

FIGURE 6-8. Combined lines, boxes, fills, and circles

Illustrations Using Video Capture   You are not limited to creating lines and other graphics primitives by hand. You can import graphics into the EGA using a television camera if you have video capture hardware such as the ICB from AT&T.

As you can see in Figure 6-9, you can achieve dramatic effects by combining images from the outside world with your internally generated graphics. The hand shown in Figure 6-9 was captured using the ICB and transferred to GRAPHIQ. After transfer, the graphics were drawn and the EGA image was printed on the Epson dot-matrix printer.

All of the hardware used to create this figure is relatively inexpensive and of the home-computer, home-video variety. The effects you can create using it are limitless.

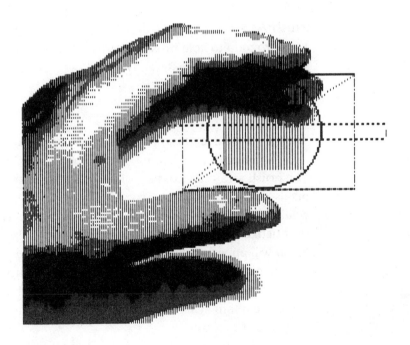

FIGURE 6-9.   Graphics elements and a video-captured hand

USING A BRUSH

A **brush** in computer graphics is a movable pattern of pixels that can change the colors on the display under control of the user. Brushes can take many forms, ranging from simple rectangular areas to free-form groupings of pixels. They can even be made of pixel patterns that are copied from the display surface.

Storing the Brush Pattern

Brush patterns are stored in arrays. A simple technique for doing this can be found in Function 6-11, BRUSH—IN.C.

Brush Array You could declare an array for general use in your program to hold brush patterns. The brush array in Function 6-11 is declared externally as follows:

long brush[16];

The long type declaration holds four bytes per array element, and 16 elements are declared. Each long integer holds 32 bits. The brush array can hold information for a pattern of 16 by 32 pixels, containing 512 positions. On the EGA display the pattern would cover one-twelfth of the display vertically and one-twentieth of the display horizontally. On the display surface the brush will appear to be roughly a square area.

You can use the brush pattern to create a locator crosshairs or an icon symbol. One interesting way to use the brush is to make it contain symbols that indicate the function to be performed by the brush.

■ FUNCTION 6-11

BRUSH—IN.C

```
/* BRUSH_IN.C defines and stores a brush given the upper left
 *   corner.  You must define brush external to main() if it is
 *   to be used in other parts of your program.  You could
 *   initialize it with your favorite brush pattern. */

long brush[16];

brush_in(x, y, color)
int x, y, color;
{
int i, j;

for (j = y; j < y + 15; ++j)
    for (i = x; i < x + 31; ++i)
        {
        if (color == readpt(x, y))
            brush[j-y] |= 0x80000000L >> (i - x);
        else brush[j-y] &= ~(0x80000000L >> (i - x));
        }
}
```

Drawing the Brush Pattern

In order to draw with a brush pattern that has been read from the display, you must reverse the procedure of Function 6-11. Function 6-12, BRUSH—OUT.C, uses the same method as that in Function 6-11 to read the brush array onto the display surface at a location specified by the brush array's upper left-hand corner.

■ FUNCTION 6-12

BRUSH—OUT.C

```
/* BRUSH_OUT.C uses a pre-defined brush to change pixel
 * colors. */

#define TRUE -1
#define FALSE 0
#define ENABLE 0x0F
#define INDEXREG 0x3CE
#define VALREG 0x3CF
#define OUTINDEX(index, val)   {outp(INDEXREG, index);\
                                 outp(VALREG, val);}
#define XORIT 0x80
#define ORIT  0x00

long brush[16];

brush_out(x, y, color, orxor)
int x, y, color, orxor;
{
int i, j;

OUTINDEX(1, ENABLE); /* enable write */
if (orxor == XORIT)
    OUTINDEX(3, 0x18);  /* code to graphics controller */

for (j = y; j < y + 15; ++j)
    for (i = x; i < x + 31; ++i)
        if (brush[j-y] && 0x80000000L >> (i - x))
            points(i, j, color);

OUTINDEX(0,0);        /* reset register */
OUTINDEX(1,0);        /* reset ENABLE */
if (orxor == XORIT)
    OUTINDEX(3, 0); /* reset XOR to unchanged */
OUTINDEX(8,TRUE);     /* reset bit mask */
}
```

Brush Color You set the desired brush color by means of the color argument passed to Function 6-12. In order to move the brush on the display, you must, as with lines and points, use an XOR method. To permanently change the brushed pixels to the brush color, you must use the brush—out( ) function without XOR.

The method used to move the brush is similar to that used to move a crosshairs on the display. The pattern is XORed against itself, moved, and then XORed at the new location. This cycle can be repeated indefinitely to give the appearance of animation.

COPYING

In using your software you will wish to copy portions of the display surface from one place to another. To do this you need a way to define the area to be copied, as well as a way to temporarily store information about the area while it is being copied to its new location.

Intermediate Buffering

You can copy with or without an intermediate buffer to store the copied area temporarily. In general, intermediate buffers are inconvenient and unnecessary for copying. Their one advantage is that they permit you to avoid thinking about the order in which the copy procedure is performed. Without an intermediate buffer, the order in which pixels are moved must be orchestrated so as to avoid copying to an area that will later be used as a source for a copy. This is seldom a problem with rectangular areas, however, because you can always control the sequence of the copy process to avoid overwriting your copy source.

If you choose to buffer your data from the display, you will need to define enough space to store the entire color specification for each pixel. This can involve quite a lot of RAM for the entire display. In the case of the EGA, to store a copy of the entire display you would need 80 times 200 times 4, or 64,000 bytes. Clearly it is not feasible, except for small areas, to copy the information contained in the display buffer into an intermediate buffer and then copy it out again. Even though you may have enough RAM for such a copy, it would take twice as long to copy to the buffer and then to copy from the buffer as it would simply to copy one area directly to another.

Copying Without an Intermediate Buffer

To avoid the need for a separate buffer to hold information from the display temporarily during a copy operation, you must know the destination of the copy relative to the source. You can specify the area to be copied by outlining it using the boxx( ) function. The source area is thus defined by two diagonally opposite corners. The destination area can then be defined by XORing the source box across the display under control of the locator. In effect, the source is outlined at the source location, identified as the source, and then moved to the destination location. The XOR capability, used earlier with lines, can create the effect of erasing the box at one location and repeatedly drawing and XORing to create the appearance that the box is moving with the locator.

Order for Copying   Once they are known, the dimensions and locations of the source and destination areas can be used to determine the order in which the pixels will be copied. The options are to copy from left to right and/or from top to bottom, or the reverse. This gives you the following possible combinations:

```
left to right, top to bottom
right to left, top to bottom
right to left, bottom to top
left to right, bottom to top
```

The destination box will be located above, below, to the right, or to the left relative to the source box. Its position may even be identical to that of the source box. You need to decide, based on the relative locations, which copying order to use and whether a copy is necessary at all.

Your first test is to see whether the location of the source box is the same as that of the destination box. If so, the copy is aborted, saving you the time necessary to read each pixel back to its own location.

If the destination box is to the right and above the source box, you will definitely wish to copy from the top of the source downward and from right to left. This will mean that destination pixels are always written to the display after any source pixels they overwrite have been copied, no matter how near the destination box is to being directly on top of the source box. The positions of the source and destination boxes dictate the copy order.

Copying in Action

Function 6-13, COPYBOX.C, illustrates how the decision as to the order of copying is made. The upper left-hand corners of the source and destination boxes are used as reference points. If they are the same, the copy is aborted. The differences between the x and y coordinates of the source and destination reference points are assigned to offset variables. The destination reference is then compared to the source reference, using these offsets.

Based on the signs of the offsets, the actual copy is achieved using readpt( ) and points( ) to transfer the color of each pixel from the source to the destination. There is no way the process can fail according to the logic of copying in sequence. No intermediate buffer is necessary.

■ FUNCTION 6-13

COPYBOX.C

```
/* COPYBOX.C copies a source box to a destination area
 *  without the need for an intermediate buffer. */

#define ENABLE 0x0F
#define INDEXREG 0x3CE
#define VALREG 0x3CF
#define OUTINDEX(index, val)    {outp(INDEXREG, index);\
                                 outp(VALREG, val);}
#define XORIT 0x80
#define ORIT  0x00

copybox(xls, yls, x2s, y2s, xld, yld, x2d, y2d)
int xls, yls, x2s, y2s, xld, yld, x2d, y2d;
{
int xuls, yuls, xlrs, ylrs;
int xuld, yuld;
int offset_x, offset_y;
int x, y;

xuls = (x2s > xls) ? xls : x2s;
yuls = (y2s > yls) ? yls : y2s;
xlrs = (x2s > xls) ? x2s : xls;
ylrs = (y2s > yls) ? y2s : yls;

xuld = (x2d > xld) ? xld : x2d;
yuld = (y2d > yld) ? yld : y2d;

offset_x = xuld - xuls;
offset_y = yuld - yuls;

if (offset_x == 0 && offset_y == 0) return(-1);

OUTINDEX(1, ENABLE); /* enable write */
if (orxor == XORIT)
    OUTINDEX(3, 0x18);  /* code to graphics controller */

/* since both offsets can't be 0, you can include 0 */

if (offset_x >= 0)             /* dest. to right */
    {                          /* copy from right to left */
    if (offset_y < 0)          /* dest. above */
        {                      /* copy from top to bottom */
        for (y = yuls+1; y < ylrs; ++y)
            for (x = xlrs-1; x > xuls; --x)
                points(x+offset_x, y+offset_y, readpt(x, y));
```

■ **FUNCTION 6-13** (continued)

COPYBOX.C

```
          }
     else {                    /* copy from bottom to top */
          for (y = ylrs-1; y > ylrs; --y)
               for (x = xlrs-1; x > xuls; --x)
                    points(x+offset_x, y+offset_y, readpt(x, y));
          }
     }
if (offset_x <  0)             /* dest. to left */
     {                         /* copy from left to right */
     if (offset_y <  0)        /* dest. above */
          {                    /* copy from top to bottom */
          for (y = yuls+1; y < ylrs; ++y)
               for (x = xuls+1; x < xlrs; ++x)
                    points(x+offset_x, y+offset_y, readpt(x, y));
          }
     else {                    /* copy from bottom to top */
          for (y = yuls+1; y < ylrs; ++y)
               for (x = xuls+1; x < xlrs; ++x)
                    points(x+offset_x, y+offset_y, readpt(x, y));
          }
     .}
OUTINDEX(0,0);      /* reset register */
OUTINDEX(1,0);      /* reset ENABLE */
if (orxor == XORIT)
     OUTINDEX(3, 0); /* reset XOR to unchanged */
OUTINDEX(8,TRUE);   /* reset bit mask */

return(0);
}
```

EDITING ORCHESTRATION

In this chapter you have seen many different functions described. These functions do not exist in a vacuum. They need to be combined together in order to work.

A successful edit mode is essential for successful graphics software. The keys to success are to use menus and other graphics techniques to make function selection easy for the user. This effort requires organizational methods similar to those used in composing music. You need to make all of your functions work together in harmony. Like musical instruments, they need to be orchestrated.

If you are successful in orchestrating your functions, you will often find that they combine together in synergistic ways. The late Buckminster Fuller coined the word **synergy** to stand for a phenomenon in which the whole appears to be greater than the sum of its parts. If your functions harmonize well, they will, in combination, spin off new uses you may not even have imagined. Just as resonance can amplify a single tone into a force that shatters glass, your functions, if resonant, can reinforce one another.

The generic prototype GRAPHIQ program in Appendix A contains most of the functions found in this chapter. It is used to illustrate how functions can be combined together into a synergistic whole.

Graphics functions in themselves are only part of the story. To understand graphics systems you need to see how functions interact with one another. You should code, compile, and run GRAPHIQ as an exercise in studying the interactive nature of graphics functions.

7

Text Mode

It can be said that all forms of visual communication are graphic, including text. The ideal graphics system would be capable of typesetting, text editing, electronic photography, and literally anything visual. Graphics systems these days are far from ideal, but they are making rapid progress.

In order to provide a full range of capabilities in your graphics software, it is necessary to include text capabilities. Text gives you the ability to invoke language, adding an important level of meaning to graphics. An all-inclusive graphics system may never become a reality, but your graphics software should, as much as possible, incorporate all visual forms.

In this chapter you will see how to represent text characters in **shape tables.** A shape table consists of lists of lines defined by endpoint coordinates. It is usually stored in an abbreviated form as an array. Characters of the alphabet and other graphics symbols are stored in shape tables and referenced by their ASCII character codes.

The theory behind shape tables was discussed in Chapter 4. In addition to presenting the concept of the shape table, this chapter will show how **stroke font** characters can be rotated, translated, and scaled just like other graphics elements and objects. A stroke font is a collection of characters that are drawn as a series of lines, like strokes of a pen on paper. The lines are *st rdcd* onto the display surface.

In addition to specifying the shape table, your software must be orchestrated to enable the user to create text. This chapter describes methods you can use to implement functions that draw text on your computer's display.

THE ASCII CHARACTER SET

In order to understand this chapter, you should know about the ASCII standard for character representation. The lower 128 characters of the ASCII character set are very standardized from computer to computer. The characters from 128 through 255 are not standardized but refer to symbols that can be defined on a particular computer. The IBM PC has a set of 256 ASCII symbols that has itself become something of a standard.

Displaying the Character Set

Function 7-1, LOCALCHR.C, will display the entire character set of your computer. DOS and the standard C library support built-in capabilities for sending and receiving characters to and from devices such as the display printer and keyboard. One such character, for example, converts the carriage return to cause the cursor to advance one line and move to the far left. With this

■ FUNCTION 7-1

LOCALCHR.C

```
/* LOCALCHR.C displays the entire 256 characters of
** the local character set in green on a blue background.
*/

/* SCREEN.H contains colors, display width and height */

#define BLACK      0x0
#define BLUE       0x1
#define GREEN      0x2
#define CYAN       0x3
#define RED     0x4
#define MAGENTA 0x5
#define BROWN      0x6
#define WHITE      0x7

#define WIDTH 160L

char far *base = (char far *)0xB8000000L;

main()
{
int mode, x, y;

mode = modeget();
modeset(3);  /* text mode */

for (x = 0; x < 16; ++x)
    for (y = 0; y < 16; ++y)
        write(x * 5, y, y + 32 * x);

getch();
modeset(mode);
}


write(x, y, character)
int x, y, character;
{
char buffer[20];
char far *offset;

offset = base + (char far *)(((long)x << 1) + WIDTH * (long)y);
*offset = GREEN << 4 | BLUE;
*++offset = (char)character;
}
```

little function you can avoid the interpretation of special characters such as CR (ASCII 3) and LF (ASCII 10).

Characters on the Display   Not all of the computer's characters can be rendered on a given printer. Therefore, the display is a good place to see the entire character set. If you enter, compile, link, and run the code in Function 7-1, you will be able to examine your computer's character set at any time from the DOS command line. In addition to displaying the characters, the function displays the ASCII value in hexadecimal for each character.

Character Hard Copy   To create a hard-copy listing of the entire character set, enter, compile, link, and run Function 7-2, PRINTCHR.C. Function 7-2 uses EGA mode 6 and BIOS interrupt 10h to do essentially the same thing as Function 7-1, but in EGA mode 6 you can use SHIFT-PRTSC to print the display on your system printer. Before you run Function 7-2, be sure to run GRAPHICS.COM. This is a program provided by IBM as a part of the DOS package. It enables you to print graphics in EGA mode 6 on the dot-matrix printer, in this case an Epson MX80. After running GRAPHICS.COM, any time you want to print graphics hold the CTRL key down and tap the PRTSC key. This is a quick method to use, as long as you are confined to EGA mode 6.

Figure 7-1 shows the result of running Function 7-2 and printing the display produced by it. These characters represent the entire ASCII set contained in ROM on an IBM PC.

Writing Text into RAM   Function 7-1, in addition to being useful for displaying the character set, also illustrates how you can write text directly into display RAM in EGA mode 3. You will want to refer to this function when you wish to print text menus for your graphics software.

■ FUNCTION 7-2

PRINTCHR.C

```c
/* PRINTCHR.C displays the entire 256 characters of
** the local character set in mode 6.  You can use
** Shift-PrtSc to print it on your dot-matrix printer.
*/

#include <dos.h>

/* SCREEN.H contains colors, display width and height */

#define BLACK     0x0
#define BLUE      0x1
#define GREEN     .0x2
#define CYAN      0x3
#define RED       0x4
#define MAGENTA 0x5
#define BROWN       0x6
#define WHITE       0x7
#define BLINK     0x8

#define WIDTH 160L
#define BASE 0xB8000000L

union REGS regs;


main()
{
int mode, x, y;

mode = modeget();
modeset(6);  /* text mode */

clearscr();

for (x = 0; x < 16; ++x)
    for (y = 0; y < 16; ++y)
        write(x * 5, y, y + 16 * x);

getch();
modeset(mode);
}


write(x, y, character)
int x, y, character;
{
char buffer[20];

sprintf(buffer, "%02X ", character);
outchar(x, y, buffer[0], WHITE);
```

■ **FUNCTION 7-2** (continued)

PRINTCHR.C

```
outchar(x+1, y, buffer[1], WHITE);
outchar(x+2, y, buffer[2], WHITE);
outchar(x+3, y, character, WHITE);
}

outchar(col, row, character, color)
int row, col, character, color;
{

regs.h.ah = 2;        /* set cursor position */
regs.h.bh = 0;        /* page */
regs.h.dh = row;      /* set row */
regs.h.dl = col;      /* set col */
int86(0x10, &regs, &regs);

regs.h.ah = 9;        /* write attribute/char */
regs.h.bh = 0;        /* page */
regs.x.cx = 1;        /* count */
regs.h.al = character;
regs.h.bl = color;
int86(0x10, &regs, &regs);
}


clearscr()
{

regs.h.ah = 7;                    /* scroll screen down */
regs.h.al = 0;                    /* entire window */
regs.h.ch = 0;                    /* upper left corner */
regs.h.cl = 0;
regs.h.dh = 24;                   /* lower right corner */
regs.h.dl = 79;
regs.h.bh = 0;                    /* use black background */
int86(0x10, &regs, &regs);       /* interrupt 10h */
}
```

Printing Text Using the BIOS In addition to showing the
ASCII character set in EGA mode 6 and allowing you to print it
on your system printer, Function 7-2 shows how to send text
characters to the graphics display in all graphics modes. This

method of displaying text is slightly slower than direct access to memory, but it has the advantage of being simple to use and very flexible.

Characters Stored in ROM The first 128 characters of the ASCII character set are stored in ROM beginning at the following address:

F000:FA6E

The second half of the character set, from 128 through 255, starts at an address pointed to by interrupt vector 1Fh. If you wish to change the character set for ASCII characters 0 through 127 by supplying your own, you can use the interrupt 44h vector to point to the substitute character set.

The IBM standard for character display is very efficient. An entire display of characters can be prepared instantaneously

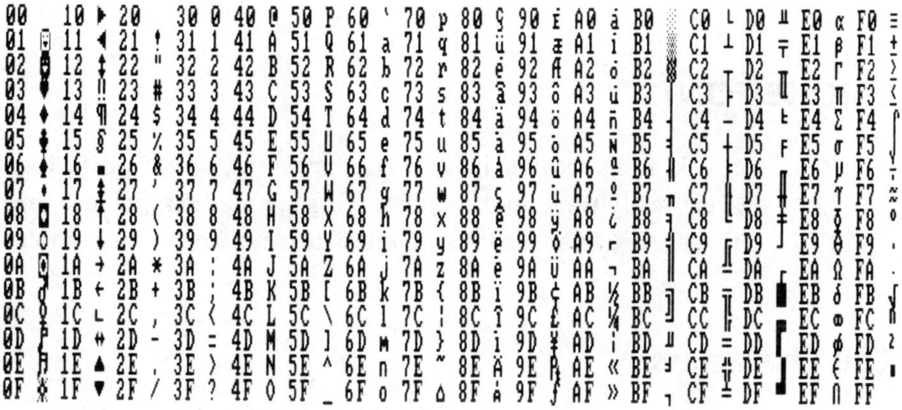

FIGURE 7-1. The ASCII character set

using cell characters. The need for cell characters is great because computers are still too slow to render graphics characters quickly enough for efficient text editing. This will not always be the case. In the near future it will become possible to use characters that are much more elaborate and highly detailed than those currently contained in the ROM BIOS.

What You See Is What You Get   It is likely that as computers become faster the trend will be toward the use of WYSIWYG (what you see is what you get) techniques. An example of an early successful attempt at WYSIWYG is, of course, the Apple Macintosh computer. Using a Mac is like using a PC entirely in graphics mode. The graphics techniques in this book will help you work with Macintosh as well as IBM graphics, with a few low-level changes.

With WYSIWYG you do not rely on tables stored in ROM to draw characters. Instead, you load fonts that are drawn using very different techniques. One of these techniques, which draws characters by simulating pen strokes, is presented in the next section.

STROKE FONTS

Stroke fonts are used in most graphics systems because the tools are already there to draw lines. To generate text, you use lines that are drawn in response to line lists contained in shape tables.

Cell Characters

You are used to seeing text characters on your computer's display. Stroke characters are not the same as these ROM-generated cell characters. The cell character is generated as a matrix of pixels that are clocked onto the display using the computer's firmware. This makes them appear quickly. Stroke characters cannot be drawn as quickly, but they are much more flexible with regard to size, angle, and location than ROM-generated cell characters are.

Pen Strokes

Think of stroke characters as though they were being drawn with a pen. The machine that holds the pen might be thought of as a robot that follows instructions from the computer. Pen plotters are literally primitive robots. They hold the pen in a raised or lowered position and move from location to location. If the pen is lowered, a line is drawn.

Stroke characters are drawn by connecting line endpoints with lines, regardless of whether the lines are drawn using a plotter or your computer's display. The coordinates of the line endpoints are contained in a list stored in the computer's memory.

The BIOS Shape Table

To use shapes in a specific piece of software, you must design your characters and code them into a specific format. An example of one kind of shape table is to be found in the ROM BIOS. As was mentioned earlier, each character displayed in the graphics modes is read from a table beginning at F000:FA6E. This is simply the table used by the PC's character-generator firmware in graphics mode.

Note that the BIOS character set contains only half of the possible ASCII characters, from 0 through 127. The characters from 128 through 255 are graphics shapes used in text mode.

Since the character set in ROM BIOS is meant to be used in graphics modes, IBM probably thought it would be unnecessary to make graphics characters a part of this set. The EGA BIOS, responding to the need for such characters, includes the complete ASCII IBM character set from 0 through 255. This corrects what some users have seen as an oversight on IBM's part.

BIOS Characters   Function 7-3, SHOWCHAR.C, displays each of the 128 character cells contained in the BIOS table. In doing so, it converts each cell in each character matrix into a coded hexadecimal number. If you enter, compile, link, and run Function 7-3, a series of matrix characters will be displayed on the screen. For example, the letter B looks like this:

```
00 01 02 03 04 05
   11 12       15 16
   21 22       25 26
   31 32 33 34 35
   41 42       45 46
   51 52       55 56
60 61 62 63 64 65
```

Notice that each cell in the character matrix is coded with its row and column position in a hexadecimal number. The origin, or 0,0 position, of the matrix is at the upper left-hand corner.

Function 7-3 is only an intermediate step intended to show you the IBM graphics character set and to provide a starting point for the creation of your own stroke font. The showchar( ) function will not be used in GRAPHIQ, the prototypical graphics application in Appendix A. It is only an illustration to make clear the method IBM uses to store its character set.

■ FUNCTION 7-3

SHOWCHAR.C

```
/* SHOWCHAR.C displays the BIOS character set
** in a form that shows row in the high part
** and column in the low part of the byte
** for each cell.  You can redirect it
** to any filename for analysis.
** */

#define TRUE -1
#define FALSE 0
#define CHARBASE 0xF000FA6EL

union
     {
     struct
          {
          unsigned char bit0 : 1;
          unsigned char bit1 : 1;
          unsigned char bit2 : 1;
          unsigned char bit3 : 1;
          unsigned char bit4 : 1;
          unsigned char bit5 : 1;
          unsigned char bit6 : 1;
          unsigned char bit7 : 1;
          } bits;
     struct
          {
          unsigned char byte;
          } bytes;
     } cell;


union
     {
     struct
          {
          unsigned char lo : 4;
          unsigned char hi : 4;
          } bits;
     struct
          {
          unsigned char byte;
          } bytes;
     } spec;
```

■ **FUNCTION 7-3** (continued)

SHOWCHAR.C

```
main()
{
int i;

for (i = 0; i <= 127; ++i)
     showchar(i);
}



showchar(ascii)
int ascii;
{
char far *table = (char far *)(CHARBASE + (long)ascii * 8L);
int row, col;
char matrix[8][8];
int drawn;

/* convert BIOS character into a matrix */

for (row = 0; row <= 7; ++row, ++table)
     for (col = 0; col <= 7; ++col)
          {
          cell.bytes.byte = *table;
          switch (col)
               {
               case 0:
                    matrix[row][col] = cell.bits.bit0;
                    break;
               case 1:
                    matrix[row][col] = cell.bits.bit1;
                    break;
               case 2:
                    matrix[row][col] = cell.bits.bit2;
                    break;
               case 3:
                    matrix[row][col] = cell.bits.bit3;
                    break;
               case 4:
                    matrix[row][col] = cell.bits.bit4;
                    break;
               case 5:
                    matrix[row][col] = cell.bits.bit5;
                    break;
```

■ **FUNCTION 7-3** (continued)

SHOWCHAR.C

```
            case 6:
                matrix[row][col] = cell.bits.bit6;
                break;
            case 7:
                matrix[row][col] = cell.bits.bit7;
                break;
            }
        }

for (row = 0; row <= 7; ++row)
    {
    for (col = 7; col >= 0; --col)
        if (matrix[row][col])
            {
            spec.bits.hi = row;
            spec.bits.lo = 7 - col;
            printf("%02X ", spec.bytes.byte);
            }
        else printf("   ");
    printf("\n\n");
    }
printf("\n\n\n");
}
```

A Stroke Font from BIOS

To understand how stroke fonts differ from character matrix fonts (or cell fonts), try converting the BIOS character shape table into a stroke character shape table. In the process, you will need to change certain aspects of the design of each character in order for the stroke font to be visually pleasing.

The BIOS character set was designed to give each character an unambiguous and natural appearance on the PC display.

When you convert the matrix into an analog version, the new characters can be viewed at different sizes, not just at the single size normally available. Instead of a matrix of dots, you will use a list of lines defined by endpoints. This creates its own set of problems and opportunities.

Creating a Stroke Character   To create a stroke character using a BIOS character matrix as a pattern, you can use the output from Function 7-3. Use the following command line from DOS to prepare a file containing the BIOS characters:

E:>showchar > chars[ENTER]

Assuming you have compiled and linked Function 7-3, this command will redirect the output of Function 7-3 into a file called CHARS. If you now use a text editor to edit the file, you will be able to change the characters into stroke characters.

Dissect the "B" character shown earlier to remove all cells except for endpoints. Remember, each cell in the matrix produced by Function 7-3 contains a number. The first part of that number is the row of the cell. The second part of the number is the column of the cell. Each cell is a potential record of a line endpoint. After you remove all cells that are not line endpoints, the letter B looks like this:

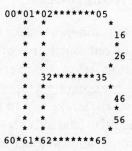

```
00*01*02*******05
   *   *            *
   *   *            16
   *   *            *
   *   *            26
   *   *            *
   *   32*******35
   *   *            *
   *   *            46
   *   *            *
   *   *            56
   *   *            *
60*61*62*******65
```

Lines to be drawn are indicated by asterisks, to help you recognize line endpoints. Use whatever method works for you.

After removing redundant cells, you prepare a list of line endpoints from the remaining cells. The list should be in the order in which you wish the lines to be drawn. Look at each line endpoint and create pairs of endpoints that are the beginnings and endings of lines that will make the final character. A line list, or stroke font representation, of the letter B follows:

```
0005
0516
1626
2635
3546
4656
5665
6560
0161
0262
3235
```

Follow the same procedure for all the characters in the BIOS, or create your own characters, if you wish. The result will be a coded line list for each character that, when put together, constitutes a finished stroke font for use in your software.

A Sample Stroke Character   Figure 7-2 shows a sample character created by using the character "B" just converted.

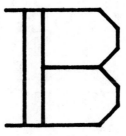

FIGURE 7-2.   *The character B expressed in stroke form*

Notice that the line endpoints that were derived for the stroke character now have lines drawn between them. The character, even at this large size, is quite readable. If it were shown as its original dot matrix, it would not be as clearly readable at this size.

The Finished Font   Figure 7-3 gives one possible version of the complete stroke font. The method just described was used as a basis, but many interpretive decisions were made to arrive at this result. These characters are only an illustration; you can change them to suit your taste. The entire listing of this stroke font is given in Appendix A, along with the source code for GRAPHIQ.

FIGURE 7-3.   The finished stroke font

Reading Stroke Fonts

In practice, your stroke fonts will be stored in arrays. You can permanently initialize a font by coding it using constants, or you can allow array space for a font that is read from disk. Most professionally designed software uses both methods. A default font is permanently coded, and space is allowed for one or more temporary fonts as well.

Reading Characters   When it is running, your software must be able to read each character coded in the array and display it at a specified location on the display surface. In order to do this you will need a function similar to the one shown as Function 7-4, READCHAR.C.

Function 7-4 will read any character from 0 through 127 from the appropriate location in the font table and draw lines of the specified color on the display. As shown, it is not capable of drawing characters of various sizes and at different rotation angles. Given the location of the upper left-hand corner of a character matrix, it will produce the same effect as the BIOS characters used in the normal manner, but more slowly. Converting to a stroke font isn't very helpful unless you wish to change size or rotation angle.

Varying Character Size and Angle   To justify the use of the stroke method, you must enable the characters to be drawn at different sizes and angles. Function 7-5, DISPCHAR.C, reads a character from the stroke font table and transforms it using xform( ) in accordance with a globally defined rotation angle, translation offset, and scale factor. The variables used to specify location are now double precision rather than integer. The origin of the coordinate system, rather than being at the upper left, is now at the lower left. The unit of measure is now 0.1 millimeter rather than an unscaled integer.

■ FUNCTION 7-4

READCHAR.C

```
/* READCHAR.C reads a stroke font character from
** the stroke font array and displays it at a
** given location in a given color.
*/

#include <font.h>

/* Example from FONT.H for letter B:
** (This file is about 900 lines long!)

unsigned stroke[128][36] = {
0x0005,0x0516,0x1626,0x2635,0x3532,0x3546,
0x4656,0x5665,0x6560,0x0161,0x0262,0xFFFF,
0x0000,0x0000,0x0000,0x0000,0x0000,0x0000,
0x0000,0x0000,0x0000,0x0000,0x0000,0x0000,
0x0000,0x0000,0x0000,0x0000,0x0000,0x0000,
0x0000,0x0000,0x0000,0x0000,0x0000,0x0000,
};
*/

#define TRUE -1
#define FALSE 0
#define ON TRUE
#define OFF FALSE
#define SOLID 0xFFFF
#define NORMIT 0

union
    {
    struct
        {
        unsigned col2 : 4;
        unsigned row2 : 4;
        unsigned col1 : 4;
        unsigned row1 : 4;
        } part;
    struct
        {
        unsigned word;
        } whole;
    } font;
readchar(x, y, character, color)
int x, y, character, color;
{

/* 0xFFFF is always last line */

while ((font.whole.word = stroke[character][i++]) != 0xFFFF)
    linef(x+font.part.row1, y+font.part.col1,
          x+font.part.row2, y+font.part.col2,
          color, SOLID, NORMIT, ON);
}
```

■ FUNCTION 7-5

DISPCHAR.C

```
/* DISPCHAR.C displays a character at a given location
** using tenths of millimeter resolution.  Rotation,
** translation and scaling are performed.
*/

#include <font.h>

#define TRUE -1
#define FALSE 0
#define ON TRUE
#define OFF FALSE
#define SOLID 0xFFFF
#define NORMIT 0
#define YMAX 199
#define XMETRIC 0.237546468
#define YMETRIC 0.096601942

union
      {
      struct
            {
            unsigned col2 : 4;
            unsigned row2 : 4;
            unsigned col1 : 4;
            unsigned row1 : 4;
            } part;
      struct
            {
            unsigned word;
            } whole;
      } font;



dispchar(x, y, character, color)
double x, y;
int character, color;
{
double x1, y1, x2, y2;
int x1_out, y1_out, x2_out, y2_out;
int i = 0;


/* find the latest version of xform()
** in Appendix A */

while ((font.whole.word = stroke[character][i++]) != 0xFFFF)
      {
      x1 = x + font.part.col1;
      y1 = y - font.part.row1;
```

■ **FUNCTION 7-5** (continued)

DISPCHAR.C

```
    x2 = x + font.part.col2;
    y2 = y - font.part.row2;

    xform(&x1, &y1);
    xform(&x2, &y2);

    x1_out = x1 * XMETRIC;
    y1_out = YMAX - y1 * YMETRIC;
    x2_out = x2 * XMETRIC;
    y2_out = YMAX - y2 * YMETRIC;

    linef(x1_out, y1_out,
        x2_out, y2_out,
        color, SOLID, NORMIT, ON);
    }
}
```

You can incorporate Function 7-5 as is into your software and use it to display any character from the character set. The character set listing is shown in Appendix A. Room has been left in the character matrices for more elaborate characters that you can create yourself.

Using Stroke Fonts

To activate the functions that read, prepare, and store strings of characters, you must create a command syntax. In other words, the functions need to be bound into a working program. The example of a working graphics application used in this book is GRAPHIQ, found in Appendix A.

In a practical application, you will use a command syntax in conjunction with pop-up menus and command files. The command to draw a string of text might look like this:

```
TEXT ("This is an example.", x1100, y1200, a30, h25, w20, s0);
```

Borrowing from C, the syntax for this command looks a lot like arguments passed to a function. The first argument is the string itself. The command syntax does not permit string pointers, but it can contain a quoted string. After the string appear the x and y coordinates for the lower left-hand corner of the first character of the string. The base angle (a), which represents the angle of the string to the horizontal, follows the origin coordinates. After the base angle, the height (h) and width (w) of each character are given. Lastly, the slant (s) is specified.

Note that the command syntax prefaces each argument with a single letter that shows what the argument means. These letters are cosmetic and, if present, are stripped off before the command is executed. Commands are insensitive to case.

The parameters passed to the TEXT command enable you to display stroke font text as character strings anywhere, at any angle, using various widths, heights, and slants for the characters in the string. Each character will be drawn using the prevailing line style, pen (or color), and other global parameters. The combination of slant, height, width, and pen give a single font many possible appearances.

Function 7-6, TESTCHAR.C, illustrates how the display of characters can be used. It displays a text string at various locations, rotations, and sizes. It will be used to illustrate how character height, width, and slant are accommodated.

Character Size   The size of each character is determined by its height and width. The native character size is 0.8 millimeter. This would result in a tiny character on the display, and so

■ FUNCTION 7-6

TESTCHAR.C

```
/* TESTCHAR.C displays a sample string at various sizes
** and rotation angles.
**      Usage:  Height defaults to 8 units.
**              May be 0 through 32767 units.
**              Width defaults to 8 units.
**              May be 0 through 32767 units.
**              Slant defaults to 0.  May be -8 <= 0 <= 8,
**              for practical purposes.
*/

/* see FONT.H in Appendix A (900 lines) */
#include <font.h>

/* SCREEN.H contains colors, display width and height */

#define BLACK      0x0
#define BLUE       0x1
#define GREEN      0x2
#define CYAN       0x3
#define RED      0x4
#define MAGENTA 0x5
#define BROWN      0x6
#define WHITE      0x7
#define WIDTH 80L
#define XMAX 639
#define YMAX 199
#define XMIN 0
#define YMIN 0


#define TRUE -1
#define FALSE 0
#define ON TRUE
#define OFF FALSE
#define SOLID 0xFFFF
#define NORMIT 0
#define XMETRIC 0.237546468
#define YMETRIC 0.096601942
#define PI 3.141592654

union
    {
    struct
        {
```

■ FUNCTION 7-6 (continued)

TESTCHAR.C

```
            unsigned col2 : 4;
            unsigned row2 : 4;
            unsigned col1 : 4;
            unsigned row1 : 4;
            } part;
        struct
            {
            unsigned word;
            } whole;
        } font;


/* These doubles are used in xform() */
double xlate_x, xlate_y;
double rot_center_x, rot_center_y;
double xform_angle, scale_factor = 1;

char test_str[] = "Stroke fonts are flexible.";


main()
{
double x, y;
int height = 8, width = 8, slant = 0, color = WHITE;
int mode;

mode = modeget();
modeset(14);

xform_angle = PI / 8;
x = 200; y = 300;
rot_center_x = x; rot_center_y = y;
height = 150; width = 80; slant = 0; color = BLUE;

display(test_str, x, y, height, width, slant, color);

xform_angle = PI / 8;
x = 300; y = 700;
rot_center_x = x; rot_center_y = y;
height = 250; width = 100; slant = 0; color = RED;

display(test_str, x, y, height, width, slant, color);

xform_angle = PI / 4;
x = 300; y = 1000;
```

■ FUNCTION 7-6 (continued)

TESTCHAR.C

```
rot_center_x = x; rot_center_y = y;
height = 250; width = 180; slant = 0; color = WHITE;

display(test_str, x, y, height, width, slant, color);

xform_angle = 0;
x = 100; y = 100;
rot_center_x = x; rot_center_y = y;
height = 180; width = 200; slant = 3; color = GREEN;

display(test_str, x, y, height, width, slant, color);

getch(); /* wait for a keypress */
modeset(mode);
}




display(string, x, y, height, width, slant, color)
char *string;
double x, y;
int height, width, slant, color;
{
int i = 0;
double xplace;

for (xplace = x;
     xplace < x + (double)strlen(test_str) * (double)width;
     xplace += (double)width)
     playchar(test_str[i++], xplace, y,
             height, width, slant, color);
}




playchar(character, x, y, height, width, slant, color)
int character;
double x, y;
int height, width, slant, color;
{
```

■ FUNCTION 7-6 (continued)

TESTCHAR.C

```c
double x1, y1, x2, y2;
double width_factor, height_factor;
int x1_out, y1_out, x2_out, y2_out;
int i = 0;

/* find the latest version of xform()
** in Appendix A */

while ((font.whole.word = stroke[character][i++]) != 0xFFFF)
    {
    width_factor = ((double)(width-1) / 7.0);
    height_factor = ((double)(height-1) / 7.0);

    y1 = (double)(height-1)
        - font.part.row1 * height_factor;
    x1 = font.part.col1 * width_factor;
    x1 += slant * width_factor * (y1 / (height-1));

    y2 = (double)(height - 1)
        - font.part.row2 * height_factor;
    x2 = font.part.col2 * width_factor;
    x2 += slant * width_factor * (y2 / (height-1));

    x1 += x;
    y1 += y;
    x2 += x;
    y2 += y;

    xform(&x1, &y1);
    xform(&x2, &y2);

    x1_out = x1 * XMETRIC;
    y1_out = YMAX - y1 * YMETRIC;
    x2_out = x2 * XMETRIC;
    y2_out = YMAX - y2 * YMETRIC;

    linef(x1_out, y1_out,
          x2_out, y2_out,
          color, SOLID, NORMIT, ON);
    }
}
```

height and width need to be increased. The function generates two factors by using the ratio of the desired height or width to the height or width of the character in the shape table (its native size):

```
width_factor = ((double)(width-1) / 7.0);
height_factor = ((double)(height-1) / 7.0);
```

It applies these scale factors to each character, not to the drawing as a whole. The function then adds the offset of the origin of the character to the character's components to derive the endpoints of the lines that create the character.

Changing Character Height   After deriving the height factor of the character from its desired height, the function uses this factor to derive the vertical component of each line endpoint in the character. Because the origin of the shape table is at the upper left and the origin of the display on which the character must appear is at the lower left, the derived height of the character is subtracted from its total height as follows:

```
y1 = (double)(height-1)
     - font.part.rowl * height_factor;
```

Changing Character Width   The character's width is derived using the width_factor and each width component from the shape table as follows:

```
x1 = font.part.coll * width_factor;
```

Because the character representation in the shape table has horizontal values originating at the left, no reversal of values is necessary for the width. Horizontal values, both in the shape table and on the display, originate with zero at the left.

Changing Character Slant   To vary the slant of each character, the user supplies a number that will be scaled and added into the horizontal endpoint values in each character. If this number is 7, it will make the top left of the character cell coincide with the top right corner, resulting in a 45-degree slant (assuming that the height and width are equal). The slant value is proportioned as follows:

```
x1 += slant * width_factor * (y1 / (height-1));
```

If you want to use italics in your text, the slant factor is invaluable. Values for slant can also be negative. It is unwise to use very large values, either positive or negative, because the distortion can make your characters unreadable.

Adding the Character Origin   After the function computes the location of the offset of each line endpoint in the character, it adds the origin of the character. Note that the shape table is read by pairs of line endpoints, and so the origin must be added as follows:

```
x1 += x;
y1 += y;
x2 += x;
y2 += y;
```

Applying Global Transformations to the Character   After the line component of each character has been scaled, it is transformed using the xform() function. You can see the xform() function in Appendix A. Pointers to the line endpoints are passed as follows:

```
xform(&x1, &y1);
xform(&x2, &y2);
```

When xform( ) is finished, the line endpoints will be rotated, translated, and scaled according to global transformation variables.

Compensating for the Display Size All computations performed on the character thus far have been double precision in a world of 0.1-millimeter units. To display the results of the above transformations, you must use a factor that relates the metric values used to the dimensions of the display horizontally and vertically. These magic numbers are based on the measurements of the display area and can be whatever you wish them to be. If you are careful, they will result in an accurate aspect ratio that renders circles as circles and squares as squares. The following sequence of operations scales and inverts the line-endpoint coordinates and assigns them to integer variables:

```
x1_out = x1 * XMETRIC;
y1_out = YMAX - y1 * YMETRIC;
x2_out = x2 * XMETRIC;
y2_out = YMAX - y2 * YMETRIC;
```

Finally, the line-endpoint coordinates are used with the standard linef( ) function to draw each character component on the display.

Text Orchestration

Each function in your program must be carefully placed and integrated with respect to the overall operation of the software. The complexity of placing and integrating a function is comparable to the crafting of a musical score. It requires orchestration. No function stand alone.

Text Tasks   To place a text function and activate it, you need to enable the user to locate the origin of a string of characters. You need to make it easy to rotate the string to various base angles so that strings can be drawn at angles other than horizontal. The font must be selectable. Further, size of the characters in the string must be made variable, and a method for changing size must be clearly implemented. Finally, the slant of the characters must be made variable.

Use a Status Menu   For text, you must consider what options are to be accessible to the user, and *when* such options will be available. One way to do this is to use a status menu that appears when the text function is selected. Such a menu shows the current settings for all aspects of the system that pertain to text. You can change settings in this menu until the desired conditions are set up and then decide whether to go ahead and enter the finished text.

Alternatively, two menus can be used in the selection of text. The status menu can be invoked at any time, even while a text string is being prepared. The text-entry menu prompts the user only for the location and content of the actual text. When the text is drawn, the current settings on the status menu are used. This process avoids the need to specify all parameters every time the user enters a text string.

Enable the Use of a Variety of Methods   Like other graphics elements, text should be capable of being invoked not only through menus but also through the use of a command line, a command file, and an abbreviated (short form) method. Experience has shown that some users like menus, others like command files, and still others like to take shortcuts. The only way to satisfy as many users as possible is to make all possible methods available.

Text Hard Copy

Samples of Stroke Fonts   Figure 7-4 shows some sample characters that were drawn on the display and then printed on a dot-matrix printer. Figure 7-5 shows the same display as it appears on a plotter.

Laser Printers Versus Pen Plotters   Judging from the difference in quality between Figure 7-4 and Figure 7-5, you would probably prefer to use a plotter for graphics work. Remember,

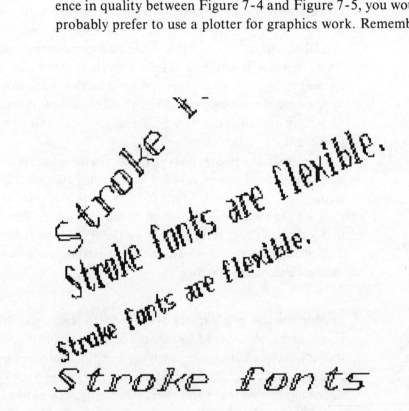

FIGURE 7-4.   Printed strings of stroke characters

however, that Figure 7-4 was prepared using a lowly dot-matrix printer. As such, it produces characters that are irregular and jagged. The plotted output is much cleaner, but the future does not belong to the pen plotter.

Laser printers are increasingly becoming capable of producing clean, smooth line art. They also have a major advantage over pen plotters. Using laser printing you can fill in large areas with shades of gray, otherwise known as halftones. Pen plotters can crosshatch areas, but they are extremely limited when it comes to filling areas.

By using appropriately formatted character strings, you can

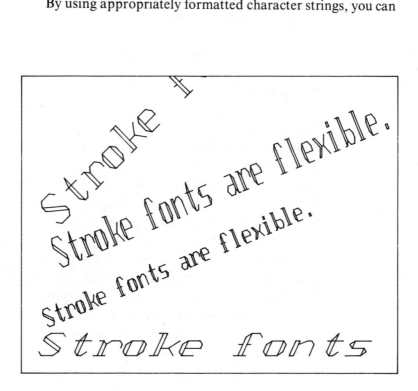

FIGURE 7-5. Plotted strings of stroke characters

use the functions in this book with pen plotters and laser printers as well as with dot-matrix printers. Graphics on laser printers are produced in much the same way as they are on dot-matrix equipment. Any function in this book that works with a dot-matrix printer can be modified to work with a laser printer.

Desktop Printing   Using the computer to produce sophisticated text fonts involves the same fundamental methods described in this chapter. There are ways to make characters more elaborate, to fill areas within characters, and to produce characters that are nearly indistinguishable from text printed on traditional presses. Desktop printing (somewhat inaccurately known as desktop publishing) is beginning to emerge as a major force in computing. The role played by desktop printing in the future will be great.

Personal computers are not the only computing devices being used in the printing industry. Many of the magazines and books you see in print today are produced by highly automated printing techniques. It is possible to produce full-color graphics at a spatial resolution that makes the product indistinguishable from a color photograph. In fact, some new equipment is capable of exceeding the resolution of photographic film.

In this chapter you have encountered some basic techniques for producing text characters on a graphics system. They are illustrated on equipment that is inexpensive and widely used. This does not mean that the functions presented here are limited to such equipment. You can extend these basic concepts far beyond the personal computer; they are written in C.

8

Printing and Plotting

After you have created a drawing, you can do many things with it. One option is to store the image in a file and use the computer to display it. This involves nothing more than dumping the display buffer into a file on disk and then reversing the process to read it back. You might use this method to create slide shows.

Another option for making the drawing useful is to use the display to create hard copy. If you have a dot-matrix printer, you can use a dithering technique to read the display buffer and turn it into a meaningful array of dots.

Dithering can also be used with laser printers. Laser printers usually have fixed dot sizes, as dot-matrix impact printers do. This makes dithering a very complex process. In the future, laser printers with variable dot sizes will appear on the market. These printers will allow direct production of a gray scale, similar to the technique used in halftone printing. Look at a photograph reproduced in any newspaper to see an example of a halftone illustration. Although laser printers are becoming more powerful and their capabilities will someday probably exceed those of pen plotters, they are still relatively expensive and have the disadvantage that they cannot print in color.

There is a better way to produce line drawings than by dumping the display buffer. If you keep a record of the lines and other objects you draw in a drawing database, you will be able to reconstruct drawings using a pen plotter. GRAPHIQ, the program in Appendix A, contains a driver that uses HP-GL (Hewlett-Packard Graphics Language) to plot on nearly any HP plotter.

The most popular means of producing hard copy are plotting and printing. Plotting has traditionally been the most visually pleasing way to produce hard copy because lines drawn using pens are smoother than dot-matrix lines. With the advent of laser printers, however, line work can be printed that is nearly as smooth as line work drawn with pens. This is because laser printers employ extremely high spatial resolution.

This chapter will first show how simple it is to create dithered screen dumps and integrate them into your software. Then you will see how to read the drawing database into formatted plotter commands. In the process of learning these techniques, you will encounter various methods of using serial and parallel ports for output. In a way, this chapter is also about the use of serial and parallel ports to communicate between your software and the outside world.

In addition to printing and plotting, your resources for presenting the display include videotape and photography. If you have a video display buffer (an ICB, for example), you can transfer images to videotape. If you use a camera, you can photograph the display. There are many ways to transfer the contents of the display buffer, including transmission over telephone lines and local area networks. This book does not cover such methods, because they are not yet commonplace. Our world is paper oriented. Until electronic paper is invented, it will be difficult to wean users away from hard copy.

Electronic paper will probably be the next step in technology after liquid crystal displays (LCDs). A flexible plastic LCD array is already available. By the turn of the century, electronic paper will be a flexible LCD array with built-in storage electronics. You will be able to write on it, erase it, and easily dump its information into a computer system. It will ultimately be so inexpensive that one sheet of it will cost less and store more data than a hundred sheets of conventional paper. Its invention is inevitable, but current technology is still a bit too primitive to make it feasible.

PRINTING DRAWINGS

At times you may want to generate hard copy from your display without having to plot your entire drawing database, or perhaps you do not even own a plotter. In any case, it is convenient to be able to dump your display buffer directly to a dot-matrix printer.

To do this, you need to know how to gain access to the display buffer, how to translate information in the display buffer into a dithering matrix, and how to convert this matrix into a format that is acceptable to your printer. Finally, you need to know how to send this information to the printer.

Although the techniques presented here are useful with any dot-matrix printer capable of graphics, the printer used as an example is the Epson MX80. This printer is the lowest common denominator in a series of printers that have been improved over the years, but which are all compatible with this early model.

Dot-Matrix Protocol

A typical dot-matrix printer uses a vertical row of pins, otherwise known as print wires, to press ink from an inked ribbon onto paper. The print wires are moved by magnetic fields generated by coils of wire. The entire assembly of print wires and coils of wire is contained in the print head that travels back and forth across the surface of the paper. Normally, each character you send to the printer results in a predefined character being sent to the print head.

In order to print graphics on your printer, you must use a special method to send characters. The entire ASCII character set can be expressed using eight-bit characters. The print wires on the Epson print head can be used to print the dot-matrix code for each column of eight dots.

Printing a Graphics Row   To print an array of graphics using the printer, you must first send an escape code. This code consists of the escape character (ASCII 27) followed by ASCII L and then two bytes. The two bytes contain, respectively, the low-order and high-order parts of a binary word (16 bits) that indicates the total number of characters to follow the escape sequence. After this four-character escape sequence, your software must send out exactly the number of characters specified in the sequence. The eight bits contained in each byte sent after the escape sequence will be translated into wire positions on the print head, as shown in Figure 8-1.

The Graphics Printer Format   The graphics format can be very confusing, and so the following detailed description is offered to help clarify the process. You must declare a string that is at least as long as the total number of characters to be sent to print one pass of the print head.

The print head contains nine print wires. Only eight of those wires are used for graphics. The high-order bit in each graphics character is the topmost print wire. The low-order bit in each graphics character is the lowest print wire.

As was mentioned previously, the first four characters required to initiate a row of graphics are as follows:

1. ASCII 27 (the escape character)

2. ASCII L (capital letter L for high-density graphics)

3. The low-order part of the number of characters to follow

4. The high-order part of the number of characters to follow

After these four characters, you must send *exactly* the number of characters specified in the last two bytes described above. For

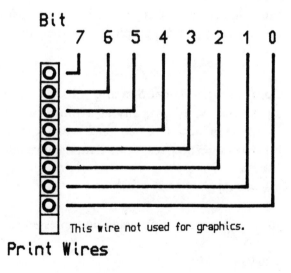

FIGURE 8-1.   Graphics print wires and the print character

example, if you wish to send 256 bytes of graphics, corresponding with a row of graphics 8 wires high by 256 wires wide, you would send the following sequence:

[Esc][L][0x00][0x01]

The representation of the number 256 in hexadecimal is 100. If this number is expressed in a 16-bit word in which the high-order 8 bits follow the low-order 8 bits, the number becomes 0010, which is expressed above as two separate bytes. In an expression in the C language, this would be expressed as follows:

\x1bL\x00\x01

Immediately after this 4-character sequence, 256 characters, no more, no less, would produce 256 vertical rows of 8 print wires. If those 256 rows were repeated, vertically spaced 8 print wires apart, you could print graphics, row after row, to make an entire display.

Controlling Vertical Spacing   To get the printer to space eight print wires vertically at a time, you must use another escape sequence. This sequence will set the printer to space down eight print wires rather than the normal nine print wires:

[Esc][A][0x8]

In the C language, this would be expressed as follows:

\x1bA\x8

You send this sequence before any graphics operations, to make sure that the print head spaces down eight wires per pass. You can, of course, vary the number of wires per pass and the amount of graphics information per pass to create many different effects. This allows you, for example, to control the aspect ratio of your hard copy, within limits, by varying the number of print wires printed per pass.

All of this seems complicated. In fact, it *is* complicated. It is one of the most complicated things you can do using a computer. If you follow the logic of Function 8-1, PRINTSCR.C, you will see how each pass of the print head is prepared before being sent out. The use of bitfields in Function 8-1 tends to simplify the complex process and make it very flexible.

No More, No Less   It is most important to emphasize that no more or less than the specified number of characters are ever printed in a given pass of the print head. If more characters are printed, you will send arbitrary information to the printer, resulting in garbage on your hard copy. If you send fewer characters than anticipated, the escape sequence for the next print pass will be missed, resulting in another kind of garbage.

Print-Wire Coding   Figure 8-1 shows the print wire positions that correspond with the bit positions in each graphics character sent. If you follow this pattern, you will be able to send any kind of dot graphics to the printer. Compare Figure 8-1 with the actual implementation in Function 8-1.

Using the Parallel Port

The parallel interface on the IBM PC is the easiest to use because its handshaking and other features are completely handled by the BIOS. You can, therefore, use built-in BIOS functions to do everything necessary to drive a parallel printer.

■ FUNCTION 8-1

PRINTSCR.C

```
/* PRINTSCR.C dithers the EGA mode 14 display to EPSON
** This function copies groups of 3 pixels horizontally,
** for each row, allowing RGB dithered photography to
** be printed. */


#include <stdio.h>
#include <dos.h>
#include <conio.h>

#define WIDTH 80L
#define XMAX 638   /* use 0 - 638 */
#define YMAX 199
#define XMIN 0
#define YMIN 0
#define CHARSOUT 800

struct {
      unsigned char i        : 4;
      unsigned char color1   : 4;
      unsigned char color2   : 4;
      unsigned char color3   : 4;
      unsigned char color4   : 4;
      unsigned char color5   : 4;
      unsigned char color6   : 4;
      unsigned char color7   : 4;
      unsigned char color8   : 4;
      } bits;

unsigned char mask = 0x80;

union SPEC {
      struct {
      unsigned char bit0 : 1;
      unsigned char bit1 : 1;
      unsigned char bit2 : 1;
      unsigned char bit3 : 1;
      unsigned char bit4 : 1;
      unsigned char bit5 : 1;
      unsigned char bit6 : 1;
      unsigned char bit7 : 1;
          } bits;
      struct {
      unsigned char byte;
```

■ **FUNCTION 8-1** (continued)

PRINTSCR.C

```
        } bytes;
    };
union SPEC spec0, spec1, spec2;

printscr(reverse)
int reverse;
{
int x, y;

/* This routine works with the EPSON MX, FX etc. printers */

fprintf(stdprn, "\x1bA\x7");   /* set linefeed in 72nds*/

for (x = XMAX; x > XMIN; x -= 24)
    {
    if (kbhit())
        {
        fputs("\x1bA\x9", stdprn);   /* 9 wires per linefeed */
        getch();    /* keeps character from console */
        break;
        }

    printrow(x, y, reverse);
    }
fputs("\x0c", stdprn);   /* page feed */
fflush(stdprn);
}




printrow(x, y, reverse)
int x, y, reverse;
{
char status();
char put_out();
unsigned i, j, newy;
/* prints CHARSOUT bits wide condensed */
/* room for header, pr_buff[],  */
/* and null character */
static unsigned char out_buff[3][9+CHARSOUT] = {
```

■ **FUNCTION 8-1** (continued)

PRINTSCR.C

```
                              "      \x1bL\x20\x03",
                              "      \x1bL\x20\x03",
                              "      \x1bL\x20\x03"};
for (y = YMIN, newy = 0; y <= YMAX*4; y+=4, ++newy)
      {
      bits.color1  = readpt(x-0, newy);
      bits.color1 |= readpt(x-1, newy);
      bits.color1 |= readpt(x-2, newy);
      bits.color2  = readpt(x-3, newy);
      bits.color2 |= readpt(x-4, newy);
      bits.color2 |= readpt(x-5, newy);
      bits.color3  = readpt(x-6, newy);
      bits.color3 |= readpt(x-7, newy);
      bits.color3 |= readpt(x-8, newy);
      bits.color4  = readpt(x-9, newy);
      bits.color4 |= readpt(x-10, newy);
      bits.color4 |= readpt(x-11, newy);
      bits.color5  = readpt(x-12, newy);
      bits.color5 |= readpt(x-13, newy);
      bits.color5 |= readpt(x-14, newy);

   if (x-14 != 0) {
      bits.color6  = readpt(x-15, newy);
      bits.color6 |= readpt(x-16, newy);
      bits.color6 |= readpt(x-17, newy);
      bits.color7  = readpt(x-18, newy);
      bits.color7 |= readpt(x-19, newy);
      bits.color7 |= readpt(x-20, newy);
      bits.color8  = readpt(x-21, newy);
      bits.color8 |= readpt(x-22, newy);
      bits.color8 |= readpt(x-23, newy);
                    }
      if (reverse)
          {
          bits.color1 = ~bits.color1;
          bits.color2 = ~bits.color2;
          bits.color3 = ~bits.color3;
          bits.color4 = ~bits.color4;
          bits.color5 = ~bits.color5;
          bits.color6 = ~bits.color6;
          bits.color7 = ~bits.color7;
          bits.color8 = ~bits.color8;
          }
```

■ **FUNCTION 8-1** (continued)

PRINTSCR.C

```
for (j = 0, bits.i = 0x8; j <= 3; ++j, bits.i >>= 1)
    {
    spec0.bits.bit7 = (bits.color1 & bits.i) >> (3-j);
    spec0.bits.bit6 = (bits.color1 & bits.i) >> (3-j);
    spec0.bits.bit5 = (bits.color1 & bits.i) >> (3-j);
    spec0.bits.bit4 = (bits.color2 & bits.i) >> (3-j);
    spec0.bits.bit3 = (bits.color2 & bits.i) >> (3-j);
    spec0.bits.bit2 = (bits.color2 & bits.i) >> (3-j);
    spec0.bits.bit1 = (bits.color3 & bits.i) >> (3-j);
    spec0.bits.bit0 = (bits.color3 & bits.i) >> (3-j);
    spec1.bits.bit7 = (bits.color3 & bits.i) >> (3-j);
    spec1.bits.bit6 = (bits.color4 & bits.i) >> (3-j);
    spec1.bits.bit5 = (bits.color4 & bits.i) >> (3-j);
    spec1.bits.bit4 = (bits.color4 & bits.i) >> (3-j);
    spec1.bits.bit3 = (bits.color5 & bits.i) >> (3-j);
    spec1.bits.bit2 = (bits.color5 & bits.i) >> (3-j);
    spec1.bits.bit1 = (bits.color5 & bits.i) >> (3-j);

  if (x-14 != 0) {
    spec1.bits.bit0 = (bits.color6 & bits.i) >> (3-j);
    spec2.bits.bit7 = (bits.color6 & bits.i) >> (3-j);
    spec2.bits.bit6 = (bits.color6 & bits.i) >> (3-j);
    spec2.bits.bit5 = (bits.color7 & bits.i) >> (3-j);
    spec2.bits.bit4 = (bits.color7 & bits.i) >> (3-j);
    spec2.bits.bit3 = (bits.color7 & bits.i) >> (3-j);
    spec2.bits.bit2 = (bits.color8 & bits.i) >> (3-j);
    spec2.bits.bit1 = (bits.color8 & bits.i) >> (3-j);
    spec2.bits.bit0 = (bits.color8 & bits.i) >> (3-j);
                }

    if (x-14 == 0) spec1.bytes.byte &= 0xFE;

    out_buff[0][y+9+j] = spec0.bytes.byte;
    out_buff[1][y+9+j] = spec1.bytes.byte;
    out_buff[2][y+9+j] = spec2.bytes.byte;
    }
  }


/* write the formatted array out printer port as characters */
for (i = 0; i < 9+CHARSOUT; ++i)
    while ((put_out(out_buff[0][i]) & 1) == 1);

put_out('\r'); /* send a carriage return */
```

■ FUNCTION 8-1 (continued)

PRINTSCR.C

```
put_out('\n'); /* send a linefeed */

for (i = 0; i < 9+CHARSOUT; ++i)
    while ((put_out(out_buff[1][i]) & 1) == 1);'

put_out('\r'); /* send a carriage return */
put_out('\n'); /* send a linefeed */

if (x-14 != 0)
    {
    for (i = 0; i < 9+CHARSOUT; ++i)
        while ((put_out(out_buff[2][i]) & 1) == 1);

    put_out('\r'); /* send a carriage return */
    put_out('\n'); /* send a linefeed */
    }
}


char status()
{
union REGS regs;

regs.h.ah = 2; /* check printer status */
regs.x.dx = 0; /* select first printer */
int86(0x17, &regs, &regs);
return(regs.h.ah & 0x80);
}


char put_out(character)
char character;
{
union REGS regs;

while(!status()); /* wait if busy */

regs.h.ah = 0; /* send a character */
regs.h.al = character;
regs.x.dx = 0; /* select first printer */

int86(0x17, &regs, &regs);
return(regs.h.ah);
}
```

Don't Use Stdprn for Graphics   Function 8-1 uses a special series of BIOS calls to control the printer port. Avoid using output to stdprn when printing graphics, because the C utilities interpret some characters specially on output. An example is the processing of new-line characters. Because the standard C function adds a carriage return when it encounters a new-line character, you can end up printing more characters than you had intended if this character is included in the group of characters sent to the printer.

Stdprn is automatically opened as a stream pointer for any compiled C function. It is opened by default in text, not binary, mode. You can use freopen( ) to reopen it in binary mode, but the fastest and best way to send graphics characters is to go directly to the BIOS. Fortunately, the C language gives you the tools to execute BIOS calls painlessly.

Parallel Port Status   The status of the parallel port can be determined using status( ). The status( ) function coded in Function 8-1 uses a DOS interrupt 17h to determine whether the printer is able to receive a character. If status( ) returns a value other than zero, it is assumed that a character cannot be sent. Any function calling status( ) should wait until status( ) is zero before trying to send a character to the selected port (in this case port 0).

Sending the Character   A character can be sent out the port by executing interrupt 17h, as shown in the put—out( ) function contained in Function 8-1. The AH register is set to zero, which causes the BIOS to send the character in the AL register out the printer port. By using status( ) and put—out( ) in combination, you can achieve a perfect interface with any parallel device, without using stdprn.

Practical Dithering Techniques

You can use many different methods to dither, as discussed in Chapter 4. In practice you will find that the EGA display can be dithered in two basic ways using EGA mode 14. Given 200 lines vertically versus 640 lines horizontally, you should preserve the vertical resolution and use the horizontal resolution to dither. If you use three horizontal pixels on the EGA display to contain RGB color values, you still have an effective dithered resolution of 213 positions horizontally by 200 vertically. The three pixels contain red, green, and blue information. The aspect ratio, it turns out, appears nearly natural if you use the printing technique described in Function 8-1.

Another possibility is to use groups of four pixels allowing 160 positions horizontally by 200 vertically. Each cell of four pixels would contain white, red, green, and blue values. Three values each for white, red, green, and blue would yield 81 colors per cell (3^4), as opposed to 27 colors per cell using three values each of red, green, and blue.

Yet another way to dither is to use all 640 by 200 positions. This yields a different kind of output that is best for line drawings and is not as good for electronic photography.

In short, Function 8-1 represents just one of the many ways to dither from the display to the printer. If you choose to modify GRAPHIQ for your own purposes, consider giving the user a choice of different methods. Function 8-1 is designed to make it easy to change dithering methods through the creative use of bitfields.

The Print Function

Function 8-1 gives you a very flexible technique that will enable graphics printing using any combination of print wires and colors. Much of what is done in this function could be achieved using loops instead of bitfields, but you will find when you try various combinations of print wires and colors that a complicated sequence of operations can evolve.

The technique used in the function relies on the modulus of the total number of passes required to complete a single rotation of colors. In other words, 3 colors printed using 8 print wires, clearly not evenly divisible, will nevertheless undergo a complete cycle every 24 wires. By designing your dithering function so that data is prepared for three passes rather than for just one, you can use a repetitive pattern of wires without going through a mind-wracking process of accounting for leftover wires. The elaborate use of bitfields will not increase code size.

Remainder Rule   As a general rule, whenever you cannot divide a number without producing a remainder, you use the lowest common denominator. By using this trick creatively, you can do a great deal using integers without the need for floating-point numbers. In digital graphics applications, integers are inevitable, and so the least-common-denominator principle will appear in many forms. Besides Function 8-1, you have seen it in action in Bresenham's algorithms for drawing a line and a circle. Consider also the use of the modulus operator.

Setting the Number of Print Wires   The first thing done in Function 8-1 is to set the number of print wires per pass. Although eight print wires will be used, the print head will be spaced down only seven print wires per pass. This is done to make the aspect ratio look normal. Although you could compute the aspect ratio by measuring the paper, measuring the display, and so on, it is better to try different approaches and see what looks best. Often what you *think* will look best is not as good as what you stumble upon by accident. The moral is that you can easily be too precise and stifle your creativity.

PRINTSCR Prints Sideways   After the number of print wires for each pass has been set, the function goes on to read the display from XMAX to XMIN in groups of 24 columns. Note that this reads the display from right to left, not from top to bottom. An odd number of columns is used, from 638 through 0, because the function reads groups of three colors. This permits dithered RGB displays to be printed accurately. It also renders horizontal and vertical lines with equal thickness.

Aborting the Print   If the user taps any key on the keyboard, the dithering process will be stopped and the printer reset to nine wires per pass. This is done so that the printing process can be easily aborted.

Bitfields   The function printrow( ) is executed once for each group of 24 columns of pixels read. The body of printrow( ) contains numerous references to bitfields that may seem redundant. In reality, since bitfields cannot be used in arrays, this repetition is necessary. It also clarifies the process that is going on: bits in various positions are being assigned to print wires. A complex pattern is being established that ends up in three separate strings that are fed, each in turn, to the printer.

Finally, after each group of three print rows has been prepared, the strings are sent to the printer. Each string contains in its first four characters the necessary graphics initialization sequence that prepares the printer to receive the precise number of graphics characters that follow.

Groups of three passes of the print head are sent until the left side of the display is reached. Because there are two print passes in the last group, rather than three, the code must accommodate this special case. The result is a nearly correct rendition of the display, printed sideways on the printer.

PLOTTING DRAWINGS

If you can afford to use a plotter, you can produce drawings that are perhaps even better than manually drafted work. In addition, you can make changes in drawings without having to erase or manually redraw your original. You can benefit from the use of a pen plotter for any kind of technical drafting, from patent drawings to engineering drawings.

Pen Plotters

In order to use pen plotters, however, you must use more information than is available from the display buffer alone. Pen plotters employ graphics languages to draw lines and other objects. The language used in GRAPHIQ (Appendix A) is HP-GL, which works with all HP plotters. It is as close to a practical standard for graphics as the industry has been able to achieve.

To use GRAPHIQ with a plotter, you should have an HP plotter, starting with the model HP7470 and including most of the HP line. If you wish to use GRAPHIQ with a plotter from another manufacturer, you must translate HP-GL into the language used by that plotter. You can easily modify the source code presented in this book to adapt to any plotter you choose.

Keep a Drawing Database   As is often suggested in this book, you should keep a database of all graphics objects you use in your editing sessions. This database can be used to regenerate the display, or it can be used to communicate with plotters.

Serial Input and Output   To communicate with the plotter, you will need to understand how to use serial input and output.

Plotters generally use the serial interface, as opposed to the parallel interface. They also allow many options for interfacing, including a variety of handshaking protocols. You will see one general method introduced here, but you should realize that many different methods are equally valid.

Using the Serial Port

For some reason, personal computers never include a completely functional serial interface in their firmware. The parallel interface is well supported by the BIOS (although it is not bidirectional), but the serial interface is always a problem.

DOS is no better. Using DOS with a serial port, you have no way of knowing the port's status. It is useless to try to use DOS to receive characters through a serial port.

Bidirectional Serial Interface   Plotters, unlike printers, usually require both input and output interfacing because you can request information from a typical plotter as well as send information to it. This makes the interface bidirectional and creates the need for buffering to and from the plotter. A buffer must be available to store information from the plotter until it can be read by your software. Likewise, a buffer must hold information from your software until it can be digested by the plotter.

In order to create a bidirectional asynchronous protocol, you need to do some very low-level programming, most of which has already been accomplished and illustrated in Function 8-2, PLOT.C. You will be able to use this technique not only with graphics software but with any software that you need to have work with serial devices.

Avoid Using stdaux for Graphics   In the standard collection of functions provided with C compilers, there is usually a way to refer to a serial port for use with standard input and output. In

■ FUNCTION 8-2

PLOT.C

```
/* PLOT.C plots a drawing using communications port 0,
** otherwise known as COM1:.
** You need to use MODE from the DOS command line prior
** to running this function:
**        MODE COM1:96,N,8,1,P
** Connect pins 2 to 3, 3 to 2, 7 to 7
** and 20 on the plotter to pin 5 on the IBM PC.
** Set the plotter switches to reflect the above mode
** setting.  Set plotter for "A" size paper (8-1/2 by 11).
** NOTE: Other elements can be added.  See GRAPHIQ in
** Appendix A for more.
*/

#include <conio.h>
#include <string.h>
#include <stdio.h>
#include <dos.h>

#define XON '\x11'
#define XOFF '\x13'

/* FILE.H contains record structures */

#define HEADER 0
#define POINT 1
#define LINE 2
#define CIRCLE 3
#define ARC 4
#define BOX 5
#define FILL 6
#define TEXT 7
#define LOC 1
#define STRG 2
#define ATTRLEN 2
#define TEXTLEN 62
#define RECLEN ATTRLEN + TEXTLEN /* in this case 64 bytes */
#define FILENAME 12

struct ELEMENT
    {
    union
        {
        struct
            {
            char attr;
            char subattr;
            } parts;

        struct
            {
            unsigned attrib;
            } whole;
        }attribute;
```

■ FUNCTION 8-2 (continued)

PLOT.C

```
union
     {
     struct
          {
          double xlate_x;
          double xlate_y;
          double rot_center_x;
          double rot_center_y;
          double xform_angle;
          double scale_factor;
          } xforms;

     struct
          {
          char filename[FILENAME+1];
          long date;
          long time;
          long records;   /* including this record */
          } header;

     struct
          {
          double x;
          double y;
          char color;
          char layer;
          } point;

     struct
          {
          double x1;
          double y1;
          double x2;
          double y2;
          int color;
          unsigned linestyle;
          char layer;
          int orxor;
          int first_pt;
          } line;

     struct
          {
          double x1;
          double y1;
          double x2;
          double y2;
          char color;
          unsigned linestyle;
          int orxor;
          char layer;
          } box;
```

■ **FUNCTION 8-2** (continued)

PLOT.C

```
        struct
            {
        double x1;
        double y1;
        double x2;
        double y2;
        char color;
        unsigned linestyle;
        int orxor;
        char layer;
        } fill;

        struct
            {
        double x_center;
        double y_center;
        double x_perim;
        double y_perim;
        char color;
        char layer;
        } circle;

        struct
            {
        double x_center;
        double y_center;
        double x_start;
        double y_start;
        double x_end;
        double y_end;
        char color;
        unsigned linestyle;
        char layer;
        } arc;

/* length of text string plus 5 determines maximum
** record length */

        struct
            {
        union
            {
            struct
                {
                double x_origin;
                double y_origin;
                double rotation;
                int height;
                int width;
                char font;
                char color;
                char layer;
                } loc;
```

■ **FUNCTION 8-2** (continued)

PLOT.C

```
                struct
                    {
                    char string[TEXTLEN]; /* governs record size */
                    } strg;
                } t_attr;
            } text;
        } attr;  /* end of attr union */
};  /* end of ELEMENT struct */


extern struct ELEMENT element;


plot(pointer)
unsigned pointer;
{
unsigned incr;
char plot_string[500];


plot_str("\x1B.P1:"); /* choose standard XON XOFF */
                      /* handshake (may vary by plotter) */
/* set plotter units to tenths of a millimeter */
/* for an 8-1/2 by 11 inch sheet */
plot_str("SC0,2500,0,1800;");


for (incr = 0; incr < pointer; ++incr)
    {
    parse(plot_string, pointer);
    plot_str(plot_string);
    }
}




parse(plot_string, pointer)
char *plot_string;
unsigned pointer;
{

strcpy(plot_string, "");

retrieve(pointer);

switch (element.attribute.parts.attr)
    {
```

■ **FUNCTION 8-2** (continued)

PLOT.C

```c
        case LINE:
            /* note: line types will not correlate
            ** with internal line styles unless you
            ** re-define the parameters for SOLID,
            ** DOTTED, etc.
            */
            sprintf(plot_string,
                "SP%d;LT%d;PAPU%f,%f;PD%f,%f;",
                element.attr.line.color+1,
                element.attr.line.linestyle,
                element.attr.line.x1,
                element.attr.line.y1,
                element.attr.line.x2,
                element.attr.line.y2);
            break;
        case BOX:
            sprintf(plot_string,
                "SP%d;LT%d;PAPU%f,%f;EA%f,%f;",
                element.attr.box.color+1,
                element.attr.box.linestyle,
                element.attr.box.x1,
                element.attr.box.y1,
                element.attr.box.x2,
                element.attr.box.y2);
            break;
        case FILL:
            sprintf(plot_string,
                "SP%d;LT%d;FT3;PAPU%f,%f;RA%f,%f;",
                element.attr.fill.color+1,
                element.attr.fill.linestyle,
                element.attr.fill.x1,
                element.attr.fill.y1,
                element.attr.fill.x2,
                element.attr.fill.y2);
            break;
        case CIRCLE:
            sprintf(plot_string,
                "SP%d;PU%f,%f;AA%f,%f,360;",
                element.attr.circle.color+1,
                element.attr.circle.x_perim,
                element.attr.circle.y_perim,
                element.attr.circle.x_center,
                element.attr.circle.y_center);
            break;
    }
}
```

■ FUNCTION 8-2 (continued)

PLOT.C

```
plot_str(plot_string)
char *plot_string;
{
unsigned far *com_base;
char outchar;
int out_element;

com_base = (unsigned far *)0x00000400L;
for (out_element = 0; out_element < strlen(plot_string);
    ++out_element)
    {
    if ((unsigned char)inp(*com_base + 5) & 0x01)
        if ((unsigned char)inp(*com_base) == XOFF)
            while ((unsigned char)inp(*com_base)
                    != XON);

    while (((unsigned char)inp(*com_base + 5) & 0x20) == NULL);

    outp(*com_base, plot_string[out_element]);
    }
}
```

the Microsoft C Compiler, you use stdaux (standard auxiliary) to send output to COM1, the logical name of the first communications adapter. One problem with stdaux is that you cannot *receive* data using input functions. Another problem is that you have no control over **handshaking** using output to stdaux. Handshaking is the use of a signal from a peripheral device to cause the sending computer to stop temporarily. Handshaking keeps the computer from sending information faster than the peripheral device can process it.

Hardwire Handshaking   When you use a plotter with a serial port, you must at least use a **hardwire handshake** to permit the plotter to tell the computer to stop while it catches up. A hardwire handshake is a wire connected between a pin on the plotter and a pin on the computer that, depending on its electrical state, can signal the computer to stop sending. If you do not do this, the plotter will work for a while, but then the pen will go crazy, drawing lines out of sequence. There are other ways to handshake, but even using these the hardwire should be connected. If you use stdaux as an output stream, you *must* use a hardwire handshake. There is no other way to enable the peripheral to tell the computer to stop sending.

Connecting a Hardwire Handshake   Although you will see many different methods described in books and manuals, the following technique has proven to be as close to universal as you can get when cabling for plotters. Figure 8-2 shows the wiring for a professionally designed universal serial interface cable for use with a plotter. Following the illustration, you first connect

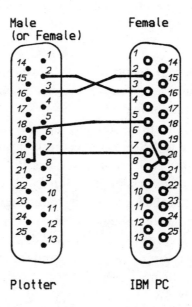

Male
(or Female)   Female

Plotter   IBM PC

FIGURE 8-2.   Wiring a serial interface for plotters

pins 7 to 7 to establish a signal ground connection. Then you wire pin 2 on the PC to pin 3 on the plotter, and pin 3 on the plotter to pin 2 on the PC. This establishes a null modem connection, allowing both the plotter and the PC to transmit and receive data. One of the excuses for the serial interface kludge is that it was originally designed for use with telephone modems. In order to use it with something else, you must "null" the modem connection (normally pins 2 to 2 and 3 to 3) by reversing it.

Pin 20 on the plotter is connected to pin 5 on the PC. Pin 20 sends a high signal (about 12 volts) to the PC and holds it there until the plotter is ready to receive more data.

The remaining connections disable two additional handshake wires that the PC would normally use with a telephone modem. You connect pins 6, 8, and 20 together on the PC connector. You can also disable these pins by setting bits on the communications chip. Some software disables these pins; other software does not. Unless these pins are disabled or held high, your handshake will not work.

Differences Using the AT   Given the difficult nature of the serial interface, you would think no one would want to make it *more* complicated. Ostensibly to save space on the IBM PC AT communications adapter, the 25-pin serial connector was changed to a 9-pin connector. It turns out that you need only nine pins for the serial interface. Pin 20 is the only pin with a number in excess of 8.

The problems caused by the change from a 9-pin to a 25-pin connector are difficult to describe. Usually, however, there is a simple way to avoid difficulty. Adapters are available to convert from this 9-pin kludge to a standard 25-pin kludge. If you have an AT, do not rewire your 25-pin connectors. Instead, use adapters.

When you make your cable, be sure to test all connections by using an ohm meter or other type of continuity tester. You test from one end of the cable to the other, as well as between pins to detect solder bridges. It can be a painstaking operation, but testing will assure you that the cable is correct.

Even if you test the cable repeatedly, however, you will often find that the interface does not work. Every kind of problem can emerge. For example, the pins can be seated too loosely and, like a stage dagger, be pushed back into the housing.

XON-XOFF Protocol   In addition to the hardwire handshake mentioned previously, GRAPHIQ uses a form of software handshake. Even if you omit the wire from pin 20 on the plotter to pin 5 on the PC, you should still establish handshaking through this secondary method.

To stop the computer from sending characters, the plotter, in addition to raising the voltage on pin 20, sends characters to the computer. What those characters are and when they are sent depends on an initialization sequence. There is usually a default method, however. The method used in GRAPHIQ is to cause the plotter to send an XOFF character when the plotter's buffer is nearly full. This character is usually ASCII 17 (DC1). The program needs to intercept this character and wait until the plotter sends an XON character, usually ASCII 19 (DC3). The mechanism for doing this is entirely contained in plot—str( ) in Function 8-2.

The first thing plot( ) does is to initialize the plotter to provide the XON-XOFF handshake. Later, in the description of plot—str( ), you will see how the handshake works.

Initializing the Serial Port

Only one serial port is used in the plot( ) function. You can make the port any of the four possible ports on the IBM PC, and with herculean ingenuity you can go beyond that. The single port is enough to illustrate how serial I/O works. The rest is up to you.

Before you use a serial port, it must be initialized. It can be initialized through DOS, using the MODE command, or it can be initialized from within your software. If you want to make your software foolproof, you may wish to initialize the ports automatically when your program starts. By automatically setting ports internally, you run the risk of interfering with settings that have been made by other programs. Unless you carefully restore those settings on exit, the user will associate things that go wrong with your program and not use it.

It is best to use DOS to initialize serial ports at the beginning of your session with the computer, even if it means explaining how to do it to a naive user. If you are able to standardize serial settings across all of your software (another argument against internal setting of ports), you need only initialize the serial port (or ports) once. A good universal setting is as follows:

MODE COM1:96,n,8,1,p

You enter this from the DOS command line, either by typing it or, preferably, by making it a part of your AUTOEXEC.BAT file. This setting uses the highest feasible baud rate (9600 baud), no parity checking, eight data bits (allowing a whole byte), one stop bit, and no device timeout testing.

Any software you use that blindly initializes serial ports will tend to interfere with the smooth running of your system. If your software needs to initialize ports internally, make sure that you give the user a way to control the initialization assumptions at least as well as the MODE command does.

The Plot Function

Function 8-2 shows a way of sending information to the plotter without using the C functions for standard output. As with printing, the conversions that occur using standard C functions often interfere with the precise expressions needed to drive peripheral devices. The function reads the GRAPHIQ database and converts it into plotter commands. These commands are then sent to the plotter, resulting in a finished drawing.

To convert the database into commands that are acceptable to the plotter, you need to initialize the plotter, read and parse the database, and finally send the parsed plotter-command strings out a serial port. The mechanism for doing this is much easier to understand than the dithering mechanism used in Function 8-1.

Setting User Units The plotter must be set up to work in units that are compatible with GRAPHIQ. To do this, the function sends the following string:

plot__str("SC0,2500,0,1800;")

This instruction scales the plotter to provide 0.1-millimeter resolution in the same scale as the data prepared using GRAPHIQ. If you are using a non-HP plotter, you will be able to set its resolution in a similar way.

The Plot Loop After initializing the plotter, plot( ) proceeds to loop through the database record by record. The variable pointer is always set to the current record number to be written, which is one more than the most recently written record. The database is read up to but not including the pointer. If the pointer is 0, of course, no plotting will occur.

First, plot__string is parsed in order to create strings that can be sent to the plotter. Second, the parsed plot__string is sent to the plotter using plot__str( ).

The Plot Switch The plot( ) function uses the following switch to select elements based on the attribute field in each element record. Notice how access to the attribute attr is gained.

```
switch (element.attribute.parts.attr)
```

You can gain access to any part of the element structure and its union in this way. The attr variable contains a number that unambiguously determines whether the element record is a line, circle, box, or other element.

For clarity, the mnemonics contained in FILE.H are repeated here, as they are in all illustrations in this book. In practice you would use an include statement, as follows:

```
#include <file.h>
```

In this book each mnemonic is defined directly in the illustration. This makes it easier to understand what is going on without your having to flip from one part of the book to another. For example, the mnemonics POINT, LINE, CIRCLE, and BOX are each given a number.

The switch contains references to these mnemonics. Each element encountered in the database will trigger the formation of an appropriate plotter instruction string, which will then be sent out the serial port to the plotter.

As an example, let's examine what happens in the case of LINE. The code for drawing a line on the plotter is as follows:

```
case LINE:
    sprintf(plot_string,
        "SP%d;LT%d;PAPU%f,%f;PD%f,%f;",
        element.attr.line.color+1,
        element.attr.line.linestyle,
        element.attr.line.x1,
        element.attr.line.y1,
        element.attr.line.x2,
        element.attr.line.y2);
    break;
```

When the switch encounters an attribute (attr) of 2, corresponding with the mnemonic LINE, it uses sprintf( ) to assemble a string that contains HP-GL plotter codes. The line specification is a self-contained unit that contains all the information necessary to draw a line. The line will be drawn with a given color (using a given pen) in a specific style. This record can be separated from the database and used elsewhere as a self-contained entity, making it a very flexible data structure.

HP-GL Plotter Codes   The codes used in HP-GL to make things happen on an HP plotter need a little explanation. HP produces some very effective documentation on HP-GL, and so this discussion will merely introduce you to plotter language. Let's look at the string SP%d;LT%d;PAPU%f,%f;PD%f,%f; for an illustration of HP-GL in action.

The English translation of this string is something like the following: select pen (SP) number (element.attr.line.color+1), and select line type (LT) (element.attr.line.linestyle). Plot absolute (PA) with the pen up (PU) to the coordinates (element.attr.line.x1, element.attr.line.y1) and then, with the pen down (PD), move to coordinates (element.attr.line.x2, element.attr.line.y2), thus drawing the line.

If you followed the preceding description successfully, you saw that the plotter language consists of simple two-character commands associated with various combinations of numbers. There are many other commands in HP-GL, making it the most widely used (and imitated) plotting language.

Plot Rotation, Translation, and Scale   To plot your drawing, you must first determine a scale factor, rotation angle, and offset for the plot. If you use default values, the contents of the display will be duplicated in an 8-1/2- by-11-inch format. You can add features to this plot function to plot within windows and at optional scale factors and rotation angles that differ from the system state. These enhancements are left to your discretion.

There's More to It   Function 8-2 is really only a small fraction of the size it would be in a commercial plotting program. It is used here only for illustration. It also appears in GRAPHIQ, the prototypical graphics program shown in Appendix A, in a more elaborate form.

Many other features must be added to the plot( ) function to make it useful. Aside from drawing lines, boxes, and circles, it must be able to set global scale factors, rotation angles, and offsets. It must be able to set the current object name using data under an object identifier attribute. Many other graphics entities, including text, arcs, and object coordinate lists, must be included. Then the entire program needs to be beta-tested and debugged. GRAPHIQ is intentionally kept simple enough to avoid the need for intensive debugging yet be reasonably functional.

Sending Strings to the Plotter

The function plot—str( ), a part of Function 8-2 that sends strings to the plotter, requires some explanation. It is in plot— str( ) that the string is taken character by character, from beginning to end, and sent to the plotter.

In the process of sending each character, two things happen. First, the port status is tested using the following expression:

```
if ((unsigned char)inp(*com __ base + 5) & 0x01)
```

In this expression, inp( ), the standard Microsoft C port input function, is used to obtain the port status from the address on the communications chip contained at com—base. Earlier, com—base was set to 0x00000400L, which is a frightening way of saying it is at an offset 400h from the beginning of RAM. A far pointer is declared to gain access to data at that location. This is where DOS keeps the addresses of various ports on the 8250 UART (universal asynchronous receiver transmitter) chip.

At *com—base + 5 a status byte reflects the current status of the communications port. Although there is more to the status than this, suffice it to say that if the first bit of the status byte is not zero, it means there is a character in the UART's receiver latch. Since the port is queried once before each character is sent, it is assumed that when the plotter sends an XOFF character (ASCII 17, or 11h) it will be received. This may not always be true, especially if the plotter is being used to send other information back to the running program. If the latter is the case, you must use a more complex serial interface than this. The interface must be interrupt-driven and buffered. For the purposes of this book, it is enough to be able to detect single XOFF and XON characters. Any other data to be received would depend on sending requests, and so the XON-XOFF protocol will usually be protected.

You can also test for timeouts and other errors, but if the interface is working properly you really need be concerned only with the presence or absence of a character in the receiver latch. When this character is XOFF, a while( ) loop repeatedly tests the UART's receiver latch until an XON character appears there. The function then continues to send the current character from plot—string.

Before the character from plot—string is actually sent, a second while( ) loop tests the status byte to determine whether bit 1 (0x02) of the byte is nonzero. If nonzero, bit 1 indicates that the interface is busy. This is where the hardwire handshake influences whether or not the computer should send more data. If bit 1 is not zero, the while( ) loop repeats until bit 1 becomes zero.

Use Both Forms of Handshaking   You can see from this that it is wise to use both software and hardware handshaking. If, for example, a glitch in synchronization between the plotter and the computer results in data being sent from the plotter out of sequence, or the wrong plotter command happens to be sent, an XOFF or XON might not be intercepted by the loop. The hardwire handshake would nevertheless catch such an error.

Timing Considerations   This simple serial interface is sensitive to timing. In other words, the time it takes to prepare a character to be written could interfere with the reception of an XOFF or XON character. The interface will be very problematic if anything *but* XON or XOFF characters is sent by the plotter. This means that the clock speed of your computer will have an effect on the serial interface. You may need to insert a timer loop to slow the interface down if you are using a fast computer. Above all, do not expect the interface to work the first time. Serial interfaces are extremely fickle.

Another option for the receiving end of the interface is to use a buffered interrupt-driven method. Chapters 11 and 12 discuss a more comprehensive approach to receiving serial characters using buffering. Using an interrupt method, serial characters are received in the background, while your software is doing other things. The characters are buffered and made available on demand. If the simple method of receiving one character at a time presented here is not working for you, read Chapters 11 and 12 for more detail.

Even with interrupt-driven bidirectional buffering, anomalous conditions do crop up from time to time. A carelessly wired cable will not matter most of the time, but when things do go wrong you will be all the more mystified.

ORCHESTRATING PRINTING AND PLOTTING FUNCTIONS

In your actual applications you will need to orchestrate printing and plotting so that they do not interfere with other functions and are clearly understood. To do this, the usual options must be made available to the user. In other words, commands must be executable from the command line, from command files, from menus, and in abbreviated form.

You might consider creating one general category for hard copy and then branching from that category into plotting and printing functions. Each subcategory would then have its own set of parameters.

Executing the Print Function

The print function could have two options. The first would be to display and modify a printer status menu. In this menu you might have a choice of dithering methods, a choice of printer ports, and the status of the printer queue. After the status for printing was set, it would become the default status for any subsequent printing. The user would begin printing by selecting a menu item to start.

Executing the Plot Function

Plotting is more complicated than printing in that more parameters govern the appearance of a final plot. You can choose a window, a plotting scale factor, an origin different from the system origin, a rotation angle, and much more.

Setting Plotter Status The first option the user could exercise might be to modify the global plotting status. The selection of plotting window, origin, and scale factor should be done interactively, if possible, so that the user can actually locate the pen on the plotter itself to select the corners of the plotter window and other features. This makes the plotter setup much easier than it would be if the user had to specify numbers.

As with the selection of printer options, the user should have an option to start the plotting process. If the user wanted only to set the status for a future plot, the start option could be ignored and the printer menu exited.

Termination of Plotting or Printing

While plotting or printing is in progress, many unforeseen events can happen. The pen could run out of ink, or the plotter ribbon could be torn. The pen could tear the paper. The user needs to be able to stop the process quickly to avoid damage to equipment or drawings.

In general, you should designate a single key for termination, and a reminder message should be shown on the display during the plot. For some functions any key could be pressed to terminate the operation, but in practice this can result in unintentional disruption. It is unlikely that the user will accidentally press the ESC key, and so this could be a standard key to use to terminate ongoing processes.

Printing and Plotting Using GRAPHIQ

In Appendix A of this book you will find a humble program called GRAPHIQ. It is intended to suggest ways in which the functions in this book can work together. In addition it contains the most current versions of all functions. It has been tested, but not exhaustively, and so you may find bugs in it.

The use of menus suggested in this chapter is illustrated in a cursory way in GRAPHIQ. In a more formal application you might want to add more status options to those shown.

In general, though, GRAPHIQ can be used for many graphics tasks even as it is. Make a project of entering, compiling, and linking it. In the process you will learn a great deal about the practical aspects of sending graphics data to peripheral devices. Above all, stay calm, be patient, and realize that serial and parallel interface standards can be very difficult to master.

9

Menu Design

Menus are used to display options to the software user. Your menus can range from being extremely descriptive to being very abbreviated. They can consist of graphics symbols, text, or a combination of graphics and text. Menus appear in many forms and serve many purposes, but all menus must be designed with one basic principle in mind: They must be clear and appropriate if they are to be useful.

There is an art as well as a science to software design. An artfully designed program is one that communicates with the user effectively and is even a joy to use. Few programs achieve status as art, perhaps because few programmers perceive themselves or train themselves as artists.

It can be said that software is essentially a communications medium. In the past it was sufficient to design a piece of software to perform a function, with little attention to the human interface. The user was presented with a command line and a technical manual. Every command had to be prepared syntactically, and explicit knowledge of the command vocabulary was required.

When personal computers became widespread, the command line became an object of fear and loathing. The term "user friendly" came to be associated with software that was designed to guide the user (who had perhaps never touched a computer keyboard) politely through a system's command hierarchy.

Strangely enough, probably because the world works in cycles, users became disenchanted with menu-based software. After people had used systems that *required* the use of menus, they wanted to take shortcuts. The buzzword **macro** was borrowed from the province of programming languages and used to identify a shorthand for executing functions (even in groups) *without* the use of menus.

Over the years it has become clear that software users have a broad range of needs and desires. No person in this marvelous universe is quite the same as any other. The only solution to the problem of supplying appropriate command-entry methods for the mass market is to include every conceivable technique in a single software offering. This tends to place most of the emphasis on user interaction rather than on substance in the design and coding of software.

As a software artist, you must make your software work with pop-up menus for mice, command lines, macro languages, command files, menus for digitizers—literally any method imaginable, and all at once. This makes the design of the user interface the most complicated part of creating a software package.

This chapter will focus on simple techniques that can be used with the EGA to display menus and select from them. It will also introduce you to more general techniques for moving blocks of memory quickly from one place to another. When your menus pop up, they do so because you know how to move memory efficiently.

CREATING MENUS

Creating a menu involves both selecting the functions to be made available and coding the menu in memory. It is most important that the functions you activate using a menu be appropriate. If you spend most of your time designing the system before you code it, you will save a great deal of time in the coding phase.

Assuming that you have taken the time to select appropriate functions to execute from the menu, your next task is to decide on the type of menu to use. In GRAPHIQ, the prototypical graphics program in Appendix A, a simple approach to pop-up menu design has been selected. This is, of course, not the only way to use menus.

Pop-Up Menus in EGA Graphics Modes

Figure 9-1 shows an actual pop-up menu used in GRAPHIQ. The source code for GRAPHIQ in Appendix A includes this menu in a somewhat more advanced form. It is declared and initialized in DECLARES.H, the header file that contains GRAPHIQ's declarations.

Declaring an Array of Pointers   Notice that the menu in Figure 9-1 is declared as an array of pointers to strings. You can declare arrays of pointers in this way and reserve space for them if you initialize the arrays explicitly. The array is initialized to contain the actual text of the menu.

Border Characters   You will see some garbage characters bordering the menu in this illustration. These are the seven-bit representations of what in the actual initialization are full eight-bit characters. These characters represent graphics characters from 128 through 255 in the extended character set; when displayed on the screen they result in a double-line box. Take a look at your computer's graphics character set for their equivalents, and substitute them if you wish to create menus surrounded by double lines.

Passing Pointers Because the menu is declared as an array of pointers, you can pass these pointers to functions. To display such menus, you need a function such as Function 9-1,

```
/* An actual menu used in GRAPHIQ.  Look in Appendix A,
** DECLARES.H for the most current version.
*/


char *main_mnu[] = {
"IMMMMMMMMMMMMMMMMM;",
": HELP  (F6)    :",
": GRID          :",
": STYLE (F7)    :",
": COLOR (F8)    :",
": MOVE  (F9)    :",
": LINE  (F10)   :",
": BOX           :",
": FILL          :",
": CIRCLE        :",
": PLAYBACK      :",
": PRINT         :",
": PUT SCREEN    :",
": GET SCREEN    :",
": COMMAND FILE  :",
": CLEAR DISPLAY :",
": EXIT THIS MENU :",
": QUIT GRAPHIQ  :",
"HMMMMMMMMMMMMMMMMM<",
""};
```

FIGURE 9-1. Initialization for a text menu

■ FUNCTION 9-1

WRITE_AR.C

```c
/* WRITE_AR.C writes an array of characters given
** a pointer to a pre-initialized pointer array,
** the upper left corner of the array, and the
** color they are to be written in.
** This file also contains functions to write
** a string and a single character using the
** EGA BIOS.  Use this in graphics modes.
*/


#include <dos.h>
#indlude "screen.h"

#define XORIT 0x80
#define NORMIT 0

union REGS regs;


int write_array(string, row, col, color)
char *string[];
int row, col, color;
{
int i, j, newcol;

for (i = 0, newcol = col; strlen(string[i]) != 0; ++i, ++row)
    for (j = 0, newcol = col; j < strlen(string[i]);
            ++j, ++newcol)
        write_char(string[i][j], row, newcol, color, XORIT);
return(i-1);
}




write_str(string, row, col, color)
char *string;
int row, col, color;
{
int j, newcol;

for (j = 0, newcol = col; j < strlen(string); ++j, ++newcol)
    write_char(string[j], row, newcol, color, XORIT);


}
```

■ **FUNCTION 9-1** (continued)

WRITE__AR.C

```
write_char(character, row, col, color, orxor)
char character;
int row, col, color, orxor;
{

set_curs(row, col);

regs.h.ah = 9;                   /* write character */
regs.x.cx = 1;                   /* one character */
regs.h.al = character;           /* character */
regs.h.bl = color | orxor;       /* set color (NORMIT, XORIT) */
int86(0x10, &regs, &regs);       /* interrupt 10h */
}




read_char(character, row, col)
char *character;
int row, col;
{

set_curs(row, col);

regs.h.ah = 8;                   /* read character */
regs.h.bh = 0;                   /* for page 0 */
int86(0x10, &regs, &regs);       /* interrupt 10h */
*character = regs.h.al;          /* character */
}




set_curs(row, col)
int row, col;
{

regs.h.ah = 2;                   /* set cursor position */

regs.h.bh = 0;                   /* for page 0 */
regs.h.dh = row;                 /* current row */
regs.h.dl = col;                 /* current col */
int86(0x10, &regs, &regs);       /* interrupt 10h */
}
```

WRITE＿AR.C. In use, a pointer to main＿mnu would be passed to write＿array( ), as in the following line of code:

```
height = write_array(main_mnu, 0, 0, color);
```

Function 9-1 takes the pointer to main＿mnu, the row and column of the upper left corner, and the color to use to write the menu. You must guarantee that the menu will fit on the display.

Finding the End of the Menu   Function 9-1 determines the total number of rows in the menu by waiting for the first null string pointed to by the menu pointer array. When it reaches this string, which is defined as having no length, the function returns to the caller. Menus are either XORed or placed normally against the background. If XORed, you can remove the menu by XORing it again at the same position. If the menu replaces the background, there is no way to recover the background. You can make menus pop up simply by XORing them to make them appear and then XORing them again to restore the background. This has some drawbacks if the background is complex, but it is the only fast way to use the EGA to display large areas of text quickly and preserve the background without the use of display paging. If you wish to evolve another technique, make sure you have enough RAM on your EGA to contain an auxiliary buffer. This book assumes that you have the minimum 64K required for a one-page display buffer.

Pop-Up Menus in EGA Text Mode

In text mode you can take advantage of the accessibility of display memory to use Microsoft C's movedata( ) function. This function makes use of the 8086 microprocessor's MOVSB instruction to move a block of data from any location in address space to any other location. You can apply the movedata( ) function to any text string. Text mode lets you appreciate the power of block memory moves. You can quickly buffer any part of the display, write anything you want there, and copy the buffer back when you are finished.

Moving Strings to the Display   Using EGA mode 3 as an example, you could move a menu onto the display by storing the menu specification as a string initialized with an array of pointers that allow you to refer conveniently to rows of characters. Function 9-2, TEXTDISP.C, shows the initialization of the string pointer array and the instructions necessary to move the string onto the display. You will find that this method works almost instantaneously. Without recourse to assembler, working entirely in C, you can create very impressive text menus with this technique.

Saving Text Background   It is fine to be able to put menus on text displays quickly, but what about removing them? To remove a menu and restore the text background, you must have saved the background in a buffer before placing the menu.

To save the background characters, you use a function similar to Function 9-3, SAVE_BKG.C. Note that instead of using an array of pointers to initialized strings, Function 9-3 uses an array that has been defined globally.

Restoring Text Background   The procedure for displaying a menu will be first to use Function 9-3 to save the background, and then to place the menu using Function 9-2. Finally, after the menu has served its purpose, you must restore the back-

■ FUNCTION 9-2

TEXTDISP.C

```
/* TEXTDISP.C displays a text menu in EGA mode 3.
**
** The menu is initialized as an array of pointers
** to type char.  In this printed version
** the graphics characters which make up the
** border can't be shown directly.  Instead,
** the characters' ASCII values plus 128 will
** determine the graphics characters to be used.
*/

#include <memory.h>
#include <dos.h>
#include <stdio.h>

#define DISPLAY_WIDTH 160


char *text[] = {
"IMMMMMMMMMMMMMMMMMMMMMMMM;",
": This sample menu    :",
": will appear within  :",
": a double-line box.  :",
":                     :",
": The characters that :",
": surround this box   :",
": refer to graphics   :",
": characters as       :",
": below:              :",
":                     :",
": Character    ASCII  :",
":    I         201    :",
":    M         205    :",
":    ;         187    :",
":    :         186    :",
":    <         188    :",
":    H         200    :",
":                     :",
"HMMMMMMMMMMMMMMMMMMMMMMMM<",};


/* In actual use you would pass the text pointer
** array to the following function, along with the
** coordinates of the upper left and lower right
** corners of the menu.  Note that coordinates are
** in character positions, not graphics units.
*/
```

■ **FUNCTION 9-2** (continued)

TEXTDISP.C

```
textdisp(txt_buff, ulx, uly, lrx, lry)
char *txt_buff[];
int ulx, uly, lrx, lry;
{
int element, posn, col;
int row_len = ((lrx - ulx) + 1) * 2;
char scr_assy[DISPLAY_WIDTH];
int mode, columns, apage;
struct SREGS segregs;
int srcseg, srcoff, destseg, destoff;

segread(&segregs);

srcseg = segregs.ds;
srcoff = (int)scr_assy;

destseg = 0xb800;  /* color/graphics text */
                   /* if monochrome use 0xb000 */

destoff = (ulx * 2) + (uly * DISPLAY_WIDTH);

for (element = 0; element <= (lry - uly);
     ++element, destoff += DISPLAY_WIDTH)
    {
        /* copy existing attributes from destination */
    movedata(destseg, destoff, srcseg, srcoff, row_len);
    for (posn = 0, col = 0; col <= (lrx - ulx);
            posn += 2, ++col)
        scr_assy[posn] = txt_buff[element][col];
    movedata(srcseg, srcoff, destseg, destoff, row_len);
    }

}
```

ground from the buffer used in Function 9-3. This is done using Function 9-2 again, but this time the pointer to the background buffer is passed instead of the pointer to the initialized menu pointer array.

■ FUNCTION 9-3

SAVE＿BKG.C

```
/* SAVE_BKG.C saves the text background where
** a menu in text mode will be placed so it can be
** restored later.
*/


#include <memory.h>
#include <dos.h>
#include <stdio.h>

#define DISPLAY_WIDTH 160

/* declare a place to store the text display
** characters.
*/
char bkgd_buffer[25][81];


/* In actual use you pass the bkgd_buffer pointer
** to the following function as buffer.
*/

save_bkg(buffer, ulx, uly, lrx, lry)
char buffer[][81];
int ulx, uly, lrx, lry;
{
int element, posn, col;
unsigned row_len = ((lrx - ulx) + 1) * 2;
char scr_assy[DISPLAY_WIDTH];
int mode, columns, apage;
struct SREGS segregs;
int srcseg, srcoff, destseg, destoff;

segread(&segregs);

srcseg = 0xb800;  /* origin for color/graphics text */
                  /* if monochrome use 0xb800 */

srcoff = (ulx * 2) + (uly * DISPLAY_WIDTH);

destseg = segregs.ds;
destoff = (int)scr_assy;

for (element = 0; element <= (lry - uly);
     ++element, srcoff += DISPLAY_WIDTH)
     {
     movedata(srcseg, srcoff, destseg, destoff, row_len);
     for (posn = 0, col = 0; col <= (lrx - ulx);
          posn += 2, ++col)
          buffer[element][col] = scr_assy[posn];
     }
}
```

SELECTING FROM MENUS

You can use several techniques to select options from menus. You could have the user move a cursor to the desired item and then press a key to select the item. Menu items can also be selected numerically.

If you decide to use a cursor selection method, you will need to design a cursor that moves from cell to cell on the menu. There are many different types of cursor, but you will find that using text characters in graphics modes on the EGA is much faster than trying to draw pixels. For color graphics on the EGA, you need to change four bit planes for each pixel. This makes block moves to save and restore areas of pixels a slow process. The design of the display controller makes it fairly easy to handle four bit planes when dealing with single pixels but harder to handle blocks of data in the display buffer.

The Display Background

Given the limitations of the EGA, the methods used in GRAPHIQ (Appendix A) are probably consistent with the way IBM originally intended the EGA to be used. Text menus are XORed onto the background. As you may already know, when you XOR a bit with another bit it reverses the target bit. XOR-ing a bit twice with the same data restores the bit to its original state. GRAPHIQ's menus are XORed because it takes too much time to buffer the background on the EGA and restore it again. On faster hardware you could save the information behind the menu, display the menu, make your menu selection, and then restore the background from its buffer. This is only feasible for small areas of the EGA display.

Dealing with Complex Backgrounds   One unfortunate implication of XORing menus over graphics is that the menus become unreadable if the background is very complex. A way to deal with this problem on the EGA is to make your menus movable so that they can be placed in a quieter area of the display, if any. Another way is to use two pages of display RAM. To do this you must have more than 64K on the EGA. See your EGA documentation for an explanation of memory options. If you use display pages, you can draw the menu on page 1, quickly switch to page 1, select from the menu, and then quickly switch back to page 0. This has the disadvantage that your menus cannot be superimposed over the graphics, requiring you to remember what the display looked like while making your selections.

Reverse-Video Text Cursors

To select from your pop-up menu, you must use a function like Function 9-4, MENUCURS.C. This function will display a reverse-video cursor at a specified initial location. It will then, under control of the arrow keys (you could substitute a mouse driver here), permit you to move the cursor up or down on the menu.

The text cursor determines where text characters and attributes are to be placed or found on the display.

Handy Cursor Functions   Function 9-4 contains a few handy functions for handling text on the display. They are really nothing more than BIOS interrupts. The first of these, re __ vid( ), actually produces the reverse-video cursor. The fol-

■ FUNCTION 9-4

MENUCURS.C

```
/*
**   MENUCURS.C
**   Display a menu cursor by changing the attribute
**   to reverse video
**   for the current menu row from ulx + 1 to lrx - 1.
**   Up arrow key moves cursor up to uly + 1.
**   Down arrow key moves cursor down to lry - 1.
**   Home key selects the function.
**   Esc key escapes from the menu.
*/


#include <stdio.h>
#include <conio.h>
#include <dos.h>

/* SCREEN.H contains colors, display width and height */

#define BLACK        0x0
#define BLUE         0x1
#define GREEN        0x2
#define CYAN         0x3
#define RED          0x4
#define MAGENTA      0x5
#define BROWN        0x6
#define WHITE        0x7

#define TRUE -1
#define FALSE 0
#define XORIT 0x80
#define NORMIT 0
#define BS 0x08
#define CR 0x0D
#define ENTER CR
#define NULLCHAR '\0'
#define ESC 0x1b
#define HOME 0x147
#define UP 0x148
#define DOWN 0x150
#define LEFT 0x14B
#define RIGHT 0x14D

union REGS regs;

int menucurs(row, ulx, uly, lrx, lry)
int *row, ulx, uly, lrx, lry;
{
int inchar;
```

■ FUNCTION 9-4 (continued)

MENUCURS.C

```
re_vid(*row, ulx, uly, lrx, lry);

do {

inchar = retkey();

switch (inchar)
    {
    case ESC:            /* escape key */
        *row = 0xffff;
        break;
    case UP:           /* move cursor up */
        if (*row == (uly + 1))
            break;
        re_vid(*row, ulx, uly, lrx, lry);
        set_curs(--*row, ulx + 1);
        re_vid(*row, ulx, uly, lrx, lry);
        break;
    case DOWN:             /* move cursor down */
        if (*row == (lry - 1))
            break;
        re_vid(*row, ulx, uly, lrx, lry);
        set_curs(++*row, ulx + 1);
        re_vid(*row, ulx, uly, lrx, lry);
        break;
    case RIGHT:      /* neutralize right and left arrow keys */
        break;
    case LEFT:
        break;
    default:
        break;
    }
}
while ((inchar != ENTER) && (inchar != ESC));

re_vid(*row, ulx, uly, lrx, lry);

return(*row);
}




/* set attribute current row to reverse video */
int re_vid(row, ulx, uly, lrx, lry)
int row, ulx, uly, lrx, lry;
```

■ **FUNCTION 9-4** (continued)

MENUCURS.C

```
{
int inchar;
int fore, back;

for (inchar = ulx + 1; inchar <= lrx - 1; ++inchar)
    {
    set_curs(row, inchar);
    set_attr(rd_attri(&fore, &back), back, fore, 1);
    }
}




set_curs(row, col)
int row, col;
{
union REGS regs;

regs.h.ah = 2;                  /* set cursor position */
regs.h.bh = 0;                  /* for page 0 */
regs.h.dh = row;               /* current row */
regs.h.dl = col;               /* current col */
int86(0x10, &regs, &regs);     /* interrupt 10h */
}




rd_attri(fore, back)
int *fore, *back;
{
union REGS regs;

regs.h.bh = 0;                  /* for page 0 */
int86(0x10, &regs, &regs);     /* interrupt 10h */
*fore = regs.h.ah & 0xF;
*back = regs.h.ah >> 4;
return(regs.h.al);
}




set_attr(character, fore, back, count)
char character;
int fore, back, count;
```

■ FUNCTION 9-4 (continued)

MENUCURS.C

```
{
union REGS regs;

/* if bit 7 is 1, character is xored onto screen */

regs.h.bh = 0;
regs.x.cx = count;
regs.h.al = character;
regs.h.bl = fore | back << 4;
int86(0x10, &regs, &regs);     /* interrupt 10h */
}



int retkey()
{
int inchar;

if (!inkey(&inchar))
     inchar += 0x100;  /* extended character add 256 */

while (kbhit()) getch();  /* flush the keyboard buffer */

return(inchar);
}



int inkey(ascii)
int *ascii;
{
union REGS regs;

regs.x.ax = 0;
int86(22, &regs, &regs);

*ascii = regs.h.ah;

if (regs.h.al == 0)
    return(0);

*ascii = regs.h.al;
return(1);
}
```

lowing listing shows the re＿vid( ) function:

```
/* set attribute current row to reverse video */
int re_vid(row, ulx, uly, lrx, lry)
int row, ulx, uly, lrx, lry;
{
char ch;
int inchar;
int fore, back;

for (inchar = ulx + 1; inchar <= lrx - 1; ++inchar)
    {
    set_curs(row, inchar);
    ch = rd_attri(&fore, &back);
    set_attr(ch, back, fore, 1);
    }
}
```

You can use re＿vid( ) in many applications, whenever you need to have reverse video appear at a location on the display. It works character by character, starting at the leftmost column (ulx + 1) and moving to the rightmost one (lrx − 1). It does this so rapidly that the row of characters appears to change color instantly.

For each character in the row, the text cursor is set using a call to the BIOS in set＿curs( ). This function is as follows:

```
set_curs(row, col)
int row, col;
{
union REGS regs;

regs.h.ah = 2;              /* set cursor position */
regs.h.bh = 0;              /* for page 0 */
regs.h.dh = row;           /* current row */
regs.h.dl = col;           /* current col */
int86(0x10, &regs, &regs); /* interrupt 10h */
}
```

After the cursor is positioned, the character and attributes at its position are read by rd＿attri( ), as follows:

```
rd_attri(fore, back)
int *fore, *back;
{
union REGS regs;
```

```
regs.h.bh = 0;              /* for page 0 */
int86(0x10, &regs, &regs);  /* interrupt 10h */
*fore = regs.h.ah & 0xF;
*back = regs.h.ah >> 4;
return(regs.h.al);
}
```

This function uses the BIOS to retrieve a character and the foreground and background attributes of that character. It returns the ASCII character code and passes pointers to the foreground and background values as arguments. This enables you to use rd＿attri( ) itself as an argument.

Finally, in order to change the color of the character, set＿attr( ) is used. The listing for set＿attr( ) is as follows:

```
set_attr(character, fore, back, count)
char character;
int fore, back, count;
{
union REGS regs;

/* if bit 7 is 1, character is xored onto screen */

regs.h.bh = 0;
regs.x.cx = count;
regs.h.al = character;
regs.h.bl = fore | back << 4;
int86(0x10, &regs, &regs);    /* interrupt 10h */
}
```

The character and its foreground and background attributes are passed to this function, along with a character count, and another BIOS interrupt is executed. Note that the background and foreground attribute positions are reversed in making this call. This is where the reverse-video effect is achieved.

Moving the Cursor If you repeat re＿vid( ), it will have the effect of restoring the foreground and background colors. All you have to do to move the reverse-video cursor is to place it at one location, and then repeat it at that location and place it at the next location. This causes the cursor to appear to move.

FAST MENU-DISPLAY TECHNIQUES

A great deal of mystery surrounds the problem of increasing the speed of a program's operation. It really shouldn't. A simple fact is that the closer you get to the processor's machine code, the faster your software will run. Stated simply, this means that functions written in assembler are often faster than functions written in high-level languages. It also implies that the processor's built-in features should be used to greatest advantage. The key to increasing speed is to avoid far calls and use near operations as much as possible. A macro in C can often be used to avoid making a call. Writing routines in assembler can give you control over short jumps.

Making Block Moves

One of the fastest instructions in the 8086 repertoire is the MOVSB instruction. This instruction moves the contents of the byte located at address DS:SI to ES:DI. In other words, it does in a few instruction cycles what would normally require several more. Further, the MOVSB instruction, in concert with the REP instruction, will repeat the move as many times (within the limits of an unsigned integer) as you wish. Thus, you can use MOVSB (or its cousin MOVSW) to perform **block** moves of data. A block move transfers data at a given series of addresses to another series of addresses offset by a given distance in memory. It is not possible here to explain this instruction in detail. If you need more information, consult your favorite books on 8086 assembler.

Working with and Around
the Graphics Controller

One of the problems with the EGA has to do with the difficulties you encounter trying to do block moves in modes 13 through 16. Everything must be done using the graphics controller chip as an intermediary. When you are working one pixel at a time, this is adequate, but if you try to take advantage of the microprocessor's built-in block-move capabilities, you will find that many things become impossible. Display techniques on the EGA could be much faster if EGA display memory were readily accessible.

Whenever you wish to change entire areas of the display to the same color and you do not need to use line styles, you can use Microsoft C's movedata( ) function. First, set the color using graphics controller function 0, and then set function 5 to mode 2, and then use movedata( ) for entire rows rather than using a repeated far call. This method works only when you wish to set all pixels to the same color, however, not when you wish to put a variety of colors on the display.

The EGA Graphics
Controller

The functions used in this book to change the EGA's display memory all manipulate the EGA graphics controller in some way. To use the graphics controller efficiently, you need to know how to do a few basic things with it.

Using Graphics Controller Registers The graphics controller itself consists of registers that are located at ports 3CCh, 3CAh, 3CEh, and 3CFh. Remember, you can write to any port by using the Microsoft C outp( ) function. For the purposes of this book, the registers at 3CCh and 3CAh (the graphics position registers) never need to be changed. Register 3CCh is automatically set to 00, and register 3CAh is automatically set to 01.

Register 3CEh on the EGA serves as an **index** to select a feature to be accessed using register 3CFh. The contents of an index register control the function of another register. This allows register 3CFh to function as though it were eight different registers.

Selecting Graphics Controller Functions In order to select a function to be performed, you output the function number as an index to register 3CEh. The following command shows a typical function index selection:

outp(0×3CE, function); outp(0×3CF, register—value);

The functions of register 3CFh are listed in Table 9-1.

To preserve compatibility with its original CGA, IBM used a great deal of ingenuity in designing the graphics controller chip. In practice, the chip is extremely difficult to use compared with other graphics products. Nevertheless, the popularity of the EGA makes it necessary to live with the labyrinthine methods you must use to program for it.

Registers Are Write Only The registers of the graphics controller chip, to add to the difficulties, are **write only.** This means that you cannot read the register to find out what is there and

Functions	Descriptions
0	For write mode 0 only. Bit planes 0 through 3 are controlled by bits 0 through 3 of this register. If on, and enabled by function 1, a bit will result in a bit in the color plane being set by function 5. This function sets the color to be written by function 5.
1	Enables the bit planes corresponding with bits 0 through 3 of this register. If disabled, no color for the disabled plane will be changed, even if a color value is selected by function 0. You normally output 0x0F to this register and then forget about it.
2	Used with reads from bit planes, this function uses bits 0 through 3 of its register to store a color value for which read mode 1 returns a 1 in any of its 8 bit positions. If you wanted to read the EGA display to find only those pixels of a given color, this is how you would do it.
3	Bits 0 through 2 of this register can contain a number from 0 through 7 that represents the number of bits that the data from the microprocessor will be rotated to the left when write function 5, mode 0 is executed. To change a single pixel, you could write a 0×01 to the display address and rotate it to one of 8 pixel positions within the byte.

Bits 3 and 4 of the register for this function select write modes as follows:

00	unmodified
01	AND against background
10	OR against background
11	XOR against background

| 4 | Selects a bit plane to read using read mode 0 and bits 0 through 2 of this register. |

TABLE 9-1. Register 3CFh Functions

Functions	Descriptions

5   Bits 0 and 1 of this register determine the write mode to be used, as follows:

00	Processor data is rotated using the number from function 3. The bit mask set using function 8 is used to set the corresponding bit in all planes enabled using function 1 according to the graphics controller latch or the value set using function 0.
01	The processor latch loaded by a previous read is written to the bit planes. This enables copying of pixels from one part of display to another using fast reads and writes.
10	The data byte you write contains color in bits 0 through 3. This function sets 8 bits in all bit planes selected by the given color. If the mask from function 8 is used, you can select which bits are from the latch and which are from the data. If you want to set up to 8 pixel positions to a specified color, this mode is for you.
11	Not used.

Bit 2 of the function 5 register specifies a test condition. It is normally 0.

Bit 3 of the function 5 register specifies the read mode. If this bit is 0, a plane selected by function 4 will be read. If it is 1, the color specified using function 2 will determine which bits are set when a byte is read from the buffer.

Bit 4 of the function 5 register specifies odd/even or sequential addressing modes. If 0, odd/even addressing is used. If 1, memory is addressed sequentially. You seldom need to change this bit.

Bit 5 can be used to create a CGA-compatible mode with four colors having two adjacent bits per pixel. Normally, you will not need to change this register.

TABLE 9-1.   Register 3CFh Functions (continued)

Functions	Descriptions
6	If bit 0 of the register is 1, character generator latches are disabled. If bit 0 is 0, alpha graphics are selected. If bit 1 of this register is 1, odd maps are chained after even maps. Otherwise, as in the CGA, map 2 follows map 0 and map 3 follows map 1 in memory. Bits 2 and 3 govern memory mapping, as follows: 00 A000h is base of 128K 01 A000h is base of 64K for high-resolution graphics 10 B000h is base for 32K monochrome text 11 B800h is base for 32K CGA-compatible graphics
7	When you are reading using read mode 1 (color compare), planes for which bits are set in bit positions 0 through 3 of this register should not be used.
8	Bits set to 0 are written from memory latches, and bits set to 1 are written using the prevailing method of color specification, as indicated by function 5. To preserve the background, you must first read at the memory location in display buffer space to load the graphics controller latches.

TABLE 9-1.   Register 3CFh Functions (continued)

OR the contents with a new value. Thus, you must carefully consider all settings, particularly for function 5, before outputting any data to the register. This results in wasted time and lots of trial and error.

Reading and Moving Display Data

A simple approach to the EGA, if you just want to get the job done with a minimum of headaches, is to leave function 5 alone and use modeset( ) to select the EGA mode you want. You would then use the other functions to set masks, change colors, and write data. If you wish to read the color of a given pixel, use BIOS interrupt 10h with BH set to the display page, DX set to the row, and CX set to the column. On exit, AH will contain the color value of the pixel. This can be done using C and the Microsoft int86( ) function as follows:

```
#include <dos.h>

int read_pix(x, y, page)
int x, y, page;
{
union REGS regs;

regs.h.bh = page;
regs.x.dx = y;
regs.x.cx = x;
int86(0x10, &regs, &regs);
return(regs.h.ah);
}
```

This use of the BIOS will slow down your display access. Unfortunately, the alternative involves knowing which of two read modes is in effect, meaning that you need to use function 5. Unless you are using a CGA-compatible EGA mode, you can set bits 4 and 5 of function 5 to 0. Bit 2 is always 0 unless you are a technician testing the EGA. This leaves bits 0, 1, and 3. Because you are concerned with reading the display buffer and not writing it, bits 0 and 1 of function 5 can also be set to 0.

Finally, you can set bit 3 of the register for function 5 to 0 (setting all other bits to 0 as well) if you wish to read a bit plane selected by function 4. If you wish to read only the color specified using function 2, you must set bit 3 of the function 5 register to 1.

Use BIOS When Possible   If you can live with the slow speed of the BIOS, it is best to avoid the hassle of using the graphics controller directly to read color values for individual pixels. Fortunately, you can use write mode 1 of function 5 to transfer bytes from one part of the display buffer to another without an intervening read. In other words, whenever you wish to transfer data, use write mode 1 of function 5. Whenever you wish to know the color of a pixel, use BIOS interrupt 10h. The BIOS reduces the amount of labor involved.

Moving an Area of the Display   To move an area of pixels on the display from one location to another, you could first read each pixel's color and duplicate that color at a new location. There is a faster method, however, that uses the internal color latches of the graphics controller chip.

To use the graphics controller as an intermediary for duplicating color values, you must set function 5 bits 0 and 1 to 01. This can be done simply by outputting a 1 to 0x3CF. Write mode 1, selected in this way, will write the contents of the color latches read at one location into the bit planes associated with another address. This allows you to use the graphics controller registers as a "bucket" to carry color from one location to another.

Copying Areas of the Display   Function 9-5, COPYAREA.C, will copy an area of color from one part of the EGA display to another. It uses write mode 1 to do the copying. The use of the on-board color latches makes the reading and writing process much faster than if there were no graphics controller. However, it still is not as fast as it would be if block moves were possible in graphics modes on the EGA.

■ FUNCTION 9-5

COPYAREA.C

```
/* COPYAREA.C copies an area on the EGA to another
** using the EGA graphics controller to buffer
** each byte.
*/


#define TRUE -1
#define FALSE 0
#define max(x,y)    (((x) > (y)) ? (x) : (y))
#define abs(x)      (((x) < 0) ? -(x) : (x))
#define sign(x)  ((x) > 0 ? 1 : ((x) == 0 ? 0 : (-1)))
#define ENABLE 0x0F
#define INDEXREG 0x3CE
#define VALREG 0x3CF
#define OUTINDEX(index, val)    {outp(INDEXREG, index); \
                                 outp(VALREG, val);}
#define EGABASE 0xA0000000L
#define WIDTH 80L
#define XMAX 639
#define YMAX 199
#define XMIN 0
#define YMIN 0
#define XORIT 0x80
#define ORIT  0x00


/* ulx, uly, lrx and lry must be on display */
copyarea(ulx, uly, lrx, lry, offsetx, offsety)
int ulx, uly, lrx, lry, offsetx, offsety;
{
int x, y;
/* exist_color is a dummy variable, */
/* no data is actually read, it is only used */
/* to CAUSE the read. */
unsigned char mask, exist_color;
char far *base;


OUTINDEX(1, ENABLE); /* enable write */

OUTINDEX(5, 1); /* select mode 1 of function 5, */
                /* to transfer bit plane values */

for (y = uly; y <= lry; ++y)
```

■ **FUNCTION 9-5** (continued)

COPYAREA.C

```
      for (x = ulx; x <= lrx; ++x)
          {
          base = (char far *)(EGABASE
                      + ((long)y * WIDTH + ((long)x / 8L)));

          /* existing color into EGA register */
          exist_color = *base;

          base = (char far *)(EGABASE
                      + ((long)(y+offsety)
                      * WIDTH + ((long)(x+offsetx) / 8L)));

          mask = 0x80 >> (x+offsetx) % 8;

          OUTINDEX(8, mask);     /* set mask */

          *base &= TRUE;         /* force a write to the EGA */
          }
OUTINDEX(0,0);      /* reset register */
OUTINDEX(1,0);      /* reset ENABLE */
OUTINDEX(8,TRUE);   /* reset bit mask */
}
```

Clearing the Display

You can use the EGA BIOS to clear the display quickly by scrolling it. This method will work in any EGA mode because the BIOS automatically keeps track of most aspects of the functioning of the EGA. The function on the next page can be used to clear the EGA display.

```
clearscr()
{

regs.h.ah = 7;                    /* scroll screen down */
regs.h.al = 0;                    /* entire window */
regs.h.ch = 0;                    /* upper left corner */
regs.h.cl = 0;
regs.h.dh = 24;                   /* lower right corner */
regs.h.dl = 79;
regs.h.bh = 0;                    /* use black background */
int86(0x10, &regs, &regs);        /* interrupt 10h */
}
```

The clearscr( ) function sets registers using the Microsoft C REGS union in concert with the int86( ) function. Register AH can be set to 6 to scroll the page up and set to 7 to scroll the page down. Register AL receives the number of lines to scroll. If AL is set to 0, the entire display is scrolled. Register CH contains the row and register CL contains the column of the upper left corner of the window in which the scroll is to take place. Register DH contains the row and register DL contains the column of the lower right corner of the scroll window. Register BH contains an attribute to be used on blank lines. If BH is set to 0, new lines will have black backgrounds as they appear on the display. You can use any of the colors defined in SCREEN.H in Appendix A.

KEYBOARD INTERACTION

In order to type text onto the display surface without destroying any graphics that might be underneath, you must use some method besides the printf( ), puts( ), or other functions available in your C library. These functions use standard methods to replace rather than XOR pixels.

If you use the methods presented here, you will be able to prompt for a command anywhere on the display surface. After the user enters the command, the entire line will disappear, without any effect on the graphics that were at the location of the command prompt.

Nondestructive Command Entry

Function 9-6, GET __ STR.C, displays a line of text as it is entered from the keyboard. Each character is XORed onto the display as it is typed. You can backspace over characters if you wish to change them.

When you press ENTER, the command will be executed and the command line will disappear. Otherwise, characters will be XORed and stored in a global command string for use after you exit Function 9-6. The command string can be used to send commands to the system or to convey text strings for various purposes.

How Nondestructive Command Entry Works   Function 9-6 includes a few useful utilities that have not been presented elsewhere in this book. The first of these, get __ curs( ), uses the BIOS to determine the text cursor location. This function is as follows:

```
get_curs(row, col)
int *row, *col;
{

regs.h.ah = 3;                  /* get cursor position */
regs.h.bh = 0;                  /* for page 0 */
int86(0x10, &regs, &regs);      /* interrupt 10h */
*row = regs.h.dh;               /* current row */
*col = regs.h.dl;               /* current col */
}
```

You can use get __ curs( ) in your software any time you want to know the cursor location in any EGA mode. It uses a standard feature of the BIOS and will not vary from computer to computer.

Another useful pair of utilities included in Function 9-6 are retkey( ) and inkey( ). The inkey( ) function uses a standard BIOS interrupt to receive the current character from the key-

■ FUNCTION 9-6

GET — STR.C

```
/* GET_STR.C uses the current cursor position to get a string
** from keyboard input.  The text can be written over graphics
** without disturbing anything.
*/

#include <stdio.h>
#include <conio.h>
#include <string.h>
#include <dos.h>

#define TRUE -1
#define FALSE 0
#define XORIT 0x80
#define NORMIT 0
#define BS 0x08
#define CR 0x0D
#define NULLCHAR '\0'

/* SCREEN.H contains colors, display width and height */

#define BLACK         0x0
#define BLUE          0x1
#define GREEN         0x2
#define CYAN          0x3
#define RED           0x4
#define MAGENTA       0x5
#define BROWN         0x6
#define WHITE         0x7

union REGS regs;



get_str(string, color)
char *string;  /* make sure string allows > 80 characters long */
int color;
{
int inchar, row, col, position = 0;
char oldchar;
extern char *command;

strcpy(command, "");
get_curs(&row, &col);
```

■ **FUNCTION 9-6** (continued)

GET__STR.C

```
while ((inchar = retkey()) != CR)
    {
    switch (inchar)
        {
        case BS:
            if (position > 0)
                {
                oldchar = string[--position];
                string[position] = NULLCHAR;
                if (col < 79)
                    write_char('_', row, col, color, XORIT);
                write_char(oldchar, row, --col, WHITE, XORIT);
                write_char('_', row, col, color, XORIT);
                }
            break;
        default:
            if (col < 79)
                {
                write_char('_', row, col, color, XORIT);
                write_char(inchar, row, col++, WHITE, XORIT);
                write_char('_', row, col, color, XORIT);
                string[position++] = inchar;
                string[position] = NULLCHAR;
                }
            else if (col == 79)
                {
                write_char(inchar, row, col, WHITE, XORIT);
                string[position] = inchar;
                }
            break;
        }
    }
}




get_curs(row, col)
int *row, *col;
{

regs.h.ah = 3;                  /* get cursor position */
regs.h.bh = 0;                  /* for page 0 */
```

■ **FUNCTION 9-6** (continued)

GET__STR.C

```c
int86(0x10, &regs, &regs);      /* interrupt 10h */
*row = regs.h.dh;               /* current row */
*col = regs.h.dl;               /* current col */
}


write_char(character, row, col, color, orxor)
char character;
int row, col, color, orxor;
{

set_curs(row, col);

regs.h.ah = 9;                  /* write character */
regs.x.cx = 1;                  /* one character */
regs.h.al = character;          /* character */
regs.h.bl = color | orxor;      /* set color (NORMIT, XORIT) */
int86(0x10, &regs, &regs);      /* interrupt 10h */
}


set_curs(row, col)
int row, col;
{

regs.h.ah = 2;                  /* set cursor position */
regs.h.bh = 0;                  /* for page 0 */
regs.h.dh = row;                /* current row */
regs.h.dl = col;                /* current col */
int86(0x10, &regs, &regs);      /* interrupt 10h */
}


int retkey()
{
int inchar;

if (!inkey(&inchar))
    inchar += 0x100;   /* extended character add 256 */

while (kbhit()) getch();   /* flush the keyboard buffer */
```

■ FUNCTION 9-6 (continued)

GET＿STR.C

```
return(inchar);
}


int inkey(ascii)
int *ascii;
{
union REGS regs;

regs.x.ax = 0;

int86(22, &regs, &regs);

*ascii = regs.h.ah;

if (regs.h.al == 0)
    return(0);

*ascii = regs.h.al;
return(1);
}
```

---

board buffer. The code for this function is as follows:

```
int inkey(ascii)
int *ascii;
{
union REGS regs;

regs.x.ax = 0;

int86(22, &regs, &regs);

*ascii = regs.h.ah;

if (regs.h.al == 0)
    return(0);

*ascii = regs.h.al;
return(1);
}
```

With the AH register set to 0, interrupt 22 (0x16) is used to receive the next character in the buffer or to wait until one is available. The character, when available, appears in AH upon return from the interrupt. If the AL register is 0 on return, it means the character from the keyboard is a standard ASCII character between 0 and 0xFF. If AL is not 0 on return, it means the character is an **extended** character peculiar to the IBM keyboard interface. Extended character codes refer to special keys and key combinations on the IBM keyboard. You can read about these extended keys in the *IBM Technical Reference* for the PC.

The retkey( ) function is used to process the output from inkey( ). The retkey( ) function is as follows:

```
int retkey()
{
int inchar;

if (!inkey(&inchar))
    inchar += 0x100;      /* extended character add 256 */

while (kbhit()) getch(); /* flush the keyboard buffer */

return(inchar);
}
```

If the value returned by inkey( ) is not 0, the value of inchar (an integer) is increased by 0x100. This enables the function that calls retkey( ) to distinguish between standard ASCII characters and IBM's special characters without an elaborate return process.

In addition to processing extended characters, retkey( ) flushes the keyboard buffer by using a while( ) to respond to each pending keyboard hit (kbhit( )) with a getch( ) to get each character without echoing it. You can use retkey( ) with or without this buffer dump, or you can even make the dump an option selected by a flag. It depends on whether or not you want the type-ahead feature of the keyboard to be used. In command-line work or selection from menus, the type-ahead buffer can cause a series of commands to be repeated accidentally if the user holds a key down for too long.

All of the tools necessary to understand Function 9-6 are included in the function as shown in this book. In practice, you do not need to duplicate each function in the file. All you need to do is refer to the function in your source code, compile it, and link it with the actual functions whose object code modules are in a library. Chapter 15 describes how to create a library for the functions described in this book.

10

Locators

A computer graphics system works through the use of **surfaces.** Surfaces are physical areas that can either display or receive graphics information. A piece of paper, by this definition, is a surface. The difference between a paper drawing surface and the surfaces used in computer graphics is that with the latter, the computer, as well as the user, can manipulate graphics.

In order for the user to communicate spatial information to the computer system, a **locator** is necessary. A locator indicates spatial position on the surface. The user employs a locator to indicate to the computer system where graphical information is to be obtained or placed.

A locator is similar to (but not the same as) a text cursor. In a coordinate system the locator indicates position, just as a text cursor in a word processing system indicates position. The units used are different, but the same methods are involved.

When you draw a line on a sheet of paper using a pencil, the process is very direct. Graphite and carbon in a beeswax binder are sheared from the pencil lead by friction between the lead and the paper. This leaves a visible deposit of material that you interpret as a line. The process of drawing using a computer is much different.

When a computer is used for drawing, material is not deposited on the display surface. Instead, a signal is sent from the drawing **stylus** to the computer system. A stylus is the computer equivalent of a pencil. It is the drawing instrument you use, whether a mouse or a digitizer stylus, when drawing with graphics software. The signal from the stylus usually goes through a wire to hardware that communicates with the computer. The effects of this signal appear as movement of the locator crosshairs.

Crosshairs are used in engineering devices of all kinds. The word "crosshairs" derives from the horse hairs, one vertical and one horizontal, that were sandwiched between plates of glass in surveying equipment and gun sights. Of course, you do not use real horse hairs in the computer. The computer's crosshairs are made of pixel patterns that simulate the appearance of crossed hairs. The computer gives you additional options for the appearance of crosshairs. Use this feature to its greatest advantage. On the computer, crosshairs can even contain messages that explain how they are to be used.

Whereas paper is passive, the computer system actively and repeatedly asks for information. When the stylus is moved, the graphics system knows about it because the system has been repeatedly asking, or **polling,** the locator device. Polling is the process of asking for the status of some part of the computer system. The computer uses polling often to ascertain whether a device is able to send information.

There are many ways to ascertain the position of the stylus. Chapter 11, which discusses interfacing, will give you more detailed information regarding the process used to read information from digitizers, mice, and light pens.

In this chapter you will see how to make locators appear on the display surface and how to move them from place to place. Different locator types will also be discussed.

LOCATOR DESIGN

Locators must be appropriate for the purposes they are intended to serve. For most purposes a simple crosshairs pattern is sufficient. The potential for creativity in the design of crosshairs is great, however. Since one of the computer's strengths is its flexibility, you should think of the crosshairs as a powerful way to provide information to the user, rather than simply as a way to locate pixels on the display surface.

Locator Types

Figure 10-1 shows a variety of locators that you might use with your software. The simplest locator (Figure 10-1c) is a simple cross, like a plus (+) sign. Another type of locator is shown in Figure 10-1d. It might be used to indicate that the system is in text mode.

Complex Locators   Figure 10-1f shows a more complex locator. Such locators might contain information about the system status, including the current drawing color, line style, coordinates, and more. Because the locator is at the point of interest of the user, it is wise to have it show as much information as possible.

Full Screen Locators   If users of your system will need to line up pixels with other pixels horizontally or vertically, you can provide a locator like the one shown in Figure 10-1e, known as a full screen locator. This locator gives the user capabilities similar to those available using drafting equipment. You might also wish to make such full screen locators rotate to the prevailing system rotation angle.

GRAPHIQ's Locator   The locator used in the prototypical system GRAPHIQ, shown in Appendix A, is a simple cross like the one shown in Figure 10-1a. The central rows of horizontal and vertical pixels have been removed, permitting the locator to surround a pixel rather than cover it. It is much easier to identify the color of a pixel if you do not cover it with the locator crosshairs. The locator takes on the characteristics of the current line style (see Figure 10-1b). The current pen number is identified using one of eight colors for the locator. This important system information is all contained in one simple locator.

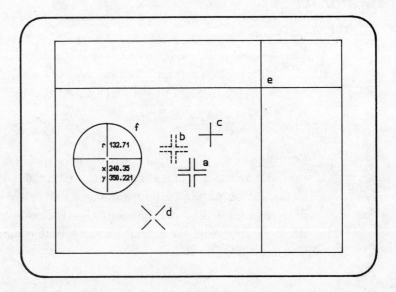

FIGURE 10-1.   Some locator types on a display surface

Smart Locators

If you design your system carefully, the locator can be the only system information that constantly needs to be on the display surface. This means that menus and even the command line can be hidden from view most of the time, leaving the entire display surface free for graphics. You might refer to this as a smart locator approach.

Instead of being conveyed through fixed menus and status information, the system state is expressed in the locator itself. This information moves about on the display under control of the locator device. When you wish to locate the beginning and ending points of a line, you know at a glance what color, line style, and other information will be used to draw the line. The locator tells you this, not a menu. If you want to see detailed descriptions of any part of the system's operation, you can display a system menu at the push of the ENTER key.

CODING LOCATORS

In order for locator crosshairs patterns to appear on the display surface, these patterns must reside somewhere in memory. The patterns are stored in matrix form. Access to a desired locator matrix is gained through the use of a pointer.

You can code a series of locator crosshairs patterns and keep them in a header that is included in the source code for each program you write. You can select any pattern you wish by passing its pointer to a function that displays it.

Moving Bit Patterns

The code for the locator used in GRAPHIQ is reproduced here as Function 10-1, LOCATOR.H. The matrix declarations are used as shown in Function 10-2, LOCATOR.C. Passing the

■ FUNCTION 10-1

LOCATOR.H

```
/* LOCATOR.H The GRAPHIQ locators are stored here */

/* solid */
unsigned long matrix1[] = {
0x00183000L,
0x00183000L,
0x00183000L,
0x00183000L,
0x00183000L,
0x00183000L,
0xFFF83FFEL,
0x00000000L,
0xFFF83FFEL,
0x00183000L,
0x00183000L,
0x00183000L,
0x00183000L,
0x00183000L,
0x00000000L};

/* dotted */
unsigned long matrix2[] = {
0x00183000L,
0x00000000L,
0x00183000L,
0x00000000L,
0x00183000L,
0x00000000L,
0x99983332L,
0x00000000L,
0x99983332L,
0x00000000L,
0x00183000L,
0x00000000L,
0x00183000L,
0x00000000L,
0x00183000L,
0x00000000L};

/* dashed */
unsigned long matrix3[] = {
0x00183000L,
0x00183000L,

0x00183000L,
0x00000000L,
0x00183000L,
0x00183000L,
```

■ FUNCTION 10-1 (continued)

LOCATOR.H

```
0xF0F83E1EL,
0x00000000L,
0xF0F83E1EL,
0x00183000L,
0x00183000L,
0x00000000L,
0x00183000L,
0x00183000L,
0x00183000L,
0x00000000L};

/* dash dot */
unsigned long matrix4[] = {
0x00183000L,
0x00000000L,
0x00183000L,
0x00183000L,
0x00183000L,
0x00183000L,
0xE6783CCEL,
0x00000000L,
0xE6783CCEL,
0x00183000L,
0x00183000L,
0x00183000L,
0x00183000L,
0x00000000L,
0x00183000L,
0x00000000L};

/* dash dot dot */
unsigned long matrix5[] = {
0x00183000L,
0x00000000L,
0x00183000L,
0x00000000L,
0x00183000L,
0x00183000L,
0xCCF83E66L,
0x00000000L,
0xCCF83E66L,
0x00183000L,
0x00183000L,
0x00000000L,
0x00183000L,
0x00000000L,
0x00183000L,
0x00000000L};
```

■ **FUNCTION 10-2**

LOCATOR.C

```
/* LOCATOR.C uses XOR to plot points from a matrix pattern.
**    You pass the x, y coordinates of the upper left corner,
**    the color of the pattern, and a pointer to an array of
**    pointers which contain the pattern as an array of
**    longs.  Bits set in the longs create the pattern. */


#define ALLON 0xFF
#define ENABLE 0x0F
#define INDEXREG 0x3CE
#define VALREG 0x3CF
#define OUTINDEX(index, val)    {outp(INDEXREG, index); \
                                 outp(VALREG, val);}
#define EGABASE 0xA0000000L
#define WIDTH 80L
#define XMAX 639
#define YMAX 199
#define XMIN 0
#define YMIN 0
#define XORPIX 0x18
#define XMETRIC 0.237546468
#define YMETRIC 0.096601942


locator(x, y, color, grid)
double x, y;
int color;
unsigned long grid[];   /* 16 by 16 bit matrix */
{
int i, j;
int xint, yint;
unsigned long mask = 0x80000000L;
extern double xlate_x, xlate_y;
extern double rot_center_x, rot_center_y;
extern double xform_angle, scale_factor;

xform(&x, &y, xlate_x, xlate_y, rot_center_x, rot_center_y,
        xform_angle, scale_factor);

x *= XMETRIC;
y = YMAX - y * YMETRIC;

xint = x -= 15;
yint = y -= 7;


OUTINDEX(3, XORPIX);  /* set index to XOR pixels */
OUTINDEX(1, ENABLE); /* enable write */
```

■ **FUNCTION 10-2** (continued)

LOCATOR.C

```
for (j = 0; j <= 15; ++j)
    for (i = 0; i <= 31; ++i)
        if (grid[j] & mask >> i)
            points(xint+i, yint+j, color);

OUTINDEX(0,0);       /* reset register */
OUTINDEX(1,0);       /* reset ENABLE */
OUTINDEX(3,0);       /* reset XOR to normal */
OUTINDEX(8,ALLON);    /* reset bit mask */
}
```

pointer for a given locator matrix to Function 10-2 will produce the desired locator crosshairs. You can see how Function 10-2 is used directly in GRAPHIQ.C if you examine the following fragment of code:

```
case F7:
    if (line_style > 5) line_style = 1;
    switch (line_style++)
        {
        case 1:
            pattern = SOLID;
            matrix = matrix1;
            break;
        case 2:
            pattern = DOTTED;
            matrix = matrix2;
            break;
        case 3:
            pattern = DASHED;
            matrix = matrix3;
            break;
        case 4:
            pattern = DASHDOT;
            matrix = matrix4;
            break;
        case 5:
            pattern = DASHDOTDOT;
            matrix = matrix5;
            break;
        }
    break;
```

This fragment is part of a switch that enables the user to select line styles. For each press of key F7, the variable line style is incremented and a series of line styles results. The variable named pattern is set to a constant for each line style. This variable (of type unsigned int) is used as a mask in drawing lines. After the pattern has been set, the pointer for the desired locator matrix is passed to the variable named matrix. The matrix pointer is passed to Function 10-2 each time the function is invoked. This results in a locator crosshairs that reflects the line style that will be used to draw lines.

The color of any lines that will be drawn (corresponding to the pen number to be used) is also passed to Function 10-2 each time the locator crosshairs are to be XORed on or off the display. In this way the user can easily see the status of lines to be drawn by looking at the locator crosshairs.

Understanding the Locator Function

To understand how Function 10-2 works, you must first understand how the locator matrix is coded. Examine Figure 10-2 to see how a solid locator crosshairs would appear as pixels in a 32-by 16-pixel grid. The black cells are binary 1, and the white cells are binary 0. Notice that because the number of pixel positions both horizontally and vertically is even, the last pixel in each row and column is left off. This is done to make a central horizontal and a central vertical row of pixels available so that the crosshairs are symmetrically placed around any pixel they are used to identify.

Binary Pixel Expression You can express the values of the bits in each horizontal row of the locator pixel grid as a single binary number. This number consists of 32 bits. A variable of type long also consists of 32 bits. If you convert the binary value derived by the above process into a hexadecimal number, you will be able to store that number in a long variable.

Table 10-1 shows binary and hexadecimal expressions for various line styles. The lines that will appear in the finished line are shown under the binary numbers. Each binary number is broken down into four-bit fields to make conversion into hex easier. To the right of each binary number is its hexadecimal expression.

The numbers in Table 10-1 create five different line styles, equivalent to the five line styles used in GRAPHIQ. Compare Table 10-1 to Function 10-1 to see how each pattern is used in its appropriate locator matrix.

Locator Matrix Appearance   Although the matrix shown in Figure 10-2 consists of 32 columns by 16 rows, it does not appear as a shallow rectangle on the display. Because data in the display buffer will appear approximately half as wide when it is

Binary	Hex
1111 1111 1111 1000 0011 1111 1111 1110	FFF83FFE
1111 0000 1111 1000 0011 1110 0001 1110	F0F83E1E
1100 1100 1111 1000 0011 1110 0110 0110	CCF83E66
1110 0110 0111 1000 0011 1100 1100 1110	E6783CCE
1001 1001 1001 1000 0011 0011 0011 0010	99983332

TABLE 10-1.   Binary and Hex Expressions for Locator Line Styles

on the display, the actual appearance of the locator crosshairs will be a square similar to the one shown in Figure 10-3.

Full Screen Locators

Full screen locators are special crosshairs that cover the entire surface of the display.

You may wish to use a locator crosshairs consisting of two long lines, one extending vertically the entire height of the display and the other extending horizontally the entire display width. It is not feasible to use a bit matrix approach for such a cursor, because the matrix would be the size of the display and would take forever to draw.

Instead of using a locator matrix with long crosshairs, you must draw two lines each time you move the crosshairs. You XOR the lines onto and off of the display just as you do with the matrix, but the method of drawing is much different.

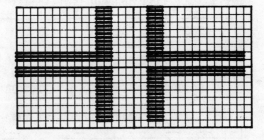

FIGURE 10-2. *The locator pixel pattern in a 32-by-16—pixel grid*

Drawing the Full Screen Locator LONGCROS.C, Function 10-3, draws a full screen crosshairs for use as a locator. The first time you draw it on the display it will XOR the colors under it. The second time you draw it at the same position it will return the colors under it to their original values.

Function 10-3 uses one of the fastest ways to draw a solid horizontal line in the EGA graphics modes. If you study the function carefully, you will see that the mask is not changed to draw individual pixels in the horizontal direction. Instead, 80 bytes are changed across the display. If the line were drawn one pixel at a time, the process would be considerably slower, resulting in a full screen locator that would appear to move sluggishly.

Using the Full Screen Locator You should implement a menu item that allows the user to change the locator from the small cross to the full screen at any time. In this way the user can select the locator style that is appropriate to the kind of work

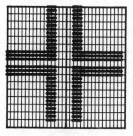

FIGURE 10-3. The locator pixel pattern as it actually appears

■ FUNCTION 10-3

LONGCROS.C

```
/* LONGCROS.C  draws a crosshairs extending
** the entire width and height of the display.
*/

#define ALLON 0xFF
#define ENABLE 0x0F
#define INDEXREG 0x3CE
#define VALREG 0x3CF
#define OUTINDEX(index, val)   {outp(INDEXREG, index); \
                                outp(VALREG, val);}

#define EGABASE 0xA0000000L
#define WIDTH 80L
#define XMAX 639
#define YMAX 199
#define XMIN 0
#define YMIN 0
#define XORPIX 0x18
#define XMETRIC 0.237546468
#define YMETRIC 0.096601942


longcros(x, y, color)
double x, y;
int color;
{
int xint, yint, xout, yout;
unsigned long mask = 0x80000000L;
extern double xlate_x, xlate_y;
extern double rot_center_x, rot_center_y;
extern double xform_angle, scale_factor;

xform(&x, &y, xlate_x, xlate_y, rot_center_x, rot_center_y,
        xform_angle, scale_factor);

x *= XMETRIC;
y = YMAX - y * YMETRIC;

xint = x;
yint = y;

OUTINDEX(3, XORPIX);  /* set index to XOR pixels */
OUTINDEX(1, ENABLE); /* enable write */
OUTINDEX(0, color);  /* set new color*/


mask = ALLON;
OUTINDEX(8, mask);   /* set mask */
```

■ FUNCTION 10-3 (continued)

LONGCROS.C

```
/* can use an abbreviated form for speed */
for (xout = XMIN; xout <= XMAX; xout += 8)
     {
     base = (char far *)(EGABASE
               + ((long)yint * WIDTH + ((long)xout / 8L)));

     *base &= TRUE;         /* force a write to the EGA */
     }
for (yout = YMIN; yout <= YMAX; ++yout)
     {
     base = (char far *)(EGABASE
               + ((long)yout * WIDTH + ((long)xint / 8L)));

     /* existing color into EGA register */
     exist_color = *base;

     mask = 0x80 >> xint % 8;

     OUTINDEX(8, mask);    /* set mask */

     *base &= TRUE;         /* force a write to the EGA */
     }
OUTINDEX(0,0);         /* reset register */
OUTINDEX(1,0);         /* reset ENABLE */
OUTINDEX(3,0);         /* reset XOR to normal */
OUTINDEX(8,ALLON);     /* reset bit mask */
}
```

being done. Full screen locators are useful when you wish to line up a locator position with other work, as might be done when using a horizontal or vertical straightedge in a drafting environment.

Rotated Full Screen Locators

You may wish to incorporate in your software a global rotation state capability. This means that all graphics portrayed on the display surface can be given a rotated frame of reference. Such rotational state capability can come in handy, for example, if you wish to use graphics that were prepared for a horizontally positioned sheet of paper on a vertically positioned sheet.

You can make your full screen locator reflect the rotated orientation of the system by transforming the crosshairs in the same way that you would transform graphics. A simple way to do this is shown in Function 10-4, ROTLOC.C, which does the same thing as Function 10-3, but with a "twist."

Understanding the rotloc( ) Function   To understand how Function 10-4 works, you need to know how rotational transformations in general are accomplished. Chapter 5 discussed transformations in detail. Function 10-4 relies on the xform( ) function discussed in Chapter 5 to transform line-endpoint coordinates.

The system rotation state is declared as externals of type double. These variables are assumed to have been declared outside of main( ) in the caller. The declarations appear as follows:

```
extern double xlate_x, xlate_y;
extern double rot_center_x, rot_center_y;
extern double xform_angle, scale_factor;
```

The width of the display surface is measured in two ways. On the physical display it has the following dimensions:

```
#define XMAX 639
#define YMAX 199
#define XMIN 0
#define YMIN 0
```

■ FUNCTION 10-4

ROTLOC.C

```
/* ROTLOC.C rotates the longhair locator to
** the system rotation state.
*/

#define TRUE -1
#define FALSE 0
#define XMAX 639
#define YMAX 199
#define XMIN 0
#define YMIN 0
#define XORIT 0x80
#define ORIT  0x00
#define XMETRIC 0.237546468
#define YMETRIC 0.096601942


rotloc(x, y, color, style)
double x, y;
int color, orxor;
unsigned style;
{
double x1, y1, x2, y2;
double disp_width, disp_height;
extern double xlate_x, xlate_y;
extern double rot_center_x, rot_center_y;
extern double xform_angle, scale_factor;

disp_width = (double)(XMAX + 1) / XMETRIC;
disp_height = (double)(YMAX + 1) / YMETRIC;

/* draw horizontal element */
x1 = x + disp_width;
x2 = x - disp_width;
y1 = y;
y2 = y;

xform(&x1, &y1, xlate_x, xlate_y, rot_center_x, rot_center_y,
        xform_angle, scale_factor);

xform(&x2, &y2, xlate_x, xlate_y, rot_center_x, rot_center_y,
        xform_angle, scale_factor);

x1 *= XMETRIC;
y1 = YMAX - y * YMETRIC;

x2 *= XMETRIC;
y2 = YMAX - y * YMETRIC;
```

■ **FUNCTION 10-4** (continued)

ROTLOC.C

```
linef((int)x1, (int)y1, (int)x2, (int)y2,
        color, style, XORIT, TRUE);

/* draw vertical element */
x1 = x;
x2 = x;
y1 = y + disp_height;
y2 = y - disp_height;

xform(&x1, &y1, xlate_x, xlate_y, rot_center_x, rot_center_y,
        xform_angle, scale_factor);

xform(&x2, &y2, xlate_x, xlate_y, rot_center_x, rot_center_y,
        xform_angle, scale_factor);

x1 *= XMETRIC;
y1 = YMAX - y * YMETRIC;

x2 *= XMETRIC;
y2 = YMAX - y * YMETRIC;

linef((int)x1, (int)y1, (int)x2, (int)y2,
        color, style, XORIT, TRUE);
}
```

These values are integers, not the double-precision type required
for the xform( ) function. To convert from integers to double
precision, you must use a conversion factor, as follows:

```
disp_width = (double)(XMAX + 1) / XMETRIC;
disp_height = (double)(YMAX + 1) / YMETRIC;
```

This conversion is based on the assumption that units used in
double precision reduce to tenths of a millimeter. A whole
number (without a decimal portion) is assumed to be expressed

in tenths of a millimeter. Under this assumption the number 10.0 would express 1 millimeter. The conversion factors that scale integer display units into a metric frame of reference are declared as follows:

```
#define XMETRIC 0.237546468
#define YMETRIC 0.096601942
```

Using the display width derived above, the horizontal and vertical lines that form the locator are drawn. First, the horizontal line is derived using the x value passed to the function. The display width is added to it to derive the rightmost x component for the line endpoint. The display width is subtracted to derive the leftmost endpoint. The y value, which is the vertical, is used as is. In the function the following fragment computes the horizontal line endpoints:

```
x1 = x + disp_width;
x2 = x - disp_width;
y1 = y;
y2 = y;

xform(&x1, &y1, xlate_x, xlate_y, rot_center_x, rot_center_y,
        xform_angle, scale_factor);

xform(&x2, &y2, xlate_x, xlate_y, rot_center_x, rot_center_y,
        xform_angle, scale_factor);
```

The line endpoints are first derived from the locator coordinates and then transformed using the standard xform( ) function. After they have been transformed to the system rotation, translation, and scaling state, the horizontal line endpoints are converted to the integer coordinate system of the display surface using the following fragment:

```
x1 *= XMETRIC;
y1 = YMAX - y * YMETRIC;

x2 *= XMETRIC;
y2 = YMAX - y * YMETRIC;
```

The coordinates of the line endpoints in integer space having been computed, the line can now be drawn. It is XORed onto the display surface using the standard linef( ) function. To find the xform( ) and linef( ) functions, consult the function index in this book. The call to linef( ) is made as follows:

```
linef((int)x1, (int)y1, (int)x2, (int)y2,
      color, style, XORIT, TRUE);
```

It is important to recognize that linef( ) can accept only integer values. The double-precision variables are cast as int types before linef( ) receives them.

8087 Numeric Coprocessor Necessary   Without the use of a numeric coprocessor, Function 10-4 will be unbearably slow. With the numeric coprocessor it will still be slow, but will be valuable for those special cases in which you need to align graphics elements at angles to one another.

Selecting the Rotated Locator   The rotated full screen locator is a special type of locator that should be distinguished from the normal full screen locator. Because it is slower, consider making it a special menu item for use under circumstances where angular alignment is desired. Your system should have a submenu for selecting the various cursor styles described in this chapter. This way you will be able to select the tools you need to accomplish the task.

11

Parallel and
Serial Interfacing

In order to create effective graphics software, you must provide ways for your computer to communicate with the outside world. Your software can communicate with the user through the use of CRT displays, printers, plotters, mice, digitizers, light pens, and a host of other devices. These devices are connected to the computer in various ways.

This chapter is about the art and science of interfacing. This subject pertains to all aspects of computer use, not just graphics. You will find that the skills required for competent graphics programming embrace all other computer skills. In other words, if you can create graphics using a computer, you will be able to do almost any other kind of computer programming.

You might think that interfacing is boring, that it has little to do with creativity. You will find, however, that interfacing of peripherals can be done in a variety of ways. Depending on your choices, you can create magic or end up with software that balks at everything. All graphics programs rely on successful interfacing techniques.

When you are working with locator devices, you will need to receive data from the serial interface. Traditionally, because of the ineffectiveness of the parallel interface on the IBM PC, the serial interface is most often used with locator devices. To receive data you can use serial interrupts, or you can use a polled interface method. The polled method, which involves using a polled serial input protocol to ask the sending device for each byte as it arrives, is the easier one to use.

The code presented in this chapter is intentionally explicit rather than containing included files and mnemonics. It is intended to help you understand what is going on in the functions, rather than serving as an example of code you would use in a program. You may find that many explicit references could be made using mnemonics or equates. By all means, feel free to change the code to reflect your own style. Just be sure that any changes you make accomplish the same things as the original code would do.

Throughout this book you have seen interfacing used implicitly in various functions. No detailed explanation of interface options was offered. In this chapter you will see how to receive information from digitizers, mice, and light pens. You will see how serial and parallel interfaces work, not only for graphics but for all of your software. Finally, you will see a serial interrupt service routine that *really works*.

PARALLEL PORTS

The parallel interface port on the IBM PC series of computers is the easiest interface to understand. Most devices that connect to it are wired at the factory to be compatible. You seldom need to worry about making cables for parallel ports.

The parallel port is used primarily for interfacing with printers. It uses eight data wires, one for each bit in a byte to be sent. The use of eight wires means that eight bits can be sent at once, in parallel. The serial interface would require you to send the same eight bits one bit at a time.

Sending Characters Through a Parallel Port

To send a character through the parallel port, you first need to determine which port you will use. You then use either the BIOS or direct access to the port registers to send the character. Because the BIOS in this instance is perfectly adequate, a BIOS interrupt is the preferred way to send characters through the parallel port.

To send a character you use BIOS interrupt 17h. Before executing the interrupt, you load AH with 0, load AL with the character to be printed, and load DX with the desired printer number. Printer numbers 0, 1, and 2 correspond with LPT1, LPT2, and LPT3, respectively.

Monitoring Printer Status

You must also be concerned with the status of the printer. If the printer cannot receive the character you wish to send, it will raise or lower one or more of its status wires. The status wires are monitored by setting AH to 2 and DX to the desired printer number. The printer status is returned in AH after you execute interrupt 17h. In practice, you first generate interrupt 17h with AH set to 2 and loop until AH returns a nonzero value for bit 8. When this occurs, you know that the printer is not busy and you

■ **FUNCTION 11-1**

PUT—OUT.C

```
/* PUT_OUT.C puts a character out the parallel
** port using the BIOS.
*/

char put_out(character)
char character;
{
union REGS regs;

while(!status()); /* wait if busy */

regs.h.ah = 0; /* send a character */
regs.h.al = character;
regs.x.dx = 0; /* select first printer */

int86(0x17, &regs, &regs);
return(regs.h.ah);
}


char status()
{
union REGS regs;

regs.h.ah = 2; /* check printer status */
regs.x.dx = 0; /* select first printer */
int86(0x17, &regs, &regs);
return(regs.h.ah & 0x80);
}
```

send the desired character. This is all the handshaking you will ever need for parallel output.

Function 11-1, PUT—OUT.C, shows a complete character output function that you can use for any software you write. It is very clean, and you seldom need more than this. You will encounter it in GRAPHIQ.C in Appendix A in the code used for dithering pictures out onto the dot-matrix printer.

Parallel Output Without Using DOS or the BIOS

To go one level further down, you can use the technique shown in Function 11-2, PRALEL — O.C, to do almost the same thing the BIOS does, but from the C language. Use this function if you wish to change low-level access for any reason.

Normally, the standard for parallel interfacing requires 36 pins. IBM wanted to use a 25-pin D connector (a female), leaving 11 pins unused. The idea was to use a male 25-pin D connector for the serial interface and a female connector for the parallel interface to make it possible to differentiate between the two without taking the cover off the computer. This strategy has backfired because users often plug serial devices into parallel ports if the serial devices happen to have male connectors. This puts ±12 volts on TTL (transistor-transistor logic) circuits capable of sinking 0 through 5 volts, and has probably destroyed many a parallel adapter.

Of course, one implication of the unfortunate choice of connectors is that all the pins necessary to support the full parallel standard are not available. In its infinite wisdom, IBM chose to make the parallel BIOS interface capable of only output! If they had used a 36-pin connector, the means of supporting full bidirectional input/output could have been parallel.

Three parallel adapters are recognized by the BIOS. Their addresses are stored starting at 0000:0408 in RAM. The best way to find the address of the port for a given adapter is to use word offsets from base 0000:0408, as follows:

```
unsigned far *base = 0x00000408L + paraport;
```

The long variable paraport is 0 for LPT1, 2 for LPT2, or 4 for LPT3. This can be expressed in definitions as follows:

```
#define PARALLEL2 0L
#define PARALLEL2 2L
#define PARALLEL3 4L
```

■ FUNCTION 11-2

PRALEL—O.C

```
/* PRALEL_O.C uses a non-BIOS method to send a
** character out the parallel port.
** This method uses no timeout checking as
** the BIOS does.
*/

/* possible values for paraport */
#define PARALLEL1 0L
#define PARALLEL2 2L
#define PARALLEL3 4L


unsigned far *base = 0x00000408L;

char stat_o();

char pralel_o(character, paraport)
char character;
long paraport;
{
union REGS regs;

while (!stat_o(paraport)); /* wait for not busy */

/* send the character */
outp(*(base + paraport), character);
}


char stat_o(paraport)
long paraport;
{

regs.h.ah = inp(*(base + paraport) + 1);
regs.h.ah &= 0xF8;
regs.h.ah ^= 0x48;
return(regs.h.ah & 0x80);
}
```

Note that LPT1, LPT2, and LPT3 are reserved DOS device names, and so it is unwise to use them as they are in your programs, unless you wish to refer to devices DOS recognizes.

LPT1 can also appear as PRN. You can send or receive bytes from the parallel port by using the OUT or IN instructions of the microprocessor. A typical output to the eight-bit parallel latch can be executed as follows:

```
outp(*base, character);
```

This assumes that you have initialized base to point to the address of the desired parallel port. The only other consideration is that you must be able to tell the sending device when to send the next character. To do this you control the same pins that the BIOS monitors when receiving a character.

One thing Function 11-2 does not do is repeatedly test the port if the character was not successfully sent. This means that there is no certainty that the receiving device is working. In practice, this usually does not create problems. You can avoid testing for device timeout in this way.

Receiving Characters from a Parallel Port

There is no support in the BIOS for receiving characters using the parallel interface. This is truly unfortunate. If most plotters, digitizers, and other devices used the parallel interface rather than the serial interface, there would be much less confusion in the computer industry. Further, the parallel interface is potentially much faster and more reliable than the RS232C serial interface. The only drawback would be the fact that cables for parallel interfaces cannot be as long as serial cables. The voltages on parallel interface wires range from 0 to +5, relying on ground potential for their off condition. The serial interface uses voltages lower than -3 volts or greater than $+3$ volts to determine the on or off state of the interface wire. The usual voltage employed in serial interfaces is ± 12 volts. The use of ground potential and a narrowly defined +5-volt signal level makes parallel input/output more susceptible to electrical noise than serial input/output.

Because most plotters and digitizers use cables that are less than 8 feet long, the use of parallel, rather than serial, interfacing for these devices would have been possible. Traditionally, though, this was just not done. It is probably a tragic case of false economy. Is one interface wire really cheaper than eight? Looking backward, with the benefit of hindsight, it probably would have been better to use serial interfacing with modems only for telephone communications (where one wire is all you get) and full 36-wire parallel interfacing for everything else.

Receiving a character through the parallel port is a more difficult task than sending one. To receive a character, you must violate the usage ground rules of the parallel interface standard. Normally, receiving would be done using pins 20 through 27 of the 36-pin standard for data. This would enable received data to be latched simultaneously with sent data. However, the kludged design of the IBM parallel interface makes this impossible.

Fortunately, although it is nonstandard, you can use the eight pins normally used for output to receive as well as send a byte. Of course, you cannot receive and send at the same time, as you can with the full 36-pin standard, but you can multiplex the interface to share the same eight pins, with some reduction in speed and improvisation of handshaking.

Function 11-3, PRALEL—I.C, is like Function 11-2 except that it receives rather than sends a character. You may need to modify Function 11-3 to meet the needs of specific sending devices. For example, a specific device may need a handshake using the strobe wire (pin 1). You cannot send acknowledge or busy signals, unfortunately, because the status port is meant to be read only. Also, you should set the bits of the status register that are not used to states that are required by the sending device. In other words, you must be careful to meet the requirements of the sending device, using a modified form of Function

■ FUNCTION 11-3

PRALEL — I.C

```
/* PRALEL_I.C uses a non-BIOS method to receive a
** character from the parallel port.
** This is a simple handshake protocol that, although
** unable to receive a null byte, is very effective.
*/

/* possible values for paraport */
#define PARALLEL1 0L
#define PARALLEL2 2L
#define PARALLEL3 4L


unsigned far *base = 0x00000408L;

char stat_i();

char pralel_i(paraport)
long paraport;
{
union REGS regs;

outp(*(base + paraport), 0); /* reset data to 0 */
while(inp(*(base + paraport)) == 0); /* wait for data */
return (inp(*(base + paraport)));
}
```

11-3. Understand that Function 11-3 is intended only as a suggestion. To make it work, you must provide initialization and handshaking that are appropriate for the sending device.

The technique in Function 11-3 assumes that the sender waits for all bits of data to be 0 before sending the next character. Because the handshake is based on setting all data bits to 0, you cannot receive a null byte. For most purposes this is adequate, but it depends on the sender recognizing this protocol. The parallel port is seldom used to receive data; you will probably use it for this only when you wire your own hardware. This protocol is suggested for those circumstances.

In order to use Function 11-3, you must create a receiver buffer of as many characters as will be received in one port access. You may read the port using Function 11-3 for each character in the buffer, until you have received as many characters as you wish.

If you plan to interface parallel equipment professionally and can create your own hardware, it is wise to use a full 36-pin standard adapter. The use of this standard is highly encouraged with the hope that someday it will replace the IBM parallel interface, to the great benefit of the computer industry.

The Parallel Interface at a Glance

Figure 11-1 shows the IBM parallel port in all its glory, with the contents of all registers and their relationships to the wires used to connect the port to external devices. The parallel port need never again be a mystery.

The diagram shows the pins on the IBM PC connector (female) as well as the three registers used to establish communication with the pins. Both the data register and the interrupt enable and strobe register can be read or written. The status register will show the current status of the wires, but you cannot use it to change the status of the wires. The fact that the status register is passive raised serious objections when the PC was first marketed. Some PCs may permit handshaking using the status register. Another way to establish a handshake is to do so using null data, because null data bytes are seldom sent. This technique will be discussed later.

Caution: Inverted Pin Status

Note that pins 17, 10, and 0 are inverted when represented in the interrupt enable and strobe register. This can be very confusing for people writing drivers because these wires are off when their bit representations are on and vice versa. It is usually a mistake to invert logic arbitrarily in designing interfaces, as has been done in the BIOS.

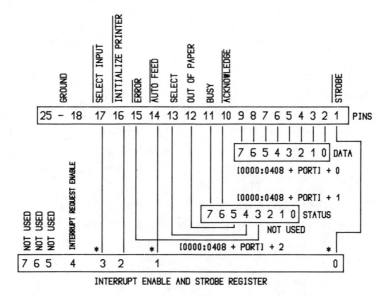

For LPT1, PORT = 0   For LPT2, PORT = 2   For LPT3, PORT = 4

* Signal inverted again in register.

FIGURE 11-1.   The parallel port system at a glance

SERIAL PORTS

The serial interface on IBM PCs is much more versatile than the parallel interface. Unlike the parallel interface, input as well as output capabilities are included by design. But the BIOS, unfortunately, has incredibly poor support for serial input/output. You can send characters, but that is about all. If you wish to receive characters, the BIOS will just wait forever, unless you happen to use the hardwire handshaking that the BIOS anticipates. It is best to ignore the BIOS altogether when working with serial communications.

Asynchronous Communications

The standard for serial data transfer (if something so confusing can be called a standard) is called **asynchronous** because two separate clocks are used, rather than a synchronization wire and one clock. The two clocks (one for the transmitter and one for the receiver) are never exactly in step, but their frequencies are close enough so that the start and stop bits that frame a word can be used to synchronize the reading of the bits in the word.

The two clocks in an asynchronous data exchange are *almost* the same frequency. Framed between the start bit and the final stop bit, your data is clocked using the local clock and the known start bit. The clock gets a little out of synchronization by the time it reaches the last stop bit. If it is too far out of step, it generates a **framing error.** A framing error indicates that the difference between the clock of the receiver and the clock of the sender is too great.

The Serial Port Registers

The IBM PC supports full interrupt handling for two serial ports and leaves space in the table of interrupts for two more. You will seldom require more than two serial ports (one for a mouse or digitizer and one for a plotter), and so this is an adequate arrangement.

Serial Adapter Base Addresses   The addresses of each installed communications adapter can be found in low memory starting at 0000:0400, in 16-bit words. The high byte of the address of the first adapter is found at 0000:0401, and the low byte is found at 0000:0400. As elsewhere in this book, you can use a far pointer to retrieve the contents of the word at this address as follows:

```
unsigned far *base = (unsigned far *)0x00000400L;
base_reg = *base;
```

The above method will transfer the port address to base_reg, assuming that base_reg is of type unsigned int. The actual address of COM1 on IBM PCs is 0x3F8. Try using DEBUG to verify this for yourself by dumping the contents of 0000:0400. It is better to refer to the base_reg value indirectly, using the far pointer, than to hardwire the port address. This way the address can be changed and your software will still work.

If you have two ports, the base address for COM2 will be stored at 0000:0402. If three or four ports are available, the addresses for the third and fourth will be at 0000:0404 and 0000:0406, respectively.

Starting at the base address for the communications adapter,

```
ADAPTER LOGICAL NAME      BASE          USUAL CONTENTS
       COM1              [0000:0400]    3F8
       COM2              [0000:0402]    2F8
   Third comm adapter    [0000:0404]
   Fourth comm adapter   [0000:0406]


OFFSET   COM1 Example    REGISTER'S FUNCTION
  0         3F8          Data
  1         3F9          Interrupt Enable
  2         3FA          Interrupt Identification
  3         3FB          Data Format
  4         3FC          Serial Control
  5         3FD          Serial Status
  6         3FE          Input Status



Data Register   (Register 0)
   Bit 0                 Data bit 0
   Bit 1                 Data bit 1
   Bit 2                 Data bit 2
   Bit 3                 Data bit 3
   Bit 4                 Data bit 4
   Bit 5                 Data bit 5
   Bit 6                 Data bit 6
   Bit 7                 Data bit 7


Interrupt Enable Register  (Register 1)
   Bit 0                 Data Ready
   Bit 1                 Transmitter Empty
   Bit 2                 Serial Status Change
   Bit 3                 Input Status Change
   Bits 4 - 7           Not Used


Interrupt Identification Register  (Register 2)
   Bit 0                 0 Means Interrupt Pending
   Bits 1 - 2           Interrupt ID:
                         00  Serial Status Int.
               [2][1]    01  Transmitter Status Int.
                         10  Data Ready Int.
                         11  Input Status Int.
   Bits 3 - 7           Not Used
```

FIGURE 11-2.   *The serial interface at a glance*

the addresses of the six registers associated with each port are
found by adding their offsets to the base. Figure 11-2 shows
most of the registers necessary to control the serial interface.

```
Data Format Register   (Register 3)
     Bits 0 - 1                Word Length:
                               00  5 bits
                         1 0   01  6 bits
                               10  7 bits
                               11  8 bits
     Bit 2                     Stop bits:
                               0   1 bit
                               1   2 bits
     Bit 3                     Parity Enable:
                               1   Parity On
                               0   Parity Off
     Bit 4                     Parity:
                               1   Even Parity
                               0   Odd Parity
     Bit 5                     Stick Parity
     Bit 6                     Set Break
     Bit 7   (selects)        Baud Rate Divisor

Serial Control Register   (Register 4)
     Bit 0                     Data Terminal Ready (pin 20)
     Bit 1                     Request To Send (pin 4)
     Bit 2                     OUT1 (user defined int. request)
     Bit 3                     OUT2 (enable interrupts)
     Bit 4                     Loop Test
     Bits 5 - 7                Not Used

Serial Status Register   (Register 5)
     Bit 0                     Data Ready
     Bit 1                     Overrun Error
     Bit 2                     Parity Error
     Bit 3                     Framing Error
     Bit 4                     Received Break
     Bit 5                     Transmitter Holding Reg. Empty
     Bit 6                     Transmitter Shift Reg. Empty
     Bit 7                     Not Used

Input Status Register   (Register 6)
     Bit 0                     Change On Pin 5
     Bit 1                     Change On Pin 20
     Bit 2                     Change On Pin 22
     Bit 3                     Change On Pin 8
     Bit 4                     Clear To Send (CTS)
     Bit 5                     Data Set Ready (DSR)
     Bit 6                     Ring Indicator (RI)
     Bit 7                     Data Carrier Detect (DCD)
```

If you compare Figure 11-2 with Figure 11-1, you will see how much more complex than the parallel interface the serial interface really is. There is a lot more to control with serial I/O.

Base Addresses for Serial Registers　Figure 11-2 shows, from top to bottom, the locations in memory of the base addresses of each of the four possible communications adapters. Of course, you could add many more serial ports if you used unreserved interrupts, but the four reserved interrupt addresses are in a place in memory where they are not likely to be interfered with. DOS recognizes two logical names, COM1 and COM2. COM1 is also called AUX. These names are shown in the figure, along with their address vectors and the addresses to which they are typically initialized on an IBM PC. Square brackets indicate the *contents* pointed to by an address. Thus, [0000:0400] *points to* the word that holds the address 3F8 (hex).

Serial Interface Registers　The registers on the communications adapter are in a series of addresses that follow the base address consecutively. You can refer to each register relative to the base address for the adapter. The second part of Figure 11-2 shows the offsets of each of the six communications registers from the base address.

The Data Register　The data register is the simplest of the six registers to understand. It holds a single byte either to send or to receive. Whether you are sending or receiving depends on whether you are writing or reading this register. If you use an outp( ) to the data register, the data will be prepared and sent to the receiving device. If you use an inp( ) from the data register, the data in it will be made available to you.

If you are sending the byte, you need to know that the receiving device has room to receive it. If you are receiving the byte, you need to know that the sending device has indeed sent something and that a byte is waiting to be read.

The Interrupt Enable Register   If you wish to install an interrupt-driven serial interface, you must select the kind of event that will signal the processor that an interrupt needs service. If any combination of these bits are set, the event or combination of events will create an interrupt. In addition, there is a priority in which these interrupt events will be served.

Interrupt Service Priorities   Any change in the input status will receive the highest priority. In other words, the input lines (wires) themselves, if they change state at the same time that any other change takes place, will be served first.

If data is received (Data Ready), its service will come next. In other words, if Data Ready occurs at the same time as Transmitter Empty, then Data Ready will be served first.

If the transmitter holding register is empty (as indicated by Transmitter Empty), it will be served next in priority after Data Ready. It has the third level of priority.

Finally, a change in the modem status (Serial Status) will be the last served by the interrupt mechanism. Serial status indicates whether translation was successful. Any of a number of errors or other important conditions can occur, and these are monitored by the serial status register.

The Interrupt Identification Register   When you have enabled interrupts by using the interrupt-enable register, the serial control register, and the 8259 interrupt mask register (at 0x21), you may wish to know when one of the interrupts occurs. You can receive the current interrupt status from the interrupt identification register. For example, you may wish to install an interrupt service routine that is executed only if an interrupt of a certain type is pending.

The Data Format Register   The data format register sets the data bits, a parity bit, stop bits, and a baud rate. These govern the way serial data will be interpreted. You have many options for these settings.

You could set this register directly or use the DOS MODE command before running your program. From an overall system standpoint, you should, as much as possible, keep your software from setting serial ports internally. From the standpoint of ease of installation, however, you may wish to set the port for your user, and then reset it when the user exits the software.

To set the number of data bits, you change bits 0 and 1 of the data format register, as shown in Figure 11-2. Values of 5 and 6 bits are seldom (if ever) used.

To set the number of stop bits, you change bit 2 of the data format register. Settings with two stop bits are seldom used. Remember, there is always one start bit (always 0) and always at least one stop bit in a complete serial transfer. The two bits, one always on and one always off, are used to establish synchronization with the clock.

You can have one or two stop bits. If you specify one stop bit, eight data bits, and no parity, you will send a total of *ten* bits per transfer cycle. There will be one start bit (always), eight data bits, and the stop bit you requested. This tends to be confusing, but the actual format is unimportant. The important part is to make sure that the format used by the receiver matches the format used by the transmitter.

Selecting Parity   To select parity, you change bit 3 of the data format register. If on, this bit enables parity checking. This means that right after the data a bit will be added that reflects the sum of the bits in the data. If parity is enabled, an automatic sum is generated each time a full eight bits is received. The status of the parity bit received will be compared with the sum of the data bits just generated. If the sum is odd and the parity bit received says it should be even, a parity error has occurred.

To select whether the expected parity will be odd or even, you set bit 4 of the data format register. If you wish it to be even, turn bit 4 on. If you expect parity to be odd, turn bit 4 off. No matter how bit 4 is set, it will mean nothing if bit 3 is not on.

The **stick parity** bit (bit 5) adds to the confusion of it all by reversing the meaning of the parity bit (bit 4). Make sure you turn it off.

Break Detection   Bit 6 of the data format register is used to send a break signal to a terminal. It does this by holding all data to space voltages (-12 volts) long enough for the terminal to detect a break in transmission.

The Baud Rate Divisor Latch   Last but not least, bit 7 of the data format register *changes the meaning of registers 0 and 1*. It selects the Baud Rate Divisor Latch. When bit 7 of register 3 is on, the data register contains the low byte of the baud rate divisor, and the interrupt enable register contains the high byte of the baud rate divisor. If you intend to receive or transmit data, make sure that bit 7 of the data format register (register 3) is off.

The Baud Rate Divisor Latch (seen in registers 0 and 1 when bit 7 of register 3 is high) contains a number that, when multiplied by 16 and divided into the magic clock frequency number 1,843,200, generates a baud rate. The baud rate divisor can be determined and set by using Function 11-4, SET__BAUD.C.

The Serial Control Register   The serial control register sets the state of two pins on the serial interface connector, enables interrupts, and places the communications adapter into test mode. If you wish to signal a sender to stop sending, you can do so by lowering pins 4 and/or 20. Of course, the wire you use

■ FUNCTION 11-4

SET＿BAUD.C

```
/* SET_BAUD.C  sets baud rate given the
** desired rate.  It computes the divisor
** necessary.  You should stick to conventional
** rates from 50 through 9600, exceeding at
** your own risk.
*/


union
      {
      struct
            {
      unsigned lobyte : 8;
      unsigned hibyte : 8;
            } byte;
      struct
            {
      unsigned word;
            } whole;
      }bytes;

set_baud(baud_rate)
int baud_rate;
{
/* use COM1 for example */
unsigned far *ser_base = (unsigned far *)0x00000400L;

/* set bit 7 high to access divisor latch */
outp((*ser_base)+3, inp((*ser_base)+3) | 8);

bytes.whole.word = 1843200L / (long)baud_rate << 4;
outp((*ser_base)+0, bytes.byte.lobyte);
outp((*ser_base)+1, bytes.byte.hibyte);

/* set bit 7 low to return to Data Format Reg */
outp((*ser_base)+3, inp((*ser_base)+3) & ~8);
}
```

must be connected to the sender's pin 5 or it will not do anything. Bit 2 of the serial control register is disabled on some boards and functions identically to bit 3 on others. Bit 3 has a very special function. It *must* be set if you wish to enable serial interrupts to be sent. You must also have selected them using the interrupt enable register (register 1). Further, you must also unmask serial interrupts on the 8259 UART (port address 0x21) in order to enable these interrupts.

The Serial Status Register   The serial status register reports the various conditions related to the conversion of serial into parallel data. If data is ready after conversion, bit 0 will be high. If no errors were encountered during the process, bits 1 through 4 will be 0. Bit 1, the OVERRUN Error, can be used to detect whether the data was sent so fast that a byte arrived in the data latch before the previous byte could be retrieved from it. Bit 2 tells us that the sum of the data bits was odd when it was expected to be even or vice versa. Bit 3, which reports framing errors, tells us that the clock of the transmitter is just a little too fast or slow to match the clock of the receiver closely enough. Bit 4 reports that a received transfer word was completely logic 0 (space) for all of its bits. This is the corollary of bit 6 of the data format register (set break). Bit 5 indicates that the transmitter register is ready to accept a new character for transmission. Bit 6 indicates that the transmitter shift register is not being used.

The Input Status Register   The input status register reports the real-time state of the control lines for the serial interface. Bits 0 through 3 indicate that a change has taken place on wires connected to pins 5, 20, 22, and/or 8 since the last time this register was read. Bit 4 indicates the status of the Clear To Send line (CTS, pin 5). Bit 5 shows the status of the Data Set Ready line (DSR, pin 20). The DSR line is traditionally used to indicate, when high, that it is clear to send information. Bit 6, the Ring Indicator (RI, pin 22), usually indicates (you guessed it) that the phone connected to a modem is ringing. Bit 7, the Data Carrier Detect line (DCD, pin 8), gives the opposite of the Received Line Signal Detect (RLSD) signal. For non-modem equipment, you normally connect pins 6 and 8 to pin 20 on the same connector for both the sender and the receiver. Plotters, digitizers, and mice are non-modem equipment.

Serial Interrupt Service

If you are stout of heart and can live with frustration, you can try to implement a serial interrupt-service routine yourself. Many books have been written about the installation of serial-interrupt service routines, but each text seems to leave something out or make mistakes. It is easy to do this because of the awkwardness of the interrupt-service mechanism on the PC. Serial interrupts are not necessary for most work that involves receiving data from serial devices. The serial interrupt service given in this book *actually works* and can be used with little modification for most (if not all) applications that require constant input from a serial port.

Creating Serial Interrupt Service   Several things must be done to install a serial interrupt-service routine. You must first create a serial interrupt handler. Function 11-5, SERISR.ASM, fits the bill. To install it you must run Function 11-6, INSTISR.C. A version of INSTISR.C, called ISR_INST.C, appears in Appendix A. To uninstall the service routine and restore the original handler, you must run Function 11-7, UNINSTAL.C. Finally, in any program that uses serial interrupts, you must include the following header:

```
struct ISRVEC
    {
    unsigned vecl;
    unsigned vech;
    unsigned type;
    };


struct ISRVEC isrvec;

unsigned char serisr(), readbuf();
unsigned buffchr();
```

■ FUNCTION 11-5

SERISR.ASM

```
; SERISR.ASM is a serial interrupt service routine.

_TEXT      SEGMENT  BYTE PUBLIC 'CODE'
_TEXT      ENDS
CONST      SEGMENT  WORD PUBLIC 'CONST'
CONST      ENDS
_BSS       SEGMENT  WORD PUBLIC 'BSS'
_BSS       ENDS
_DATA      SEGMENT  WORD PUBLIC 'DATA'
_DATA      ENDS
DGROUP     GROUP    CONST,    _BSS,     _DATA
     ASSUME  CS: _TEXT, DS: DGROUP, SS: DGROUP, ES: DGROUP

           TOTAL    equ  64
           TOP      equ  63
           BOTTOM   equ  0

_DATA      SEGMENT
           buffer   db   TOTAL dup('@')
           front    dw   BOTTOM
           back     dw   BOTTOM
           count    dw   BOTTOM
       _DATA ENDS

_TEXT SEGMENT
     PUBLIC _serisr
_serisr    PROC     FAR
           push     ax
           push     dx
           push     si
           push     ds
           mov      ax, DGROUP
           mov      ds, ax

           mov      dx, 3F8h        ; base register address
           in       al, dx          ; input a character

           mov      si, front
           mov       buffer[si], al

           inc      front
           inc      count
           cmp      front, TOP
           jbe      front_below
           mov      front, BOTTOM
```

■ **FUNCTION 11-5** (continued)

SERISR.ASM

```
front_below:
        cmp     count, TOTAL
        jbe     count_below
        mov     count, TOTAL
count_below:

        mov     al, 20h         ; signal interrupt mask
        out     20h, al         ; register complete

        pop     ds
        pop     si
        pop     dx
        pop     ax
        iret
_serisr ENDP




PUBLIC  _buffchr
_buffchr PROC   FAR
        cli
        push    bp
        mov     bp, sp
        push    ds
        mov     ax, DGROUP
        mov     ds, ax
        xor     ax, ax

        mov     ax, count

        pop     ds
        mov     sp, bp
        pop     bp
        sti
        ret
_buffchr ENDP




PUBLIC  _readbuf
_readbuf PROC   FAR
        cli
        push    bp
        mov     bp, sp
        push    si
```

■ FUNCTION 11-5 (continued)

SERISR.ASM

```
            push    ds
            mov     ax, DGROUP
            mov     ds, ax
            xor     ax, ax

            cmp     count, BOTTOM
            jz      back_below

            mov     si, back
            mov     al, buffer[si]

            dec     count
            inc     back
            cmp     back, TOP
            jbe     back_below
            mov     back, BOTTOM
back_below:
            pop     ds
            pop     si
            mov     sp, bp
            pop     bp
            sti
            ret
_readbuf    ENDP


        _TEXT ENDS

END
```

The ISRVEC Structure   If you study Functions 11-6 and 11-7, you will see that they share the ISRVEC structure. The values placed in this structure by Function 11-6 are used in Function 11-7 just before you exit from your program back to DOS. In this way the original interrupt vector is restored in a clean and responsible way.

■ FUNCTION 11-6

INSTISR.C

```
/* INSTISR.C installs the serial interrupt service
** routine.  Refer to "serial interface at a glance"
** for register offsets used.
*/


#include <stdio.h>
#include <conio.h>
#include <dos.h>


struct ISRVEC
      {
      unsigned vecl;
      unsigned vech;
      unsigned type;
      };


extern struct ISRVEC isrvec;


instisr(service, request, port)
unsigned (*service)();
unsigned request;
unsigned long port;
{
unsigned far *base = (unsigned far *)port;
int i = 2;

outp((*base)+1, 1);  /* select interrupts */

/* maskable hardware interrupts must be unmasked */
/* in the 8259 interrupt mask register */
outp(0x21, inp(0x21) & ~0x10); /* unmask COM1 interrupt */

/* set the interrupt vector using DOS */
setvect(request, service);

/* enable interrupts selected */
outp((*base)+4, inp((*base)+4) | 8);

/* clear pending interrupts */
inp(*base);
inp(*base);
inp(*base);

return(0);
}
```

■ **FUNCTION 11-6** (continued)

INSTISR.C

```
setvect(vector, service)
int vector;
unsigned (*service)();
{
union REGS regs;
struct SREGS sregs;

regs.h.al = vector;
regs.h.ah = 0x35;
int86x(0x21, &regs, &regs, &sregs);
isrvec.vech = sregs.es; /* segment */
isrvec.vecl = regs.x.bx; /* offset */
isrvec.type = vector;

sregs.ds = FP_SEG(service); /* segment */
regs.x.dx = FP_OFF(service); /* offset */
regs.h.al = vector;
regs.h.ah = 0x25;
int86x(0x21, &regs, &regs, &sregs);
}
```

The buffchr() Function   The word at offset 68 contains a nonzero value when there is data in the buffer. You can check it while your program is running to see if any goodies have been gathered from the sending device. To read the count variable, because it is not public, you must use the buffchr() function contained in Function 11-5. If this function returns a nonzero value, it indicates that there is at least one character in the rotating buffer. This count is never allowed to exceed the total number of characters in the buffer.

■ **FUNCTION 11-7**

UNINSTAL.C

```
/* UNINSTAL.C uninstalls the serial interrupt service
** routine.
*/


#include <stdio.h>
#include <dos.h>
#include <conio.h>

#define SERPORT1 0x00000400L
#define SERPORT2 0x00000402L
#define SERVEC1 12
#define SERVEC2 11

struct ISRVEC
    {
    unsigned vecl;
    unsigned vech;
    unsigned type;
    };


extern struct ISRVEC isrvec;

uninstal(port)
unsigned long port;
{
unsigned far *base = (unsigned far *)port;

/* disable interrupts selected */
outp(*base+4, inp(*base+4) & ~0x8);

outp(0x21, inp(0x21) | 0x10); /* mask IRQ4 */

outp((*base)+1, 0);  /* reset interrupts to 0 */

unsetvec();

return(0);
}
unsetvec()
{
union REGS regs;
struct SREGS sregs;

sregs.ds = isrvec.vech; /* segment */
regs.x.dx = isrvec.vecl; /* offset */
regs.h.al = isrvec.type;
regs.h.ah = 0x25;
int86x(0x21, &regs, &regs, &sregs);
}
```

The readbuf( ) Function   To read a character from the *back* of the buffer, you must use the readbuf( ) function, which is given in Function 11-5. The interrupt service buffer is intentionally kept local so that it does not interact with external data. This means that you must read the buffer with a function that knows where the buffer is. Interrupts must be turned off before the buffer is read and turned on again before the function returns to its caller.

Function 11-5 will handle interrupts from each occurrence of a full data latch, intercepting each byte as it arrives from the sender, until the buffer is full. The current character is placed at the front of the buffer, and the back of the buffer is read by your program. The delay between the receipt of characters from the sender and their retrieval by your program can be decreased by decreasing the size of the receiver buffer. The buffer shown is 64 bytes long. You can change the number of bytes, but be sure to reflect the change throughout the routine. If you make the buffer 20 bytes long, the offsets 64, 66, and 68 must be made 20, 22, and 24, respectively. The buffer never overflows, but if you do not check it before it goes through one complete cycle, you will lose one cycle's worth of data.

Overrun Errors   If a byte arrives in the latch before the current byte has been read from the latch, the interrupt-service routine will receive garbled data. If you find that garbled data is being received, lower the sender's and receiver's baud rates. The interrupt-service routine is generally able to accommodate 9600 baud easily, however.

Making Interrupt-Service Routines Work   Making interrupt-service routines work can be a difficult undertaking. The primary frustration is that not only must you debug your program, but you must be aware that the interrupt-service routine is working constantly while your software is running. Interrupts can occur at any time. Unless you carefully coordinate the interrupt service so that it does not interfere with the processes that are being interrupted, you will find that mysterious things happen. Function 11-5 has been carefully designed to use *variables that are never public.* If public variables or calls are used, interrupt-service routines can become interactive in a very negative way.

Serial Interrupt Service Works Well   Be assured that Functions 11-5 through 11-7 will work well if you take the time to compile, assemble, and link them exactly as they are. The serial interrupt service they install and maintain will be the primary source of input from your serial devices. These functions represent one easy technique to make serial input fast and easy for every application. The advantage of serial interrupts is that they can keep up with the fastest senders and give you information only when you want it. 9600 baud is IBM's recommended limit, but it can be exceeded at your own risk. Since most C compilers do not support interrupt-service handling, Functions 11-5 through 11-7 should prove to be very valuable to you in all applications, not just for graphics.

Digitizer Interfacing

It is difficult to speak in general terms about digitizer interfacing. Digitizers are perhaps the least standardized of all computer devices. The tradition in digitizer design is very liberal. For this reason, as with other devices, a specific digitizer is used here as an example. This does not constitute an endorsement of the product, but the digitizer chosen is very popular.

The Kurta Series One digitizer uses a serial interface to communicate with the computer. If you use it as it is shipped from the factory, its cable will plug into your COM1 port, and so it will be easy to interface. If you wish to employ hardwire handshaking, follow the user manual to learn how to connect pin 4 (the orange wire inside the connector shell) to the orange wire coming from the digitizer. This connection is not made at the factory, but it will enable your software to stop and start the digitizer using bit 1 of register 4. (See Figure 11-2 for details.)

Setting the Digitizer's Switches   To work with serial inter- rupt input from the digitizer, you should set the switches on the back of the digitizer for 1200 baud. There are two banks of switches. One has four positions, and the other has eight.

On the four-position switch, set all the switches to off. On the eight-position switch, set positions 2, 3, and 8 to on and all the others off. These switches govern option settings and baud rate. Read about them in the digitizer manual.

Setting the Baud Rate   In the early days of the IBM PC, applications were designed to set the baud rate within most programs, ignoring the needs of the operating system. These days, although it is less convenient, the user is encouraged to establish a system-wide serial interface initialization. If software changes this system-wide setting, it should restore it on exit. Function 11-8, TEST_DIG.C, will configure the port for 1200 baud, no parity, 8 data bits, 1 stop bit, and no device timeouts.

Testing the Digitizer   Using Function 11-5 as shown in Func- tion 11-8, you can see a data stream from the digitizer. Assemble, compile, and link Functions 11-5 through 11-8. Raw data from the digitizer (or any other properly configured serial transmit- ter) should appear rapidly on the display. As you move the digitizer stylus, the characters will change. If they jump around wildly from value to value, you are getting overrun errors, and you should lower the baud rates of the receiver and sender.

■ FUNCTION 11-8

TEST __ DIG.C

```
/* TEST_DIG.C tests the digitizer using
** serial interrupt service.
*/


#include <stdio.h>
#include <conio.h>
#include <string.h>


#define SERPORT1 0x00000400L /* COM1 interrupt address */
#define SERPORT2 0x00000402L /* COM2 interrupt address */
#define SERVEC1 12  /* COM1 interrupt request (IRQ4)    */
#define SERVEC2 11  /* COM2 interrupt request (IRQ3)    */

struct ISRVEC
     {
     unsigned vecl;
     unsigned vech;
     unsigned type;
     };


struct ISRVEC isrvec;

unsigned char serisr(), readbuf();
unsigned buffchr();

main()
{
unsigned far *outbase = (unsigned far *)SERPORT1;
unsigned char baudlo, baudhi, bits;
unsigned char thisbuff[200];
unsigned x, y, i;

/* turn pins 4 and 20 off */
outp((*outbase)+4, inp((*outbase)+4) & ~3);

bits = inp(*outbase + 3);
/* turn on baud divisor latch selector bit */
bits |= 0x80;
outp(*outbase + 3, bits);

/* set 8 data bits, 1 stop bit, no parity */
/* and select divisor latch */
outp(*outbase + 3, 0x83);

/* save existing baud rate */
baudlo = inp(*outbase + 0);
baudhi = inp(*outbase + 1);
```

■ **FUNCTION 11-8** (continued)

TEST — DIG.C

```
/* set 9600 baud using 0x00C divisor */
/* set 1200 baud using 0x060 divisor */
outp(*outbase + 0, 0x60);
outp(*outbase + 1, 0x00);

/* turn off baud divisor latch selector bit */
outp(*outbase + 3, inp(*outbase + 3) & 0x7F);

/* install interrupt service routine */
instisr(serisr, SERVEC1, SERPORT1);

/* turn pins 4 and 20 on */
outp((*outbase)+4, inp((*outbase)+4) | 3);

/* display raw input from rotating */
/* interrupt service buffer */

while (!kbhit())
    {
    while(!buffchr());
    if ((thisbuff[0] = readbuf()) >= 0x80)
        {
        for (i = 1; i <= 5; ++i)
            {
            while(!buffchr());
            thisbuff[i] = readbuf();
            }
        if (thisbuff[5] >= 0x80)
            {
            x = thisbuff[1];
            x += (unsigned)thisbuff[2] << 7;
            y = thisbuff[3];
            y += (unsigned)thisbuff[4] << 7;

            printf("x = %u   y = %u\n", x, y);
            }
        }

    }

getch();  /* dispose of pending character */

uninstal(SERPORT1);

/* restore port settings */
outp(*outbase + 3, bits);
outp(*outbase + 0, baudlo);
outp(*outbase + 1, baudhi);
/* turn off divisor latch select bit */
outp(*outbase + 3, inp(*outbase + 3) & 0x7F);
}
```

When you make a legal exit by pressing a key (other than a control or shift key) on the keyboard, the original baud rate and other settings of the serial port will be restored. To make sense of the binary numbers, read your digitizer's documentation and study GRAPHIQ.C in Appendix A.

Polled Serial Interfacing

If you do not need the elaborate services of an interrupt-driven serial input routine, you can easily implement polled serial input. Polled serial input is an input method that waits for a byte to enter the receiver latch before receiving it. Using polled serial input, you ask for each character as it becomes ready.

For most purposes, polled serial I/O is perfectly adequate, as long as you keep the sender's baud rate low enough so as not to overrun the byte in the latch before it is read. You can always test the overrun error bit (bit 1) in the status register (register base+5). If it is on, data is being sent too fast for your software to receive it. Your software can report overrun errors to the user and explain how to lower the baud rate.

Function 11-9, COM__STR.ASM, gets as many characters as you specify from the serial port and then lets the port continue receiving data until the next poll. This function is particularly good for use with digitizers because it always returns data that is currently being sent. When using a digitizer or mouse, you do not want data that has been buffered, because you do not want a time delay between the coordinates you receive and the actual position of the digitizer stylus.

Function 11-9 is written in assembler because it must run as fast as possible. If it runs too slowly, it will be unable to receive a character from the data latch before the next one arrives. This overrun condition will result in garbled data. You use Function 11-9, after assembling it, just as though it were a function written in C.

■ FUNCTION 11-9

COM＿STR.ASM

```
; COM_STR.ASM  fetches a desired number of bytes
; (0 to 32767) from the serial input device.
; Usage from C:
;
;         char buffer[200];
;         int count;
;
;         com_str(buffer, count);
;
; Returns:
;         string of count characters in buffer
;         return value 0


COM_STR_TEXT      SEGMENT  BYTE PUBLIC 'CODE'
COM_STR_TEXT      ENDS
CONST     SEGMENT  WORD PUBLIC 'CONST'
CONST     ENDS
_BSS      SEGMENT  WORD PUBLIC 'BSS'
_BSS      ENDS
_DATA     SEGMENT  WORD PUBLIC 'DATA'
_DATA     ENDS
DGROUP      GROUP      CONST,    _BSS,      _DATA
     ASSUME  CS: COM_STR_TEXT, DS: DGROUP, SS: DGROUP, ES: DGROUP
PUBLIC    _com_str

COM_STR_TEXT    SEGMENT
     PUBLIC      _com_str
_com_str  PROC      FAR
          push      bp
          mov       bp,sp
                              ; get pointer from stack
          mov       bx, [bp + 6]
                              ; get count from stack
          mov       cx, Word Ptr [bp + 8]
          cmp       cx, 0
          je        exit

          and       cx,7FFFh ; strip off high bit in
                             ; case negative int was passed

not_ready:
                             ; test for character
                             ; in latch and no errors
          mov       dx, 3F8h ; Register 0 (base)
          add       dx, 5    ; Register 5
          in        al, dx   ; Serial Status Register
          test      al, 1    ; Is only Data Ready set?
          jz        not_ready
```

■ **FUNCTION 11-9** (continued)

COM＿STR.ASM

```
                            ; receive the character
            mov     dx, 3F8h  ; Register 0 (base)
            add     dx, 3     ; Register 3
            in      al, dx    ; Data Format Register
            and     al, 7Fh   ; make sure divisor latch
            out     dx, al    ; not selected
            mov     dx, 3F8h  ; Register 0 (base)
            in      al, dx    ; input the byte
                            ; store byte in public string
            mov     Byte Ptr [bx], al
            inc     bx        ; point to next character
                            ; supply ASCIIZ string
                            ; terminator (null byte)
            mov     Byte Ptr [bx], 0
            dec     cx
            cmp     cx, 0
            jbe     exit      ; exit when cx reached
            loop    not_ready
exit:
            mov     ax, 0     ; always returns 0
            mov     sp,bp
            pop     bp
            ret
_com_str    ENDP

COM_STR_TEXT    ENDS
END
```

Mouse Interfacing

The mouse, which is perhaps even more ubiquitous than the digitizer, can also be used as a locator. The advantage in using a mouse is that it is inexpensive, convenient, and supported by most modern software. The only real disadvantage in using a mouse is that you can work only with **relative coordinates.**

Relative coordinates are derived from the last known position of the locator, rather than from a constant reference point. In other words, the mouse knows only its last position and the distance it has moved from it, not its absolute location on a grid.

Unless you are tracing drawings, you will not need a locator that has absolute position-reporting capabilities. To select from menus, you need only to sense the direction of each successive movement of the locator — whether *up, down, left,* or *right.*

The Mouse   The mouse used for the purposes of this description is made by Mouse Systems. As with the digitizer, this does not constitute an endorsement of this particular mouse, but it does recognize that this mouse is very popular and thus suitable for a general description of mouse interfacing techniques.

Function 11-9 will be used to receive a stream of characters from the port to which your mouse is connected. For purposes of demonstration, this will be COM1, but you can modify the source code as you choose. You are strongly encouraged to try the mouse with the serial interrupt-service routines of Functions 11-5 through 11-7 as well.

Receiving a Single Character   To receive one character at a time quickly from a serial port, you should use a function like Function 11-10, GET_SER.ASM. Written in assembler and callable from C, this function waits for a character to appear in the data latch and then reads the character. You could use Microsoft C's inp( ) function to do the same thing, but it would be slower, especially using the Medium memory model, as is done throughout this book. If you are receiving characters one at a time this way, the baud rates of receiver and sender may need to be kept very low in order not to overrun the data latch. If you use the serial interrupt-service routine of Functions 11-5 through 11-7, you will not encounter this problem for baud rates of up to 9600.

■ FUNCTION 11-10

GET—SER.ASM

```
; GET_SER.ASM gets a single character from COM1.
; Declaration:
;        char get_ser();
;        char character;
; Usage:
;        character = get_ser();

GET_SER_TEXT      SEGMENT  BYTE PUBLIC 'CODE'
GET_SER_TEXT      ENDS
CONST      SEGMENT  WORD PUBLIC 'CONST'
CONST      ENDS
_BSS       SEGMENT  WORD PUBLIC 'BSS'
_BSS       ENDS
_DATA      SEGMENT  WORD PUBLIC 'DATA'
_DATA      ENDS
DGROUP     GROUP    CONST,    _BSS,      _DATA
     ASSUME  CS: GET_SER_TEXT, DS: DGROUP, SS: DGROUP, ES: DGROUP
PUBLIC    _get_ser

GET_SER_TEXT      SEGMENT
     PUBLIC    _get_ser
_get_ser  PROC      FAR
          push      bp
          mov       bp,sp

not_ready:
                              ; test for character
                              ; in latch and no errors
          mov       dx, 3F8h  ; Register 0 (base)
          add       dx, 5     ; Register 5
          in        al, dx    ; Serial Status Register
          test      al, 1     ; Is only Data Ready set?
          jz        not_ready

                              ; receive the character
          mov       dx, 3F8h  ; Register 0 (base)
          add       dx, 3     ; Register 3
          in        al, dx    ; Data Format Register
          and       al, 7Fh   ; make sure divisor latch
          out       dx, al    ; not selected
          mov       dx, 3F8h  ; Register 0 (base)
          in        al, dx    ; input the byte
          mov       sp,bp
          pop       bp
          ret
_get_ser  ENDP

GET_SER_TEXT      ENDS
END
```

Getting Mouse Data   Function 11-11, GET_MOUS.C, gets bytes sent from the mouse over the serial interface and displays them using standard output to the display. This function also shows how to initialize the serial port and restore it on exit. The mouse operates at 1200 baud with 8 data bits, 1 start bit, and 1 stop bit. It uses no parity checking.

Compile Function 11-11 and link it with Function 11-10 to see the mouse in action. As you move the mouse on its little pad, you will see characters on the display that reflect its movement. As you press buttons on the mouse, characters will appear that reflect the button pressed.

The Limitations of Polled Mouse Interface   Function 11-11 is only an example that gets some data from the mouse. It shows only one way to interface the mouse. You can also use an interrupt-service routine that you write yourself, like Function 11-5, or you can use software tools provided by the mouse manufacturer. Since such tools solve most of your low-level problems, they are highly recommended.

Light Pen Interfacing

A light pen interface is perhaps the easiest interface of all. The EGA supports light pens from a wide range of manufacturers, and so no specific piece of hardware need be discussed. The EGA BIOS service 4 of interrupt 10 (hex) is adequate to report both the row and column number of the light pen in character positions and the location of the pen in pixels.

Reading the Light Pen Position and Switch   Function 11-12, READ_PEN.C, reads the light pen position and indicates whether the pen switch is pressed or not. The code is very direct and will work no matter what mode the EGA is in.

■ FUNCTION 11-11

GET_MOUS.C

```
/* GET_MOUS.C  gets an input stream of characters from
** the scurrying mouse.  To make sense of the characters
** see your mouse documentation.  Try modifying this
** function to report the x, y location and buttons.
*/

#include <stdio.h>
#include <conio.h>


#define SERPORT1 0x00000400L
#define SERPORT2 0x00000402L


main()
{
char get_ser();
char buffer[20];
unsigned far *base = (unsigned far *)SERPORT1;
unsigned char baudlo, baudhi, bits;
int i;

bits = inp(*base + 3);
/* turn on baud divisor latch selector bit */
bits |= 0x80;
outp(*base + 3, bits);

/* set 8 data bits, 1 stop bit, no parity */
/* and select divisor latch */
outp(*base + 3, 0x83);

/* save existing baud rate */
baudlo = inp(*base + 0);
baudhi = inp(*base + 1);

/* set 1200 baud using 0x0060 divisor */
outp(*base + 0, 0x60);
outp(*base + 1, 0x00);

/* display data */
while (!kbhit())
    {
    /* use GET_SER.C to get characters from mouse */
    putch(get_ser());
    }

getch(); /* waste character from keyboard */
/* restore port settings */
outp(*base + 3, bits);
```

■ **FUNCTION 11-11** (continued)

GET__MOUS.C

```
outp(*base + 0, baudlo);
outp(*base + 1, baudhi);
/* turn off divisor latch select bit */
outp(*base + 3, inp(*base + 3) & 0x7F);
}
```

■ **FUNCTION 11-12**

READ__PEN.C

```
/* READ_PEN.C reads the light pen position
** and switch status.  Return value is 1
** if switch has been triggered.
*/

#include <conio.h>
#include <dos.h>


read_pen(row, col, x, y)
int *row, *col, *x, *y;
{
int timer;
union REGS regs;

for (;;)
    {
    regs.h.ah = 4;        /* service 4, light pen */
    int86(0x10, &regs, &regs);
    *row = regs.h.dh;
    *col = regs.h.dl;
    *y = regs.h.ch;
    *x = regs.x.bx;
    }
return(regs.h.ah)
}
```

Serial Output Interfacing

Receiving information from the outside world is usually much more difficult than sending it. That is why so much attention has been given to receiving data from the parallel and serial ports.

You can send data out a serial port merely by outputting bytes to the serial port's base register. You will face two major problems if you try this. First, you must make sure that there is nothing in the data latch that should be read. Second, you must know if the receiving device has room for the data you are about to send.

Output Verification and Handshaking   If you refer to Figure 11-2, you will see the serial status register (register 5). Bit 0 of this register, data ready, indicates that a byte is available in the latch and can be read. If this bit is high and you are interested in the information in the latch, you must receive it before attempting to transmit a byte. Likewise, if bit 5 of register r is 0, it means there is a byte in the transmitter holding register that has not yet been sent. If you care about the contents of this register, you must wait for this bit to be set to high before trying to send a character.

The device to which you are sending will usually control pin 5 of the interface, setting it to high if you are clear to send data and low if you are not clear to send. You must monitor pin 5 to see if the receiving device will permit you to send a byte. You can do this by monitoring bit 4 of the input status register (register 6). This register keeps track of the real-time status of the handshake wires connected to the interface pins.

Sending Characters Interactively   Function 11-13, SEND___SER.ASM, is a function, written in assembler and callable from C, that sends a byte, but will do so only after it has received any pending characters from the data latch. It is useful for commu-

■ FUNCTION 11-13

SEND_SER.ASM

```
; SEND_SER.ASM  sends and receives characters interactively.
; Declaration:
;         char send_char();
;         char character;
; Usage:
;         rec_char = send_ser(character);
;
; Returns:
;         if not zero, return is received character
; Note:
;         requires pin 4 held high by destination to send
;         no control of pins 5 or 20


SEND_SER_TEXT     SEGMENT  BYTE PUBLIC 'CODE'
SEND_SER_TEXT     ENDS
CONST      SEGMENT  WORD PUBLIC 'CONST'
CONST      ENDS
_BSS       SEGMENT  WORD PUBLIC 'BSS'
_BSS       ENDS
_DATA      SEGMENT  WORD PUBLIC 'DATA'
_DATA      ENDS
DGROUP     GROUP    CONST,     _BSS,      _DATA
     ASSUME  CS: SEND_SER_TEXT, DS: DGROUP, SS: DGROUP, ES: DGROUP
PUBLIC     _send_ser

SEND_SER_TEXT     SEGMENT
     PUBLIC     _send_ser
_send_ser  PROC       FAR
           push       bp
           mov        bp,sp

           xor        ax, ax       ; clear AX
                                   ; test for character
                                   ; in latch and no errors
           mov        dx, 3F8h     ; Register 0 (base)
           add        dx, 5        ; Register 5
           in         bh, dx       ; Serial Status Register
           test       bh, 1        ; Is only Data Ready set?
           jz         no_receive

                                   ; receive the character
           mov        dx, 3F8h     ; Register 0 (base)
           add        dx, 3        ; Register 3
           in         al, dx       ; Data Format Register
           and        al, 7Fh      ; make sure divisor latch
           out        dx, al       ; not selected
           mov        dx, 3F8h     ; Register 0 (base)
           in         al, dx       ; input the byte
```

■ **FUNCTION 11-13** (continued)

SEND_SER.ASM

```
no_receive:
        mov     dx, 3F8h  ; Register 0 (base)
        add     dx, 6     ; Input Status Register
        in      bh, dx    ; examine register 6
        test    bh, 10h   ; is bit 4 (pin 5) on?
        jz      no_receive      ; if not, wait until it is

not_empty:
        mov     dx, 3F8h  ; Register 0 (base)
        add     dx, 5     ; Serial Status Register
        in      bh, dx    ; examine register 5
        test    bh, 90h   ; are bits 5 and 6 on?
        jz      not_empty ; if not, wait until they are

                          ; get character from stack
        mov     bl, [bp + 6]
        mov     dx, 3F8h  ; Register 0 (base)
        out     dx, bl    ; send the character

                          ; if char was received in al
                          ; it will be returned on exit
        mov     sp,bp
        pop     bp
        ret
_send_ser  ENDP

SEND_SER_TEXT    ENDS
END
```

nications programs where you wish to send and receive characters interactively. The function has no way to stop the sender from sending more characters, however, and should be used only in situations where you know that the number of characters to be received will be limited. If you want full control, you must implement a handshake and hold wire 20 to the destination low until you can accept more characters. Function 11-13 must be called in rapid succession in a tight loop if you are to avoid overrun errors. If the loop does not run fast enough and will work only at an extremely low baud rate, implement more of the loop directly in assembler.

If at First You Don't Succeed Serial interfacing can be extremely frustrating. Keep in mind that there are many complex variables involved and that the functions in this book, although they work in isolated test situations, may not work if any of a million combinations of factors are changed. It is impossible to give examples of all the possible combinations here. On the other hand, the functions are all sound in principle and thoroughly illustrate the options available using serial interface programming. If you carefully assemble, compile, and link Functions 11-5 through 11-7 and use serial interrupt service in your software, you can have done with serial input once and for all.

12

Maintenance Modes

Graphics software involves much more than using a few functions to draw lines. All the tools you use to create graphics must be carefully stored in convenient places so that you can easily gain access to them. The context for graphics tools is easily as important as the tools themselves.

The GRAPHIQ program in Appendix A demonstrates how graphics software is orchestrated. If you think of your software as a symphony of functions that share information, with yourself as the composer, you will share the point of view of this book. This chapter discusses the overall organization of a program like GRAPHIQ. It is about placing functions in the context of a complete graphics system.

From the time the user copies your software to his or her working environment to the time a graphics editing session is complete, your software must make it easy to find and use functions. Functions are interdependent, especially in graphics systems. Maintenance modes govern the system's housekeeping by tying graphics tools together. Maintenance modes are used to maintain the picture database. You can update the database on disk, clear the system of data, and change the locations of graphics entities using the maintenance modes.

FUNCTIONS IN CONTEXT

Think of GRAPHIQ, the prototypical program given in Appendix A, as a programmer's sketch. Many of the functions and techniques discussed in this book are bound into GRAPH-IQ so that you can see them in operation. Creating the functions themselves is not nearly as complicated as getting them to work together.

Using the Locator

In GRAPHIQ the locator is, like a pen, pencil, or brush, the primary device for both drawing and overall system operation. Except for a few things that need to be typed (such as text strings), the locator is the only tool needed to run GRAPHIQ.

The Kurta Series One digitizer is the locator for the sample program in this book. Because you have the entire source code, however, you can easily substitute a mouse (as described in Chapter 11) or a light pen, or just use the arrow keys. Serial interfacing is made extremely easy through the use of a universal serial interrupt-service routine. The creation and installation of serial interrupt service is discussed in Chapter 11.

Simple Selection Options The locator can report only two things. It can return the x,y coordinates of the location to which it is pointing, and it can indicate when a switch has been pressed.

This operation is kept simple on purpose. It means you only need to remember to move the locator to a desired position and press its button when you wish to select from a menu.

The Numeric Keypad   At any time, whether you have a digitizer or not, you can use the arrow keys on the numeric keypad as a locator. If you have a digitizer, you must turn it off using the LOCATOR ON/OFF command when you wish to use the arrow keys, or the crosshairs will jump back to the digitizer's coordinates. If you are using the numeric keypad, the ENTER key functions in the same way as the button on the digitizer or mouse. You can use either the ENTER key or the locator button at any time.

Command Entry

You can enter commands by selecting from menus, or you can enter them directly from a command line.

Selecting from Menus   Menu selection involves using either the arrow keys on the numeric keypad or the locator device. If no prompts or menus are on the display and you press the locator's button or the ENTER key, you will select the main menu. To move the menu cursor, you move the locator up or down. To select an item from the menu, you press the ENTER key or the locator button. The process is very direct.

The Command Line   To display a command line at which commands can be entered, press the ESC key while no menus are displayed. The commands can be executed by name using a command language. You can expand on this command language by changing the source code of GRAPHIQ to fit your needs.

Command Files   You can put a collection of commands in a command file and run the file. In this case each command in the file will be executed as though from the command line.

Notice that GRAPHIQ supports a variety of methods for executing commands. You can add to these methods. The important thing is that all the methods be interactive. Switching from one method to another is very easy. You can run the entire system by typing commands, selecting from menus, or running command files in any combination.

Functions Included

Lines, Boxes, and Rectangular Fills   You will find in GRAPH-IQ functions to draw lines in five styles using eight colors (including black). Boxes and rectangular filled areas can be drawn using the line styles and colors. To delete a line or other entity or object, set the color to black (you will not be able to see the crosshairs) and execute the same function you used to draw the entity. This will cover it with black, thus erasing it. Granted, there are better ways to erase and edit, and given unlimited time they can be implemented. This is left as an exercise for you to do.

Full Rotation and Scaling   Unlike simple pixel-paint software, GRAPHIQ allows you to change the height, width, slant, and rotation base angle for text drawn using the built-in stroke font.

Circles   Circles can be drawn using Bresenham's circle algorithm, which is presented in Chapter 4. This method is fast but limits you to full circles.

Playback   The playback function enables you to regenerate the display from the vector database. This is different from putting and getting the display itself. As each element is drawn, a vector database receives all of the information about it. This database can be transformed if you implement functions to make transformations happen.

Drawing Text   The stroke-based text capabilities of GRAPHIQ rival the best graphics software on the market. You are not limited to characters of one size always drawn along a horizontal baseline. You can change the rotation, translation, and scaling of the system to place text anywhere and at any angle. Text mode is perhaps the best feature of the program.

Grids   Grids help you to visualize where graphics will be placed on the display. You can generate grids at any angle and in any supported color.

Rotation, Translation, and Scaling   You can change the system origin, rotation origin, rotation angle, and scaling factor at any time. After you change it, graphics will be drawn at the prevailing angle, origin, and scale. You can add a function to report the system state.

Grid Snap   You can **snap** the locator crosshairs to a grid if the snap feature is enabled. Snap is the rounding of coordinate numbers to the nearest grid node. You can enable or disable snap. If enabled, both the arrow keys on the numeric keypad and the locator device (mouse, digitizer, or light pen) will snap to the prevailing grid. When the crosshairs snap to a grid point, they cannot be located between grid points.

Printing   You can print the display at any time on your dot-matrix line printer. The printer driver discussed in Chapter 8 is used to dither the display onto the Epson printer.

Picture Files   Two types of picture files are supported. The first is a simple dump of the display to disk (PUT DISPLAY) and simple retrieval (GET DISPLAY). The PUT DATABASE and GET DATABASE commands put and get the vector database, which contains the specifications for each element in your drawing. You can change the contents of the vector database if you implement functions to do so. This will allow you to move, rotate, and scale elements as well as to put and get them.

Because GRAPHIQ is available to you in source code, you can expand the above functions. If there is something you do not understand in this text, you can see the details in GRAPHIQ's source code. GRAPHIQ is a work in progress.

Functions Not Included

GRAPHIQ does not include many of the functions that are necessary in a complete system. As presented in this book, GRAPHIQ gives you a framework that serves as a starting point for more powerful, specialized software. The user interface is the primary concern. Given this framework, you can improvise your own extended capabilities.

Copying   You will need to install a function to copy one part of a drawing to another. You also need a function to append drawings from files. Chapter 6 will help you add copying features.

Change Scale   You should provide the ability to change the scale of objects in the drawing, as well as to rotate and translate them.

Delete Object You will need to implement a function to locate and delete objects. This is a major editing feature that takes a great deal of time to implement.

Complex Fills Only rectangular fills are included in GRAPHIQ. You could add complex fill capabilities as described in Chapter 4.

Chorded Circles and Arcs The circle function implemented in GRAPHIQ is a simple Bresenham's circle generator. You could substitute the circle generator shown in Chapter 4. Aside from being able to draw arcs, this generator can also rotate and change the scale of circles. Ellipses and elliptical arcs are also possible.

Three-Dimensional Database You could expand the database to be three-dimensional. This is not an easy task, but the system is designed to make it easier than you might imagine. Everything you need to add three-dimensional capability is available in this book. See Chapters 4 and 5 for the necessary transformations.

Automatic Drawing Depending on your specific interest, you may wish to implement functions that automatically draw grids, charts, or dimension lines. The needs of a chemist will differ from those of an architect, for example. Carefully choose a selection of automatic drawing features appropriate to the needs of anticipated users.

Plotting Although the plotter driver is described in Chapter 8, it is not implemented in GRAPHIQ. You can easily include it, however. When you do so, you can add commands appropriate to your plotter's language.

PROGRAM STARTUP
AND TERMINATION

When you run a graphics program, a lot needs to be done by the software before the crosshairs appear on the display. Depending on the specific design of your system, various functions will require initialization. The initialization parameters can be entirely self-contained, or many of them can come from an initialization file.

Included Files

The necessary header files included in GRAPHIQ.C consist of the standard Microsoft C headers, which are located in another directory. Figure 12-1 shows the entire collection. The GRAPHIQ headers are all contained in the local directory. Some of these are GRAPHIQ.H, which contains definitions and structure

```
#include <stdio.h>
#include <dos.h>
#include <conio.h>
#include <malloc.h>
#include <process.h>
#include <string.h>
#include <memory.h>
#include <math.h>
#include "graphiq.h"
#include "file.h"
#include "screen.h"
#include "locator.h"
#include "declares.h"
#include "font.h"
```

FIGURE 12-1. Headers included in GRAPHIQ source

tags; FILE.H, which contains the file structure declaration and structure tag; and SCREEN.H, which contains the colors available for use with the EGA. In addition, LOCATOR.H contains the various locator matrixes, DECLARES.H contains most global declarations, and FONT.H (900 lines) contains the declaration of the system's stroke-font character set.

Definitions

Mnemonics for numbers used throughout the system can be found in Function 12-1, GRAPHIQ.H. The usual definitions are provided for TRUE and FALSE. The extended keystrokes for the arrow keys and other special keys are shown. If a key is extended, it will have a value in excess of 0x100 upon return from retkey( ).

System Resolution   The drawing surface is an 8 1/2- by 11-inch sheet of paper. Drawing units are in millimeters. NDCXMAX and NDCYMAX contain the maximum measurements, in millimeters, of a sheet of standard typing paper. You could, of course, use other values for larger paper sizes. Function 12-2, DECLARES.H, declares most global variables used in GRAPHIQ. The origin for the drawing unit system is in the lower-hand left corner, but you can move it by changing the values of xlate—x and xlate—y, declared in Function 12-2. The values XMETRIC and YMETRIC are used to convert from millimeters to display units.

Display Resolution   The values XMAX and YMAX do not refer to millimeters but to display units. The EGA in mode 14 has a resolution of 640 by 200 display units. The origin for the display system is in the upper left-hand corner; thus, the origins of the drawing system and the display system are different.

■ FUNCTION 12-1

GRAPHIQ.H

```
/* GRAPHIQ.H is the main header for GRAPHIQ.C */

#define TRUE -1
#define FALSE 0
#define ON TRUE
#define OFF FALSE
#define ESC 0x1b
#define HOME 0x147
#define UP 0x148
#define DOWN 0x150
#define LEFT 0x14B
#define RIGHT 0x14D
#define NDCXMAX 2690.0    /* conforms to 8-1/2 by 11 inch paper */
#define NDCYMAX 2060.0
#define NDCXMIN 0
#define NDCYMIN 0
#define CENTERX (NDCXMAX / 2.0)
#define CENTERY (NDCYMAX / 2.0)
#define WIDTH 80L
#define XMAX 639
#define YMAX 199
#define XMIN 0
#define YMIN 0
#define CROSS 0
#define OUTLINE 1
#define LOCOFF 3
#define TENTHMM 1
#define MILLIMETER 10
#define FIVEMM 50
#define TENMM 100
#define TWENTYMM 200
#define F1 0x13B
#define F2 0x13C
#define F3 0x13D
#define F4 0x13E
#define F5 0x13F
#define F6 0x140
#define F7 0x141
#define F8 0x142
#define F9 0x143
#define F10 0x144
#define COMMAND TRUE
#define NOCOMMAND FALSE
#define XMETRIC 0.237546468
#define YMETRIC 0.096601942
#define PI 3.141592654
#define XORIT 0x80
#define NORMIT 0
#define CR 0x0D
#define LF 0x0A
```

■ FUNCTION 12-1 (continued)

GRAPHIQ.H

```
#define BS 0x8
#define NEWLINE LF
#define NULLCHAR '\0'
#define SOLID 0xFFFF
#define DOTTED 0x8888
#define DASHED 0xF0F0
#define DASHDOT 0xFAFA
#define DASHDOTDOT 0xEAEA
#define ENTER 0x0D
#define RETURN ENTER
#define QUIT 0x11
#define MAIN_MNU 0
#define FILE_MNU 1

/* utilities for access to EGA controller */

#define ENABLE 0x0F
#define INDEXREG 0x3CE
#define VALREG 0x3CF
#define OUTINDEX(index, val)   {outp(INDEXREG, index);\
                                outp(VALREG, val);}
#define EGABASE 0xA0000000L

#define SERPORT1 0x00000400L /* COM1 interrupt address */
#define SERPORT2 0x00000402L /* COM2 interrupt address */
#define SERVEC1 12   /* COM1 interrupt request (IRQ4)   */
#define SERVEC2 11   /* COM2 interrupt request (IRQ3)   */

struct ISRVEC
     {
     unsigned vecl;
     unsigned vech;
     unsigned type;
     };

/* miscellaneous macros */
#define SQ(x) ((x) * (x))

union

     {
     struct
          {
          unsigned char lo : 4;
          unsigned char hi : 4;
          } hilo;
     struct
          {
          unsigned char byte;
          } whole;
     } colr;
```

■ FUNCTION 12-2

DECLARES.H

```c
/* DECLARES.H contains declarations for GRAPHIQ.C */

int height = 30, width = 25, slant = 0, color = 0x7;
int in_menu = FALSE;
double x, y, radius;
double lastx, lasty;
double tempx, tempy;
double oldx, oldy;
double corner_x, corner_y;
double x_center, y_center;
double x_perim, y_perim;
double inc = 200.0;
unsigned pointer;
FILE *cmd_stream;
int reading_cmd;
int line_style = 1;
unsigned pattern = SOLID;
int oldmode;
int main_select = 1;
int file_select = 1;
char command[81];
char *colarray;
char mess[25][30];
unsigned allowed, dwg_seg;
double xlate_x, xlate_y;
double rot_center_x, rot_center_y;
double xform_angle, scale_factor = 1.0;
double xlate_xb, xlate_yb;
double rot_center_xb, rot_center_yb;
double xform_angleb, scale_factorb;
int reverse = FALSE;
unsigned long *matrix;

char *put_msg[] = {"Filename to PUT screen: _", ""};
char *get_msg[] = {"Filename to GET screen: _", ""};
char *put_data_msg[] = {"Filename to PUT database: _", ""};
char *get_data_msg[] = {"Filename to GET database: _", ""}; .
char *cmd_msg[] = {"Command: _", ""};
char *file_msg[] = {"Command Filename: _", ""};
char *file_error[] = {"Can't open file. Press a key...", ""};
char *exists_msg[]
  = {"File by that name exists, or access error. \
        Enter Y to replace...",""};

char *replace_msg[]
  = {"Do you wish to replace work in progress? \
        Enter Y to replace...",""};
```

■ FUNCTION 12-2 (continued)

DECLARES.H

```
char *quit_msg[] = {"ENTER Y or Yes if you wish to quit: _", ""};
char *height_msg[] = {"ENTER Height: _", ""};
char *width_msg[] = {"ENTER Width: _", ""};
char *slant_msg[] = {"ENTER Slant: _", ""};
char *text_msg[] = {"ENTER Text: _", ""};
char *rot_msg[] = {"ENTER Rotation Angle: _", ""};
char *scale_msg[] = {"ENTER Scale Factor: _", ""};
char *print_msg[] = {"Reverse works for photos. \
Reverse? (y/n) _", ""};
char *too_big[] = {"Too many elements. Save drawing. \
Press a key...",""};
char *circl_msg[] = {"Locate center of circle, press ENTER.",""};
char *circ2_msg[] = {"Locate perimeter of circle, \
press ENTER.",""};
char *box1_msg[] = {"Locate corner of box, press ENTER.",""};
char *box2_msg[] = {"Locate other corner, press ENTER.",""};
char *welcome[] = {
"IMMMMMMMMMMMMMMMMMMMMMM;",
": Welcome   to  GRAPHIQ. :",
": Press   function  keys :",
": or ENTER DY command. :",
":                        :",
": F1    0.1mm increment   :",
": F2    1.0mm             :",
": F3    5.0mm             :",
": F4   10.0mm             :",
": F5   20.0mm             :",
": F6   Help               :",
": F7   Line Style         :",
": F8   Change Color       :",
": F9   Move (no line)     :",
": F10  Draw Line          :",
"HMMMMMMMMMMMMMMMMMMMMMM<",
""};

char *help[] = {
"IMMMMMMMMMMMMMMMMMMMMMMMMMMMMMMMMMMMMMMMMMMMMMMMMMMMMMMMMMMMMMMMM\
MMMM;",
": HELP (F6)                                                   \
    :",
":                                                             \
    :",
": Press Function Keys      Press ENTER DY to select a funct\
ion.:",
":                          Press Esc to enter a command.   \
    :",
```

■ **FUNCTION 12-2** (continued)

DECLARES.H

```
":  F1   0.1mm increment      Hold Ctrl down, hit Q to quit, or\
    :",
":  F2   1.0mm                     enter the QUIT command.      \
    :",
":  F3   5.0mm                                                  \
    :",
":  F4  10.0mm                                                  \
    :",
":  F5  20.0mm                                                  \
    :",
":  F6  Help                                                    \
    :",
":  F7  Line Style                                              \
    :",
":  F8  Change Color                                            \
    :",
":  F9  Move (no line)                                          \
    :",
":  F10 Draw Line             Press a key to leave this menu...\
    :",
"HMMMMMMMMMMMMMMMMMMMMMMMMMMMMMMMMMMMMMMMMMMMMMMMMMMMMMMMMMMMMMM\
MMMM<",
""};

char *main_mnu[] = {
"IMMMMMMMMMMMMMMMMM;",
":  HELP   (F6)       :",
":  GRID              :",
":  SNAP ON/OFF       :",
":  LOCATOR ON/OFF  :",
":  STYLE  (F7)       :",
":  COLOR  (F8)       :",
":  LOCATE (F9)       :",
":  LINE   (F10)      :",
":  BOX               :",
":  FILL              :",
":  CIRCLE            :",
":  TEXT              :",
":  ROTATION Angle  :",
":  ROTATION Origin:",
":  OFFSET +X, +Y   :",
":  SCALE             :",
":  PLAYBACK          :",
":  PRINT             :",
":  PICTURE FILES   :",
":  COMMAND FILE    :",
":  CLEAR DISPLAY   :",
```

■ **FUNCTION 12-2** (continued)

DECLARES.H

```
":  QUIT GRAPHIQ    :",
":  EXIT THIS MENU :",
"HMMMMMMMMMMMMMMMMM<",
""};


char *file_mnu[] = {
"IMMMMMMMMMMMMMMMM;",
":  PUT DISPLAY     :",
":  GET DISPLAY     :",
":  PUT DATABASE    :",
":  GET DATABASE    :",
"HMMMMMMMMMMMMMMMMM<",
""};


struct ELEMENT element;
struct SREGS segs;
union REGS regs;


struct ISRVEC isrvec;

unsigned char serisr(), readbuf(), get_dig();
unsigned buffchr();

unsigned far *outbase = (unsigned far *)SERPORT1;
unsigned char baudlo, baudhi, bits;
unsigned char serbuff[20];
int digitizer = FALSE;
int snap = FALSE;
```

Line-Style Masks   Values for SOLID, DOTTED, DASHED, and others hold bit masks for use in drawing lines of different styles. These masks are passed to the line-drawing functions to produce the various line styles.

EGA Controller Mnemonics and Macro   Utilities for direct access to the EGA controller are contained in the GRAPHIQ.H header. The OUTINDEX( ) macro is implemented as a macro to speed up access to the display controller.

Serial Port Mnemonics   Mnemonics for the two serial ports that support serial interrupts are included. You can switch these values to enable COM2 if you wish, or you can make the serial service work for both ports. As it stands, GRAPHIQ uses COM1 to receive data from a mouse or digitizer.

After the serial interface mnemonics, the ISRVEC tag is declared as a structure. The ISRVEC structure retains the original settings of the interrupt vector so that they can be restored when you exit GRAPHIQ and return to DOS.

Declarations

GRAPHIQ has no external initialization. If a serial port for COM1 is installed and no device is connected to COM1, GRAPHIQ will install the interrupt service routine and wait for input that will never be received. It will not interfere with the use of the arrow keys on the numeric keypad.

Declaration Header   To avoid taking up space in GRAPHIQ.C (the main GRAPHIQ module), a separate header file called Function 12-2 has been created. This file is kept in the directory in which you are working. If you wish to use an included file from the default directory only and nowhere else, you must surround the file specifications with double quotes, as follows:

```
#include "declares.h"
```

If you were to put Function 12-2 in another directory that was accessible from a path, however, you would refer to it as follows:

```
#include <declares.h>
```

In this case Function 12-2 would not be found if it were in the local directory, only if it were in another directory that the compiler knew about.

Function 12-2 contains explicitly initialized declarations for most of the global variables used in GRAPHIQ. Note that if a variable is not initialized when it is declared outside of main( ), it is automatically initialized to 0. In some cases explicit initializations are used even though they might not be necessary. This is done to make the initial state of the variable clear and will not interfere with the initialization.

Function 12-2 contains the complete initialization header. The following are the first variables to be initialized:

```
int height = 30, width = 25, slant = 0, color = 0x7;
```

Height, width, and slant pertain to attributes of stroke-font text characters. The color variable is the main variable controlling color in the system. It is initialized to be white (7). You can change these initializations if you wish to change the initial appearance of characters or the default color.

The in—menu variable indicates whether or not the user is in a menu rather than in drawing mode. If in—menu is TRUE, the locator generates *up* and *down* characters, rather than changed x and y values, as the stylus is moved up or down on the tablet.

The x, y, and radius variables contain the current x and y values reported by the locator and the current radius that would be used to draw circles or arcs.

The lastx and lasty variables contain the last x and y values stored for use as the beginning point of a future line or other element. To use lastx and lasty you can invoke the LOCATE command. These coordinates are stored for later use, but nothing is drawn.

The Database Pointer   The system pointer is an unsigned integer, allowing storage of up to 65,535 drawing elements in the database. Because the database is stored in RAM, you will not be able to store that many elements at one time. Memory allocated for drawings is 128K, allowing approximately 2000 elements of 64 bytes each. If you have more system RAM, you may allocate more paragraphs of memory, using the ALLOCATE.C function.

Grid Increment   The system increment for construction of grids and movement using the numeric keypad, a variable named inc, is initialized to 200 units. System units are in tenths of a millimeter. Thus, each press of an arrow key on the numeric keypad will move the locator 20 millimeters in system units. This will not, of course, appear as exactly 20 millimeters on the display, but it will be so on the plotter.

Memory is initialized to store the current cursor row in each available menu (main__select, file__select). A command string is initialized and given the name command. It will later hold commands received from the display( ) function.

System State Variables   The system state variables xlate__x, xlate__y, rot__center__x, rot__center__y, xform__angle, and scale__factor are initialized. Following them is a set of backups that retain the system state when it needs to be changed temporarily. All the state variables are initialized to 0 except for the scale factor. If this is set to 0, it will have the effect of multiplying every entity by 0, with the result that only a point at the system origin will be drawn.

After the state variables are initialized, all of the system menus are declared. All text for prompts and menus must be contained here and displayed using write—array().

Finally, the ELEMENT structure tag is assigned to a pointer for use as a global reference to the database. The ELEMENT structure is contained in FILE.H. The SREGS and REGS structures are contained in DOS.H, supplied by Microsoft.

In order to return the desired types, serisr( ), readbuf( ), get—dig( ), and buffchr( ) must be declared. These functions can be found in Chapter 11. They control the serial interrupt service.

The main( ) Function

When GRAPHIQ begins execution starting with the main( ) call, it first uses a DOS interrupt to allocate 8192 **paragraphs** (0x2000) of system memory. A paragraph is 16 bytes. This means that a total of 131,072 (0x20000) bytes, or exactly 128K of RAM, is allocated for use as a storage buffer. If this amount is not available, the system exits back to DOS with an error message. You could, by the way, allocate as much as possible and set a limit to the maximum value of the database pointer instead of requiring 128K. It's just more complicated to do.

After the database buffer has been allocated, segread( ), a standard Microsoft C library function, is used to find out which segments are in use by the program. These values may be used later. The data segment (DS) is constant in a Medium model C program. The Medium model is used to compile GRAPHIQ.

Preserving the EGA Mode The EGA mode in effect upon entry to GRAPHIQ is stored in oldmode, and the new mode (14) is set. You can easily make GRAPHIQ work in modes 15 or 16 if you have full memory on your EGA. Working with a CGA is more difficult, but working with mode 6 on the EGA is quite easy. Managing modes other than 14 is left to you.

The center of the display is derived next. The system is initialized so that if a line is drawn it will extend from the system origin, unless its starting point is located first. To draw a line, you must first locate its starting point using the LOCATE command. Subsequent lines will use the previous line's ending point as a starting point.

Enabling the Digitizer Next, the serial interrupt service is installed. If no COM1 serial card is installed, the global variable named digitizer will be set to 0, disabling the digitizer or mouse.

After the digitizer (if any) is enabled, the locator is displayed. It will be XORed repeatedly to remove and then redisplay it. If it is ever turned off without being turned on again, its appearance and disappearance order will be reversed. The functions in GRAPHIQ have been carefully orchestrated to prevent this from happening.

Just before the executive loop, a friendly welcoming message appears. If the user presses any key or presses the mouse or digitizer button, the welcome menu will disappear. If the locator button or ENTER key is pressed, the system main menu will appear.

The Executive Loop

The executive loop in GRAPHIQ contains the primary keyboard and digitizer access function. Depending on the strings pointed to by the pointer named command, all the system functions are executed from the executive loop.

If the QUIT command is received, the executive loop terminates. Figure 12-2 shows the sequence of events when this occurs. First, the program frees the memory allocated by allocate( ) at the beginning of the program. It does this by passing its segment pointer to frealloc( ). The screen is then cleared. A call is made to modeset( ) to restore the EGA mode that prevailed upon entry. The serial interrupt service is uninstalled by a call to uninstal( ). A call to restport( ) restores the baud rate, parity, data bits, and stop bits of the original serial port setting. Finally, a legal exit is made with the termination variable set to 0. From beginning to end, GRAPHIQ sets up a complex series of parameters and exits without leaving a trace of its having run.

Putting the Tools Away   One of the reasons for producing a prototypical piece of software for a book such as this is that it can be used to illustrate a proper way of initializing and terminating the procedure. Few books emphasize this extremely important aspect of software development. The way in which functions are put together is more important than the functions themselves.

```
frealloc(dwg_seg);

clearscr();

modeset(oldmode);

uninstal(SERPORT1);

restport(); /* restore port settings */

exit(0);
```

FIGURE 12-2.   Program termination sequence

FILES FOR DRAWINGS AND COMMANDS

Within the executive loop, you will find maintenance functions that preserve the contents of the display buffer as well as the contents of the database. Command files can be read in order to set up conditions for a drawing as well as to duplicate sets of instructions.

The Display and Database Files

The contents of the display buffer can be dumped into and retrieved from a file. Figure 12-3 shows a fragment of code taken from the executive loop. It shows how the FILES command leads to four subcommands that enable you to handle the display and database files.

Putting the Display   To put the display to disk, you execute the PUT DISPLAY command. To dump the display to memory, all you need is a filename and the putega( ) function. This function puts the EGA display buffer into a file. The process takes longer than it should, however. Can you make it run faster?

Getting the Display   To get the display from disk, you execute the GET DISPLAY command. To retrieve the display buffer from a file to which it has been put, you use the getega( ) function with the desired filename. The putega( ) and getega( ) functions were first introduced in Chapter 3.

```
if (!strcmp(command, "FILES"))
    {
    file_mess(0, 0, color, inchar);

    if (!strcmp(command, "PUT SCREEN"))
        {
        message(put_msg, 24, 0, RED, ESC);
        if (strlen(command))
            {
            if (putega(command))
                message(file_error, 24, 0,
                            RED, ESC);
            }
        }

    if (!strcmp(command, "GET SCREEN"))
        {
        message(get_msg, 24, 0, RED, ESC);
        if (strlen(command))
            {
            if (getega(command))
                message(file_error, 24, 0,
                                RED, ESC);
            }
        }

    if (!strcmp(command, "PUT DATABASE"))
        {
        message(put_data_msg, 24, 0, RED, ESC);
        if (strlen(command))
            {
            if (putdata(command))
                message(file_error, 24, 0,
                                RED, ESC);
            }
        }

    if (!strcmp(command, "GET DATABASE"))
        {
        message(get_data_msg, 24, 0, RED, ESC);

        if (strlen(command))
            {
            if (getdata(command))
            message(file_error, 24, 0,
                                RED, ESC);
            }
        }
    }
```

FIGURE 12-3.   File access mechanism

■ FUNCTION 12-3

PUTDATA.C

```
/* PUTDATA.C puts the GRAPHIQ database to disk.
*/

putdata(filename)
char *filename;
{
FILE *putstream;
unsigned i;

if ((putstream = fopen(filename, "r+b")) == NULL)
    {
    message(exists_msg, 24, 0, GREEN, ESC);
    if (!strchr(command, 'y') && !strchr(command, 'Y'))
        return(FALSE);
    if ((putstream = fopen(filename, "wb")) == NULL)
        return(TRUE);
    }

for (i = 0; i < pointer; ++i)
    {
    retrieve(i);
    fwrite(&element, sizeof(char), sizeof(element),
                putstream);
    }

fclose(putstream);

return(FALSE);
}
```

Putting the Database   To put the vector database (declared by the ELEMENT structure tag) to a file, you use the PUT DATABASE command, which is intercepted as shown in Figure 12-3. Function 12-3, PUTDATA.C, contains the code necessary to take 64-byte records indirectly referenced by the variable named pointer and store them in a file.

■ FUNCTION 12-4

GETDATA.C

```
/* GETDATA.C gets the GRAPHIQ database from a file.
*/

getdata(filename)
char *filename;
{
FILE *getstream;
unsigned i;

if ((getstream = fopen(filename, "rb")) == NULL)
        return(TRUE);

message(replace_msg, 24, 0, RED, ESC);

if (!strchr(command, 'y') && !strchr(command, 'Y'))
    return(FALSE);

pointer = 0;
while (fread(&element, sizeof(char), sizeof(element), getstream))
    store(pointer++);

fclose(getstream);

return(FALSE);
}
```

Getting the Database   The command used to get the database from disk is GET DATABASE. To get the vector database from a file, you must use Function 12-4, GETDATA.C. Records at record numbers 0 through pointer are read into the database until the end of the file is encountered. The new pointer value is preserved as the system data pointer.

■ FUNCTION 12-5

RETRIEVE.C

```
/* RETRIEVE.C retrieves a drawing element from
** allocated buffer. */

#include <dos.h>
#include "file.h"

extern struct ELEMENT element;
extern struct SREGS segs;
extern union REGS regs;

retrieve(record)
unsigned record;
{
int srcseg, srcoff, destseg, destoff;
extern unsigned dwg_seg;

srcseg = dwg_seg + ((unsigned)sizeof(element) >> 4) * record;
srcoff = 0;
destseg = segs.ds;
destoff = (int)&element;

movedata(srcseg, srcoff, destseg, destoff,
    (unsigned)sizeof(element));
}
```

Function 12-3 uses Function 12-5, RETRIEVE.C, and Function 12-4 uses Function 12-6, STORE.C, to place records incrementally in the GRAPHIQ database external buffer. This buffer will hold up to about 2000 records in 128K of RAM. The retrieve( ) and store( ) functions access the external segment reserved for GRAPHIQ's database.

■ FUNCTION 12-6

STORE.C

```
/* STORE.C stores a record in the database in
** allocated memory.
*/

#include <dos.h>
#include "file.h"

extern struct ELEMENT element;
extern struct SREGS segs;
extern union REGS regs;

extern unsigned pointer;
extern unsigned dwg_seg;


store()
{
int srcseg, srcoff, destseg, destoff;

if (pointer > 2048)
    {
    message(too_big, 24, 0, RED, ESC);
    return;
    }

srcseg = segs.ds;
srcoff = (int)&element;
destseg = dwg_seg + ((unsigned)sizeof(element) >> 4) * pointer++;
destoff = 0;

movedata(srcseg, srcoff, destseg, destoff,
        (unsigned)sizeof(element));
}
```

Command Files

Command files are necessary to allow the construction of extended commands, otherwise known (somewhat inaccurately) as macros. The command file contains commands you could normally enter from the keyboard. When the command file is read, the software reads and executes commands from the file instead of from the keyboard.

The command language for GRAPHIQ is not complete. The skeleton for a full implementation is in place, however, and you could extend the command language dramatically. Because the code is written for the Medium memory model, you are essentially unlimited with regard to code space. The entire memory of your machine can be populated by code, with the exception of reserved memory and 128K for the database buffer. This leaves lots of room if you have 512K of RAM.

Figure 12-4 shows a fragment of code showing how the system responds to the COMMAND FILE command. The command file must be there or an error message will be generated. If it is there, the reading—cmd flag is set. Input from the keyboard and mouse or digitizer will now be ignored, and the

```
if (!strcmp(command, "COMMAND FILE"))
    {
    message(file_msg, 24, 0, RED, ESC);
    if (strlen(command))
        {
        if ((cmd_stream = fopen(command,"rt"))
                        == NULL)
            message(file_error, 24, 0, RED, ESC);
        reading_cmd = TRUE;
        }
    }
```

FIGURE 12-4. Access to a command file

contents of the command file will be processed by the system. The following code fragment is found in the message( ) function:

```
if (reading_cmd)
    if (fread(command, 80, cmd_stream) == 0)
        {
        fclose(cmd_stream);
        reading_cmd = FALSE;
        }
    else command[strlen(command)-1] = NULLCHAR;
```

This fragment, if reading__cmd is TRUE, reads each command from the command file until a new-line terminator character is encountered in a command. At the end of the file, the file is closed and reading__cmd is set to FALSE. If a command is received, a null character is substituted for the returned new-line character.

13

Graphics Documentation

There are as many schools of thought on the subject of documentation as there are people who use software. Everyone has his or her likes and dislikes. For this reason you should not expect everyone to like everything about your documentation. You can describe a function one way and someone will suggest that you change it. As soon as you change it, someone will suggest that it be described the way you had it previously.

Many users do not bother to read documentation, and so no matter how well it is written it will have no effect on them. Many problems are caused by users who are provided with the best of documentation but are not motivated to read it before trying to use the software. After all, you are providing software to be used on the marvelous, omniscient, powerful computer, yet the user must use printed material, the invention of an earlier age, to gain access to this marvel.

"If computers are so good," a user might say, "why do I need to read a manual to use one?" If you have used computers regularly for many years, you can skip over much of the documentation and get started quickly. There is a wide range of experience levels among computer users, however. Some need a lot of hand-holding, others do not need any. The trick is to provide enough information of the right kind to serve the needs of everyone.

It is not possible, given the scope of this book, to go into the details of the art of documentation. It would be remiss, however, not to bring to your attention the importance of carefully and completely describing your software to users. Documentation is often the weakest part of a software offering.

GRAPHICS TASK DIFFERENTIATION

Task differentiation is a concept that comes from the realm of **ergonomics.** Ergonomics is a field of study that crosses boundaries between art, architecture, social science, psychology, and industrial design. It is one of our contemporary buzzwords. Ergonomics is concerned with the way in which objects in the environment are fitted to human use. Task differentiation relates to the ways in which objects enhance or detract from the user's ability to discriminate between a variety of options in solving problems. A task is related to problem solving and is directed toward achieving a goal.

Allocating Tasks

Task differentiation helps you discover the best way to allocate tasks a user must perform. For example, if a mouse and the keyboard are both used, avoid making it necessary for the user to type commands while using the mouse because the two tasks require separate hand positions.

Another example of task differentiation occurs when a user is required to read a manual while also operating a computer. The book and the computer are located in two separate places and are each used differently. If the user constantly needs to switch between reading the book and operating the computer, the user's body must be physically repositioned. Repeated body position changes produce a small amount of stress. Although the amount of stress may be acceptable, under certain circumstances it may not be. Differentiating tasks helps you to analyze what your software is asking a user to do and in what sequence.

Friendly Versus Unfriendly

If the user is constantly frustrated in understanding which tasks he or she must perform and the performance of those tasks produces unacceptable stress, the software will be perceived as unfriendly. If, however, the user can clearly differentiate between tasks, and the performance of those tasks in combination produces minimal stress, the software will be perceived as friendly.

The Task of Using Documentation

In using documentation a person needs to shift attention from what is happening in a dynamic, running system to static printed material. This constant switching back and forth produces stress, which, in turn, leads to fatigue. People tend to avoid stress whenever possible, and this is one explanation for the fact that large numbers of people do not read documentation.

On-Screen Help   Ideally, the program and documentation could be seen together. One way to accomplish this is for your software to have as many on-screen instructions as possible. This would make it less necessary for the user to turn away from the display and look something up in the manual. Yet it is not recommended that you abandon the manual altogether. A disadvantage of on-screen documentation is that the user must often interrupt the program to see it. Interrupting a task to see a help screen can be very frustrating. On-screen help and written documentation are thus not mutually exclusive. You can and should use both.

Levels of Help   It is common practice to provide the user with several levels of help, from novice to expert, to reduce the distraction and reduction of efficiency that the extra overhead of menus and instruction screens can cause. Create an appropriate system for your program to implement various levels of on-screen help. It is safe to say that on-screen instructions are mandatory for today's commercial applications.

Printed Documentation

Figure 13-1 summarizes the major sections that should be included in a typical manual. This is not the only way to do it, but most of the necessary ingredients are there. If you provide nothing else, always give printed installation instructions. Until the user can make the system run on a computer, even the most extensive on-screen help will not be of any use.

Installation   Printed documentation is most useful for installation and off-line training. Before you install the software, you must know what switches to set, what wires to solder, how much memory you need, and much more. These items should be available in the front of your manual, in a separate section.

Command Summary   After the all-important installation instructions, the documentation should include a command summary on a single card or sheet. This command summary can consist of a template that attaches to the keyboard, a set of key caps with function designations on them, or any of a number of

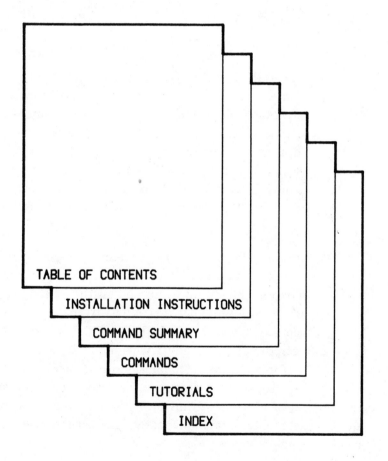

FIGURE 13-1.   *The parts of a typical software manual*

other clever devices that aid the user in quickly identifying the keys to press to perform program functions.

Command Descriptions After the command summary, a complete, page-by-page description of all possible options should be made available. Each keyword in a command language, for example, could be described on its own page. Design this section so that the keyword always occupies the same part of the page and is in a large, bold type font to make recognition easy.

Tutorial Finally, a tutorial section should be included, with a written narrative that describes more than one typical session with the system. The tutorial is extremely important, particularly for inexperienced users, because it can show them a great deal about how functions work together to solve problems. Isolated functions may be powerful, but unless you know how they work together you will not know how to use them or be able to extend their use to solve different problems.

Index An index is of the utmost importance. Without an index the reader will be unable to cross-reference information or to locate important words and instructions. Your index should have entries for all words in the text that are meaningful in the context of your program. These words should lead the reader to descriptions that convey meaning.

In all forms of technical writing, an index is the part of the work that the reader uses most often. Technical manuals are not read like other forms of literature, from front to back. They contain information that the reader will use piecemeal for solving problems.

GRAPHICS PROGRAMS
FOR YOUR OWN USE

It is easy to neglect documentation for programs you write for your own use. You are usually too busy trying to solve problems using temporary batch files and kludges to spend any time on documentation.

Build Documentation
into the Program

You will find that building the documentation into your programs helps a great deal. Try to imagine that the utility you are writing is intended to be used by someone else far away, and that you must send it to this person. In a few weeks or months, when you remember that little utility you wrote, you will thank yourself for being so careful in using comments in your source code.

Provide Useful Comments   Your source code should contain numerous meaningful comments. Try to distill your comments down to what is absolutely essential. This practice will help you to think through problems as well as to visualize what is going on in the program.

Default Documentation

Why should you have to look at the source code just to remind yourself how to use a function? If you follow this simple formula, you will create self-documenting programs with a minimum of pain, and you will not need to look at the source to use them.

The following method will help you remember:

1. When you create a program, use the command line to pass information to main( ) using the argc and argv variables.

2. When argc is equal to 1, meaning that no arguments were supplied on the command line, make the documentation for the program appear by printing a series of lines of text. The utility then returns to the command line.

3. When you run the utility at a later date and you want to know what it does, simply enter the command name and view the "usage" rules you created for it.

If you use this approach consistently, it will become a powerful tool. With this method you should not need to keep paper documentation. Paper usually gets lost. The human brain varies in its ability to remember details, and you should not feel that you have to remember everything. Let the computer do it for you.

If the program can be run without arguments (like DIR), this trick will not work, but you can still use a variation of the technique by providing a flag (like -?) that will display the documentation.

GRAPHICS PROGRAMS FOR INDIVIDUAL CLIENTS

Your clients will need as much documentation as you can give them. Be careful to include an estimate of the time required for documentation in every job you do. You will find that documentation can be a real headache because it must be changed every time the program is changed. Errors in the documentation, even if the program runs well, will lead the client astray and frustrate your efforts.

Large Projects

If a project is large, consider collaborating with an experienced technical writer who is not involved in the coding. Few programmers, if any, are equipped with the nerves of steel required to write and debug code and then write and debug the documentation as well. If only one person is involved in writing both code and documentation, many errors will be missed. It is easy to develop blind spots for errors that can easily be seen by another person.

Small Projects

The small project requires a clear understanding between you and the client of how much documentation will be necessary. For simple jobs a program may simply be well documented from within, for example, provided with meaningful prompts.

Remember, you will never be able to supply enough documentation for users with whom you will not have frequent contact. You should emphasize to the client that no amount of written documentation will be adequate, explain why, and encourage the client to contact you or your associates whenever help is needed. A recognition of the importance of technical support should be written into your contract.

GRAPHICS PROGRAMS FOR THE MASS MARKET

Programs for the mass market are the most difficult and expensive to document. If you are lucky enough to find a venture capitalist who is brave enough to invest in your enterprise, be sure to allocate copious amounts of money for advertising, documentation, and software development.

Admittedly, it should be the other way around. The software, being the purpose behind all the commotion, should get the biggest share of the pie. But that is not how it works. Often you will benefit from documenting a function before you code it. The process of describing it to others tends to clarify the requirements of the function. Unfortunately, there is seldom enough time to work out the details before beginning to code. You are usually too busy to be organized.

Seeing What the Customer Sees

In commercial enterprises of all kinds, it is what the prospective customer *sees* that sells the product. Even if you have the best system in the world, if the consumer does not see it over and over again, you will not sell much. Your documentation is, in addition to (or in spite of) being a description of the functions in the program, a sales tool. People will judge your software by the appearance of your documentation.

Documentation Styles

Commercial software documentation seems to have progressed from a period of medieval incoherence, through a renaissance (when typesetting was invented), to a period of baroque exuberance, and beyond, to the excesses of rococo and mannerism, in but a few years. It is still almost the same software, but the manuals are getting larger, with every conceivable combination of color printing, icons, logos, and complicated tutorials. One popular package has beautifully designed icons whose meanings are completely obscure and an index with page number codes that are not explained anywhere. In most cases the manuals are excessive, and meaning gets lost in clutter. Avoid overdoing it.

An excellent example of thorough, clear documentation is the Microsoft C Compiler manual. The style in this manual is appropriate for the documentation of a programming language.

Perfect-bound Manuals

When personal computers first became popular, it was fashionable to provide commercial documentation in small three-ring binders. The binder would slide into a box. In theory, the binder allowed pages to be removed and inserted for each update. In reality, there were very few such updates. Each revision required the user to purchase a new program, generally at a discount.

The box was supposed to provide a storage place for floppy disks, but in reality the disks are usually taken out of the box, copied, and put in a safe place.

Binders permit the manual to be opened flat, but there are ways to bind books so that they open flat too. The problem with loose-leaf binders is that with heavy use the rings invariably tear through the paper. This results in lost pages, pages out of sequence, and an irregular edge. It is nearly impossible to thumb through a loose-leaf—bound manual. It is easy to argue for manuals that look and behave more like books. Manuals can and should be perfect-bound. The perfect-bound book is stitched or glued at its binding, much like the book you are reading now.

Eventually, each software package will be accompanied by — you may have guessed it — a book. Many successful descriptive techniques have been worked out in the designs of the billions of books that have been printed over the centuries. Books have been around for a long time, but it appears that the software industry in general has not discovered them yet. A good example of successful perfect-bound documentation is in Borland's documentation for SideKick and Turbo Pascal, among others.

GRAPHICS ICONS AND WORDS

An **icon** is a pictorial symbol that is used to identify an item on a menu. Icons are fashionable in graphics software. The user is expected to recognize what a function does by looking at its icon. If the icon is well designed, the picture will tell the story without a written description.

Unfortunately, it is difficult to make a tiny icon take on enough varied appearances to convey the needed unique meanings. As a result, too often the icon means something to the programmer but fails to mean the same thing to the user.

Visual and Verbal Meaning

Visual meaning and verbal meaning are completely different. In graphics programming you can, and should, use both. Some people remember images more easily than they remember words. For others, words are easier to deal with than images. Each of us is unique.

Identifying Icons with Words   A simple rule to remember is to make sure that each icon you use has one simple word to identify it. Use both the word *and* the icon wherever possible. Figure 13-2 shows a few obvious icons and the words that might describe what each one means. You will have no difficulty putting these words in an alphabetical index, but the icons alone would be impossible to categorize.

You don't need to abandon language when you construct a graphics system. It is too easy to take an either/or attitude, abandoning words or icons, when in reality both ways of conveying information are necessary.

What You See Is What You Get

One approach to graphics programming is popularly known as "what you see is what you get," abbreviated WYSIWYG. More accurately, the approach is a hybrid of WYSIWYG and command language. The idea behind WYSIWYG programming is to make the image on the computer display similar or identical to the image on hard copy. The ideal WYSIWYG display is the same size as hard copy. For example, a WYSIWYG system for standard typing paper would measure 8 1/2 by 11 inches. What you saw on the display surface would be identical to what you got on paper. WYSIWYG systems can be very hard to document because they are not run by a verbal command set. They rely on icons.

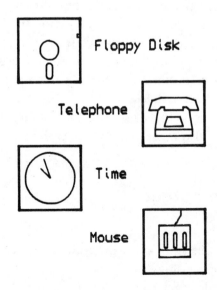

FIGURE 13-2.   Icons with their associated names

WYSIWYG Limitations There are limitations to the WYSIWYG approach. During the creation of a graphics display, you may want text and graphics to appear as they will on finished copy. The problem is that once your text is on the display surface it has been made into an array of dots that cannot easily be taken back off the display and used for another purpose. The only way to reuse your data is to generate it from a command file or buffer.

Growing Popularity of WYSIWYG WYSIWYG is very popular in desktop publishing using laser, ink-jet, and dot-matrix impact printers. The technique is part of the overall trend toward realism in graphics systems. The declining cost of television equipment seems to be bringing with it some very exciting prospects for computer display enhancement. You can expect improved color options, real-time animation, typeset-quality printing, and much more in the years to come.

Because GRAPHIQ is a hybrid WYSIWYG system, you can easily combine text with your icons. Figure 13-3 shows a typical icon combined with its name as it might appear on the menu of a typical graphics system. By combining the icon with its name, you have not lost anything. Instead, you have increased the likelihood that a user will understand what the icon means. You have also made your system easier to document.

Programmers Forget What It's Like

For the most part, programmers specialize in making magic happen using computers. This task is exhausting in itself. It is no wonder that most programmers cannot write documentation that really helps users. They are too close to the problem.

Placing Proper Emphasis   It is not easy to adopt the point of view of the user when you are working night and day to perfect your software. It is always easy to assume that something you understand will be easily understood by someone else. You need to communicate your ideas to the user, but it is hard to know where to place emphasis.

The budget for software documentation is seldom adequate. To do it right, the amount of time spent describing how to use the software could be greater than that required to code it. Yet much documentation is done as a kind of afterthought.

The reader of your documentation will thank you for your efforts in taking his or her point of view. If you are unable to obtain the assistance of an independent writer, it may be helpful

FIGURE 13-3.   An icon used with its name

to put some distance between yourself and the writing of documentation. Did you ever go back to an application you wrote several months ago, try to demonstrate it, and end up having to use your own documentation to find out how to execute a function? If so, you probably saw it from the reader's perspective, perhaps for the first time. Try to look at all of your documentation from this objective point of view.

14

Using the Compiler

The functions presented in this book make up a toolkit that you can use in many ways. This toolkit contains nearly everything you need to create graphics using the EGA. You can use it on a function-by-function basis without altering source code, or you can take the functions apart. GRAPHIQ, the prototypical graphics program in Appendix A, can be used like a wrecking yard for cars. You can take the transmission, the steering wheel, the tires, and the carburetor and use the parts in your own vehicle.

Certain assumptions have been made for the compiled form of the toolkit. If you have the source code and library in magnetic form, you must adhere to the assumptions made in compiling the modules because the library was created using those compiler assumptions. If you enter and compile the functions yourself, you can modify them to work with any memory model you choose.

THE MICROSOFT C COMPILER

The Microsoft C compiler was chosen because it is popular, advanced, very well debugged, and well documented. It is wise to use a compiler designed by the same company that created and maintains the operating system. One can only assume that such a compiler will better match the environment in which it is used. This may not always be of benefit, but you can at least be assured that changes to the operating system will be known by Microsoft before they are known by the outside world.

Early C compilers were poorly documented. Programmers had to rely on other programmers for explanations when a compiler did not perform as expected. Recently, however, C has become well enough entrenched and standardized to enable the development of comprehensive documentation. With current versions of C, you can trace a problem through to its origin nearly every time. C has gone from being a very obscure, sparsely documented language to being a language that, more than any other, enables you to know what is happening at all levels. The C language gives you hardware independence and control.

Because of the universality of C, you are not limited to the Microsoft compiler. You will be able to compile the functions in this book on most other C compilers. Certain features (such as the far and near keywords) must be changed for other C compilers, but there is usually a way to use alternative techniques.

The Compiler's Environment

In order to run your C compiler efficiently, you should take the time to set up your computer's environment to allow you to use the compiler from any subdirectory on your hard disk. If you are not using a hard disk, your task will be more difficult. It is strongly recommended that you use a hard disk if you plan to do more than a small amount of programming. The reason for this is that C programs usually consist of numerous modules rather than single source files. A **module** is a file that contains object code for functions that can be linked together to form an executable program. By breaking your programs down into modules, you can dramatically decrease the time required to recompile a program after you have made changes to it.

Setting the Environment   The following discussion describes the specific settings you must use to compile the functions in this book. You can read about the compiler environment in detail in your Microsoft C documentation.

The C functions in this book were consistently compiled using the environment presented here. To duplicate this environment, you must create an AUTOEXEC.BAT file that contains the following information:

```
echo off
path \;\sysfiles;\exe
set include=\include
set lib=\msc;\agic
set tmp=\temp
set icb=::I:::I:::I:
set icbset=g
graphics
modega 3
prompt $p$g
mode com1:9600,n,8,1,p
echo on
```

Setting the Path   The path setting determines which paths are used to gain access to executable files. The setting used here causes the operating system to look in the root directory first, and then in the SYSFILES directory, and finally in the EXE directory for any command you invoke. The path environmental setting is used by all of your software, not just the C compiler.

Setting Include   When you use the #include compiler directive, the compiler needs to know where to look for included files. If you put all compiler files that have the .H extension in a directory named \INCLUDE, the compiler will look for them there. Any filename that is enclosed in pointed brackets in the include command, as follows, will be taken from your \INCLUDE directory:

#include <stdio.h>

If you wish to include files from the current directory (the default directory) only, and to ignore all other directories, enclose the filename in quotation marks, as follows:

#include "myfile.h"

This technique will help you to discriminate between included files that belong to the C compiler or to *all* of your C programs and those that are to be used by a program within its own subdirectory only. It allows you to keep the program you are creating isolated in its own subdirectory, preventing confusion from arising if duplicate filenames are used.

Setting Lib   C programs can be compiled and linked using libraries as well as object files. The C compiler has its own libraries that it uses internally. It needs to know where they are. You tell the compiler where its libraries are by making a subdirectory for them and setting the lib environmental variable to indicate the name of that subdirectory. In this case the Microsoft C library is in a subdirectory called \MSC, and the *Advanced Graphics in C* library is in a subdirectory called \AGIC.

Setting Tmp While it is compiling, the C compiler creates temporary files as needed. It does this to keep track of the variables, constants, and code used in the program. Temporary files are marked by .TMP extensions. You should specify where the compiler is to create its .TMP files. In this case the temporary files are to be created in the root directory.

Electronic Photography Settings If you have an AT&T ICB and wish to use the programs contained in Appendix E, you will need to add two environmental settings. The first of these, icb, sets jumpers on the ICB using colons and capital I's in an ingenious way. Where a capital I is shown, it represents a jumper on jumper blocks documented in the ICB manual. The colons represent unjumpered positions on jumper blocks. You can change jumper settings artificially in this way through software without having to physically change the jumper positions on the boards. If you wish to know what the jumper settings are for, consult the ICB documentation.

The second setting for the ICB is the icbset environment variable. The setting shown enables genlock, which locks the synchronization of the ICB with the signal from a video source such as a television receiver.

Miscellaneous Environment Settings The remainder of the AUTOEXEC.BAT file shown performs a few miscellaneous tasks. If you have a system clock, you will probably want to run an enabler program, to make the clock known to DOS, as part of your AUTOEXEC file. Running GRAPHICS.COM, a graphics enabler program that comes with DOS, is a good idea because it enables you to print EGA mode 6 graphics by pressing SHIFT-PRTSC. You can also use the AUTOEXEC file to set an EGA mode with the MODEGA.EXE program described in

Chapter 2. The system prompt, as you may already know, can be changed to show more than the currently logged drive. For example, the sample AUTOEXEC file shown earlier sets the prompt to show the current path. Finally, it is wise to specify a standard setting for your serial port or ports. As discussed elsewhere in this book, serial ports should be initialized and used with one setting, if possible. If you need to redirect I/O to a serial port and it is not initialized, you will run into headaches.

If you use an environment similar to the one just described, you will be able to compile any source code in this book. You will also be able to use the C compiler from any path at any time, rather than from one directory only. If you keep the executable portion of the C compiler in your \EXE directory, it will always be accessible because the path setting reveals its location.

The Compiler Batch File

To simplify compilation, you should construct a separate batch file for each compiler assumption you use. Each batch file will invoke all the necessary compiler options. The compiler batch file used to construct the library for the toolkit is as follows:

```
echo off
:label
MSC %1, %1 /FPi /AM /Ze; > %1.err
if errorlevel 1 goto edit
goto end
:edit
e %1.c %1.err
goto label
:end
echo on
```

This batch file, called COMPILE.BAT, contains two parts. The first part is the compiler invocation itself. The second part determines what will happen when an error is encountered.

You can, of course, use the make command to compile a series of source files automatically, depending on the date they were last compiled. Read your Microsoft C documentation to find out how to do this.

Invoking the C Compiler   To compile your C source file, you must execute MSC.EXE. The MSC.EXE file should be in your \EXE directory. The following shows the actual invocation:

```
MSC %1, %1 /FPi /AM /Ze; > %1.err
```

The argument you pass to the batch file is substituted for the %1 reference in the two places shown. This means that the name of the C source file that is passed as an argument to the batch file will be used as the name of the source to be compiled as well as the name of the .OBJ file produced by the compiler.

The three sets of characters that begin with a slash (/) are option designations. You can select a variety of options with the Microsoft C compiler. Read about all of the possible options in the Microsoft C manual.

In-line code is generated for use with the 8087 or 80287 coprocessor. If a math coprocessor is not present, the /FPi option will substitute a library to emulate one. If the coprocessor is present, it will be used. Most graphics functions need all the help they can get to run fast and so a math coprocessor is highly recommended. If you do not have one, however, the code will still run if you use the /FPi option.

Using the Medium Memory Model   The /AM compiler option selects the Medium memory model. The Medium memory model was used for the graphics toolkit library because it allows the maximum code size while permitting less space but faster access to data. With the Medium model, the compiler assigns the code segment by module *file* rather than by using a constant code segment (s is done in the Small model). No code module can be greater than 64K, but you can have as many code segments as you have modules. This means that you can group functions together within files and thus expand the size of your program; you are limited only by available memory and over-head. Because your data always uses a near pointer, it can be accessed as rapidly as possible.

In graphics applications data often cannot be accessed fast enough, and so you must use near pointers wherever possible. One way to use memory in the Medium model is to maintain buffers in the constant data segment and swap blocks from memory allocated outside the fixed data segment. This enables you to use near pointers within C's fixed data segment while you are manipulating graphics, but you can also maintain as much data in RAM as you desire. Thus, you can have your cake and eat it, too.

Enabling the Far Keyword   To enable the far keyword used in many functions in this book, you must employ the /Ze compiler option. The far keyword is used in conjunction with the Medium model to obtain direct access to data anywhere in RAM, even though near pointers for data are maintained by C in this model. The far keyword is invaluable because it avoids the use of calls, with their attendant pushes and pops, which take much more time. The near and far keywords take the place of the peek( ) and poke( ) functions often found in standard C compiler libraries. After you become comfortable with the far keyword, you will not miss peeks and pokes.

Handling Errors   When the compiler encounters errors in your source code, it will set the DOS ERRORLEVEL variable to 1. Your COMPILE.BAT batch file will test the ERROR-LEVEL variable and branch according to its status. If its value is 1, the batch file will to :edit, where you can use your text editor to edit both the C source file and the .ERR file. When you have made your corrections, the batch file jumps to :label and restarts the compiler.

If no errors are encountered in your source file, the COM-PILE.BAT file jumps over the edit loop and exits back to DOS command level. At this point you have an object file with the same name as your source file, except that it has the .OBJ extension.

THE GRAPHICS TOOLKIT

The C functions shown in this book were developed with two goals in mind. They were designed to fit into an evolving proto-typical graphics program that grew during the several months required to write the book, and they were also intended to go into a toolkit for you to use in your own graphics programming.

The tools consist of functions to draw lines in various styles and colors, to draw boxes, to fill areas, to draw circles, and even to draw the various graphic elements in true perspective. An entire stroke-font character set is included, along with a function to draw characters at any size or angle. Functions to handle serial and parallel interfacing are also provided.

Functions in the Toolkit

This section contains a summary of the functions in the code library for this book (AGIC.LIB). It is included to give you an understanding of how the library is used in this book and how you can use it for your own purposes. See the index for page references to each function.

You can enter each of the functions in the library from this book and create a library. The library and source code are also available on magnetic media for your convenience. See the order form in the front of this book for details.

allocate( )   The allocate( ) function allocates the desired number of paragraphs of RAM; a paragraph consists of 16 bytes. It is used to allocate buffer space outside the C data segment.

boxx2( )   The boxx2( ) function draws a box given the real coordinates of two diagonal corners. It uses line style, color, and logic to place the lines that form the box.

brush—in( )   The brush—in( ) function copies a brush pattern from the display surface.

brush—out( )   The brush—out( ) function places a brush pattern on the display using a previously copied brush. See brush—in( ).

center( )   The center( ) function finds the center of a circle given three points on the perimeter of the circle.

circle( )   The circle( ) function draws a circle using Bresenham's circle algorithm. See also the symmetry( ) function.

circle—r( )   The circle—r( ) function draws a circle by rotating chords around the perimeter. This function contains the linec( ) and rotatec( ) functions.

clearscr( )   The clearscr( ) function clears the EGA display. This function is part of the CHARHDLR.C module. See also get—curs( ), get—str( ), read—char( ), set—curs( ), write—array( ), write—char( ), and write—str( ).

com—fill( )   The com—fill( ) function generates a complex area fill, allowing other than rectangular boundaries. This function contains the line—int( ) function.

com—str( )   The com—str( ) function fetches the desired number of bytes from a serial device. This function is written in assembler and can be called from C.

copybox( )   The copybox( ) function copies a desired area on the display surface from one location to another.

cross—it( )   The cross—it( ) function is part of the retkey( ) function and generates a cross locator as opposed to a box locator. See also line—it( ), lineloc( ), and locate( ).

disp—curs( )   The disp—curs( ) function is called from the mnu—curs( ) function to display a reverse-video cursor on a pop-up text menu.

display( )   The display( ) function displays entities from the graphics database, given pointers to desired records.

draw—text( )   The draw—text( ) function draws a string of stroke-font text characters using the playchar( ) function.

fillbox2( )   The fillbox2( ) function fills a rectangular area using the prevailing color and line style. It accepts real coordinate values and converts them to the current system transformation states.

frealloc( )   The frealloc( ) function frees paragraphs of memory allocated using the allocate( ) function.

get—curs( )   The get—curs( ) function gets the location of the text cursor. This function is part of the CHARHDLR.C module.

getdata( )   The getdata( ) function gets data from a given file and stores it in a drawing database in allocated RAM.

get—dig( )   The get—dig( ) function gets a data stream from the Kurta digitizer. It demonstrates how the serial port can be used to receive characters.

getega( )   The getega( ) function gets the contents of the EGA display buffer from a file on disk. The file is assumed to have been put there by putega( ).

get—row( )   The get—row( ) function is part of getega( ). It gets a row of graphics from a file.

get—ser( )   The get—ser( ) function gets the specified number of characters from a polled serial port. See also the SERISR. ASM module for an interrupt-driven approach.

get_str( )   The get_str( ) function gets a string of characters from the keyboard. It echoes the characters nondestructively as they are typed. To do this it XORs the characters onto the display. This function is part of the CHARHDLR.C module.

horline( )   The horline( ) function draws only horizontal lines. For such lines it is quicker than the linef( ) function because it involves less computation.

icbega( )   The icbega( ) function transfers a television picture from the AT&T ICB to the IBM EGA. In doing so it compresses a range of 32,768 colors down to a range of 27 colors.

inkey( )   The inkey( ) function receives a keystroke from the keyboard.

isr_inst( )   The isr_inst( ) function installs a serial interrupt-service routine (ISR) for the GRAPHIQ program. It shows everything you need to do to get a serial ISR to work.

linec( )   The linec( ) function is the part of the circle_r( ) function that draws the chords that make up a circle.

linef( )   The linef( ) function draws lines quickly. It is the general-purpose line-drawing function.

line_int( )   A part of com_fill( ), line_int( ) draws lines at intervals using lists of line endpoints. It draws the actual fill lines for complex fills.

line—it( )   A part of retkey( ), line—it( ) draws box locators under keyboard or digitizer control.

lineloc( )   Part of the retkey( ) function, lineloc( ) draws a line locator. It can be used to preview the location of a line to be drawn.

linep( )   The linep( ) function draws a line in space and projects it onto a projection plane. Each point in the line is drawn in perspective.

locate( )   The locate( ) function is part of retkey( ). It directs the locator, using a selection of locator types. It also monitors the function keys on the keyboard.

locator( )   The locator( ) function generates the locator pattern. A pointer to the desired locator pattern is passed to locator( ).

message( )   The message( ) function displays a pop-up menu and permits the selection of menu items with a reverse-video cursor. This function also allows commands to be processed from a command file as well as keyboard entry of commands.

mnu—curs( )   The mnu—curs( ) function displays a menu cursor in reverse video and enables you to move it. The cursor can be moved under either keyboard or digitizer control.

modeget( )   The modeget( ) function gets the current EGA mode.

modeset( )   The modeset( ) function sets the EGA mode.

playchar( )   Part of the TEXTOUT.C mode, playchar( ) displays a stroke-font character on the EGA display surface.

point( )   The point( ) function uses the EGA BIOS to set the color of a pixel. It is usually slower than the other pixel-drawing functions (such as pointf( ) and points( )) in this book.

pointf( )   The pointf( ) function draws a point quickly. If you need to draw multiple points, use the points( ) function instead.

pointp( )   The pointp( ) function draws a point in space and projects it onto a projection plane. The point is drawn in true perspective.

points( )   The points( ) function does not contain EGA initialization; it expects the EGA to be initialized before the function is used. Because it does not initialize and restore the EGA state each time the color of a pixel is changed, points( ) works faster than pointf( ). Be sure to initialize and restore the EGA state before and after each set of calls to points( ).

pop_dbl( )   Used in concert with push_dbl( ), pop_dbl( ) pops a double-precision number from a stack you specify. The pop_dbl( ) function is contained in the PUSHPOP.C module.

printrow( )   The printrow( ) function is a part of the PRINTSCR.C module. It prints a row of graphics on the Epson dot-matrix printer.

printscr( )   The printscr( ) function prints the EGA display on the Epson dot-matrix printer.

pr—line( )   The pr—line( ) function is part of the ICBEGA.C module. It displays a line of graphics (a graphics row) on the EGA.

projectr( )   The projectr( ) function projects points defined in three-dimensional space onto a projection plane.

push—dbl( )   Used in concert with pop—dbl( ), push—dbl( ) pushes a double-precision number onto a stack you specify. The push—dbl( ) function is contained in the PUSHPOP.C module.

putdata( )   You can use putdata( ) to write the graphics data-base to disk under a specified filename.

putega( )   The putega( ) function writes the EGA display buffer to disk under a specified filename.

put—out( ) Part of the printscr( ) function, put—out( ) sends characters to the parallel port.

putrow( )   Part of the printscr( ) function, put—row( ) prepares a row of graphics characters and sends the row to the printer.

readbuf( )   The readbuf( ) function is written in assembler and can be called from C. It is part of the SERISR.ASM module.

read—char( ) The read—char( ) function, part of the CHARHDLR.C module, reads a character at a given row and column location on the EGA display surface.

read—pix2( ) The read—pix2( ) function reads the color of a pixel without using the BIOS.

readpt( ) The readpt( ) function uses the EGA BIOS to read a pixel's color on the EGA display surface.

rectangl( ) The rectangl( ) function draws a rectangle given the coordinates of two diagonal corners.

restport( ) The restport( ) function is used in GRAPHIQ to restore the serial port to the settings in effect when GRAPHIQ was started.

retkey( ) The retkey( ) function returns a keystroke from the keyboard. It also handles simultaneous monitoring of the locator. This function is the heart of GRAPHIQ. All system commands originate in retkey( ).

retrieve( ) The retrieve( ) function retrieves a record from the database in RAM. The record must have been stored at a pointer location using the store( ) function.

rotate( ) The rotate( ) function rotates a single point around the origin of a two-dimensional coordinate system.

rotatec( ) The rotatec( ) function is a part of circle—r( ). It rotates the chords of the circle to their destinations for drawing.

rotate3d( ) The rotate3d( ) function rotates a point around the origin of a three-dimensional coordinate system. You can use it to show rotation of an object in space.

scale( ) The scale( ) function performs a scale transformation on the coordinates of a point.

SERISR.ASM Written in assembler and *not* callable from C, SERISR.ASM is a serial interrupt-service routine. When installed, serisr intercepts incoming characters from a serial port. Each character, when received, generates an interrupt that is served by the serisr interrupt-service routine.

set—curs( ) The set—curs( ) function sets the text cursor location on the EGA using the BIOS. It is a part of the CHARHDLR.C module.

setvect( ) The setvect( ) function sets the desired interrupt vector using DOS functions for interrupt 21 (hex).

status( ) A part of printscr( ), status( ) uses the BIOS to check the printer port status.

store( ) Records are stored in the graphics database using store( ) and retrieved using retrieve( ). A pointer identifies each record.

stretch( ) The stretch( ) function multiplies coordinates by a factor that elongates an object in the desired direction. You can use it to selectively distort objects.

swap( )   The swap( ) function swaps the contents of two double-precision variables.

symmetry( )   Part of the circle( ) function, symmetry( ) reproduces one octant of the circle to derive the seven other octants. In doing so, it flips the circle as necessary to complete the perimeter.

textout( )   The textout( ) function sends stroke-font text to the display surface. It also processes text to conform to the current character height, width, and slant, as well as calculating the text baseline, scale, and translation relative to the system origin.

translate( )   The translate( ) function offsets a point from its position relative to the system origin to a new location.

uninstal( )   The uninstal( ) function uninstalls an interrupt service routine.

unsetvec( )   Part of uninstal( ), unsetvec( ) restores the interrupt address present at a specified interrupt vector.

verline( )   The verline( ) function draws only vertical lines. It is faster than linef( ) when your line drawing involves vertical lines only.

write—array( )   The write—array( ) function writes an array of characters for use in the display of pop-up menus or system prompts. It is part of the CHARHDLR.C module.

write—char( ) Part of the CHARHDLR.C module, write—char( ) draws a text character on the display surface.

write—str( ) Part of the CHARHDLR.C module, write—str( ) uses write—char( ) to write character strings.

xform( ) The xform( ) function performs rotation, translation, and scaling operations using currently defined global parameters. By passing pointers to double-precision reals to xform( ), you can transform coordinates to appear at the current system transformation locations.

The above functions are all discussed at length elsewhere in this book. You will see most of them in action as part of the GRAPH-IQ program in Appendix A.

15

Linking the Toolkit

If you have entered all of the functions in this book and compiled them, you will have object code for each function. As was mentioned in Chapter 14, you can consolidate these functions into a library to make them easy to use in your programs.

When you compile GRAPHIQ, or any other software, you must link the functions together using your system's linker program. The linker used with Microsoft C, LINK.EXE, is included with your C compiler to ensure that it will handle the requirements of the current version of C. You must use LINK. EXE to resolve any external symbolic references.

This chapter will show you how to bind functions together into a library and link them using the Microsoft linker. You can use other linkers if you wish, with minor modifications. This chapter shows how to use the linker by "thinking in simples."

Most things that look complicated are really quite simple when taken apart carefully and examined piece by piece. You can work creatively and enhance your software if you know how to control your linker.

CREATING A LIBRARY

Linkable code is so attractive to programmers because it provides code worlds that are either public or private. A code reference is public if it is available to any external process that wants it. A code reference is private, or local, when it cannot be known by or influence external processes.

If a reference is declared to be PUBLIC in an assembler program, or declared outside of all functions in a C program, it is known to the program as a whole. With symbolic references the symbolic name identifies a storage place (if it refers to data) or an entry point (if it refers to code). If the reference is to data, the symbolic name represents the starting address of the data. If the reference is to code, the symbolic name refers to an entry address to which the code segment (CS) and instruction pointer (IP) will be set. Libraries can contain any combination of publicly and locally defined information.

Programming is greatly simplified if you can control the worlds in which information is known. If everything in the program is known everywhere, anything can change it at any time. If you can create sheltered regions that perform functions but that are guaranteed not to change anything else, code becomes much more predictable. Predictability, fortunately or unfortunately, engenders confidence.

Information in a library should be carefully coordinated. If you are careless in constructing libraries, confusion will inevitably result. Don't worry—if you are not careful, the library manager (LIB.EXE) will teach you to "put your ducks in a row."

Understanding Symbolic
Names and Linking

To understand how the linker works with a library, you need to understand how symbolic references are processed. Many words used by programmers, such as "symbolic," "recursive," "near," and "far," can be intimidating. As with all scientific jargon, the meanings behind the words are usually very simple.

Symbols Are Words That Replace Numbers   There are two reasons for using symbolic names. First, they allow you to use words that have meaning to identify locations and values. Second, they free you of the need to locate your code and data in one and only one place. The linker will give your code addressability, making it unnecessary for you to waste your time computing addresses.

When you identify a function by its address, you must use two numbers, the code segment and the instruction pointer. These two numbers identify the exact location of the code in memory. The code segment either changes or remains constant, depending on the memory model you use.

In Small memory model programs, the code segment is assumed to be constant. It is set at the beginning of the program and stays set (from the standpoint of the C language) until the program ends. The CS register contains the code segment number.

In Medium or Large memory model programs, the code segment changes depending on the module of code that is in use. Each module in the library contains information about its own code segment.

Compiler References and the Library   Symbolically, the compiler refers to the code segment as _TEXT for Small model programs and [modulename]_TEXT for Medium and Large model programs. A module named MYMOD_TEXT would identify code that required its own segment, rather than the single code segment (_TEXT) allotted for Small model programs.

Do you see how symbolic names work? When only one segment is assumed, _TEXT identifies that segment. When more segments are desired, each has its own symbol that incorporates _TEXT in it. The linker's job is to allocate a code segment by setting the CS register appropriately. To do this the linker first determines an acceptable entry point and then adds offsets from that entry point to derive the contents of the CS register. The instruction pointer (IP) register controls execution. When the linker encounters the symbolic name for a function, it sets the IP register as required to reach that function.

The Advantages of External References   Code that must be defined strictly internally has certain limitations. Suppose that you are working on the code for an accounting system and you wish to use a printer driver routine you developed earlier for a text editor package. If all references must be internal, you have no easy way to include the printer driver. Its source code must be combined with the source code on which you are working.

A function written in the C language, or for that matter any executable code module, begins at a certain address in memory and ends at another address. If the code *always* begins at the same address, it does not need to be put in a library. It does not even need to be linked. Such code is said to be **internally referenced** because all of its addressing is self-contained. It is not easy to reuse functions with internally referenced codes. If **external references** are permitted, however, you can refer to code that is *not* part of the source code for your specific application. The symbolic name is used instead of the beginning address of an external piece of code.

Linking Externally Referenced Code   When you compile your program, any symbolic names that are found in it will be placed in the code so that the linker can find them. Later, when you link your code, the linker will seek to resolve those external references by finding matching symbolic names. The linker can look in one of two places for such symbolic names. It can refer to an explicit list of object modules that is passed to the linker, or it can refer to modules that are contained in a library.

   If you choose to link code modules directly from object files, the list of files could grow until your command line became unreasonably long. Libraries make such long linker invocations unnecessary. Instead of listing the name of each object module on the command line, you can use LIB.EXE to combine the desired object modules together into a library.

Using Consistent Memory Models   The modules in a given library should all be compiled using the same memory model. Although it is possible to mix memory models in a library, you should never do so. If you use different assumptions regarding the contents of the code segment, data segment, and other registers, the linker will generate peculiar errors. If you see the phrase "Fixup Errors" in your linker error file (.ERR), you can bet that they were caused by inconsistent use of memory models. A procedure that uses assembler FAR calls, for example, will generate linker fixup errors if you try to link it with a procedure that is declared to be NEAR.

Assumptions Can Cause Confusion   Much confusion is caused by assumptions made in the design of microprocessors and assemblers. Although they are necessary and make the system more powerful, assumptions are often not clearly documented by the manufacturer or understood by the programmer.

The C language assumes nothing, requiring you to declare almost everything. Assembler is just the opposite. Many tacit assumptions are made when code is assembled. This is one of the reasons why assembler is so hard to master. You never see all that is going on. A great deal must be inferred.

One example of the unseen mechanisms used by the microprocessor is the fact that you cannot change the contents of the CS (code segment) register directly using the 8086 microprocessor. When you wish to execute a procedure, you must use a CALL statement, and a lot happens behind the scenes when this statement is processed. The CALL first pushes the address (an offset) of the next instruction in the current procedure onto the stack. If it is a FAR CALL, the code segment register and then the offset are pushed. The microprocessor then sets the CS and IP registers as necessary, transferring control to the new process. All you did was generate a CALL, but the microprocessor changed some registers and pushed some information onto the stack. The inferred processor activity is important, yet it is completely hidden when you write the program.

Managing Your Library

A simple way to understand how program modules are linked together is to examine a typical library of functions created using LIB.EXE, the Microsoft library manager. A **library** is a collection of functions whose symbolic names are publicly known. To understand how these functions are identified, you must understand how symbolic names are used in the library.

In order to add, delete, and substitute library modules, you must use LIB.EXE in accordance with its documentation. There are many ways to use the library manager program, not all of which are described here. The following discussion describes routine use of the library manager, particularly as it applies to the graphics toolkit.

Creating a Sample Library   To illustrate the commands you will use to create a library, let's write a simple function in C and compile it. The following function is trivial, consisting only of an initialized string pointer:

```
yourmod()
{
char *string = "This is a dummy object module.";
}
```

After you compile this C program, you will have a module called YOURMOD.OBJ. You can now create a library that contains this simple module alone. You create and add modules to a library by using a command line like the following:

```
lib yourlib +yourmod;
```

The .OBJ extension is assumed for all modules added to the library. The library manager program also checks to determine whether the object code is in the proper format for linkable code.

Adding Modules   If you wish to add more modules to the library, you can do so by using the same type of command line for each one. Notice the semicolon at the end of the command. This tells the library manager that no more options are required. If you omit it, you will be prompted for additional information. The semicolon also indicates that you want the library manager to perform a consistency check. If the library manager finds inconsistencies in the library, they will be reported at the end of the session. You need only press ENTER for each additional prompt if you forget to include the semicolon.

   The library manager will create, in the above example, a library named YOURLIB.LIB that contains a single reference to a module named yourmod. You can add modules to the library until the 64K available is filled.

Listing the Contents of a Library   To see the contents of a library and to see how much of the memory available to the library has been used, you can enter the following command:

```
lib yourlib, yourlib
```

This will create a file called YOURLIB that contains a listing of all the modules in the library. The listing looks like this:

```
_yourmod..........yourmod

yourmod              Offset: 00000010H  Code and data size: 33H
  _yourmod
```

You can see that the only function in the library is __yourmod. Modules and routines within modules are cross-referenced in library listings. You can also view the offset of the start of the module in memory along with the module's size. See Figure 15-1 for a more elaborate example of this.

Removing Modules   Removing modules from a library is as easy as adding them. You can use the following command line to remove the yourmod module from the library:

```
lib yourlib -yourmod;
```

If you wish to *replace* rather than delete a library module, all you need to do is the following:

```
lib yourlib -+yourmod;
```

You now know all you need to know to add, delete, and revise library modules for the purposes of this book. You can do many other useful things with LIB.EXE. If you wish to know more, please consult your documentation.

```
_allocate.........allocate        _boxx2............boxx2
_brush_in.........brush_in        _brush_out.......brush_out
_BUFFCHR..........serisr          _center..........center
_circle..........circle           _circle_r........circle_r
_clearscr........charhdlr         _com_fill........com_fill
_COM_STR.........com_str          _copybox.........copybox
_cross_it........retkey           _display.........display
_disp_curs.......mnu_curs         _draw_text.......textout
_fillbox2........fillbox2         _frealloc........frealloc
_getdata.........getdata          _getega..........getega
_get_curs........charhdlr         _get_dig.........get_dig
_get_row.........getega           _GET_SER.........get_ser
_get_str.........charhdlr         _horline.........horline
_icbega..........icbega           _inkey...........inkey
_instisr.........instisr          _isr_instal......isr_inst
_linec...........circle_r         _linef...........linef
_lineloc.........retkey           _linep...........linep
_line_int........com_fill         _line_it.........retkey
_locate..........retkey           _locator.........locator
_message.........message          _mnu_curs........mnu_curs
_modeget.........modeget          _modeset.........modeset
_playchar........textout          _point...........point
_pointf..........pointf           _pointp..........pointp
_points..........points           _pop_dbl.........pushpop
_printrow........printscr         _printscr........printscr
_projectr........projectr         _pr_line.........icbega
_push_dbl........pushpop          _putdata.........putdata
_putega..........putega           _put_out.........printscr
_put_row.........putega           _READBUF.........serisr
_readpt..........readpt           _read_char.......charhdlr
_read_pix2.......read_pix2        _rectangl........rectangl
_restport........restport         _retkey..........retkey
_retrieve........retrieve         _rotate..........rotate
_rotate3d........rotate3d         _rotatec.........circle_r
_scale...........scale            _SERISR..........serisr
_setvect.........instisr          _set_curs........charhdlr
_status..........printscr         _store...........store
_stretch.........stretch          _swap............swap
_symmetry........circle           _textout.........textout
_translate.......translat         _uninstal........uninstal
_unsetvec........uninstal         _verline.........verline
_write_array.....charhdlr         _write_char......charhdlr
_write_str.......charhdlr         _xform...........xform
```

FIGURE 15-1.   Cross-reference listing of GRAPHIQ.LIB

```
point          Offset: 00000010H  Code and data size: 43H
  _point

center         Offset: 00000160H  Code and data size: 1E9H
  _center

modeset        Offset: 00000670H  Code and data size: 2AH
  _modeset

circle         Offset: 000007C0H  Code and data size: 279H
  _circle          _symmetry

rectangl       Offset: 00000C60H  Code and data size: 5BH
  _rectangl

horline        Offset: 00000DF0H  Code and data size: C5H
  _horline

verline        Offset: 00001000H  Code and data size: C5H
  _verline

swap           Offset: 00001210H  Code and data size: 28H
  _swap

scale          Offset: 00001330H  Code and data size: 68H
  _scale

stretch        Offset: 00001530H  Code and data size: 4BH
  _stretch

translat       Offset: 00001700H  Code and data size: 2CH
  _translate

rotate         Offset: 00001890H  Code and data size: BBH
  _rotate

rotate3d       Offset: 00001AE0H  Code and data size: 2A4H
  _rotate3d

points         Offset: 00002070H  Code and data size: D7H
  _points

linep          Offset: 00002280H  Code and data size: 445H
  _linep

pointp         Offset: 00002AB0H  Code and data size: 16CH
  _pointp
```

FIGURE 15-1.   Cross-reference listing of GRAPHIQ.LIB (continued)

```
modeget          Offset: 00002DC0H   Code and data size: 30H
  _modeget

projectr         Offset: 00002F00H   Code and data size: CFH
  _projectr

linef            Offset: 000031E0H   Code and data size: 206H
  _linef

allocate         Offset: 00003530H   Code and data size: 5DH
  _allocate

frealloc         Offset: 000036B0H   Code and data size: 30H
  _frealloc

copybox          Offset: 00003800H   Code and data size: 2AEH
  _copybox

com_fill         Offset: 00003C20H   Code and data size: 2CCH
  _com_fill          _line_int

circle_r         Offset: 00004060H   Code and data size: 898H
  _circle_r          _linec              _rotatec

brush_out        Offset: 00004EE0H   Code and data size: 13BH
  _brush_out

brush_in         Offset: 000051A0H   Code and data size: 9BH
  _brush_in

putega           Offset: 00005390H   Code and data size: DDH
  _putega            _put_row

getega           Offset: 000055F0H   Code and data size: 14FH
  _getega            _get_row

readpt           Offset: 000058E0H   Code and data size: 3CH
  _readpt

icbega           Offset: 00005A30H   Code and data size: 2E8H
  _icbega            _pr_line

xform            Offset: 00005EC0H   Code and data size: 135H
  _xform

inkey            Offset: 00006290H   Code and data size: 48H
  _inkey
```

FIGURE 15-1.   Cross-reference listing of GRAPHIQ.LIB (continued)

```
read_pix2        Offset: 000063E0H  Code and data size: D1H
  _read_pix2

com_str          Offset: 000065F0H  Code and data size: 40H
  _COM_STR

get_ser          Offset: 000066D0H  Code and data size: 20H
  _GET_SER

instisr          Offset: 00006790H  Code and data size: 122H
  _instisr          _setvect

uninstal         Offset: 00006A30H  Code and data size: B2H
  _uninstal         _unsetvec

serisr           Offset: 00006C50H  Code and data size: D3H
  _BUFFCHR          _READBUF           _SERISR

retrieve         Offset: 00006E30H  Code and data size: 43H
  _retrieve

restport         Offset: 00006FB0H  Code and data size: 7AH
  _restport

isr_inst         Offset: 000071B0H  Code and data size: 159H
  _isr_instal

pushpop          Offset: 00007510H  Code and data size: 5AH
  _pop_dbl          _push_dbl

locator          Offset: 00007700H  Code and data size: 206H
  _locator

get_dig          Offset: 00007B70H  Code and data size: 18AH
  _get_dig

store            Offset: 00008010H  Code and data size: 69H
  _store

boxx2            Offset: 000081F0H  Code and data size: 1D9H
  _boxx2

textout          Offset: 00008630H  Code and data size: 563H
  _draw_text        _playchar          _textout

retkey           Offset: 00009100H  Code and data size: C68H
  _cross_it         _lineloc           _line_it            _locate
  _retkey
```

FIGURE 15-1.   Cross-reference listing of GRAPHIQ.LIB (continued)

```
fillbox2            Offset: 0000A6D0H   Code and data size: 15AH
  _fillbox2

pointf              Offset: 0000AA80H   Code and data size: 192H
  _pointf

display             Offset: 0000AD70H   Code and data size: 23CH
  _display

putdata             Offset: 0000B2D0H   Code and data size: D1H
  _putdata

getdata             Offset: 0000B560H   Code and data size: B1H
  _getdata

message             Offset: 0000B7D0H   Code and data size: 2B2H
  _message

charhdlr            Offset: 0000BD40H   Code and data size: 373H
  _clearscr            _get_curs            _get_str             _read_char
  _set_curs            _write_array         _write_char          _write_str

mnu_curs            Offset: 0000C3C0H   Code and data size: 149H
  _disp_curs           _mnu_curs

printscr            Offset: 0000C6A0H   Code and data size: 14CEH
  _printrow            _printscr            _put_out             _status
```

FIGURE 15-1.   Cross-reference listing of GRAPHIQ.LIB (continued)

Creating the Toolkit Library   To create your own toolkit library from the functions in this book, you must first choose, copy, and compile the functions you wish to use. You then create and maintain your library as described above. You can obtain the library on magnetic media, if you wish to avoid manually entering the functions. An order form is supplied in the front of this book.

USING THE LINKER

Program modules need to be linked together if you have written code that contains any external symbolic references. Unless you use an assembler or compiler that produces code in which all references are internal, you will need to link your code to make it executable. It is safe to assume that most code you create using modern tools will make use of external references, and so you will need to know how to use the linker.

Functions written in C must be linked because they become modules that rely on symbolic names. Another reason for linking them is that the compiler provides the code necessary to create an executable (.EXE) file. The code that enables the main( ) function, supplied by the C compiler, is linked together with all the functions in a C program to produce an executable piece of software.

The Linker Command Line

It helps to have a standard batch file that contains the linker command line to be used for a given project. You could, for example, create a file called LK.BAT that contained the following command line:

```
link   /STACK:%2 %1,%1,,agic; > %1.err
type %1.err
```

This command line invokes the linker (LINK.EXE) and specifies a series of options. The first option declares a stack size. The stack will contain the number of bytes you designate in the command you use to start the batch file. This number is specified after the name of the file to be linked. The following is an example of the command you would use to start the batch process and create a stack:

```
lk myprog 10000
```

This command would link a file called MYPROG.OBJ to modules contained in a library called AGIC.LIB and, if successful, would create a file called MYPROG.EXE containing an executable program.

Controlling the Stack   The size of the stack used in the preceding example is 10,000 bytes. When you link GRAPHIQ, try using a 10,000-byte stack. As you change GRAPHIQ, you will need to change the stack size, depending on how much your new functions use the stack or on how recursive they are. A **recursive** function will execute itself from within itself. Remember, each time a function is called by C, the stack is used to store the information required on return. If calls to the calling function recur during the execution of any C function, the stack pointer will move downward in memory. If this occurs too many times, the allocated stack size will be exceeded, and the program will terminate with a stack overflow error. *Always* use recursion consciously, rather than by accident, or you will generate code that is extremely unpredictable. An example of an extremely recursive function follows:

```
recursion()
{
recursion();
}
```

The recursion( ) function is designed to do one thing only—use up the stack. It will run until the stack pointer exceeds its allocated offset, and then it will generate a stack overflow error and terminate. A non-restrictive call is made to the same address as the calling function. The result is that the function simply continues to call itself indefinitely.

When the Linker Encounters Errors   If the linker session is not successful, any errors encountered during the session will be listed in a file called MYPROG.ERR. After the linker session, MYPROG.ERR will automatically be typed to show such errors.

The above method, using LK.BAT, will be useful for most work you do in C. You can keep LK.BAT in the directory you use for executable programs (with a path set to that directory) so that it will be available from any subdirectory. You will probably accumulate a collection of different linker batch files for different circumstances. Your linker's operations manual will give more information regarding the options available to you.

Linking GRAPHIQ

If you wish to run the GRAPHIQ program given in Appendix A, you must first compile each module used in it. After compiling the source code using the options described in Chapter 14, you must create a library that contains the object code for each function external to GRAPHIQ.C. You then link GRAPHIQ.OBJ with the library.

Using Functions from This Book   A library has already been created and is available on magnetic media, if you wish to avoid compiling each function. You will learn a lot by copying the functions from this book, however, and you are encouraged to do so. If you choose to do this, be sure to use the functions contained in Appendix A and not their counterparts in the examples in the chapters. The functions in Appendix A are essentially the same as the ones in the illustrations, but they have been "tweaked" to work well within the tested version of GRAPHIQ. In other words, look to the chapters in this book to find out how typical graphics functions work, but look to Appendix A for functions that have been combined together into a working program.

Contents of AGIC.LIB   The *Advanced Graphics in C* library, AGIC.LIB, contains all references that are external to GRAPHIQ. Figure 15-1 shows the complete contents of this library. This list was generated by having the LIB.EXE program list the library's contents. If you wish to link GRAPHIQ successfully, you must provide most of the functions shown in this listing. Certain functions, particularly those dealing with three-dimensional operations and plotting, are contained in the library but are not used in GRAPHIQ. It is left to you to incorporate such functions if you wish to use them.

Software Must Be Abandoned to Be Finished   What you see in this book is a program that is frozen at one stage in its evolution. Almost any software project could literally continue forever. Like a work of art, a work of software must be abandoned to be finished.

The references shown in Figure 15-1 are those that were used when GRAPHIQ was debugged and tested. This means that the code linked using the library corresponding to this listing actually worked. If you stick to the library as shown, you too will stand a good chance of achieving success.

If you successfully copy, compile, and link all of the modules shown in Appendix A, you will enjoy the use of a powerful little piece of graphics software. Feel free to use GRAPHIQ as the basis for any software you like. It is intended to give you a platform from which you can build your own applications.

GRAPHIQ Source Code Listing

This appendix contains the source code for GRAPHIQ, a simple graphics program. The name "GRAPHIQ" was derived from the word "graph" and the abbreviation "IQ," which stands for "intelligence quotient." Pronounce it as graph-IQ, or, if you like, you can pronounce it as though it were the French word "graphique" (sounds like "grafeek"). The Larousse French dictionary defines "graphique," a masculine noun, as "design applied to the sciences." The name symbolizes the purpose of the program: to help you raise your graphics intelligence quotient. GRAPHIQ was designed to serve as a launching pad for your own applications. It supplies information you cannot get with a collection of separate functions. GRAPHIQ illustrates the most important aspect of graphics programming—how functions work together in a program.

You can use GRAPHIQ as it is, or you can add your own special features to it. You can also take GRAPHIQ apart and use its components for different purposes. Whether you use it as a launching platform or a wrecking yard, GRAPHIQ gives you ready-made solutions that can speed up your work.

If you are a C programmer with little experience with or interest in graphics, but you have a specific project that requires some graphics programming, GRAPHIQ is for you. You can borrow its techniques in lieu of spending valuable hours developing them yourself. Most graphics toolkits on the market are deficient in two major areas. They do not provide you with source code, and they do not show you how to use their isolated functions in the context of a complete, working program.

The source code in this appendix was developed from scratch, starting in September 1986. It was finished and "frozen" in December 1986. All of the functions contained in this book are original, and no license fee is required for you to use them and incorporate them in your work. The functions cover the entire range of capabilities of the IBM PC. They enable you to use the keyboard, the EGA, serial communications ports, parallel printer ports, interrupts, allocated memory, and much more. In effect, you do not need anything more than this book (and its companion disk) to program the IBM PC using your C compiler and assembler. This book was designed to provide, in one convenient place, all the functions that cannot be found on the shelves of bookstores.

HOW TO USE THE GRAPHIQ
SOURCE CODE

GRAPHIQ's source code is organized starting with the program itself (GRAPHIQ.C), followed by the source code for each module and function. They are listed in the same order in which they appear in the AGIC.LIB library shown in Chapter 15. After the C and assembler code, you will find listings for all headers.

If you choose to compile from this listing, you should create a library of all object code (except GRAPHIQ.OBJ) so that the program can be linked. Read Chapters 14 and 15 for information regarding the compiler and linker assumptions.

The contents of this appendix supersede all of the code shown elsewhere in this book and are the most current versions of the code. In order to make the functions work together, they have been "tweaked." This does not mean that the functions described in detail in the chapters are inaccurate. It just means that in some cases the functions have been modified to add features or to make them appropriate for specific uses.

Listing of All C and Assembler Modules

The C and assembler source code required to produce the complete GRAPHIQ program comprise a formidable collection of routines. The following pages contain complete source code for GRAPHIQ.

Within the various code modules, reference is made to several headers. These headers contain global declarations, definitions, and lookup tables for use by the C and assembler modules. A complete list of headers for GRAPHIQ follows the source code.

Remember that the modules shown here, although complete, require a suitable C compiler library. The Microsoft C compiler was used to compile the program shown. You can use other compilers, but you will need to modify the code in order to do so.

GRAPHIQ SOURCE CODE

GRAPHIQ.C

```
/* GRAPHIQ.C is a simple graphics program that provides
** a prototype for your custom applications.
** As many functions as possible are implemented, the rest
** are up to you.  This version works with the eight
** low-intensity colors available with typical low-cost RGB
** monitors.  You might wish to make your first project the
** improvement of GRAPHIQ to work with sixteen colors. */

#include <stdio.h>
#include <dos.h>
#include <conio.h>
#include <malloc.h>
#include <process.h>
#include <string.h>
#include <memory.h>
#include <math.h>
#include "graphiq.h"
#include "file.h"
#include "screen.h"
#include "locator.h"
#include "declares.h"
#include "font.h"

main()
{
int inchar;
int welcome_on = TRUE;
double i, j, k;
int incr;
double int_portion;

if (allocate(0x2000, &allowed, &dwg_seg)
    && allowed)  /* allocate 128K for drawing data */
    {
    printf("Not enough memory to run program.");
    exit(1);
    }

segread(&segs); /* get segments in use by program */
```

```
oldmode = modeget();

modeset(14);

/* put last x and y positions at */
/* center of display */
modf(CENTERX / inc, &int_portion);
lastx = x = int_portion * inc;
modf(CENTERY / inc, &int_portion);
lasty = y = int_portion * inc;

/* install serial interrupt service */
isr_instal();

/* initialize the locator matrix */
matrix = matrix1;

/* display the first locator */
locator(x, y, color, matrix);

/* display the welcome message */
write_array(welcome, 0, 0, BLUE);

/* the main loop for GRAPHIQ */
do   {

    strcpy(command, "");

    if (!reading_cmd) inchar = retkey(CROSS);
    else inchar = ESC;

    if (welcome_on)
        {
        welcome_on = FALSE;
        write_array(welcome, 0, 0, BLUE);
        }

    if (inchar != DOWN
    &&  inchar != UP
    &&  inchar != LEFT
    &&  inchar != RIGHT
    &&  inchar != HOME)
        {
    locator(x, y, color, matrix);   /* locator off */

    tempx = x; tempy = y;
```

```
switch (inchar)
    {
    case ESC:
    case ENTER:
        message(cmd_msg, 24, 0, GREEN, inchar);
        break;
    }


if (strlen(strupr(command)))
    {

    if (!strcmp(command, "HELP"))
        {
        write_array(help, 0, 0, GREEN);
        getch();
        write_array(help, 0, 0, GREEN);
        }

    if (!strcmp(command, "GRID"))
        {
        message(grid_msg, 24, 0, RED, ESC);
        if (strlen(command))
            inc = atof(command);

        for (i = NDCXMIN-xlate_x;
                i <= NDCXMAX-xlate_x; i += inc)
            {
            if (kbhit()) break;
            for (j = NDCYMIN-xlate_y;
                    j <= NDCYMAX-xlate_y; j += inc)
                draw_line(i,j,i,j, color,
                    pattern, XORIT, ON);
            }
        }

    if (!strcmp(command, "SNAP"))
        snap = (!snap) ? TRUE : FALSE;

    if (!strcmp(command, "LOCATOR"))
        digitizer = (!digitizer) ? TRUE : FALSE;

    if (!strcmp(command, "TENTHMM"))
        inc = TENTHMM;
```

```
if (!strcmp(command, "MILLIMETER"))
    inc = MILLIMETER;

if (!strcmp(command, "FIVEMM"))
    inc = FIVEMM;

if (!strcmp(command, "TENMM"))
    inc = TENMM;

if (!strcmp(command, "TWENTYMM"))
    inc = TWENTYMM;

if (!strcmp(command, "STYLE"))
    {
    if (line_style > 4) line_style = 0;
    switch (++line_style)
        {
        case 1:
            pattern = SOLID;
            matrix = matrix1;
            break;
        case 2:
            pattern = DOTTED;
            matrix = matrix2;
            break;
        case 3:
            pattern = DASHED;
            matrix = matrix3;
            break;
        case 4:
            pattern = DASHDOT;
            matrix = matrix4;
            break;
        case 5:
            pattern = DASHDOTDOT;
            matrix = matrix5;
            break;
        }
    }

if (!strcmp(command, "COLOR"))
    {
    color -= 1;
    color = (color < 0) ? 0x7 : color;
    }
```

```
if (!strcmp(command, "MOVE"))
    {
    x = tempx; y = tempy;
    lastx = x;
    lasty = y;
    }

if (!strcmp(command, "LINE"))
    {
    x = tempx; y = tempy;
    corner_x = lastx; corner_y = lasty;

    draw_line(lastx, lasty, x, y, color,
         pattern, XORIT, ON);

    while (retkey(LINELOC) != ENTER);

    draw_line(lastx, lasty, x, y, color,
         pattern, NORMIT, ON);

    element.attribute.parts.attr = LINE;
    element.attribute.parts.subattr = 0;
    element.attr.line.x1 = lastx;
    element.attr.line.y1 = lasty;
    element.attr.line.x2 = x;
    element.attr.line.y2 = y;
    element.attr.line.color = color;
    element.attr.line.linestyle = pattern;
    element.attr.line.orxor = NORMIT;
    element.attr.line.first_pt = ON;
    element.attr.line.layer = 0;   /* layering not */
                                   /* implemented  */

    store();

    lastx = x;
    lasty = y;

    }

if (!strcmp(command, "BOX"))
    {
    x = tempx; y = tempy;
    boxit();
```

```
                /* replace box when located */
                boxx2(corner_x, corner_y, x, y, pattern,
                        color, NORMIT);

                /* store record of box in database */
                element.attribute.parts.attr = BOX;
                element.attribute.parts.subattr = 0;
                element.attr.box.x1 = corner_x;
                element.attr.box.y1 = corner_y;
                element.attr.box.x2 = x;
                element.attr.box.y2 = y;
                element.attr.box.color = color;
                element.attr.box.linestyle = pattern;
                element.attr.box.orxor = NORMIT;
                element.attr.box.layer = 0;

                store();

                }

        (!strcmp(command, "FILL"))
                {
                x = tempx; y = tempy;
                boxit();

                /* remove box when located */
                boxx2(corner_x, corner_y, x, y,
                        pattern, color, XORIT);

                /* draw the fill */
                fillbox2(corner_x, corner_y, x, y,
                        pattern, color, NORMIT);

                /* store record of fill in database */
                element.attribute.parts.attr = FILL;
                element.attribute.parts.subattr = 0;
                element.attr.fill.x1 = corner_x;
                element.attr.fill.y1 = corner_y;
                element.attr.fill.x2 = x;
                element.attr.fill.y2 = y;
                element.attr.fill.color = color;
                element.attr.fill.linestyle = pattern;
                element.attr.fill.orxor = NORMIT;
                element.attr.fill.layer = 0;
```

```
        store();

        }

if (!strcmp(command, "CIRCLE"))
        {
        x = tempx; y = tempy;
        locate_circ(&x_center, &y_center,
                        &x_perim, &y_perim);

        draw_circ(x_center, y_center,
            x_perim, y_perim, color);

        /* store record of circle in database */
        element.attribute.parts.attr = CIRCLE;
        element.attribute.parts.subattr = 0;
        element.attr.circle.x_center = x_center;
        element.attr.circle.y_center = y_center;
        element.attr.circle.x_perim = x_perim;
        element.attr.circle.y_perim = y_perim;
        element.attr.circle.color = color;
        element.attr.circle.layer = 0;

        store();

        }

if (!strcmp(command, "TEXT"))
        {
        locator(x, y, color, matrix); /* locator on */

        write_array(loc_text, 24, 0, color);

        while ((inchar = retkey(CROSS)) != ENTER);

        write_array(loc_text, 24, 0, color);

        locator(x, y, color, matrix); /* locator off */

        tempx = x; tempy = y;

        textout(x, y);

        /* store record of text in database */
```

```
element.attribute.parts.attr = TEXT;
element.attribute.parts.subattr = 0;
element.attr.text.t_attr.loc.x_origin = tempx;
element.attr.text.t_attr.loc.y_origin = tempy;
element.attr.text.t_attr.loc.rot_angle
                          = xform_angle;
element.attr.text.t_attr.loc.height = height;
element.attr.text.t_attr.loc.width = width;
element.attr.text.t_attr.loc.slant = slant;
element.attr.text.t_attr.loc.color = color;
element.attr.text.t_attr.loc.layer = 0;

store();

element.attribute.parts.attr = TEXT;
element.attribute.parts.subattr = 0;
strcpy(element.attr.text.t_attr.strg\
    .string, command);
strcpy(command, "");

store();

}


(!strcmp(command, "ROTATION"))
  {
  x = tempx; y = tempy;

  locator(x, y, color, matrix); /* locator on */

  write_array(loc_rot, 24, 0, color);

  while ((inchar = retkey(CROSS)) != ENTER);

  write_array(loc_rot, 24, 0, color);

  locator(x, y, color, matrix); /* locator off */

  rot_center_x = x;
  rot_center_y = y;

  write_array(rot_msg, 24, 0, color);
  corner_x = rot_center_x;
  corner_y = rot_center_y;
```

```
        draw_line(rot_center_x, rot_center_y, x, y, color,
            pattern, XORIT, ON);

        while (retkey(LINELOC) != ENTER);

        draw_line(rot_center_x, rot_center_y, x, y, color,
            pattern, XORIT, ON);

        write_array(rot_msg, 24, 0, color);

        xform_angle = atan2(x-rot_center_x, y-rot_center_y);

        xform_angle = (xform_angle < 0)
                        ? PI - xform_angle : xform_angle;

        element.attribute.parts.attr = XFORMS;
        element.attribute.parts.subattr = 0;
        element.attr.xforms.xlate_x = xlate_x;
        element.attr.xforms.xlate_y = xlate_y;
        element.attr.xforms.rot_center_x = rot_center_x;
        element.attr.xforms.rot_center_y = rot_center_y;
        element.attr.xforms.xform_angle = xform_angle;
        element.attr.xforms.scale_factor = scale_factor;

        store();
        }


    if (!strcmp(command, "RESET"))
        {

        element.attribute.parts.attr = XFORMS;
        element.attribute.parts.subattr = 0;
        element.attr.xforms.xlate_x = xlate_x = 0;
        element.attr.xforms.xlate_y = xlate_y = 0;
        element.attr.xforms.rot_center_x = rot_center_x
                            = 0;
        element.attr.xforms.rot_center_y = rot_center_y
                            = 0;
        element.attr.xforms.xform_angle = xform_angle
                            = 0;
        element.attr.xforms.scale_factor = scale_factor
                            = 1;
```

```
            store();
            }


if (!strcmp(command, "SYSORIGIN"))
            {
            x = tempx; y = tempy;

            locator(x, y, color, matrix); /* locator on */

            write_array(loc_sys, 24, 0, color);

            while ((inchar = retkey(CROSS)) != ENTER);

            write_array(loc_sys, 24, 0, color);

            locator(x, y, color, matrix); /* locator off */

            xlate_x = x;
            xlate_y = y;

            x = 0; y = 0;

            element.attribute.parts.attr = XFORMS;
            element.attribute.parts.subattr = 0;
            element.attr.xforms.xlate_x = xlate_x;
            element.attr.xforms.xlate_y = xlate_y;
            element.attr.xforms.rot_center_x = rot_center_x;
            element.attr.xforms.rot_center_y = rot_center_y;
            element.attr.xforms.xform_angle = xform_angle;
            element.attr.xforms.scale_factor = scale_factor;

            store();
            }


if (!strcmp(command, "SCALE"))
            {
            write_array(scale_msg1, 24, 0, color);

            draw_line(rot_center_x, rot_center_y, x, y, color,
                  pattern, XORIT, ON);

            while (retkey(LINELOC) != ENTER);
```

```
            draw_line(rot_center_x, rot_center_y, x, y, color,
                pattern, XORIT, ON);

            oldx = x; oldy = y;

            write_array(scale_msg1, 24, 0, color);
            write_array(scale_msg2, 24, 0, color);

            draw_line(rot_center_x, rot_center_y, x, y, color,
                pattern, XORIT, ON);

            while (retkey(LINELOC) != ENTER);

            draw_line(rot_center_x, rot_center_y, x, y, color,
                pattern, XORIT, ON);

            write_array(scale_msg2, 24, 0, color);

            scale_factor = hypot(x, y) / hypot(oldx, oldy);

            element.attribute.parts.attr = XFORMS;
            element.attribute.parts.subattr = 0;
            element.attr.xforms.xlate_x = xlate_x;
            element.attr.xforms.xlate_y = xlate_y;
            element.attr.xforms.rot_center_x = rot_center_x;
            element.attr.xforms.rot_center_y = rot_center_y;
            element.attr.xforms.xform_angle = xform_angle;
            element.attr.xforms.scale_factor = scale_factor;

            store();
            }


    if (!strcmp(command, "PLAYBACK"))
        {
        x = tempx; y = tempy;
        xlate_xb = xlate_x;
        xlate_x = 0;
        xlate_yb = xlate_y;
        xlate_y = 0;
        rot_center_xb = rot_center_x;
        rot_center_x = 0;
        rot_center_yb = rot_center_y;
        rot_center_y = 0;
        xform_angleb = xform_angle;
```

```
        xform_angle = 0;
        scale_factorb = scale_factor;
        scale_factor = 1;

        for (incr = 0; incr < pointer; ++incr)
            display(&incr);

        xlate_x = xlate_xb;
        xlate_y = xlate_yb;
        rot_center_x = rot_center_xb;
        rot_center_y = rot_center_yb;
        xform_angle = xform_angleb;
        scale_factor = scale_factorb;
        }

if (!strcmp(command, "PRINT"))
    {
    message(print_msg, 24, 0, BROWN, ESC);

    if (strlen(strupr(command))
        && (!strcmp("Y", command)
        || !strcmp("YES", command)))
            reverse = TRUE;
    else reverse = FALSE;

    printscr(reverse);

    }

if (!strcmp(command, "FILES"))
    {
    file_mess(0, 0, color, inchar);

    if (!strcmp(command, "PUT SCREEN"))
        {
        message(put_msg, 24, 0, RED, ESC);
        if (strlen(command))
            {
            if (putega(command))
                message(file_error, 24, 0,
                        RED, ESC);
            }
        }

    if (!strcmp(command, "GET SCREEN"))
```

```
                        {
                message(get_msg, 24, 0, RED, ESC);
                if (strlen(command))
                    {
                    if (getega(command))
                        message(file_error, 24, 0,
                                        RED, ESC);
                    }
                }

        if (!strcmp(command, "PUT DATABASE"))
            {
            message(put_data_msg, 24, 0, RED, ESC);
            if (strlen(command))
                {
                if (putdata(command))
                    message(file_error, 24, 0,
                                    RED, ESC);
                }
            }

         if (!strcmp(command, "GET DATABASE"))
            {
            message(get_data_msg, 24, 0, RED, ESC);
            if (strlen(command))
                {
                if (getdata(command))
                message(file_error, 24, 0,
                                RED, ESC);
                }
            }
        }

    if (!strcmp(command, "COMMAND FILE"))
        {
        message(file_msg, 24, 0, RED, ESC);
        if (strlen(command))
            {
            if ((cmd_stream = fopen(command,"rt"))
                        == NULL)
                message(file_error, 24, 0, RED, ESC);
            reading_cmd = TRUE;
            }
        }
```

```
        if (!strcmp(command, "CLEAR DISPLAY"))
            {
            inchar = NULLCHAR;
            clearscr();
            }

        if (!strcmp(command, "EXIT"))
            inchar = NULLCHAR;

        if (!strcmp(command, "QUIT"))
            inchar = QUIT;


        }

    if (inchar == QUIT)
        {
        message(quit_msg, 24, 0, BROWN, ESC);

        if (strchr(command, 'y') || strchr(command, 'Y'));
        else inchar = NULLCHAR;
        }

        locator(x, y, color, matrix); /* locator on again */
        } /* inchar not DOWN, UP, LEFT, RIGHT OR HOME */

    } while (inchar != QUIT);

frealloc(dwg_seg);

clearscr();

modeset(oldmode);

uninstal(SERPORT1);

restport(); /* restore port settings */

exit(0);
}


boxit()
{
```

```
int inchar;

locator(x, y, color, matrix); /* locator on */
/* locate a corner */

write_array(box1_msg, 24, 0, color);

while ((inchar = retkey(CROSS)) != ENTER);
locator(x, y, color, matrix); /* locator off */

boxx2(x, y, x, y, pattern, color, XORIT);
corner_x = x;
corner_y = y;

write_array(box1_msg, 24, 0, color);
write_array(box2_msg, 24, 0, color);

while ((inchar = retkey(OUTLINE)) != ENTER);

write_array(box2_msg, 24, 0, color);
}


locate_circ(x_center, y_center, x_perim, y_perim)
double *x_center, *y_center, *x_perim, *y_perim;
{
int inchar;

write_array(circl_msg, 24, 0, color);

locator(x, y, color, matrix); /* locator on */
/* locate center */
while ((inchar = retkey(CROSS)) != ENTER);

*x_center = x;
*y_center = y;

write_array(circl_msg, 24, 0, color);
write_array(circ2_msg, 24, 0, color);

/* locate radius */
while ((inchar = retkey(CROSS)) != ENTER);

*x_perim = x;
```

```
*y_perim = y;

locator(x, y, color, matrix); /* locator off */

write_array(circ2_msg, 24, 0, color);
}


draw_line(x1, y1, x2, y2, color, pattern, orxor, first_on)
double x1, y1, x2, y2;
int color, orxor, first_on;
unsigned pattern;
{

xform_it(&x1, &y1, &x2, &y2);

linef((int)x1, (int)y1, (int)x2, (int)y2,
        color, pattern, orxor, first_on);

}


draw_circ(xc, yc, xp, yp, color)
double xc, yc, xp, yp;
int color;
{
double radius, aspect = 2.0;

xform_it(&xc, &yc, &xp, &yp);

radius = sqrt(SQ((xp - xc) / (aspect + 0.5)) + SQ(yp - yc));

circle((int)xc, (int)yc, (int)radius, aspect, color);
}


xform_it(x1, y1, x2, y2)
double *x1, *y1, *x2, *y2;
{

xform(x1, y1);

xform(x2, y2);
```

```
*x1 *= XMETRIC;
*y1 = YMAX - *y1 * YMETRIC;
*x2 *= XMETRIC;
*y2 = YMAX - *y2 * YMETRIC;
}



file_mess(row, col, color, inchar)
int row, col, color, inchar;
{
file_menu(color);
switch(file_select)
    {
    case 1:
        strcpy(command, "PUT SCREEN");
        break;
    case 2:
        strcpy(command, "GET SCREEN");
        break;
    case 3:
        strcpy(command, "PUT DATABASE");
        break;
    case 4:
        strcpy(command, "GET DATABASE");
        break;
    }
}



main_menu(color)
int color;
{
int depth;

in_menu = TRUE;
depth = write_array(main_mnu, 0, 0, color);
mnu_curs(1, 1, depth-2, 16, color, MAIN_MNU);
write_array(main_mnu, 0, 0, color);
in_menu = FALSE;
}
```

```
file_menu(color)
int color;
{
int depth;

in_menu = TRUE;
depth = write_array(file_mnu, 0, 0, color);
mnu_curs(1, 1, depth-2, 16, color, FILE_MNU);
write_array(file_mnu, 0, 0, color);
in_menu = FALSE;
}


/********  End of GRAPHIQ.C  ********/
```

POINT.C

```
/* POINT.C reads or writes a dot at x,y in given color */

#include <dos.h>

point(x, y, read_write, color)
int x, y, read_write, *color;
{
union REGS regs;

regs.x.cx = x;              /* column number */
regs.x.dx = y;              /* set row number */
regs.h.ah = read_write;     /* 13 is READPT, 12 is WRITEPT */
regs.h.al = *color;         /* color of the dot (0 - F) */
int86(0x10, &regs, &regs);  /* invoke int10h */
*color = regs.h.al;
}
```

CENTER.C

```
/* CENTER.C derives the coordinates of the center of a
** circle and its radius from the coordinates of three points on
** the circle's circumference. */

#include <math.h>

center(x, y, xc, yc, r)
double x[], y[], *xc, *yc, *r;
{
double x2[2], xh[2], y2[2], yk[2];
double x2y2[2], xnyn, ykn;

x2[0] = x[0]*x[0] - x[1]*x[1];
xh[0] = 2.0 * x[0] - 2.0 * x[1];
y2[0] = y[0]*y[0] - y[1]*y[1];
yk[0] = 2.0 * y[0] - 2.0 * y[1];

x2[1] = x[1]*x[1] - x[2]*x[2];
xh[1] = 2.0 * x[1] - 2.0 * x[2];
y2[1] = y[1]*y[1] - y[2]*y[2];
yk[1] = 2.0 * y[1] - 2.0 * y[2];

x2y2[0] = x2[0] + y2[0];
x2y2[1] = x2[1] + y2[1];

xnyn = x2y2[0];
ykn = yk[0];

x2y2[0] *= xh[1];
yk[0] *= xh[1];

x2y2[1] *= xh[0];
yk[1] *= xh[0];

*yc = (x2y2[0] - x2y2[1]) / (yk[0] - yk[1]);
*xc = (xnyn - *yc * ykn) / xh[0];

x[0] -= *xc;
y[0] -= *yc;

*r = sqrt(x[0]*x[0] + y[0]*y[0]);
}
```

MODESET.C

```
/* MODESET.C sets EGA modes */

#include <dos.h>

modeset(mode)
int mode;
{
union REGS regs;

regs.h.al = mode;
regs.h.ah = 0;
int86(0x10, &regs, &regs);
}
```

CIRCLE.C

```
/* CIRCLE.C is a generalized function to draw a circle
** using Bresenham's Octant method.  Note that an aspect
** ratio is accommodated and that it expands the horizontal
** pixel from one dot to several as required to fill in when
** the aspect ratio is greater than 1.0. */

#define TRUE 0xFF
#define ENABLE 0x0F
#define INDEXREG 0x3CE
#define VALREG 0x3CF
#define OUTINDEX(index, val)   {outp(INDEXREG, index);\
                                 outp(VALREG, val);}
#define EGABASE 0xA0000000L
#define WIDTH 80L
#define XMAX 639
#define YMAX 199
#define XMIN 0
```

```
#define YMIN 0

double ratio;

circle(xc, yc, radius, aspect, color)
int xc, yc, radius, color;
double aspect;
{
int x, y, d;
unsigned char mask, exist_color;
char far *base;

ratio = aspect + 0.5;

y = radius;
d = 3 - 2 * radius;

OUTINDEX(1, ENABLE); /* enable write */

for (x = 0; x < y;)
    {
    symmetry(x, y, xc, yc, color);

    if (d < 0)
        d += 4 * x + 6;
    else {
        d += 4 * (x - y) + 10;
        --y;
        }
    ++x;
    }

if (x = y) symmetry(x, y, xc, yc, color);

OUTINDEX(0,0);       /* reset register */
OUTINDEX(1,0);       /* reset ENABLE */
OUTINDEX(8,TRUE);    /* reset bit mask */
}



symmetry(x, y, xc, yc, color)
int x, y, xc, yc, color;
{
```

```
int x_start, x_end, x_out;
int y_start, y_end, y_out;

x_start = x * ratio;
x_end = (x + 1) * ratio;
y_start = y * ratio;
y_end = (y + 1) * ratio;

for (x_out = x_start; x_out < x_end; ++x_out)
    {
    points(x_out+xc, y+yc, color);
    points(x_out+xc, -y+yc, color);
    points(-x_out+xc, -y+yc, color);
    points(-x_out+xc, y+yc, color);
    }

for (y_out = y_start; y_out < y_end; ++y_out)
    {
    points(y_out+xc, x+yc, color);
    points(y_out+xc, -x+yc, color);
    points(-y_out+xc, -x+yc, color);
    points(-y_out+xc, x+yc, color);
    }

}
```

RECTANGL.C

```
/* RECTANGL.C   draws a rectangular box. */

rectangl(x1, y1, x2, y2, color)
int x1, y1, x2, y2, color;
{

horline(x1, x2, y1, color);
horline(x1, x2, y2, color);
verline(x1, y1, y2, color);
verline(x2, y1, y2, color);
}
```

HORLINE.C

```c
/* HORLINE.C draws a fast horizontal line. */

#define TRUE -1
#define FALSE 0
#define max(x,y)    (((x) > (y)) ? (x) : (y))
#define abs(x)      (((x) < 0) ? -(x) : (x))
#define sign(x)  ((x) > 0 ? 1 : ((x) == 0 ? 0 : (-1)))
#define ENABLE 0x0F
#define INDEXREG 0x3CE
#define VALREG 0x3CF
#define OUTINDEX(index, val)   {outp(INDEXREG, index); \
                                outp(VALREG, val);}
#define EGABASE 0xA0000000L
#define WIDTH 80L
#define XMAX 639
#define YMAX 199
#define XMIN 0
#define YMIN 0



horline(x1, x2, y, color)
int x1, x2, y, color;
{
int i;

if (x1 > x2) swap(&x1, &x2);

OUTINDEX(1, ENABLE); /* enable write */

for (i = x1; i <= x2; ++i)
     points(i, y, color);

OUTINDEX(0,0);        /* reset register */
OUTINDEX(1,0);        /* reset ENABLE */
OUTINDEX(8,TRUE);     /* reset bit mask */
}
```

VERLINE.C

```
/* VERLINE.C draws a fast line. */

#define TRUE -1
#define FALSE 0
#define max(x,y)    (((x) > (y)) ? (x) : (y))
#define abs(x)       (((x) < 0) ? -(x) : (x))
#define sign(x)  ((x) > 0 ? 1 : ((x) == 0 ? 0 : (-1)))
#define ENABLE 0x0F
#define INDEXREG 0x3CE
#define VALREG 0x3CF
#define OUTINDEX(index, val)   {outp(INDEXREG, index);\
                                 outp(VALREG, val);}
#define EGABASE 0xA0000000L
#define WIDTH 80L
#define XMAX 639
#define YMAX 199
#define XMIN 0
#define YMIN 0

verline(x, y1, y2, color)
int x, y1, y2, color;
{
int i;

if (y1 > y2) swap(&y1, &y2);

OUTINDEX(1, ENABLE); /* enable write */

for (i = y1; i <= y2; ++i)
     points(x, i, color);

OUTINDEX(0,0);        /* reset register */
OUTINDEX(1,0);        /* reset ENABLE */
OUTINDEX(8,TRUE);     /* reset bit mask */
}
```

SWAP.C

```
/* SWAP.C swaps two integers.  */

swap(x, y)
int *x, *y;
{
int z;

z = *x;
*x = *y;
*y = z;
}
```

SCALE.C

```
/* SCALE.C scales the size of an object. */

scale(x, y, offset_x, offset_y, factor)
double *x, *y, offset_x, offset_y, factor;
{

*x -= offset_x;
*y -= offset_y;

*x *= factor;
*y *= factor;

*x += offset_x;
*y += offset_y;
}
```

STRETCH.C

```c
/* STRETCH.C scales the size of an object along either the X
or Y axes. */

#define X 0
#define Y 1

stretch(x, y, offset_x, offset_y, factor, axis)
double *x, *y, offset_x, offset_y, factor, axis;
int axis;
{

if (axis == Y)
    {
    *x -= offset_x;

    *x *= factor;

    *x += offset_x;

    }
else {
    *x -= offset_x;

    *x *= factor;

    *x += offset_x;
    }
}
```

TRANSLATE.C

```c
/* TRANSLATE.C translates a point by a specified offset. */

translate(x, y, offset_x, offset_y)
double *x, *y, offset_x, offset_y;
{

*x += offset_x;
*y += offset_y;
}
```

ROTATE.C

```
/* ROTATE.C rotates a single point around the origin of the
** two-dimensional coordinate system.  Angle is in radians.*/

#include <math.h>

rotate(x, y, angle)
double *x, *y, angle;
{
double x_temp = *x;

*x = x_temp * cos(angle) - *y * sin(angle);
*y = x_temp * sin(angle) + *y * cos(angle);
}
```

ROTATE3D.C

```
/* ROTATE3D.C rotates a single point around the origin of the
** three-dimensional coordinate system.
** Angles are in radians.*/

#include <math.h>

#define X 0
#define Y 1
#define Z 2
#define FNX(x, y, theta) ((x) * cos(theta) -  (y) * sin(theta));
#define FNY(x, y, theta) ((x) * sin(theta) +  (y) * cos(theta));

struct
    {
```

```
       double home[3];
       } state;

rotate3d(x, y, z, angle)
double *x, *y, *z, angle[];
{
double rotx, roty, rotz;
double tempx, tempy;

if (angle[X] == 0.0 && angle[Y] == 0.0 && angle[Z] == 0.0)
                return;

rotx = *x - state.home[X];
roty = *y - state.home[Y];
rotz = *z - state.home[Z];

tempy = roty;
roty = FNX(tempy,rotz,angle[X]);   /* around X axis */
rotz = FNY(tempy,rotz,angle[X]);
tempx = rotx;
rotx = FNX(tempx,rotz,angle[Y]);   /* around Y axis */
rotz = FNY(tempx,rotz,angle[Y]);
tempx = rotx;
rotx = FNX(tempx,roty,angle[Z]);   /* then around Z axis */
roty = FNY(tempx,roty,angle[Z]);

*x = rotx + state.home[X];
*y = roty + state.home[Y];
*z = rotz + state.home[Z];
}
```

POINTS.C

```
/* POINTS.C is used to plot points when OUTINDEX will be used
** in the calling function to set and reset the controller.
** If set and reset can be done only once for a set of points
** it saves time for each point. */

#define TRUE 0xFF
#define ENABLE 0x0F
```

```
#define INDEXREG 0x3CE
#define VALREG 0x3CF
#define OUTINDEX(index, val)    {outp(INDEXREG, index);\
                                   outp(VALREG, val);}
#define EGABASE 0xA0000000L
#define WIDTH 80L
#define XMAX 639
#define YMAX 199
#define XMIN 0
#define YMIN 0


points(x, y, color)
int x, y, color;
{
unsigned char mask = 0x80, exist_color;
char far *base;

/* If coordinates are off display, abort. */

if (x < XMIN || x > XMAX || y < YMIN || y > YMAX) return;

base = (char far *)(EGABASE
                    + ((long)y * WIDTH + ((long)x / 8L)));

mask >>= x % 8;

exist_color = *base; /* existing color into EGA register */

OUTINDEX(0, color);   /* set new color*/
OUTINDEX(8, mask);    /* set mask */

*base &= TRUE;        /* force a write to the EGA */

}
```

LINEP.C

```
/* LINEP.C plots a line in 3-space and projects it, point by
point, onto a projection plane.  It is a 3-dimensional
```

```
version of Bresenham's algorithm. */

#define TRUE -1
#define FALSE 0
#define max(x,y)    (((x) > (y)) ? (x) : (y))
#define abs(x)       (((x) < 0.0) ? -(x) : (x))
#define sign(x)  ((x) > 0.0 ? 1 : ((x) == 0 ? 0 : (-1)))
#define ENABLE 0x0F
#define INDEXREG 0x3CE
#define VALREG 0x3CF
#define OUTINDEX(index, val)   {outp(INDEXREG, index);\
                                 outp(VALREG, val);}
#define EGABASE 0xA0000000L
#define WIDTH 80L
#define XMAX 639
#define YMAX 199
#define XMIN 0
#define YMIN 0


linep(x, y, z, xo, yo, zo, d, color, cell)
double x[], y[], z[], xo, yo, zo, d, cell;
int color;
{
double i, ix, iy, iz, incl, inc2, inc, xt, yt, zt;
double dx, dy, dz, plotx, ploty, plotz;
int plot;

/* cell is physical dimension of single raster cell */
cell = (cell <= 0.0) ? 1.0 : cell;

OUTINDEX(1, ENABLE); /* enable write */

dx = x[1] - x[0];
dy = y[1] - y[0];
dz = z[1] - z[0];
ix = abs(dx) / cell;
iy = abs(dy) / cell;
iz = abs(dz) / cell;
incl = max(ix, iy);
inc2 = max(ix, iz);
inc = max(incl, inc2);

plotx = x[0];
ploty = y[0];
```

```
plotz = z[0];

xt = yt = zt = 0.0;

pointp(plotx, ploty, plotz, xo, yo, zo, d, color);

for (i = 0.0; i <= inc; i += cell)
     {
     xt += ix;
     yt += iy;
     zt += iz;
     plot = FALSE;

     if (xt > inc)
         {
         plot = TRUE;
         xt -= inc;
         plotx += sign(dx);
         }

     if (yt > inc)
         {
         plot = TRUE;
         yt -= inc;
         ploty += sign(dy);
         }

     if (zt > inc)
         {
         plot = TRUE;
         zt -= inc;
         plotz += sign(dz);
         }

     if (plot)
         pointp(plotx, ploty, plotz, xo, yo, zo, d, color);
     }

OUTINDEX(0,0);        /* reset register */
OUTINDEX(1,0);        /* reset ENABLE */
OUTINDEX(8,TRUE);     /* reset bit mask */
}
```

POINTP.C

```
/* POINTP.C projects a point in perspective.  */

#define TRUE 0xFF
#define ENABLE 0x0F
#define INDEXREG 0x3CE
#define VALREG 0x3CF
#define OUTINDEX(index, val)  {outp(INDEXREG, index);\
                                 outp(VALREG, val);}
#define EGABASE 0xA0000000L
#define WIDTH 80L
#define XMAX 639
#define YMAX 199
#define XMIN 0
#define YMIN 0

pointp(x, y, z, xo, yo, zo, d, color)
double x, y, z, xo, yo, zo, d;
int color;
{
int xout, yout;
double xp, zp;
unsigned char mask = 0x80, exist_color;
char far *base;

projectr(x, y, z, xo, yo, zo, d, &xp, &zp);

xout = xp + 0.5;
yout = zp + 0.5;

yout = YMAX - yout; /* invert the display */
                    /* so 0,0 is at lower left */

/* If coordinates are off display, abort. */

if (xout < XMIN || xout > XMAX || yout < YMIN || yout > YMAX)
                    return;

base = (char far *)(EGABASE
                    + ((long)yout * WIDTH + ((long)xout / 8L)));
```

```
mask >>= xout % 8;

exist_color = *base; /* read existing color into EGA register */

OUTINDEX(0, color);   /* set new color*/
OUTINDEX(8, mask);    /* set mask */

*base &= TRUE;        /* force a write to the EGA */
}
```

MODEGET.C

```
/* MODEGET.C gets EGA modes */

#include <dos.h>

modeget()
{
union REGS regs;

regs.h.al = 0;
regs.h.ah = 0x0f;
int86(0x10, &regs, &regs);
return(regs.h.al);
}
```

PROJECTR.C

```
/* PROJECTR.C projects a point onto a projection plane given
the X,Y,Z location of the point, the location of the
observer, and the distance from the observer to the plane of
projection. */

#define TINY 1.0E-306
#define ABS(a) (((a) < 0.0) ? -(a) : (a))
```

```
projectr(x, y, z, xo, yo, zo, d, xp, zp)
double x, y, z, xo, yo, zo, d, *xp, *zp;
{
double ratio;

x -= xo;  /* bring observer to origin */
y -= yo;
z -= zo;

y = (y < TINY) ? TINY : y; /* eliminates points behind */
                          /* observer */

ratio = ABS(d) / y;  /* you can eliminate ABS() if you */
                     /* guarantee d is positive */ .

*xp = x * ratio;
*zp = z * ratio;

*xp += xo;  /* return observer to old location */
*zp += zo;
}
```

LINEF.C

```
/* LINEF.C is a generalized function to draw a line
** using Bresenham's Algorithm.
** Line can be XORed against background.  First point, if
** XORed would produce gaps at endpoints, so no XOR for it.
** Style mask, if 0, gives solid line.  If not 0 the style
** mask produces a bit-pattern line as desired.
*/

#define TRUE -1
#define FALSE 0
#define max(x,y)    (((x) > (y)) ? (x) : (y))
#define abs(x)      (((x) < 0) ? -(x) : (x))
#define sign(x)  ((x) > 0 ? 1 : ((x) == 0 ? 0 : (-1)))
#define ENABLE 0x0F
#define INDEXREG 0x3CE
```

```
#define VALREG 0x3CF
#define OUTINDEX(index, val)   {outp(INDEXREG, index); \
                                   outp(VALREG, val);}
#define EGABASE 0xA0000000L
#define WIDTH 80L
#define XMAX 639
#define YMAX 199
#define XMIN 0
#define YMIN 0
#define XORIT 0x80
#define ORIT  0x00


linef(x1, y1, x2, y2, color, style, orxor, first_on)
int x1, y1, x2, y2, color, orxor, first_on;
unsigned style;
{
int ix, iy, i, inc, x, y, dx, dy, plot, plotx, ploty;
unsigned style_mask;

style = (style == 0) ? 0xFFFF : style;

style_mask = style;

OUTINDEX(1, ENABLE); /* enable write */
if (orxor == XORIT)
    OUTINDEX(3, 0x18);  /* code to graphics controller */

dx = x2 - x1;
dy = y2 - y1;
ix = abs(dx);
iy = abs(dy);
inc = max(ix, iy);

plotx = x1;
ploty = y1;
x = y = 0;

if (first_on)  /* first point can be left off if needed */
    points(plotx, ploty, color);

for (i = 0; i <= inc; ++i)
    {
    if (style_mask == 0) style_mask = style;
    x += ix;
```

```
        y += iy;
        plot = FALSE;

        if (x > inc)
                {
                plot = TRUE;
                x -= inc;
                plotx += sign(dx);
                }

        if (y > inc)
                {
                plot = TRUE;
                y -= inc;
                ploty += sign(dy);
                }

        if (plot && style_mask & 0x0001)
                points(plotx, ploty, color);

        style_mask >>= 1;
        }

OUTINDEX(0,0);          /* reset register */
OUTINDEX(1,0);          /* reset ENABLE */
if (orxor == XORIT)
        OUTINDEX(3, 0); /* reset XOR to unchanged */
OUTINDEX(8,TRUE);       /* reset bit mask */
}
```

ALLOCATE.C

```
/* ALLOCATE.C allocates a block of memory using
 *  DOS function 48h. */

#include <dos.h>

int allocate(paragraphs, allowed, segment)
unsigned paragraphs, *allowed, *segment;
{
```

```
int error_code;
union REGS inregs, outregs;

inregs.h.ah = 0x48;
inregs.x.bx = paragraphs;
intdos(&inregs, &outregs);    /* DOS function 0x48h */
error_code = outregs.x.cflag;

if (error_code == 0)
    {
    *allowed = outregs.x.bx;    /* size */
    *segment = outregs.x.ax;    /* segment */
    }
else if (error_code == 8)
    *allowed = outregs.x.bx;    /* not enough memory */
else *allowed = 0;

return(error_code);
}
```

FREALLOC.C

```
/* FREALLOC.C frees space allocated using allocate(). */

#include <dos.h>

int frealloc(segment)
unsigned segment;
{
union REGS inregs, outregs;
struct SREGS segregs;

inregs.h.ah = 0x49;    /* DOS function 49h */
segregs.es = segment;
intdosx(&inregs, &outregs, &segregs);

return(outregs.x.cflag);
}
```

COPYBOX.C

```
/* COPYBOX.C copies a source box to a destination area
 *  without the need for an intermediate buffer. */

#define ENABLE 0x0F
#define INDEXREG 0x3CE
#define VALREG 0x3CF
#define OUTINDEX(index, val)   {outp(INDEXREG, index);\
                                  outp(VALREG, val);}
#define XORIT 0x80
#define ORIT   0x00

copybox(x1s, y1s, x2s, y2s, x1d, y1d, x2d, y2d)
int x1s, y1s, x2s, y2s, x1d, y1d, x2d, y2d;
{
int xuls, yuls, xlrs, ylrs;
int xuld, yuld;
int offset_x, offset_y;
int x, y;

xuls = (x2s > x1s) ? x1s : x2s;
yuls = (y2s > y1s) ? y1s : y2s;
xlrs = (x2s > x1s) ? x2s : x1s;
ylrs = (y2s > y1s) ? y2s : y1s;

xuld = (x2d > x1d) ? x1d : x2d;
yuld = (y2d > y1d) ? y1d : y2d;

offset_x = xuld - xuls;
offset_y = yuld - yuls;

if (offset_x == 0 && offset_y == 0) return(-1);

OUTINDEX(1, ENABLE); /* enable write */
if (orxor == XORIT)
    OUTINDEX(3, 0x18);  /* code to graphics controller */

/* since both offsets can't be 0, you can include 0 */

if (offset_x >= 0)              /* dest. to right */
```

```
        {                       /* copy from right to left */
     if (offset_y <  0)         /* dest. above */
        {                       /* copy from top to bottom */
        for (y = yuls+1; y < ylrs; ++y)
            for (x = xlrs-1; x > xuls; --x)
                points(x+offset_x, y+offset_y, readpt(x, y));
        }
     else {                     /* copy from bottom to top */
        for (y = ylrs-1; y > ylrs; --y)
            for (x = xlrs-1; x > xuls; --x)
                points(x+offset_x, y+offset_y, readpt(x, y));
        }
     }

if (offset_x <  0)             /* dest. to left */
    {                          /* copy from left to right */
     if (offset_y <  0)        /* dest. above */
        {                      /* copy from top to bottom */
        for (y = yuls+1; y < ylrs; ++y)
            for (x = xuls+1; x < xlrs; ++x)
                points(x+offset_x, y+offset_y, readpt(x, y));
        }
     else {                    /* copy from bottom to top */
        for (y = yuls+1; y < ylrs; ++y)
            for (x = xuls+1; x < xlrs; ++x)
                points(x+offset_x, y+offset_y, readpt(x, y));
        }
     }

OUTINDEX(0,0);        /* reset register */
OUTINDEX(1,0);        /* reset ENABLE */
if (orxor == XORIT)
    OUTINDEX(3, 0); /* reset XOR to unchanged */
OUTINDEX(8,TRUE);     /* reset bit mask */

return(0);
}
```

COM—FILL.C

```
/* COM_FILL.C creates a complex fill for non-regular
 * boundaries.  The procedure is tolerant of inclusions and
 * incursions as long as boundaries are continuous (they
 * connect) and do not intersect or touch each other.
 * Lengths of arrays must be predicted carefully.
 */

#define TRUE -1
#define FALSE 0
#define ON TRUE
#define OFF FALSE
#define X 0
#define Y 1

com_fill(line_array, coord_array, length, style, color, orxor)
int line_array[][4], coord_array[][2];
unsigned length, style;
int color, orxor;
{
unsigned pointer, element = 0, sorted = FALSE, new_start = 1;

for (pointer = 0; pointer < length; ++pointer)
    line_int(line_array[pointer], coord_array, &element);

while(!sorted)  /* sort on y */
    {
    sorted = TRUE;
    for (pointer = 1; pointer < element; ++pointer)
        if (coord_array[pointer-1][Y]
            > coord_array[pointer][Y])
            {
            swap(&coord_array[pointer-1][Y],
                &coord_array[pointer][Y]);
            swap(&coord_array[pointer-1][X],
                &coord_array[pointer][X]);
            sorted = FALSE;
            }
    }

sorted = FALSE;
while(!sorted)  /* sort on x within y */
    {
    sorted = TRUE;
    for (pointer = new_start; pointer < element; ++pointer)
        if (coord_array[pointer-1][Y]
```

```
                        == coord_array[pointer][Y])
                    if (coord_array[pointer-1][X]
                        > coord_array[pointer][X])
                        {
                        swap(&coord_array[pointer-1][Y],
                            &coord_array[pointer][Y]);
                        swap(&coord_array[pointer-1][X],
                            &coord_array[pointer][X]);
                        sorted = FALSE;
                        }
                else {
                    if (sorted == TRUE) new_start = pointer;
                    sorted = FALSE;
                    break;
                    }
            }

for (pointer = 0; pointer < element; pointer += 2)
    linef(coord_array[pointer][X],
            coord_array[pointer][Y],
            coord_array[pointer+1][X],
            coord_array[pointer+1][Y],
            color, style, orxor, ON);
}



line_int(line_array, coord_array, element)
int line_array[4], coord_array[][2], *element;
{
int ix, iy, i, inc, x, y, dx, dy, plot, plotx, ploty;

dx = line_array[2] - line_array[0];
dy = line_array[3] - line_array[1];
ix = abs(dx);
iy = abs(dy);
inc = max(ix, iy);

plotx = line_array[0];
ploty = line_array[1];
x = y = 0;

/* first pixel on line is not plotted */
/* last pixel on line is not plotted */
/* thus endpoints are not included */
```

```
for (i = 0; i < inc; ++i)
    {
    x += ix;
    y += iy;
    plot = FALSE;

    if (x > inc)
        {
        plot = TRUE;
        x -= inc;
        plotx += sign(dx);
        }

    if (y > inc)
        {
        plot = TRUE;
        y -= inc;
        ploty += sign(dy);
        }

    if (plot)
        {
        coord_array[*element][X] = plotx;
        coord_array[*element++][Y] = ploty;
        }
    }
}
```

CIRCLE—R.C

```
/* CIRCLE_R.C  generates a circle or arc given the location
 *  of the center and the radius, or the locations of any
 *  three points assumed to be on the perimeter.  The circle
 *  can also be specified as an inside or outside arc drawn
 *  between two points.  The angular resolution (chording) of
 *  the circle can also be specified.
 *
 *  Usage:  values of r      values of arc      action taken
 *             > 0                 0             full radial circle
```

```
*                > 0            1              interior arc
*                > 0            2              exterior arc
*                  0            0              full 3-point circle
*                  0            1              interior arc
*                  0            2              exterior arc
*/

#include <math.h>

#define TRUE -1
#define FALSE 0
#define max(x,y)    (((x) > (y)) ? (x) : (y))
#define min(x,y)    (((x) < (y)) ? (x) : (y))
#define abs(x)      (((x) < 0) ? -(x) : (x))
#define sign(x)   ((x) > 0 ? 1 : ((x) == 0 ? 0 : (-1)))
#define PI 3.141592654
#define ON TRUE
#define OFF FALSE


int circle_r(xc, yc, r, x_list, y_list, arc, increment,
        color, style, orxor)
double xc, yc, r, x_list[], y_list[], increment;
int arc, color, style, orxor;
{
int xnew, ynew;
double angle[3], angle_a, angle_b, max_angle, min_angle;
double inc_angle;
double xrot, yrot;
double local_min, local_max;
int i;


if (r != 0)  /* if radius specified, no 3 points */
    {
    x_list[2] = x_list[1];
    y_list[2] = y_list[1];
    }

for (i = 0; i <= 2; ++i)  /* find subtended angles */
    {
    angle[i] = atan2(y_list[i], x_list[i]);
    if (sign(angle[i]) == -1)
        angle[i] += 2 * PI;
    }
```

```
if (r == 0) /* derive xc, yc and r using list */
    {
    center(x_list, y_list, &xc, &yc, &r);

    angle_a = max(angle[0], angle[1]);
    angle_b = max(angle[1], angle[2]);
    max_angle = max(angle_a, angle_b);

    angle_a = min(angle[0], angle[1]);
    if (angle_a == angle[1])
        {
        swap(x_list[0], x_list[1]);
        swap(y_list[0], y_list[1]);
        }
    angle_b = min(angle[1], angle[2]);
    if (angle_b == angle[2])
        {
        swap(x_list[1], x_list[2]);
        swap(y_list[1], y_list[2]);
        }
    min_angle = min(angle_a, angle_b);
    }
else {
    max_angle = max(angle[0], angle[1]);
    min_angle = min(angle[0], angle[1]);
    if (angle_a == angle[1])
        {
        swap(x_list[0], x_list[1]);
        swap(y_list[0], y_list[1]);
        }

    }

/* now (xlist[0], ylist[0]) has the coordinates with the
 *   smallest angle from 0 */

/* draw circle or arc */
switch(arc)
    {
    case 0:  /* full circle */
        lastx = r - xc;
        lasty = 0;

        for (inc_angle = 0; inc_angle < 2 * PI;
                inc_angle += increment)
```

```
            {
            rotate(r - xc, 0 - yc,
                    &xrot, &yrot, inc_angle);
            linef(lastx, lasty, xrot+xc, yrot+yc,
                    color, style, orxor, OFF);
            lastx = xrot;
            lasty = yrot;
            }
        linef(lastx, lasty, r+xc, 0+yc,
                color, style, orxor, OFF);
        break;

case 1:  /* interior arc */
        lastx = x_list[0];
        lasty = y_list[0];
        local_min = 0;
        local_max = max_angle - min_angle;
        for (inc_angle = local_min; inc_angle < local_max;
                inc_angle += increment)
            {
            rotate(x_list[0]-xc, y_list[0]-yc,
                    &xrot, &yrot, inc_angle+min_angle);
            linef(lastx, lasty, xrot+xc, yrot+yc,
                    color, style, orxor, OFF);
            lastx = xrot;
            lasty = yrot;
            }
        rotate(x_list[0]-xc, y_list[0]-yc,
                &xrot, &yrot, max_angle);
        linef(lastx, lasty, xrot+xc, yrot+yc,
                    color, style, orxor, OFF);
        break;

case 2:  /* exterior arc */
        lastx = x_list[2];
        lasty = y_list[2];
        local_min = 0;
        local_max = max_angle - min_angle;
        for (inc_angle = local_max; inc_angle < 2 * PI;
                inc_angle += increment)
            {
            rotate(x_list[2]-xc, y_list[2]-yc,
                    &xrot, &yrot, inc_angle+min_angle);
            linef(lastx, lasty, xrot+xc, yrot+yc,
                    color, style, orxor, OFF);
```

```
                  lastx = xrot;
                  lasty = yrot;
              }
          rotate(x_list[2]-xc, y_list[2]-yc,
                  &xrot, &yrot, min_angle);
          linef(lastx, lasty, xrot+xc, yrot+yc,
                       color, style, orxor, OFF);
          break;
    }
}



rotatec(xin, yin, x, y, angle)
double xin, yin, *x, *y, angle;
{

*x = xin * cos(angle) - yin * sin(angle);
*y = xin * sin(angle) + yin * cos(angle);
}



swap(x, y)
double *x, *y;
{
double t;

t = *x;
*x = *y;
*y = t;
}
```

BRUSH—OUT.C

```
/* BRUSH_OUT.C uses a pre-defined brush to change pixel
*  colors. */

#define TRUE -1
```

```
#define FALSE 0
#define ENABLE 0x0F
#define INDEXREG 0x3CE
#define VALREG 0x3CF
#define OUTINDEX(index, val)   {outp(INDEXREG, index);\
                                outp(VALREG, val);}
#define XORIT 0x80
#define ORIT  0x00

long brush[32];

brush_out(x, y, color, orxor)
int x, y, color, orxor;
{
int i, j;

OUTINDEX(1, ENABLE); /* enable write */
if (orxor == XORIT)
    OUTINDEX(3, 0x18);  /* code to graphics controller */

for (j = y; j < y + 32; ++j)
    for (i = x; i < x + 32; ++i)
        if (brush[j-y] && 0x80000000L >> (i - x))
            points(i, j, color);

OUTINDEX(0,0);         /* reset register */
OUTINDEX(1,0);         /* reset ENABLE */
if (orxor == XORIT)
    OUTINDEX(3, 0); /* reset XOR to unchanged */
OUTINDEX(8,TRUE);     /* reset bit mask */
}
```

BRUSH—IN.C

```
/* BRUSH_IN.C defines and stores a brush given the upper left
 * corner.  You must define brush external to main() if it is
 * to be used in other parts of your program.  You could
 * initialize it with your favorite brush pattern. */

long brush[32];
```

```
brush_in(x, y, color)
int x, y, color;
{
int i, j;

for (j = y; j < y + 32; ++j)
    for (i = x; i < x + 32; ++i)
            {
            if (color == readpt(x, y))
                    brush[j-y] |= 0x80000000L >> (i - x);
            else brush[j-y] &= ~(0x80000000L >> (i - x));
            }
}
```

PUTEGA.C

```
/* PUTEGA.C puts the contents of the EGA buffer to disk
** given a filename.  This version works with EGA mode 14,
** but you can easily modify it.  Storage is limited to
** page 0.  Remember to use the /Ze option when you compile. */

#include <stdio.h>
#include <memory.h>
#include <dos.h>


#define TRUE -1
#define FALSE 0
#define XMAX 639
#define YMAX 199
#define XCOUNT (XMAX>>1)+1

union
    {
    struct
        {
        unsigned char lobyte : 4;
        unsigned char hibyte : 4;
        } parts;
```

```
       struct
            {
            unsigned char allbyte;
            } whole;
       } dbl;


putega(filename)
char *filename;
{
FILE *file_stream;
int y;

/* if any error opening file, abort with error set   */
/* Any existing file by this name will be lost!!      */
/* Test for existing files before using this function. */


if ((file_stream = fopen(filename, "wb")) == NULL)
     return(-1);

for (y = 0; y <= YMAX; ++y)
     put_row(y, file_stream);

fclose(file_stream);
return(0);
}


put_row(y, file_stream)
int y;
FILE *file_stream;
{
char buffer[XCOUNT];
int x;

     for (x = 0; x < XMAX; x += 2)
          {
          dbl.parts.hibyte = readpt(x, y);
          dbl.parts.lobyte = readpt(x+1, y);
          buffer[x>>1] = dbl.whole.allbyte;
          }

     fwrite(buffer, 1, XCOUNT, file_stream);
}
```

GETEGA.C

```
/* GETEGA.C gets the contents of the EGA buffer from disk
** given a filename.  This version works with EGA mode 14,
** but you can easily modify it.  Storage is limited to
** page 0.  Remember to use the /Ze option when you compile. */

#include <stdio.h>
#include <memory.h>
#include <dos.h>


#define TRUE -1
#define FALSE 0
#define ENABLE 0x0F
#define EGAMEMSEG 0xA0000000L /* Works for mode 14 */
#define EGAWIDTH 80L
#define XMAX 639
#define YMAX 199
#define XCOUNT (XMAX>>1)+1
#define INDEXREG 0x3CE
#define VALREG 0x3CF
#define OUTINDEX(index, val) { outp(INDEXREG, index);\
                               outp(VALREG, val); }

union
     {
     struct
          {
          unsigned char lobyte : 4;
          unsigned char hibyte : 4;
          } parts;
     struct
          {
          unsigned char allbyte;
          } whole;
     } dbl;
```

```
getega(filename)
char *filename;
{
FILE *file_stream;
int y;


/* if any error opening file, abort with error set */
if ((file_stream = fopen(filename, "rb")) == NULL)
    return(-1);

/*
** This example uses only one monitor type, RGB.
** You could add the Enhanced Display or Monochrome monitor.
** Likewise, only two modes are used.
** You could add other modes.
** The EGA graphics spec is VERY flexible.
*/

OUTINDEX(1, ENABLE); /* enable write */

for (y = 0; y <= YMAX; ++y)
    get_row(y, file_stream);

OUTINDEX(0,0);          /* reset register */
OUTINDEX(1,0);          /* reset ENABLE */
OUTINDEX(8,0xFF);       /* reset bit mask */

fclose(file_stream);
return(0);
}


get_row(y, file_stream)
int y;
FILE *file_stream;
{
char buffer[XCOUNT];
int x;


fread(buffer, 1, XCOUNT, file_stream);

for (x = 0; x < XMAX; x += 2)
    {
```

```
        dbl.whole.allbyte = buffer[x>>1];
        points(x, y, dbl.parts.hibyte);
        points(x+1, y, dbl.parts.lobyte);
        }
}
```

READPT.C

```
/* READPT.C  reads a point at x,y and returns color using
** BIOS. */

#include <dos.h>

int readpt(x, y)
int x, y;
{
union REGS regs;

regs.h.ah = 0xD;
regs.h.bh = 0;   /* display page is 0 */
regs.x.cx = x;
regs.x.dx = y;

int86(0x10, &regs, &regs);

return(regs.h.al);
}
```

ICBEGA.C

```
/* ICBEGA.C dithers from ICB to EGA.
** You can use this simple program to prepare EGA menus from
** real-world images if you have an ICB and a home TV camera!
** This function assumes a properly initialized ICB.
** See your AT&T manual for details. EGA mode is 14.
```

```
** Use the /Ze option on compile to enable 'far' keyword.
** See "Exploring the EGA" in PC Magazine, August and
** September, 1986 for more detail about this technique.
** Charles Petzold describes the use of the 'far' keyword to
** rapidly move graphic data.  Also see IBM's Technical
** Reference for the Enhanced Graphics Controller Adapter. */

#include <dos.h>
#include <conio.h>

#define TRUE -1
#define FALSE 0
#define ENABLE 0x0F
#define ICBWIDTH 256L
#define EGAWIDTH 80L
#define TOTALROWS 350
#define TOTALCOLS 640
#define EGAMAXRO 199
#define ICBMAXCOL 212
#define EGAMAXCOL 79
#define INDEXREG 0x3CE
#define VALREG 0x3CF
#define ICBASE 0X3A8   /* Depends on jumper settings, */
                       /* factory default */
#define ICBMEMSEG 0xD0000000L /* Depends on jumper settings. */
                       /* Factory default is 0xA000, but */
                       /* 0xD000 avoids conflict with EGA! */
#define EGAMEMSEG 0xA0000000L /* Works for mode 14 */
#define ICBCORRECT 0x2CL /* add offset to center image */
#define OUTINDEX(index, val) {outp(INDEXREG, index);\
                              outp(VALREG, val);}
#define RED   0
#define GREEN 1
#define BLUE 2

union           /* ICB bits */
    {
    struct
        {
        unsigned blue : 5;
        unsigned green : 5;
        unsigned red : 5;
        unsigned overlay : 1;
        } colors;
    struct
```

```
            {
            unsigned colrs;
            } all;
} icbwd;

/*
**   This is one of many ways in which color values can be
**   set on the EGA.  Direct modification of RAM is possible,
**   as is the use of Int 10h, with varying speed and
**   complexity problems.  Transfer from other video capture
**   sources can be done by customizing this technique.
*/

icbega()
{
int icb_row;
int ega_row = 0;

/* The ICB display is read from top down. */

/* select pg 2     */
outp(ICBASE, 0xcc | 2);  /* forces display on, genlock on */

for (icb_row = 71; icb_row >= 0; --icb_row, ++ega_row)
     pr_line(icb_row, ega_row);

/* select pg 1     */
outp(ICBASE, 0xcc | 3);


for (icb_row = 127; icb_row >= 0; --icb_row, ++ega_row)
     pr_line(icb_row, ega_row);

return(0);
}



pr_line(icb_row, ega_row)
int icb_row, ega_row;
{
unsigned far *icb_dat
          = (unsigned far *)(ICBMEMSEG + ICBCORRECT
          + (long)((ICBWIDTH << 1)
          * (long)icb_row));
```

```
char far *ega_dat
        = (char far *)(EGAMEMSEG + EGAWIDTH
        * (long)ega_row);
static char red[] =    "0000000000111111111111122222222222";
static char green[] = "0000000000111111111111122222222222";
static char blue[] =  "0000000000111111111111122222222222";
unsigned char dither, color, exist_color;
unsigned char mask;
int icb_count;

/* initialize the mask */
mask = 0x80;

for (icb_count = 0; icb_count <= ICBMAXCOL; ++icb_count)
    {
    icbwd.all.colrs = *icb_dat++;

    /* red, green and blue values are extracted */

    for (dither = 0; dither <= 2; ++dither)
        {
        switch (dither)
            {
            case RED:
                switch (red[icbwd.colors.red])
                    {
                    case '0':
                            color = 0x0;
                            break;
                    case '1':
                            color = 0x4;
                            break;
                    case '2':
                            color = 0xC;
                            break;
                    }
                break;

            case GREEN:
                switch (green[icbwd.colors.green])
                    {
                    case '0':
                            color = 0x0;
                            break;
                    case '1':
```

```
                              color = 0x2;
                              break;
                      case '2':
                              color = 0xA;
                              break;
                }
          break;

      case BLUE:
          switch (blue[icbwd.colors.blue])
                {
                case '0':
                        color = 0x0;
                        break;
                case '1':
                        color = 0x1;
                        break;
                case '2':
                        color = 0x9;
                        break;
                }
          break;
      }

exist_color = *ega_dat;   /* read a color byte*/
                          /* into register */

OUTINDEX(0, color);       /* set reg to color value */
OUTINDEX(1, ENABLE);      /* ENABLE output */
OUTINDEX(8, mask);        /* set bit mask */

*ega_dat &= TRUE;         /* force a write to EGA */

/* rotate the mask */

if ((mask >>= 1) == 0)
    {
    mask = 0x80;
    ++ega_dat;   /* every 8 bits (colors) the
                 ** pointer is incremented */
    }
  }
}

OUTINDEX(0, 0);    /* reset register */
```

```
OUTINDEX(1, 0);      /* reset ENABLE */
OUTINDEX(8, TRUE);   /* reset bit mask */
}
```

XFORM.C

```
/* XFORM.C transforms a point's location including rotation,
** translation and scaling.  */

#include <math.h>


xform(x, y)
double *x, *y;
{
double x_temp;
extern double xlate_x, xlate_y;
extern double rot_center_x, rot_center_y;
extern double xform_angle, scale_factor;

x_temp = *x -= rot_center_x;
*y -= rot_center_y;

*x = x_temp * cos(xform_angle) - *y * sin(xform_angle);
*y = x_temp * sin(xform_angle) + *y * cos(xform_angle);

*x += rot_center_x;
*y += rot_center_y;

*x += xlate_x;
*y += xlate_y;

*x *= scale_factor;
*y *= scale_factor;
}
```

INKEY.C

```
/* INKEY.C fetches pending keypress. */

#include <dos.h>


int inkey(ascii)
int *ascii;
{
union REGS regs;

regs.x.ax = 0;

int86(22, &regs, &regs);

*ascii = regs.h.ah;

if (regs.h.al == 0)
    return(0);

*ascii = regs.h.al;
return(1);
}



read_pix2(x, y)
int x, y;
{
int color;
unsigned char mask = 0x80 >> x % 8;
char far *base = (char far *)(0xA0000000L + (long)y * 80L
                 + (long)x / 8L);

/* select read mode 1 using function 5 */
outp(0x3CE, 5); outp(0x3CF, 0x8);

outp(0x3CE, 2); /* select function 2 */

for (color = 0; color <= 0xF; ++color)
    {
    outp(0x3CF, color);
    if (*base & mask == mask) break;
```

```
        }

return(color);
}
```

COM—STR.ASM

```
; COM_STR.ASM   fetches a desired number of bytes
; (0 to 32767) from the serial input device.
; Usage from C:
;
;            char buffer[200];
;            int count;
;
;            com_str(buffer, count);
;
; Returns:
;            string of count characters in buffer
;            return value 0


COM_STR_TEXT      SEGMENT  BYTE PUBLIC 'CODE'
COM_STR_TEXT      ENDS
CONST      SEGMENT  WORD PUBLIC 'CONST'
CONST      ENDS
_BSS       SEGMENT  WORD PUBLIC 'BSS'
_BSS       ENDS
_DATA      SEGMENT  WORD PUBLIC 'DATA'
_DATA      ENDS
DGROUP     GROUP    CONST,     _BSS,     _DATA
    ASSUME  CS: COM_STR_TEXT, DS: DGROUP, SS: DGROUP,
            ES: DGROUP
PUBLIC     _com_str

COM_STR_TEXT   SEGMENT
    PUBLIC      _com_str
_com_str PROC   ..  FAR
         push      bp
         mov       bp,sp
                                  ; get pointer from stack
```

```
            mov        bx, [bp + 6]
                                  ; get count from stack
            mov        cx, Word Ptr [bp + 8]
            cmp        cx, 0
            je         exit

            and        cx,7FFFh  ; strip off high bit in
                                 ; case negative int was passed

not_ready:
                                 ; test for character
                                 ; in latch and no errors
            mov        dx, 3F8h  ; Register 0 (base)
            add        dx, 5     ; Register 5
            in         al, dx    ; Serial Status Register
            test       al, 1     ; Is only Data Ready set?
            jz         not_ready

                                 ; receive the character
            mov        dx, 3F8h  ; Register 0 (base)
            add        dx, 3     ; Register 3
            in         al, dx    ; Data Format Register
            and        al, 7Fh   ; make sure divisor latch
            out        dx, al    ; not selected
            mov        dx, 3F8h  ; Register 0 (base)
            in         al, dx    ; input the byte
                                 ; store byte in public string
            mov        Byte Ptr [bx], al
            inc        bx    .   ; point to next character
                                 ; supply ASCIIZ string
                                 ; terminator (null byte)
            mov        Byte Ptr [bx], 0
            dec        cx
            cmp        cx, 0
            jbe        exit      ; exit when cx reached
            loop       not_ready
exit:
            mov        ax, 0     ; always returns 0
            mov        sp,bp
            pop        bp
            ret
_com_str    ENDP

COM_STR_TEXT    ENDS
END
```

GET—SER.ASM

```
; GET_SER.ASM gets a single character from COM1.
; Declaration:
;          char get_ser();
;          char character;
; Usage:
;          character = get_ser();

GET_SER_TEXT    SEGMENT  BYTE PUBLIC 'CODE'
GET_SER_TEXT    ENDS
CONST       SEGMENT  WORD PUBLIC 'CONST'
CONST       ENDS
_BSS        SEGMENT  WORD PUBLIC 'BSS'
_BSS        ENDS
_DATA       SEGMENT  WORD PUBLIC 'DATA'
_DATA       ENDS
DGROUP      GROUP    CONST,    _BSS,    _DATA
      ASSUME  CS: GET_SER_TEXT, DS: DGROUP, SS: DGROUP,
              ES: DGROUP
PUBLIC     _get_ser

GET_SER_TEXT    SEGMENT
      PUBLIC    _get_ser
_get_ser  PROC      FAR
          push      bp
          mov       bp,sp

not_ready:
                              ; test for character
                              ; in latch and no errors
          mov       dx, 3F8h  ; Register 0 (base)
          add       dx, 5     ; Register 5
          in        al, dx    ; Serial Status Register
          test      al, 1     ; Is only Data Ready set?
          jz        not_ready

                              ; receive the character
          mov       dx, 3F8h  ; Register 0 (base)
```

```
        add     dx, 3       ; Register 3
        in      al, dx      ; Data Format Register
        and     al, 7Fh     ; make sure divisor latch
        out     dx, al      ; not selected
        mov     dx, 3F8h    ; Register 0 (base)
        in      al, dx      ; input the byte

        mov     sp,bp
        pop     bp
        ret
_get_ser  ENDP

GET_SER_TEXT   ENDS
END
```

INSTISR.C

```
/* INSTISR.C installs the serial interrupt service
** routine.  Refer to "serial interface at a glance"
** for register offsets used.
*/

#include <stdio.h>
#include <conio.h>
#include <dos.h>

struct ISRVEC
     {
     unsigned vecl;
     unsigned vech;
     unsigned type;
     };


extern struct ISRVEC isrvec;


instisr(service, request, port)
unsigned (*service)();
unsigned request;
```

```
unsigned long port;
{
unsigned far *base = (unsigned far *)port;
int i = 2;

outp((*base)+1, 1);  /* select interrupts */

/* maskable hardware interrupts must be unmasked */
/* in the 8259 interrupt mask register */
outp(0x21, inp(0x21) & ~0x10); /* unmask COM1 interrupt */

/* set the interrupt vector using DOS */
setvect(request, service);

/* enable interrupts selected */
outp((*base)+4, inp((*base)+4) | 8);

/* clear pending interrupts */

inp(*base);
inp(*base);
inp(*base);

return(0);
}


setvect(vector, service)
int vector;
unsigned (*service)();
{
union REGS regs;
struct SREGS sregs;

regs.h.al = vector;
regs.h.ah = 0x35;
int86x(0x21, &regs, &regs, &sregs);
isrvec.vech = sregs.es; /* segment */
isrvec.vecl = regs.x.bx; /* offset */
isrvec.type = vector;

sregs.ds = FP_SEG(service); /* segment */
regs.x.dx = FP_OFF(service); /* offset */
regs.h.al = vector;
regs.h.ah = 0x25;
```

```
int86x(0x21, &regs, &regs, &sregs);
}
```

UNINSTAL.C

```
/* UNINSTAL.C uninstalls the serial interrupt service
** routine.
*/

#include <stdio.h>
#include <dos.h>
#include <conio.h>

#define SERPORT1 0x00000400L
#define SERPORT2 0x00000402L
#define SERVEC1 12
#define SERVEC2 11

struct ISRVEC
     {
     unsigned vecl;
     unsigned vech;
     unsigned type;
     };

extern struct ISRVEC isrvec;

uninstal(port)
unsigned long port;
{
unsigned far *base = (unsigned far *)port;

/* disable interrupts selected */
outp(*base+4, inp(*base+4) & ~0x8);

outp(0x21, inp(0x21) | 0x10); /* mask IRQ4 */

outp((*base)+1, 0);  /* reset interrupts to 0 */

unsetvec();
```

```
return(0);
}


unsetvec()
{
union REGS regs;
struct SREGS sregs;

sregs.ds = isrvec.vech; /* segment */
regs.x.dx = isrvec.vecl; /* offset */
regs.h.al = isrvec.type;
regs.h.ah = 0x25;
int86x(0x21, &regs, &regs, &sregs);
}
```

SERISR.ASM

```
; SERISR.ASM is a serial interrupt service routine.

_TEXT     SEGMENT   BYTE PUBLIC 'CODE'
_TEXT     ENDS
CONST     SEGMENT   WORD PUBLIC 'CONST'
CONST     ENDS
_BSS      SEGMENT   WORD PUBLIC 'BSS'
_BSS      ENDS
_DATA     SEGMENT   WORD PUBLIC 'DATA'
_DATA     ENDS
DGROUP      GROUP      CONST,      _BSS,      _DATA
      ASSUME  CS: _TEXT, DS: DGROUP, SS: DGROUP, ES: DGROUP

            TOTAL     equ   64
            TOP       equ   63
            BOTTOM    equ   0

_DATA       SEGMENT
            buffer    db    TOTAL dup('@')
            front     dw    BOTTOM
```

```
            back        dw      BOTTOM
            count       dw      BOTTOM
        _DATA ENDS

    _TEXT SEGMENT
        PUBLIC  _serisr
    _serisr     PROC    FAR
            push        ax
            push        dx
            push        si
            push        ds
            mov         ax, DGROUP
            mov         ds, ax

            mov         dx, 3F8h        ; base register address
            in          al, dx          ; input a character

            mov         si, front
            mov           buffer[si], al

            inc         front
            inc         count
            cmp         front, TOP
            jbe         front_below
            mov         front, BOTTOM
    front_below:
            cmp         count, TOTAL
            jbe         count_below
            mov         count, TOTAL
    count_below:

            mov         al, 20h         ; signal interrupt mask
            out         20h, al         ; register complete

            pop         ds
            pop         si
            pop         dx
            pop         ax
            iret
    _serisr     ENDP



        PUBLIC      _buffchr
```

```
_buffchr    PROC       FAR
            cli
            push       bp
            mov        bp, sp
            push       ds
            mov        ax, DGROUP
            mov        ds, ax
            xor        ax, ax

            mov        ax, count

            pop        ds
            mov        sp, bp
            pop        bp
            sti
            ret
_buffchr    ENDP




PUBLIC      _readbuf
_readbuf    PROC       FAR
            cli
            push       bp
            mov        bp, sp
            push       si
            push       ds
            mov        ax, DGROUP
            mov        ds, ax
            xor        ax, ax

            cmp        count, BOTTOM
            jz         back_below

            mov        si, back
            mov        al, buffer[si]

            dec        count
            inc        back
            cmp        back, TOP
            jbe        back_below
            mov        back, BOTTOM
back_below:
            pop        ds
```

```
            pop        si
            mov        sp, bp
            pop        bp
            sti
            ret
_readbuf    ENDP


      _TEXT ENDS

END
```

RETRIEVE.C

```
/* RETRIEVE.C retrieves a drawing element from
** allocated buffer. */

#include <dos.h>
#include "file.h"

extern struct ELEMENT element;
extern struct SREGS segs;
extern union REGS regs;

retrieve(record)
unsigned record;
{
int srcseg, srcoff, destseg, destoff;
extern unsigned dwg_seg;

srcseg = dwg_seg + ((unsigned)sizeof(element) >> 4) * record;
srcoff = 0;
destseg = segs.ds;
destoff = (int)&element;

movedata(srcseg, srcoff, destseg, destoff,
          (unsigned)sizeof(element));
}
```

RESTPORT.C

```
/* RESTPORT.C restores the port settings for GRAPHIQ.
*/

#include <conio.h>
#include "graphiq.h"

extern unsigned far *outbase;
extern unsigned char baudlo, baudhi, bits;


restport()
{
/* restore port settings */
outp(*outbase + 3, bits);
outp(*outbase + 0, baudlo);
outp(*outbase + 1, baudhi);
/* turn off divisor latch select bit */
outp(*outbase + 3, inp(*outbase + 3) & 0x7F);
}
```

ISR—INST.C

```
/* ISR_INST.C installs serial ISR for GRAPHIQ.
*/

#include <conio.h>
#include "graphiq.h"

extern unsigned far *outbase;
extern unsigned char baudlo, baudhi, bits;
extern int digitizer;
extern unsigned char serisr(), readbuf(), get_dig();
extern unsigned buffchr();
```

```
isr_instal()
{
unsigned i;

if (*outbase == 0)
    {
    digitizer = FALSE;
    return(FALSE);
    }


/* turn pins 4 and 20 off */
outp((*outbase)+4, inp((*outbase)+4) & ~3);

bits = inp(*outbase + 3);
/* turn on baud divisor latch selector bit */
bits |= 0x80;
outp(*outbase + 3, bits);

/* set 8 data bits, 1 stop bit, no parity */
/* and select divisor latch */
outp(*outbase + 3, 0x83);

/* save existing baud rate */
baudlo = inp(*outbase + 0);
baudhi = inp(*outbase + 1);

/* set 9600 baud using 0x00C divisor */
/* set 1200 baud using 0x060 divisor */
outp(*outbase + 0, 0x0C);
outp(*outbase + 1, 0x00);

/* turn off baud divisor latch selector bit */
outp(*outbase + 3, inp(*outbase + 3) & 0x7F);

/* install interrupt service routine */
instisr(serisr, SERVEC1, SERPORT1);

/* turn pins 4 and 20 on */
outp((*outbase)+4, inp((*outbase)+4) | 3);
}
```

PUSHPOP.C

```
/* PUSHPOP.C  gives you the ability to push and
** pop doubles to a stack defined globally.
*/

push_dbl(pointer)
double *pointer;
{
extern double stack[];
extern int stack_ptr;

stack[stack_ptr++] = *pointer;
}


pop_dbl(pointer)
double *pointer;
{
extern double stack[];
extern int stack_ptr;

*pointer = stack[stack_ptr--];
}
```

LOCATOR.C

```
/* LOCATOR.C uses XOR to plot points from a matrix pattern.
**     You pass the x, y coordinates of the upper left corner,
**     the color of the pattern, and a pointer to an array of
**     pointers which contain the pattern as an array of
**     longs.  Bits set in the longs create the pattern. */

#define TRUE 0xFF
#define FALSE 0
#define ALLON TRUE
#define ENABLE 0x0F
#define INDEXREG 0x3CE
```

```
#define VALREG 0x3CF
#define OUTINDEX(index, val)   {outp(INDEXREG, index); \
                                 outp(VALREG, val);}

#define EGABASE 0xA0000000L
#define WIDTH 80L
#define XMAX 639
#define YMAX 199
#define XMIN 0
#define YMIN 0
#define XORPIX 0x18
#define XMETRIC 0.237546468
#define YMETRIC 0.096601942



locator(x, y, color, grid)
double x, y;
int color;
unsigned long grid[];   /* 16 by 16 bit matrix */
{
int i, j;
int xint, yint;
unsigned long mask = 0x80000000L;
extern double xlate_x, xlate_y;
extern double rot_center_x, rot_center_y;
extern double xform_angle, scale_factor;

xform(&x, &y);

x *= XMETRIC;
y = YMAX - y * YMETRIC;

xint = x -= 15;
yint = y -= 7;

OUTINDEX(3, XORPIX);  /* set index to XOR pixels */
OUTINDEX(1, ENABLE); /* enable write */

for (j = 0; j <= 15; ++j)
    for (i = 0; i <= 31; ++i)
        if (grid[j] & mask >> i)
            points(xint+i, yint+j, color);

OUTINDEX(0,0);        /* reset register */
OUTINDEX(1,0);        /* reset ENABLE */
```

```
OUTINDEX(3,0);          /* reset XOR to normal */
OUTINDEX(8,ALLON);      /* reset bit mask */
}
```

GET—DIG.C

```
/* GET_DIG.C gets a coordinate pair from Kurta
*/

#include <math.h>

#define DIGICVT 1.27  /* factor converts from inches */
                      /* on digitizer to millimeters */

extern double x, y;
extern int digitizer;
extern int snap;
extern double inc;
extern unsigned char serbuff[];
extern double xlate_x, xlate_y;

extern unsigned char serisr(), readbuf(), get_dig();
extern unsigned buffchr();

unsigned char get_dig()
{
int i;

if (!digitizer) return(0);

while(!buffchr());
if ((serbuff[0] = readbuf()) >= 0x80)
    {
    for (i = 1; i <= 5; ++i)
        {
        while(!buffchr());
        serbuff[i] = readbuf();
        }
    if (serbuff[5] >= 0x80)
        {
```

```
        x = serbuff[1];
        x += (unsigned)serbuff[2] << 7;
        y = serbuff[3];
        y += (unsigned)serbuff[4] << 7;

        x *= DIGICVT;
        y *= DIGICVT;

        if (snap)
            {
            modf((x / inc) + 0.5, &x);
            x *= inc;
            modf((y / inc) + 0.5, &y);
            y *= inc;
            }

        x -= xlate_x;
        y -= xlate_y;

        return (serbuff[0]);
        }
    }
return (0);
}
```

STORE.C

```
/* STORE.C stores a record in the database in
** allocated memory.
*/

#include <dos.h>
#include "graphiq.h"
#include "screen.h"
#include "file.h"

extern struct ELEMENT element;
extern struct SREGS segs;
extern union REGS regs;
```

```
extern unsigned pointer;
extern unsigned dwg_seg;
extern char *too_big[];

store()
{
int srcseg, srcoff, destseg, destoff;

if (pointer > 2048)
    {
    message(too_big, 24, 0, RED, ESC);
    return;
    }

srcseg = segs.ds;
srcoff = (int)&element;
destseg = dwg_seg + ((unsigned)sizeof(element) >> 4)
                    * pointer++;
destoff = 0;

movedata(srcseg, srcoff, destseg, destoff,
                (unsigned)sizeof(element));
}
```

BOXX2.C

```
/* BOXX2.C draws a box given the coordinates of two diagonal
 * corners. */

#define TRUE -1
#define FALSE 0
#define ON TRUE
#define OFF FALSE

boxx2(x1, y1, x2, y2, style, color, orxor)
double x1, y1, x2, y2;
int color, orxor;
unsigned style;
{
double xul, yul, xlr, ylr;
```

```
        double xur, yur, xll, yll;

        xul = (x2 > x1) ? x1 : x2;
        yul = (y2 > y1) ? y1 : y2;
        xlr = (x2 > x1) ? x2 : x1;
        ylr = (y2 > y1) ? y2 : y1;

        xur = xlr; yur = yul;
        xll = xul; yll = ylr;

        xform_it(&xul, &yul, &xlr, &ylr);
        xform_it(&xur, &yur, &xll, &yll);

        linef((int)xul, (int)yul, (int)xur, (int)yur,
                color, style, orxor, OFF);
        linef((int)xur, (int)yur, (int)xlr, (int)ylr,
                color, style, orxor, OFF);
        linef((int)xlr, (int)ylr, (int)xll, (int)yll,
                color, style, orxor, OFF);
        linef((int)xll, (int)yll, (int)xul, (int)yul,
                color, style, orxor, OFF);
}
```

TEXTOUT.C

```
/*  TEXTOUT.C  gets a string of text from a prompt and
**  displays the string given prevailing transforms.
**  The command string receives the text for GRAPHIQ.
*/

#include <stdio.h>
#include <math.h>
#include <dos.h>
#include "graphiq.h"
#include "file.h"
#include "screen.h"

#define ABS(a)  ((a) > 0 ? (a) : (-(a)))

union
```

```
        {
        struct
                {
                unsigned col2 : 4;
                unsigned row2 : 4;
                unsigned col1 : 4;
                unsigned row1 : 4;
                } part;
        struct
                {
                unsigned word;
                } whole;
        } font;
extern char command[];
extern char *height_msg[];
extern char *slant_msg[];
extern char *text_msg[];
extern unsigned stroke[][36];
extern int height, width, slant, color;
extern double rot_center_x, rot_center_y;
extern double x, y;
extern double corner_x, corner_y;
extern unsigned pattern;

unsigned char get_dig();


textout(xout, yout)
double xout, yout;
{
unsigned char timer = 0;

write_array(height_msg, 24, 0, color);

/* use box locator to show character box */
boxx2(x, y, x, y, pattern, color, XORIT);
corner_x = xout;
corner_y = yout;

while (retkey(OUTLINE) != ENTER);

/* box off */
boxx2(corner_x, corner_y, x, y, pattern, color, XORIT);
```

```
width = ABS(x - xout);
height = ABS(y - yout);

write_array(height_msg, 24, 0, color);
write_array(slant_msg, 24, 0, color);

/* line on */
draw_line(xout, yout, x, y, color,
              pattern, XORIT, ON);

/* move line */
while (retkey(LINELOC) != ENTER);

/* line off */
draw_line(xout, yout, x, y, color,
              pattern, XORIT, ON);

slant = (x - xout) / width * 8;

write_array(slant_msg, 24, 0, color);
message(text_msg, 24, 0, color, ESC);

draw_text(command, xout, yout, height, width,
          slant, NORMIT, color);

}


draw_text(string, xout, yout, height, width,
              slant, orxor, color)
char *string;
double xout, yout;
int height, width, orxor, slant, color;
{
int i = 0;
double xplace;

for (xplace = xout;
     xplace < xout + (double)strlen(string) * (double)width;
     xplace += (double)width)
     playchar(string[i++], xplace, yout,
              height, width, slant, orxor, color);
}
```

```
playchar(character, xout, yout, height, width,
                slant, orxor, color)
char character;
double xout, yout;
int height, width, orxor, slant, color;
{
double x1, y1, x2, y2;
double width_factor, height_factor;
int x1_out, y1_out, x2_out, y2_out;
unsigned i = 0;


while ((font.whole.word = stroke[(unsigned)character][i++])
                != 0xFFFF)
    {
    width_factor = ((double)(width-1) / 7.0);
    height_factor = ((double)(height-1) / 7.0);

    y1 = (double)(height-1)
         - font.part.row1 * height_factor;
    x1 = font.part.col1 * width_factor;
    x1 += slant * width_factor * (y1 / (height-1));

    y2 = (double)(height - 1)
         - font.part.row2 * height_factor;
    x2 = font.part.col2 * width_factor;
    x2 += slant * width_factor * (y2 / (height-1));

    x1 += xout;
    y1 += yout;
    x2 += xout;
    y2 += yout;

    xform(&x1, &y1);
    xform(&x2, &y2);

    x1_out = x1 * XMETRIC;
    y1_out = YMAX - y1 * YMETRIC;
    x2_out = x2 * XMETRIC;
    y2_out = YMAX - y2 * YMETRIC;

    linef(x1_out, y1_out,
```

```
            x2_out, y2_out,
            color, SOLID, orxor, ON);
      }
}
```

RETKEY.C

```
/* RETKEY.C returns the extended key code.  */

#include <conio.h>
#include <math.h>
#include "graphiq.h"

#define KBD 1
#define DIG 2

extern double x, y;
extern double oldx, oldy;
extern double corner_x, corner_y;
extern double xlate_x, xlate_y;
extern double topy, boty;
extern double inc;
extern int color;
extern long *matrix;
extern int in_menu;
extern char command[];
extern unsigned pattern;
extern int digitizer;

unsigned char get_dig();

int retkey(loc_form)
int loc_form;
{
int inchar;
unsigned char pswitch;
unsigned char timer = 0;

oldx = x; oldy = y;
topy = y; boty = y;
```

```
/* wait for digitizer switches to go off */
/* this loop is the digitizer damper */
while (digitizer && get_dig() != 0x80)
     while (++timer);

while (!kbhit())
     {
     if (digitizer) {
     pswitch = get_dig();

     if (in_menu)
         {
         modf((y / 80) + 0.5, &y);
         y *= 80;

         if (y > topy)
             {
             topy = y;
             return (UP);
             }
         if (y < boty)
             {
             boty = y;
             return (DOWN);
             }
         }
     else if (oldx != x || oldy != y)
             locate(0, loc_form, DIG);

     oldx = x; oldy = y;
     topy = y; boty = y;

     if (pswitch & 0x01)
             return(ENTER);

         } /* end of if digitizer */
     }

if (kbhit()) if (!inkey(&inchar))
     inchar += 0x100;  /* extended character add 256 */

while (kbhit()) getch();  /* flush the keyboard buffer */

locate(inchar, loc_form, KBD);
```

```
        return(inchar);
        }


locate(inchar, crossbox, digiboard)
int inchar, crossbox, digiboard;
{

switch (crossbox)
        {
        case CROSS:
                cross_it(inchar, digiboard);
                break;
        case OUTLINE:
                line_it(inchar, digiboard);
                break;
        case LINELOC:
                lineloc(inchar, digiboard);
                break;
        case NOLOC:
                break;
        }

if (digiboard == DIG) return (0);

switch(inchar)
        {
        case F1:
                strcpy(command, "TENTHMM");
                break;
        case F2:
                strcpy(command, "MILLIMETER");
                break;
        case F3:
                strcpy(command, "FIVEMM");
                break;
        case F4:
                strcpy(command, "TENMM");
                break;
        case F5:
                strcpy(command, "TWENTYMM");
                break;
        case F6:
```

```
                        strcpy(command, "HELP");
                        break;
              case F7:
                        strcpy(command, "STYLE");
                        break;
              case F8:
                        strcpy(command, "COLOR");
                        break;
              case F9:
                        strcpy(command, "MOVE");
                        break;
              case F10:
                        strcpy(command, "LINE");
                        break;
              }
return (strlen(command));
}




cross_it(inchar, digiboard)
int inchar, digiboard;
{

if (digiboard == DIG)
        {
        locator(oldx, oldy, color, matrix);
        locator(x, y, color, matrix);
        return (0);   ·
        }

switch (inchar)
        {
        case DOWN:
                locator(x, y, color, matrix);
                locator(x, y-=inc, color, matrix);
                break;
        case UP:
                locator(x, y, color, matrix);
                locator(x, y+=inc, color, matrix);
                break;
        case LEFT:
                locator(x, y, color, matrix);
                locator(x-=inc, y, color, matrix);
                break;
```

```
        case RIGHT:
            locator(x, y, color, matrix);
            locator(x+=inc, y, color, matrix);
            break;
        case HOME:
            locator(x, y, color, matrix);
            locator(x=0, y=0, color, matrix);
            break;
    }
}



line_it(inchar, digiboard)
int inchar, digiboard;
{

if (digiboard == DIG)
    {
    boxx2(corner_x, corner_y, oldx, oldy, pattern,
        color, XORIT);
    boxx2(corner_x, corner_y, x, y, pattern,
        color, XORIT);
    return (0);
    }

/* XOR boxes to surround desired area */
switch(inchar)
    {
    case DOWN:
        if (y < NDCYMIN) break;
        boxx2(corner_x, corner_y, x, y, pattern,
            color, XORIT);
        boxx2(corner_x, corner_y, x, y-=inc, pattern,
            color, XORIT);
        break;
    case UP:
        if (y > NDCYMAX) break;
        boxx2(corner_x, corner_y, x, y, pattern,
            color, XORIT);
        boxx2(corner_x, corner_y, x, y+=inc, pattern,
        .   color, XORIT);
        break;
    case LEFT:
        if (x < NDCXMIN) break;
```

```
            boxx2(corner_x, corner_y, x, y, pattern,
                color, XORIT);
            boxx2(corner_x, corner_y, x-=inc, y, pattern,
                color, XORIT);
            break;
    case RIGHT:
            if (x > NDCXMAX) break;
            boxx2(corner_x, corner_y, x, y, pattern,
                color, XORIT);
            boxx2(corner_x, corner_y, x+=inc, y, pattern,
                color, XORIT);
            break;
    case HOME:
            boxx2(corner_x, corner_y, x, y, pattern,
                color, XORIT);
            x = 0;
            y = 0;
            boxx2(corner_x, corner_y, x, y, pattern,
                color, XORIT);
            break;
            }
}


lineloc(inchar, digiboard)
int inchar, digiboard;
{

if (digiboard == DIG)
    {
    draw_line(corner_x, corner_y, oldx, oldy,
            color, pattern, XORIT, ON);
    draw_line(corner_x, corner_y, x, y,
            color, pattern, XORIT, ON);
    return (0);
    }

/* XOR lines from corner to current x,y */
switch(inchar)
    {
    case DOWN:
            if (y < NDCYMIN) break;
            draw_line(corner_x, corner_y, x, y, color,
                pattern, XORIT, ON);
```

```
        draw_line(corner_x, corner_y, x, y-=inc, color,
            pattern, XORIT, ON);
        break;
    case UP:
        if (y > NDCYMAX) break;
        draw_line(corner_x, corner_y, x, y, color,
            pattern, XORIT, ON);
        draw_line(corner_x, corner_y, x, y+=inc, color,
            pattern, XORIT, ON);
        break;
    case LEFT:
        if (x < NDCXMIN) break;
        draw_line(corner_x, corner_y, x, y, color,
            pattern, XORIT, ON);
        draw_line(corner_x, corner_y, x-=inc, y, color,
            pattern, XORIT, ON);
        break;
    case RIGHT:
        if (x > NDCXMAX) break;
        draw_line(corner_x, corner_y, x, y, color,
            pattern, XORIT, ON);
        draw_line(corner_x, corner_y, x+=inc, y, color,
            pattern, XORIT, ON);
        break;
    case HOME:
        draw_line(corner_x, corner_y, x, y, color,
            pattern, XORIT, ON);
        x = 0;
        y = 0;
        draw_line(corner_x, corner_y, x, y, color,
            pattern, XORIT, ON);
        break;
        }
    }
```

FILLBOX2.C

```
/* FILLBOX2.C draws a box given the coordinates of two diagonal
 * corners and fills the box. */
```

```
#include "graphiq.h"

#define TRUE -1
#define FALSE 0
#define ON TRUE
#define OFF FALSE

fillbox2(x1, y1, x2, y2, style, color, orxor)
double x1, y1, x2, y2;
int color, orxor;
unsigned style;
{
double xul, yul, xlr, ylr;
double xult, yult, xlrt, yurt;
int row, local_inc = 1.0 / YMETRIC;

xul = (x2 > x1) ? x1 : x2;
yul = (y2 > y1) ? y1 : y2;
xlr = (x2 > x1) ? x2 : x1;
ylr = (y2 > y1) ? y2 : y1;

++xul;
--xlr;

for (; yul < ylr; yul += local_inc)
    {
    xult = xul; yult = yul; xlrt = xlr; yurt = yul;
    xform_it(&xult, &yult, &xlrt, &yurt);

    linef((int)xult, (int)yult, (int)xlrt, (int)yurt,
            color, style, orxor, ON);
    }
}
```

POINTF.C

```
/* POINTF.C is a function to draw a point on the EGA display.
** This function assumes you are using Mode 14.
** It is faster than using the BIOS INT10h method. */
```

```c
#define TRUE 0xFF
#define ENABLE 0x0F
#define INDEXREG 0x3CE
#define VALREG 0x3CF
#define OUTINDEX(index, val)   {outp(INDEXREG, index);\
                                 outp(VALREG, val);}
#define EGABASE 0xA0000000L
#define WIDTH 80L
#define XMAX 639
#define YMAX 199
#define XMIN 0
#define YMIN 0

pointf(x, y, color, orxor)
int x, y, color, orxor;
{
unsigned char mask = 0x80, exist_color;
char far *base;

/* If coordinates are off display, abort. */

if (x < XMIN || x > XMAX || y < YMIN || y > YMAX) return;

base = (char far *)(EGABASE
                + ((long)y * WIDTH + ((long)x / 8L)));

mask >>= x % 8;

exist_color = *base; /* read existing color into EGA register */

OUTINDEX(0, color);   /* set new color*/
OUTINDEX(1, ENABLE); /* enable write */
OUTINDEX(3, orxor);   /* XOR = 0x18, OR = 0x10, AND = 0x08 */
OUTINDEX(8, mask);    /* set mask */

*base &= TRUE;        /* force a write to the EGA */

/* To gain additional speed you can omit this in
** pointf(), but make sure the function calling
** resets the controller before trying to exit to DOS. */

OUTINDEX(0,0);        /* reset register */
OUTINDEX(1,0);        /* reset ENABLE */
OUTINDEX(3,0);        /* reset interaction logic, bit rotation */
OUTINDEX(8,TRUE);     /* reset bit mask */

}
```

DISPLAY.C

```
/* DISPLAY.C displays from the drawing database.
*/

#include "graphiq.h"
#include "file.h"

extern int height, width, slant, color;
extern double xform_angle;
extern double xlate_x, xlate_y;
extern double rot_center_x, rot_center_y;
extern double scale_factor;
extern struct ELEMENT element;


display(pointer)
unsigned *pointer;
{
double xtemp, ytemp;

retrieve(*pointer);

switch (element.attribute.parts.attr)
     {
     case LINE:
          draw_line(
               element.attr.line.x1,
               element.attr.line.y1,
               element.attr.line.x2,
               element.attr.line.y2,
               element.attr.line.color,
               element.attr.line.linestyle,
               element.attr.line.orxor);
          break;
     case BOX:
          boxx2(
               element.attr.box.x1,
               element.attr.box.y1,
               element.attr.box.x2,
               element.attr.box.y2,
```

```
                element.attr.box.linestyle,
                element.attr.box.color,
                element.attr.box.orxor);
        break;
case FILL:
        fillbox2(
                element.attr.fill.x1,
                element.attr.fill.y1,
                element.attr.fill.x2,
                element.attr.fill.y2,
                element.attr.fill.linestyle,
                element.attr.fill.color,
                element.attr.fill.orxor);
        break;
case CIRCLE:
        draw_circ(
                element.attr.circle.x_center,
                element.attr.circle.y_center,
                element.attr.circle.x_perim,
                element.attr.circle.y_perim,
                element.attr.circle.color);
        break;
case TEXT:
        xtemp = element.attr.text.t_attr.loc.x_origin;
        ytemp = element.attr.text.t_attr.loc.y_origin;
        xform_angle = element.attr.text.t_attr.loc.rot_angle;
        height = element.attr.text.t_attr.loc.height;
        width =  element.attr.text.t_attr.loc.width;
        slant =  element.attr.text.t_attr.loc.slant;
        color = element.attr.text.t_attr.loc.color;

        retrieve(++*pointer);

        draw_text(element.attr.text.t_attr.strg.string,
                xtemp, ytemp, height, width, slant,
                                        NORMIT, color);

        xform_angle -= element.attr.text.t_attr.loc.rot_angle;
        break;
case XFORMS:
        xlate_x = element.attr.xforms.xlate_x;
        xlate_y = element.attr.xforms.xlate_y;
```

```
                    rot_center_x = element.attr.xforms.rot_center_x;
                    rot_center_y = element.attr.xforms.rot_center_y;
                    xform_angle = element.attr.xforms.xform_angle;
                    scale_factor = element.attr.xforms.scale_factor;
                    break;
            }
    }
```

PUTDATA.C

```
/* PUTDATA.C  puts data from database to file.
*/

#include <stdio.h>
#include <string.h>
#include "graphiq.h"
#include "screen.h"
#include "file.h"

extern char *exists_msg[];
extern char command[];
extern unsigned pointer;
extern struct ELEMENT element;


putdata(filename)
char *filename;
{
FILE *putstream;
unsigned i;

if ((putstream = fopen(filename, "r+b")) != NULL)
    {
    message(exists_msg, 24, 0, GREEN, ESC);
    if (!strchr(command, 'y') && !strchr(command, 'Y'))
        return(FALSE);
    }

if (putstream == NULL)
    if ((putstream = fopen(filename, "wb")) == NULL)
```

```
            return(TRUE);

for (i = 0; i < pointer; ++i)
      {
      retrieve(i);
      fwrite(&element, sizeof(char), sizeof(element),
                  putstream);
      }

fclose(putstream);

return(FALSE);
}
```

GETDATA.C

```
/* GETDATA.C  gets data from file to database.
*/

#include <stdio.h>
#include <string.h>
#include "graphiq.h"
#include "screen.h"
#include "file.h"

extern char *replace_msg[];
extern char command[];
extern unsigned pointer;
extern struct ELEMENT element;

getdata(filename)
char *filename;
{
FILE *getstream;
unsigned i;

if ((getstream = fopen(filename, "rb")) == NULL)
          return(TRUE);

message(replace_msg, 24, 0, RED, ESC);
```

```
if (!strchr(command, 'y') && !strchr(command, 'Y'))
    return(FALSE);

pointer = 0;
while (fread(&element, sizeof(char), sizeof(element),
                                            getstream))
    store(pointer++);

fclose(getstream);

return(FALSE);
}
```

MESSAGE.C

```
/* MESSAGE.C displays a message and waits for a string.
*/

#include <stdio.h>
#include "graphiq.h"
#include "screen.h"

extern int reading_cmd;
extern int main_select;
extern char command[];
extern FILE *cmd_stream;

message(mess, row, col, color, inchar)
char *mess[];
int row, col, color, inchar;
{

switch (inchar)
    {
    case ESC:
        if (reading_cmd)
            if (fread(command, 80, cmd_stream) == 0)
                {
                fclose(cmd_stream);
```

```
                reading_cmd = FALSE;
                }
        else command[strlen(command)-1] = NULLCHAR;

  if (!reading_cmd)
        {
        /* XOR message onto background */
        write_array(mess, row, col, color);
        get_str(command, color); /* get the command */
        /* XOR message off of background */
        write_array(mess, row, col, color);
        }

  if (strlen(command) && !reading_cmd)
        {
        write_str("_", row, col+strlen(mess[0])-1,color);
        write_str(command, row, col+strlen(mess[0])-1,
                                            WHITE);
        write_str("_", row,
            col+strlen(mess[0])-1+strlen(command),
                                            color);
        }
  break;
case ENTER:
  main_menu(color);
  switch(main_select)
        {
        case 1:
                strcpy(command, "HELP");
                break;
        case 2:
                strcpy(command, "GRID");
                break;
        case 3:
                strcpy(command, "SNAP");
                break;
        case 4:
                strcpy(command, "LOCATOR");
                break;
        case 5:
                strcpy(command, "STYLE");
                break;
        case 6:
                strcpy(command, "COLOR");
                break;
```

```
case 7:
     strcpy(command, "MOVE");
     break;
case 8:
     strcpy(command, "LINE");
     break;
case 9:
     strcpy(command, "BOX");
     break;
case 10:
     strcpy(command, "FILL");
     break;
case 11:
     strcpy(command, "CIRCLE");
     break;
case 12:
     strcpy(command, "TEXT");
     break;
case 13:
     strcpy(command, "ROTATION");
     break;
case 14:
     strcpy(command, "RESET");
     break;
case 15:
     strcpy(command, "SYSORIGIN");
     break;
case 16:
     strcpy(command, "SCALE");
     break;
case 17:
     strcpy(command, "PLAYBACK");
     break;
case 18:
     strcpy(command, "PRINT");
     break;
case 19:
     strcpy(command, "FILES");
     break;
case 20:
     strcpy(command, "COMMAND FILE");
     break;
case 21:
     strcpy(command, "CLEAR DISPLAY");
     break;
```

```
        case 22:
               strcpy(command, "QUIT");
               break;
        case 23:
               strcpy(command, "EXIT");
               break;
        }
    break;
    }
}
```

CHARHDLR.C

```
/* CHARHDLR.C handles characters on display for GRAPHIQ.
*/

#include <dos.h>
#include "graphiq.h"
#include "screen.h"

extern char command[];

union REGS regs;

int write_array(string, row, col, color)
char *string[];
int row, col, color;
{
int i, j, newcol;

for (i = 0, newcol = col; strlen(string[i]) != 0; ++i, ++row)
    for (j = 0, newcol = col; j < strlen(string[i]);
                                        ++j, ++newcol)
        write_char(string[i][j], row, newcol, color, XORIT);
return(i-1);
}


write_str(string, row, col, color)
char *string;
```

```
int row, col, color;
{
int j, newcol;

for (j = 0, newcol = col; j < strlen(string); ++j, ++newcol)
     write_char(string[j], row, newcol, color, XORIT);

}




write_char(character, row, col, color, orxor)
char character;
int row, col, color, orxor;
{

set_curs(row, col);

regs.h.ah = 9;                  /* write character */
regs.x.cx = 1;                  /* one character */
regs.h.al = character;          /* character */
regs.h.bl = color | orxor;      /* set color (NORMIT, XORIT) */
int86(0x10, &regs, &regs);      /* interrupt 10h */
}



read_char(character, row, col)
char *character;
int row, col;
{

set_curs(row, col);

regs.h.ah = 8;                  /* read character */
regs.h.bh = 0;                  /* for page 0 */
int86(0x10, &regs, &regs);      /* interrupt 10h */
*character = regs.h.al;         /* character */
}



set_curs(row, col)
int row, col;
{
```

```
regs.h.ah = 2;                    /* set cursor position */
regs.h.bh = 0;                    /* for page 0 */
regs.h.dh = row;                  /* current row */
regs.h.dl = col;                  /* current col */
int86(0x10, &regs, &regs);        /* interrupt 10h */
}


get_curs(row, col)
int *row, *col;
{

regs.h.ah = 3;                    /* get cursor position */
regs.h.bh = 0;                    /* for page 0 */
int86(0x10, &regs, &regs);        /* interrupt 10h */
*row = regs.h.dh;                  /* current row */
*col = regs.h.dl;                  /* current col */
}


/* get_str() uses the current cursor position to get a string
from keyboard input.  The text can be written over graphics
without disturbing anything. */

get_str(string, color)
char *string;  /* make sure string allows > 80 characters */
int color;
{
int inchar, row, col, position = 0;
char oldchar;

strcpy(command, "");

get_curs(&row, &col);

while ((inchar = retkey(NOLOC)) != CR)
    {
    switch (inchar)
        {
        case BS:
            if (position > 0)
                {
```

```
                        oldchar = string[--position];
                        string[position] = NULLCHAR;
                        if (col < 79)
                             write_char('_', row, col, color,
                                                        XORIT);
                        write_char(oldchar, row, --col, WHITE,
                                                        XORIT);
                        write_char('_', row, col, color, XORIT);
                        }
                break;
            default:
                if (col < 79)
                        {
                        write_char('_', row, col, color, XORIT);
                        write_char(inchar, row, col++, WHITE,
                                                        XORIT);
                        write_char('_', row, col, color, XORIT);
                        string[position++] = inchar;
                        string[position] = NULLCHAR;
                        }
                else if (col == 79)
                        {
                        write_char(inchar, row, col, WHITE, XORIT);
                        string[position] = inchar;
                        }
                break;
            }
        }
}


clearscr()
{

regs.h.ah = 7;                  /* scroll screen down */
regs.h.al = 0;                  /* entire window */
regs.h.ch = 0;                  /* upper left corner */
regs.h.cl = 0;
regs.h.dh = 24;                 /* lower right corner */
regs.h.dl = 79;
regs.h.bh = 0;                  /* use black background */
int86(0x10, &regs, &regs);     /* interrupt 10h */
}
```

MNU—CURS.C

```c
/* MNU_CURS.C manages the cursor on a menu.
*/

#include "graphiq.h"

mnu_curs(row, col, depth, width, color, menu_key)
int row, col, depth, width, color, menu_key;
{
int inchar, select;
extern int main_select;   /* external allows repeat of same */
                          /* menu item */
extern int file_select;

switch (menu_key)
    {
    case MAIN_MNU:
        select = main_select;
        break;
    case FILE_MNU:
        select = file_select;
        break;
    }

row += select - 1;

disp_curs(row, col, width, color);

do    {
    switch (inchar = retkey(NOLOC))
        {
        case DOWN:
            if (select <= depth)
                {
                ++select;
                disp_curs(row, col, width, color);
                disp_curs(++row, col, width, color);
                }
            break;
```

```
            case UP:
                if (select > 1)
                    {
                    --select;
                    disp_curs(row, col, width, color);
                    disp_curs(--row, col, width, color);
                    }
                break;
            case ESC:
                select = depth+1; /* exit menu always last */
                break;
            }
        }
while (inchar != RETURN && inchar != ESC);

switch (menu_key)
    {
    case MAIN_MNU:
        main_select = select;
        break;
    case FILE_MNU:
        file_select = select;
        break;
    }

disp_curs(row, col, width, color);
}


disp_curs(row, col, width, color)
int row, col, width, color;
{
int i;

for (i = 0; i < width; ++i)
    write_char(219, row, col+i, color, XORIT);
}
```

PRINTSCR.C

```c
/* PRINTSCR.C dithers the EGA mode 14 display to EPSON
** This function copies groups of 3 pixels horizontally,
** for each row, allowing RGB dithered photography to
** be printed. */


#include <stdio.h>
#include <dos.h>
#include <conio.h>

#define WIDTH 80L
#define XMAX 638    /* use 0 - 638 */
#define YMAX 199
#define XMIN 0
#define YMIN 0
#define CHARSOUT 800

struct {
     unsigned char i         : 4;
     unsigned char color1    : 4;
     unsigned char color2    : 4;
     unsigned char color3    : 4;
     unsigned char color4    : 4;
     unsigned char color5    : 4;
     unsigned char color6    : 4;
     unsigned char color7    : 4;
     unsigned char color8    : 4;
     } bits;

union SPEC {
     struct {
     unsigned char bit0 : 1;
     unsigned char bit1 : 1;
     unsigned char bit2 : 1;
     unsigned char bit3 : 1;
     unsigned char bit4 : 1;
     unsigned char bit5 : 1;
     unsigned char bit6 : 1;
     unsigned char bit7 : 1;
          } bits;
     struct {
     unsigned char byte;
          } bytes;
     };
```

```
union SPEC spec0, spec1, spec2;

printscr(reverse)
int reverse;
{
int x, y;

/* This routine works with the EPSON MX, FX etc. printers */

fprintf(stdprn, "\x1bA\x7");   /* set linefeed in 72nds*/

for (x = XMAX; x > XMIN; x -= 24)
    {
    if (kbhit())
        {
        fputs("\x1bA\x9", stdprn);   /* 9 wires per linefeed */
        getch();   /* keeps character from console */
        break;
        }

    printrow(x, y, reverse);
    }

fputs("\x0c", stdprn);   /* page feed */
fflush(stdprn);
}



printrow(x, y, reverse)
int x, y, reverse;
{
char status();
char put_out();
unsigned i, j, newy;
/* prints CHARSOUT bits wide condensed */
/* room for header, pr_buff[], */
/* and null character */
static unsigned char out_buff[3][9+CHARSOUT] = {
                    "    \x1bL\x20\x03",
                    "    \x1bL\x20\x03",
                    "    \x1bL\x20\x03"};

for (y = YMIN, newy = 0; y <= YMAX*4; y+=4, ++newy)
```

```
    {
    bits.color1  = readpt(x-0,  newy);
    bits.color1 |= readpt(x-1,  newy);
    bits.color1 |= readpt(x-2,  newy);
    bits.color2  = readpt(x-3,  newy);
    bits.color2 |= readpt(x-4,  newy);
    bits.color2 |= readpt(x-5,  newy);
    bits.color3  = readpt(x-6,  newy);
    bits.color3 |= readpt(x-7,  newy);
    bits.color3 |= readpt(x-8,  newy);
    bits.color4  = readpt(x-9,  newy);
    bits.color4 |= readpt(x-10, newy);
    bits.color4 |= readpt(x-11, newy);
    bits.color5  = readpt(x-12, newy);
    bits.color5 |= readpt(x-13, newy);
    bits.color5 |= readpt(x-14, newy);

if (x-14 != 0) {
    bits.color6  = readpt(x-15, newy);
    bits.color6 |= readpt(x-16, newy);
    bits.color6 |= readpt(x-17, newy);
    bits.color7  = readpt(x-18, newy);
    bits.color7 |= readpt(x-19, newy);
    bits.color7 |= readpt(x-20, newy);
    bits.color8  = readpt(x-21, newy);
    bits.color8 |= readpt(x-22, newy);
    bits.color8 |= readpt(x-23, newy);
                    }
    if (reverse)
        {
        bits.color1 = ~bits.color1;
        bits.color2 = ~bits.color2;
        bits.color3 = ~bits.color3;
        bits.color4 = ~bits.color4;
        bits.color5 = ~bits.color5;
        bits.color6 = ~bits.color6;
        bits.color7 = ~bits.color7;
        bits.color8 = ~bits.color8;
        }


for (j = 0, bits.i = 0x8; j <= 3; ++j, bits.i >>= 1)
    {
    spec0.bits.bit7 = (bits.color1 & bits.i) >> (3-j);
    spec0.bits.bit6 = (bits.color1 & bits.i) >> (3-j);
```

```
        spec0.bits.bit5 = (bits.color1 & bits.i) >> (3-j);
        spec0.bits.bit4 = (bits.color2 & bits.i) >> (3-j);
        spec0.bits.bit3 = (bits.color2 & bits.i) >> (3-j);
        spec0.bits.bit2 = (bits.color2 & bits.i) >> (3-j);
        spec0.bits.bit1 = (bits.color3 & bits.i) >> (3-j);
        spec0.bits.bit0 = (bits.color3 & bits.i) >> (3-j);
        spec1.bits.bit7 = (bits.color3 & bits.i) >> (3-j);
        spec1.bits.bit6 = (bits.color4 & bits.i) >> (3-j);
        spec1.bits.bit5 = (bits.color4 & bits.i) >> (3-j);
        spec1.bits.bit4 = (bits.color4 & bits.i) >> (3-j);
        spec1.bits.bit3 = (bits.color5 & bits.i) >> (3-j);
        spec1.bits.bit2 = (bits.color5 & bits.i) >> (3-j);
        spec1.bits.bit1 = (bits.color5 & bits.i) >> (3-j);

    if (x-14 != 0) {
        spec1.bits.bit0 = (bits.color6 & bits.i) >> (3-j);
        spec2.bits.bit7 = (bits.color6 & bits.i) >> (3-j);
        spec2.bits.bit6 = (bits.color6 & bits.i) >> (3-j);
        spec2.bits.bit5 = (bits.color7 & bits.i) >> (3-j);
        spec2.bits.bit4 = (bits.color7 & bits.i) >> (3-j);
        spec2.bits.bit3 = (bits.color7 & bits.i) >> (3-j);
        spec2.bits.bit2 = (bits.color8 & bits.i) >> (3-j);
        spec2.bits.bit1 = (bits.color8 & bits.i) >> (3-j);
        spec2.bits.bit0 = (bits.color8 & bits.i) >> (3-j);
                 }

        if (x-14 == 0) spec1.bytes.byte &= 0xFE;

        out_buff[0][y+9+j] = spec0.bytes.byte;
        out_buff[1][y+9+j] = spec1.bytes.byte;
        out_buff[2][y+9+j] = spec2.bytes.byte;
        }
    }


/* write the formatted array out printer port as characters */
for (i = 0; i < 9+CHARSOUT; ++i)
    while ((put_out(out_buff[0][i]) & 1) == 1);

put_out('\r'); /* send a carriage return */
put_out('\n'); /* send a linefeed */

for (i = 0; i < 9+CHARSOUT; ++i)
    while ((put_out(out_buff[1][i]) & 1) == 1);
```

```
put_out('\r'); /* send a carriage return */
put_out('\n'); /* send a linefeed */


if (x-14 != 0)
    {
    for (i = 0; i < 9+CHARSOUT; ++i)
        while ((put_out(out_buff[2][i]) & 1) == 1);

    put_out('\r'); /* send a carriage return */
    put_out('\n'); /* send a linefeed */
    }
}



char status()
{
union REGS regs;

regs.h.ah = 2; /* check printer status */
regs.x.dx = 0; /* select first printer */
int86(0x17, &regs, &regs);
return(regs.h.ah & 0x80);
}



char put_out(character)
char character;
{
union REGS regs;

while(!status()); /* wait if busy */

regs.h.ah = 0; /* send a character */
regs.h.al = character;
regs.x.dx = 0; /* select first printer */

int86(0x17, &regs, &regs);
return(regs.h.ah);
}
```

GRAPHIQ HEADERS

GRAPHIQ.H

```
/* GRAPHIQ.H is the main header for GRAPHIQ.C  */

#define TRUE -1
#define FALSE 0
#define ON TRUE
#define OFF FALSE
#define ESC 0x1b
#define HOME 0x147
#define UP 0x148
#define DOWN 0x150
#define LEFT 0x14B
#define RIGHT 0x14D
#define NDCXMAX 2690.0   /* conforms to 8-1/2 by 11 inch paper */
#define NDCYMAX 2060.0
#define NDCXMIN 0
#define NDCYMIN 0
#define CENTERX (NDCXMAX / 2.0)
#define CENTERY (NDCYMAX / 2.0)
#define WIDTH 80L
#define XMAX 639
#define YMAX 199
#define XMIN 0
#define YMIN 0
#define CROSS 0
#define OUTLINE 1
#define LINELOC 2
#define NOLOC 3
#define TENTHMM 1
#define MILLIMETER 10
#define FIVEMM 50
#define TENMM 100
#define TWENTYMM 200
#define F1 0x13B
#define F2 0x13C
#define F3 0x13D
#define F4 0x13E
#define F5 0x13F
#define F6 0x140
#define F7 0x141
#define F8 0x142
#define F9 0x143
#define F10 0x144
```

```
#define COMMAND TRUE
#define NOCOMMAND FALSE

#define XMETRIC 0.237546468
#define YMETRIC 0.096601942
#define PI 3.141592654
#define XORIT 0x80
#define NORMIT 0
#define CR 0x0D
#define LF 0x0A
#define BS 0x8
#define NEWLINE LF
#define NULLCHAR '\0'
#define SOLID 0xFFFF
#define DOTTED 0x8888
#define DASHED 0xF0F0
#define DASHDOT 0xFAFA
#define DASHDOTDOT 0xEAEA
#define ENTER 0x0D
#define RETURN ENTER
#define QUIT 0x11
#define MAIN_MNU 0
#define FILE_MNU 1

/* utilities for access to EGA controller */

#define ENABLE 0x0F
#define INDEXREG 0x3CE
#define VALREG 0x3CF
#define OUTINDEX(index, val)    {outp(INDEXREG, index);\
                                 outp(VALREG, val);}
#define EGABASE 0xA0000000L

#define SERPORT1 0x00000400L /* COM1 interrupt address */
#define SERPORT2 0x00000402L /* COM2 interrupt address */
#define SERVEC1 12  /* COM1 interrupt request (IRQ4)   */
#define SERVEC2 11  /* COM2 interrupt request (IRQ3)   */

struct ISRVEC
     {
     unsigned vecl;
     unsigned vech;
     unsigned type;
     };

/* miscellaneous macros */
#define SQ(x) ((x) * (x))
```

```
union
    {
    struct
        {
        unsigned char lo : 4;
        unsigned char hi : 4;
        } hilo;
    struct
        {
        unsigned char byte;
        } whole;
    } colr;
```

DECLARES.H

```
/* DECLARES.H contains declarations for GRAPHIQ.C */

int height = 30, width = 25, slant = 0, color = 0x7;
int in_menu = FALSE;
unsigned curs_toggle = FALSE;
double x, y, radius;
double lastx, lasty;
double tempx, tempy;
double oldx, oldy;
double topy, boty;
double corner_x, corner_y;
double x_center, y_center;
double rot_center_x, rot_center_y;
double x_perim, y_perim;
double xlate_x, xlate_y;
double xform_angle, scale_factor = 1.0;
double xlate_xb, xlate_yb;
double rot_center_xb, rot_center_yb;
double xform_angleb, scale_factorb;
double inc = 200.0;
unsigned pointer;
FILE *cmd_stream;
int reading_cmd;
int line_style = 1;
unsigned pattern = SOLID;
```

```
int oldmode;
int main_select = 1;
int file_select = 1;
char command[81];
char *colarray;
char mess[25][30];
unsigned allowed, dwg_seg;
int reverse = FALSE;
unsigned long *matrix;

char *put_msg[] = {"Filename to PUT screen: _", ""};
char *get_msg[] = {"Filename to GET screen: _", ""};
char *put_data_msg[] = {"Filename to PUT database: _", ""};
char *get_data_msg[] = {"Filename to GET database: _", ""};
char *cmd_msg[] = {"Command: _", ""};
char *file_msg[] = {"Command Filename: _", ""};
char *file_error[] = {"Can't open file. Press a key...", ""};
char *exists_msg[]
  = {"File by that name exists, or access error. Enter Y to\
replace...",""};
char *replace_msg[]
  = {"Do you wish to replace work in progress?  Enter Y to\
 replace...",""};
char *quit_msg[] = {"ENTER Y or Yes if you wish to quit: _", ""};
char *height_msg[] = {"ENTER Height and width...", ""};
char *slant_msg[] = {"ENTER Slant...", ""};
char *loc_text[] = {"Locate Text...", ""};
char *text_msg[] = {"ENTER Text: _", ""};
char *loc_rot[] = {"Locate Rotation Center...", ""};
char *rot_msg[] = {"ENTER Rotation Baseline...",""};
char *scale_msg1[] = {"ENTER Original Size...", ""};
char *scale_msg2[] = {"ENTER Destination Size...", ""};
char *loc_sys[] = {"Locate System Origin...", ""};
char *print_msg[] = {"Color Reverse? (y/n) _", ""};
char *too_big[] = {"Too many elements. Save drawing. \
Press a key...",""};
char *circl_msg[] = {"Locate center of circle, press ENTER.",""};
char *circ2_msg[] = {"Locate perimeter of circle, press \
ENTER.",""};
char *box1_msg[] = {"Locate corner of box, press ENTER.",""};
char *box2_msg[] = {"Locate other corner, press ENTER.",""};
char *grid_msg[] = {"ENTER Grid Interval \
(default current): _",""};
char *welcome[] = {
"IMMMMMMMMMMMMMMMMMMMMMMMMMMMMMMMMMMMMMMMMMMMMMMMMMMMMMMMMMMMMMMM;",
```

```
": Welcome to GRAPHIQ.                                           :",
":                                                               :",
": The programs contained herein are adapted from \"Advanced     :",
": Graphics in C\" by Nelson Johnson, published by               :",
": Osborne/McGraw-Hill, copyright 1987 by Osborne/McGraw-Hill.   :",
": Used with the permission of Osborne/McGraw-Hill.  Program     :",
": adaptations are solely the work of Imagimedia Technologies,   :",
": Inc. and are not a publication of Osborne/McGraw-Hill.        :",
":                                                               :",
"HMMMMMMMMMMMMMMMMMMMMMMMMMMMMMMMMMMMMMMMMMMMMMMMMMMMMMMMMMMMMMM<",
""};

char *help[] = {
"IMMMMMMMMMMMMMMMMMMMMMMMMMMMMMMMMMMMMMMMMMMMMMMMMMMMMMMMMMMMMMMMMM;",
": HELP (F6)                                                     :",
":                                                               :",
": Press Function Keys        Press ENTER DY to select a function.:",
":                            Press Esc to enter a command.      :",
": F1    0.1mm increment      Hold Ctrl down, hit Q to quit, or  :",
": F2    1.0mm                    enter the QUIT command.        :",
": F3    5.0mm                                                   :",
": F4   10.0mm                                                   :",
": F5   20.0mm                                                   :",
": F6   Help                                                     :",
": F7   Line Style                                               :",
": F8   Change Color                                             :",
": F9   Move (no line)                                           :",
": F10 Draw Line              Press a key to leave this menu...   :",
"HMMMMMMMMMMMMMMMMMMMMMMMMMMMMMMMMMMMMMMMMMMMMMMMMMMMMMMMMMMMMMMMMM<",
""};

char *main_mnu[] = {
"IMMMMMMMMMMMMMMMMMM;",
": HELP   (F6)    :",
": GRID           :",
": SNAP ON/OFF    :",
": LOCATOR ON/OFF :",
": STYLE  (F7)    :",
": COLOR  (F8)    :",
": LOCATE (F9)    :",
": LINE   (F10)   :",
": BOX            :",
": FILL           :",
": CIRCLE         :",
": TEXT           :",
```

```
":  ROTATION        :",
":  RESET           :",
":  OFFSET +X, +Y   :",
":  SCALE           :",
":  PLAYBACK        :",
":  PRINT           :",
":  PICTURE FILES   :",
":  COMMAND FILE    :",
":  CLEAR DISPLAY   :",
":  QUIT GRAPHIQ    :",
":  EXIT THIS MENU  :",
"HMMMMMMMMMMMMMMMM<",
""};


char *file_mnu[] = {
"IMMMMMMMMMMMMMMMM;",
":  PUT DISPLAY     :",
":  GET DISPLAY     :",
":  PUT DATABASE    :",
":  GET DATABASE    :",
"HMMMMMMMMMMMMMMMM<",
""};

struct ELEMENT element;
struct SREGS segs;
union REGS regs;

struct ISRVEC isrvec;

unsigned char serisr(), readbuf(), get_dig();
unsigned buffchr();

unsigned far *outbase = (unsigned far *)SERPORT1;
unsigned char baudlo, baudhi, bits;
unsigned char serbuff[20];
int digitizer = FALSE;
int snap = FALSE;
```

FILE.H

```
/* FILE.H contains record structures for GRAPHIQ.C */

#define HEADER 0
#define POINT 1
#define LINE 2
#define CIRCLE 3
#define ARC 4
#define BOX 5
#define FILL 6
#define TEXT 7
#define XFORMS 8
#define LOC 1
#define STRG 2
#define ATTRLEN 2
#define TEXTLEN 62
#define RECLEN ATTRLEN + TEXTLEN /* in this case 64 bytes */
#define FILENAME 12

struct ELEMENT
    {
    union
        {
        struct
            {
            char attr;
            char subattr;
            } parts;

        struct
            {
            unsigned attrib;
            } whole;
        }attribute;

    union
        {
        struct
            {
            double xlate_x;
            double xlate_y;
            double rot_center_x;
            double rot_center_y;
            double xform_angle;
```

```
        double scale_factor;
        } xforms;
struct
      {
      char filename[FILENAME+1];
      long date;
      long time;
      long records;   /* including this record */
      } header;

struct
      {
      double x;
      double y;
      char color;
      char layer;
      } point;

struct
      {
      double x1;
      double y1;
      double x2;
      double y2;
      int color;
      unsigned linestyle;
      char layer;
      int orxor;
      int first_pt;
      } line;

struct
      {
      double x1;
      double y1;
      double x2;
      double y2;
      char color;
      unsigned linestyle;
      int orxor;
      char layer;
      } box;

struct
```

```
            {
            double x1;
            double y1;
            double x2;
            double y2;
            char color;
            unsigned linestyle;
            int orxor;
            char layer;
            } fill;

      struct
            {
            double x_center;
            double y_center;
            double x_perim;
            double y_perim;
            char color;
            char layer;
            } circle;

      struct
            {
            double x_center;
            double y_center;
            double x_start;
            double y_start;
            double x_end;
            double y_end;
            char color;
            unsigned linestyle;
            char layer;
            } arc;

/* length of text string plus 5 determines maximum
** record length */

      struct
            {
            union
                  {
                  struct
                        {
                        double x_origin;
                        double y_origin;
```

```
                    double rot_angle;
                    int height;
                    int width;
                    int slant;
                    int color;
                    char font;
                    char layer;
                    } loc;

             struct
                  {
                  char string[TEXTLEN]; /* governs record
                                                size */

                  } strg;
                } t_attr;
            } text;
        } attr;  /* end of attr union */
    };  /* end of ELEMENT struct */
```

CURSOR.H

```
/* CURSOR.H the GRAPHIQ cursor is stored here */

unsigned long matrix[] = {
0x00183000L,
0x00183000L,
0x00183000L,
0x00183000L,
0x00183000L,
0x00183000L,
0xFFF83FFEL,
0x00000000L,
0xFFF83FFEL,
0x00183000L,
0x00183000L,
0x00183000L,
0x00183000L,
0x00183000L,
0x00183000L,
0x00000000L};
```

LOCATOR.H

```
/* LOCATOR.H The GRAPHIQ locators are stored here */

/* solid */
unsigned long matrix1[] = {
0x00183000L,
0x00183000L,
0x00183000L,
0x00183000L,
0x00183000L,
0x00183000L,
0xFFF83FFEL,
0x00000000L,
0xFFF83FFEL,
0x00183000L,
0x00183000L,
0x00183000L,
0x00183000L,
0x00183000L,
0x00000000L};

/* dotted */
unsigned long matrix2[] = {
0x00183000L,
0x00000000L,
0x00183000L,
0x00000000L,
0x00183000L,
0x00000000L,
0x99983332L,
0x00000000L,
0x99983332L,
0x00000000L,
0x00183000L,
0x00000000L,
0x00183000L,
0x00000000L,
```

```
0x00183000L,
0x00000000L};

/* dashed */
unsigned long matrix3[] = {
0x00183000L,
0x00183000L,
0x00183000L,
0x00000000L,
0x00183000L,
0x00183000L,
0xF0F83E1EL,
0x00000000L,
0xF0F83E1EL,
0x00183000L,
0x00183000L,
0x00000000L,
0x00183000L,
0x00183000L,
0x00183000L,
0x00000000L};

/* dash dot */
unsigned long matrix4[] = {
0x00183000L,
0x00000000L,
0x00183000L,
0x00183000L,
0x00183000L,
0x00183000L,
0xE6783CCEL,
0x00000000L,
0xE6783CCEL,
0x00183000L,
0x00183000L,
0x00183000L,
0x00183000L,
0x00000000L,
0x00183000L,
0x00000000L};

/* dash dot dot */
unsigned long matrix5[] = {
0x00183000L,
0x00000000L,
```

```
0x00183000L,
0x00000000L,
0x00183000L,
0x00183000L,
0xCCF83E66L,
0x00000000L,
0xCCF83E66L,
0x00183000L,
0x00183000L,
0x00000000L,
0x00183000L,
0x00000000L,
0x00183000L,
0x00000000L};
```

SCREEN.H

```
/* SCREEN.H contains colors, display width and height */

#define BLACK      0
#define BLUE       1
#define GREEN      2
#define CYAN       3
#define RED        4
#define MAGENTA    5
#define BROWN      6
#define WHITE      7
```

FONT.H

```
/* FONT.H contains the standard character set from
** ASCII 0 through 127. */

unsigned stroke[128][36] = {
/* 00 */
```

```
0xFFFF,0xFFFF,0xFFFF,0xFFFF,0xFFFF,0xFFFF,
0xFFFF,0xFFFF,0xFFFF,0xFFFF,0xFFFF,0xFFFF,
0xFFFF,0xFFFF,0xFFFF,0xFFFF,0xFFFF,0xFFFF,
0xFFFF,0xFFFF,0xFFFF,0xFFFF,0xFFFF,0xFFFF,
0xFFFF,0xFFFF,0xFFFF,0xFFFF,0xFFFF,0xFFFF,
0xFFFF,0xFFFF,0xFFFF,0xFFFF,0xFFFF,0xFFFF,
/* 01 */
0x0106,0x0617,0x1767,0x6776,0x7671,0x7160,
0x6010,0x1001,0x2232,0x2535,0x4245,0x4554,
0x5453,0x5342,0xFFFF,0xFFFF,0xFFFF,0xFFFF,
0xFFFF,0xFFFF,0xFFFF,0xFFFF,0xFFFF,0xFFFF,
0xFFFF,0xFFFF,0xFFFF,0xFFFF,0xFFFF,0xFFFF,
0xFFFF,0xFFFF,0xFFFF,0xFFFF,0xFFFF,0xFFFF,
/* 02 */
0x0106,0x0617,0x1767,0x6776,0x7671,0x7160,
0x6010,0x1001,0x1113,0x1323,0x2321,0x2111,
0x1416,0x1626,0x2624,0x2414,0x4146,0x4655,
0x5552,0x5241,0xFFFF,0xFFFF,0xFFFF,0xFFFF,
0xFFFF,0xFFFF,0xFFFF,0xFFFF,0xFFFF,0xFFFF,
0xFFFF,0xFFFF,0xFFFF,0xFFFF,0xFFFF,0xFFFF,
/* 03 */
0x0102,0x0213,0x1304,0x0405,0x0516,0x1636,
0x3663,0x6330,0x3010,0x1001,0xFFFF,0xFFFF,
0xFFFF,0xFFFF,0xFFFF,0xFFFF,0xFFFF,0xFFFF,
0xFFFF,0xFFFF,0xFFFF,0xFFFF,0xFFFF,0xFFFF,
0xFFFF,0xFFFF,0xFFFF,0xFFFF,0xFFFF,0xFFFF,
0xFFFF,0xFFFF,0xFFFF,0xFFFF,0xFFFF,0xFFFF,
/* 04 */
0x0336,0x3663,0x6330,0x3003,0xFFFF,0xFFFF,
0xFFFF,0xFFFF,0xFFFF,0xFFFF,0xFFFF,0xFFFF,
0xFFFF,0xFFFF,0xFFFF,0xFFFF,0xFFFF,0xFFFF,
0xFFFF,0xFFFF,0xFFFF,0xFFFF,0xFFFF,0xFFFF,
0xFFFF,0xFFFF,0xFFFF,0xFFFF,0xFFFF,0xFFFF,
0xFFFF,0xFFFF,0xFFFF,0xFFFF,0xFFFF,0xFFFF,
/* 05 */
0x0204,0x0415,0x1524,0x2434,0x3436,0x3646,
0x4664,0x6462,0x6240,0x4030,0x3032,0x3222,
0x2211,0x1102,0xFFFF,0xFFFF,0xFFFF,0xFFFF,
0xFFFF,0xFFFF,0xFFFF,0xFFFF,0xFFFF,0xFFFF,
0xFFFF,0xFFFF,0xFFFF,0xFFFF,0xFFFF,0xFFFF,
0xFFFF,0xFFFF,0xFFFF,0xFFFF,0xFFFF,0xFFFF,
/* 06 */
0x0313,0x1346,0x4664,0x6475,0x7571,0x7162,
0x6240,0x4013,0xFFFF,0xFFFF,0xFFFF,0xFFFF,
0xFFFF,0xFFFF,0xFFFF,0xFFFF,0xFFFF,0xFFFF,
```

```
0xFFFF,0xFFFF,0xFFFF,0xFFFF,0xFFFF,0xFFFF,
0xFFFF,0xFFFF,0xFFFF,0xFFFF,0xFFFF,0xFFFF,
0xFFFF,0xFFFF,0xFFFF,0xFFFF,0xFFFF,0xFFFF,
/* 07 */
0x2324,0x2435,0x3545,0x4554,0x5453,0x5342,
0x4232,0x3223,0xFFFF,0xFFFF,0xFFFF,0xFFFF,
0xFFFF,0xFFFF,0xFFFF,0xFFFF,0xFFFF,0xFFFF,
0xFFFF,0xFFFF,0xFFFF,0xFFFF,0xFFFF,0xFFFF,
0xFFFF,0xFFFF,0xFFFF,0xFFFF,0xFFFF,0xFFFF,
0xFFFF,0xFFFF,0xFFFF,0xFFFF,0xFFFF,0xFFFF,
/* 08 */
0x0007,0x0777,0x7770,0x7000,0x2225,0x2536,
0x3646,0x4655,0x5552,0x5241,0x4131,0x3122,
0xFFFF,0xFFFF,0xFFFF,0xFFFF,0xFFFF,0xFFFF,
0xFFFF,0xFFFF,0xFFFF,0xFFFF,0xFFFF,0xFFFF,
0xFFFF,0xFFFF,0xFFFF,0xFFFF,0xFFFF,0xFFFF,
0xFFFF,0xFFFF,0xFFFF,0xFFFF,0xFFFF,0xFFFF,
/* 09 */
0x1215,0x1525,0x2526,0x2656,0x5655,0x5565,
0x6562,0x6252,0x5251,0x5121,0x2122,0x2212,
0xFFFF,0xFFFF,0xFFFF,0xFFFF,0xFFFF,0xFFFF,
0xFFFF,0xFFFF,0xFFFF,0xFFFF,0xFFFF,0xFFFF,
0xFFFF,0xFFFF,0xFFFF,0xFFFF,0xFFFF,0xFFFF,
0xFFFF,0xFFFF,0xFFFF,0xFFFF,0xFFFF,0xFFFF,
/* 0A */
0x0001,0x0111,0x1110,0x1000,0x0607,0x0717,
0x1716,0x1606,0x6061,0x6171,0x7170,0x7060,
0x6667,0x6777,0x7776,0x7666,0x2324,0x2435,
0x3545,0x4554,0x5453,0x5342,0x4232,0x3223,
0xFFFF,0xFFFF,0xFFFF,0xFFFF,0xFFFF,0xFFFF,
0xFFFF,0xFFFF,0xFFFF,0xFFFF,0xFFFF,0xFFFF,
/* 0B */
0x0407,0x0727,0x3307,0x3134,0x3445,0x4565,
0x6574,0x7471,0x7160,0x6040,0x4031,0xFFFF,
0xFFFF,0xFFFF,0xFFFF,0xFFFF,0xFFFF,0xFFFF,
0xFFFF,0xFFFF,0xFFFF,0xFFFF,0xFFFF,0xFFFF,
0xFFFF,0xFFFF,0xFFFF,0xFFFF,0xFFFF,0xFFFF,
0xFFFF,0xFFFF,0xFFFF,0xFFFF,0xFFFF,0xFFFF,
/* 0C */
0x0205,0x0516,0x1636,0x3654,0x5331,0x3111,
0x1102,0x5373,0x5474,0x6166,0xFFFF,0xFFFF,
0xFFFF,0xFFFF,0xFFFF,0xFFFF,0xFFFF,0xFFFF,
0xFFFF,0xFFFF,0xFFFF,0xFFFF,0xFFFF,0xFFFF,
0xFFFF,0xFFFF,0xFFFF,0xFFFF,0xFFFF,0xFFFF,
0xFFFF,0xFFFF,0xFFFF,0xFFFF,0xFFFF,0xFFFF,
```

```
/* 0D */
0x0207,0x0727,0x2722,0x2202,0x2262,0x6271,
0x7170,0x7060,0x6051,0x5152,0xFFFF,0xFFFF,
0xFFFF,0xFFFF,0xFFFF,0xFFFF,0xFFFF,0xFFFF,
0xFFFF,0xFFFF,0xFFFF,0xFFFF,0xFFFF,0xFFFF,
0xFFFF,0xFFFF,0xFFFF,0xFFFF,0xFFFF,0xFFFF,
0xFFFF,0xFFFF,0xFFFF,0xFFFF,0xFFFF,0xFFFF,
/* 0E */
0x0207,0x0757,0x5766,0x6665,0x6555,0x5546,
0x4647,0x2227,0x0262,0x6271,0x7170,0x7060,
0x6051,0x5152,0xFFFF,0xFFFF,0xFFFF,0xFFFF,
0xFFFF,0xFFFF,0xFFFF,0xFFFF,0xFFFF,0xFFFF,
0xFFFF,0xFFFF,0xFFFF,0xFFFF,0xFFFF,0xFFFF,
0xFFFF,0xFFFF,0xFFFF,0xFFFF,0xFFFF,0xFFFF,
/* 0F */
0x2225,0x2555,0x5552,0x5222,0x0022,0x0323,
0x0424,0x0725,0x3735,0x4745,0x7755,0x7454,
0x7353,0x7052,0x4042,0x3032,0xFFFF,0xFFFF,
0xFFFF,0xFFFF,0xFFFF,0xFFFF,0xFFFF,0xFFFF,
0xFFFF,0xFFFF,0xFFFF,0xFFFF,0xFFFF,0xFFFF,
0xFFFF,0xFFFF,0xFFFF,0xFFFF,0xFFFF,0xFFFF,
/* 10 */
0x0036,0x3660,0xFFFF,0xFFFF,0xFFFF,0xFFFF,
0xFFFF,0xFFFF,0xFFFF,0xFFFF,0xFFFF,0xFFFF,
0xFFFF,0xFFFF,0xFFFF,0xFFFF,0xFFFF,0xFFFF,
0xFFFF,0xFFFF,0xFFFF,0xFFFF,0xFFFF,0xFFFF,
0xFFFF,0xFFFF,0xFFFF,0xFFFF,0xFFFF,0xFFFF,
0xFFFF,0xFFFF,0xFFFF,0xFFFF,0xFFFF,0xFFFF,
/* 11 */
0x0630,0x3066,0xFFFF,0xFFFF,0xFFFF,0xFFFF,
0xFFFF,0xFFFF,0xFFFF,0xFFFF,0xFFFF,0xFFFF,
0xFFFF,0xFFFF,0xFFFF,0xFFFF,0xFFFF,0xFFFF,
0xFFFF,0xFFFF,0xFFFF,0xFFFF,0xFFFF,0xFFFF,
0xFFFF,0xFFFF,0xFFFF,0xFFFF,0xFFFF,0xFFFF,
0xFFFF,0xFFFF,0xFFFF,0xFFFF,0xFFFF,0xFFFF,
/* 12 */
0x0304,0x0426,0x2624,0x2454,0x5456,0x5674,
0x7473,0x7351,0x5153,0x5323,0x2321,0x2103,
0xFFFF,0xFFFF,0xFFFF,0xFFFF,0xFFFF,0xFFFF,
0xFFFF,0xFFFF,0xFFFF,0xFFFF,0xFFFF,0xFFFF,
0xFFFF,0xFFFF,0xFFFF,0xFFFF,0xFFFF,0xFFFF,
0xFFFF,0xFFFF,0xFFFF,0xFFFF,0xFFFF,0xFFFF,
/* 13 */
0x0102,0x0242,0x4241,0x4101,0x6162,0x0506,
0x0646,0x4645,0x4505,0x6566,0xFFFF,0xFFFF,
```

```
0xFFFF,0xFFFF,0xFFFF,0xFFFF,0xFFFF,0xFFFF,
0xFFFF,0xFFFF,0xFFFF,0xFFFF,0xFFFF,0xFFFF,
0xFFFF,0xFFFF,0xFFFF,0xFFFF,0xFFFF,0xFFFF,
0xFFFF,0xFFFF,0xFFFF,0xFFFF,0xFFFF,0xFFFF,
/* 14 */
0x0107,0x0767,0x0110,0x1020,0x2031,0x3137,
0x0464,0xFFFF,0xFFFF,0xFFFF,0xFFFF,0xFFFF,
0xFFFF,0xFFFF,0xFFFF,0xFFFF,0xFFFF,0xFFFF,
0xFFFF,0xFFFF,0xFFFF,0xFFFF,0xFFFF,0xFFFF,
0xFFFF,0xFFFF,0xFFFF,0xFFFF,0xFFFF,0xFFFF,
0xFFFF,0xFFFF,0xFFFF,0xFFFF,0xFFFF,0xFFFF,
0xFFFF,0xFFFF,0xFFFF,0xFFFF,0xFFFF,0xFFFF,
/* 15 */
0x1706,0x0602,0x0211,0x1122,0x2224,0x2435,
0x3545,0x4554,0x6071,0x7174,0x7465,0x6554,
0x5452,0x5241,0x4131,0x3122,0xFFFF,0xFFFF,
0xFFFF,0xFFFF,0xFFFF,0xFFFF,0xFFFF,0xFFFF,
0xFFFF,0xFFFF,0xFFFF,0xFFFF,0xFFFF,0xFFFF,
0xFFFF,0xFFFF,0xFFFF,0xFFFF,0xFFFF,0xFFFF,
/* 16 */
0x4146,0x4666,0x6661,0x6141,0x5156,0xFFFF,
0xFFFF,0xFFFF,0xFFFF,0xFFFF,0xFFFF,0xFFFF,
0xFFFF,0xFFFF,0xFFFF,0xFFFF,0xFFFF,0xFFFF,
0xFFFF,0xFFFF,0xFFFF,0xFFFF,0xFFFF,0xFFFF,
0xFFFF,0xFFFF,0xFFFF,0xFFFF,0xFFFF,0xFFFF,
0xFFFF,0xFFFF,0xFFFF,0xFFFF,0xFFFF,0xFFFF,
/* 17 */
0x0304,0x0426,0x2624,0x2444,0x4446,0x4664,
0x6463,0x6341,0x4143,0x4323,0x2321,0x2103,
0x7077,0xFFFF,0xFFFF,0xFFFF,0xFFFF,0xFFFF,
0xFFFF,0xFFFF,0xFFFF,0xFFFF,0xFFFF,0xFFFF,
0xFFFF,0xFFFF,0xFFFF,0xFFFF,0xFFFF,0xFFFF,
0xFFFF,0xFFFF,0xFFFF,0xFFFF,0xFFFF,0xFFFF,
/* 18 */
0x0304,0x0426,0x2624,0x2464,0x6463,0x6323,
0x2321,0x2103,0xFFFF,0xFFFF,0xFFFF,0xFFFF,
0xFFFF,0xFFFF,0xFFFF,0xFFFF,0xFFFF,0xFFFF,
0xFFFF,0xFFFF,0xFFFF,0xFFFF,0xFFFF,0xFFFF,
0xFFFF,0xFFFF,0xFFFF,0xFFFF,0xFFFF,0xFFFF,
0xFFFF,0xFFFF,0xFFFF,0xFFFF,0xFFFF,0xFFFF,
/* 19 */
0x0304,0x0444,0x4446,0x4664,0x6463,0x6341,
0x4143,0x4303,0xFFFF,0xFFFF,0xFFFF,0xFFFF,
0xFFFF,0xFFFF,0xFFFF,0xFFFF,0xFFFF,0xFFFF,
0xFFFF,0xFFFF,0xFFFF,0xFFFF,0xFFFF,0xFFFF,
0xFFFF,0xFFFF,0xFFFF,0xFFFF,0xFFFF,0xFFFF,
```

```
0xFFFF,0xFFFF,0xFFFF,0xFFFF,0xFFFF,0xFFFF,
/* 1A */
0x1314,0x1436,0x3654,0x5453,0x5335,0x3513,
0x3035,0xFFFF,0xFFFF,0xFFFF,0xFFFF,0xFFFF,
0xFFFF,0xFFFF,0xFFFF,0xFFFF,0xFFFF,0xFFFF,
0xFFFF,0xFFFF,0xFFFF,0xFFFF,0xFFFF,0xFFFF,
0xFFFF,0xFFFF,0xFFFF,0xFFFF,0xFFFF,0xFFFF,
0xFFFF,0xFFFF,0xFFFF,0xFFFF,0xFFFF,0xFFFF,
/* 1B */
0x1213,0x1331,0x3153,0x5352,0x5230,0x3012,
0x3136,0xFFFF,0xFFFF,0xFFFF,0xFFFF,0xFFFF,
0xFFFF,0xFFFF,0xFFFF,0xFFFF,0xFFFF,0xFFFF,
0xFFFF,0xFFFF,0xFFFF,0xFFFF,0xFFFF,0xFFFF,
0xFFFF,0xFFFF,0xFFFF,0xFFFF,0xFFFF,0xFFFF,
0xFFFF,0xFFFF,0xFFFF,0xFFFF,0xFFFF,0xFFFF,
/* 1C */
0x5121,0x2120,0x2050,0x5056,0xFFFF,0xFFFF,
0xFFFF,0xFFFF,0xFFFF,0xFFFF,0xFFFF,0xFFFF,
0xFFFF,0xFFFF,0xFFFF,0xFFFF,0xFFFF,0xFFFF,
0xFFFF,0xFFFF,0xFFFF,0xFFFF,0xFFFF,0xFFFF,
0xFFFF,0xFFFF,0xFFFF,0xFFFF,0xFFFF,0xFFFF,
0xFFFF,0xFFFF,0xFFFF,0xFFFF,0xFFFF,0xFFFF,
/* 1D */
0x1252,0x5230,0x3012,0x1537,0x3755,0x5515,
0x3235,0xFFFF,0xFFFF,0xFFFF,0xFFFF,0xFFFF,
0xFFFF,0xFFFF,0xFFFF,0xFFFF,0xFFFF,0xFFFF,
0xFFFF,0xFFFF,0xFFFF,0xFFFF,0xFFFF,0xFFFF,
0xFFFF,0xFFFF,0xFFFF,0xFFFF,0xFFFF,0xFFFF,
0xFFFF,0xFFFF,0xFFFF,0xFFFF,0xFFFF,0xFFFF,
/* 1E */
0x1314,0x1447,0x4757,0x5750,0x5040,0x4013,
0xFFFF,0xFFFF,0xFFFF,0xFFFF,0xFFFF,0xFFFF,
0xFFFF,0xFFFF,0xFFFF,0xFFFF,0xFFFF,0xFFFF,
0xFFFF,0xFFFF,0xFFFF,0xFFFF,0xFFFF,0xFFFF,
0xFFFF,0xFFFF,0xFFFF,0xFFFF,0xFFFF,0xFFFF,
0xFFFF,0xFFFF,0xFFFF,0xFFFF,0xFFFF,0xFFFF,
/* 1F */
0x1017,0x1727,0x2754,0x5453,0x5320,0x2010,
0xFFFF,0xFFFF,0xFFFF,0xFFFF,0xFFFF,0xFFFF,
0xFFFF,0xFFFF,0xFFFF,0xFFFF,0xFFFF,0xFFFF,
0xFFFF,0xFFFF,0xFFFF,0xFFFF,0xFFFF,0xFFFF,
0xFFFF,0xFFFF,0xFFFF,0xFFFF,0xFFFF,0xFFFF,
0xFFFF,0xFFFF,0xFFFF,0xFFFF,0xFFFF,0xFFFF,
/* 20 */
0xFFFF,0xFFFF,0xFFFF,0xFFFF,0xFFFF,0xFFFF,
```

```
0xFFFF,0xFFFF,0xFFFF,0xFFFF,0xFFFF,0xFFFF,
0xFFFF,0xFFFF,0xFFFF,0xFFFF,0xFFFF,0xFFFF,
0xFFFF,0xFFFF,0xFFFF,0xFFFF,0xFFFF,0xFFFF,
0xFFFF,0xFFFF,0xFFFF,0xFFFF,0xFFFF,0xFFFF,
0xFFFF,0xFFFF,0xFFFF,0xFFFF,0xFFFF,0xFFFF,
/* 21 */
0x0203,0x0314,0x1424,0x2433,0x3343,0x4342,
0x4232,0x3221,0x2111,0x1102,0x6263,0xFFFF,
0xFFFF,0xFFFF,0xFFFF,0xFFFF,0xFFFF,0xFFFF,
0xFFFF,0xFFFF,0xFFFF,0xFFFF,0xFFFF,0xFFFF,
0xFFFF,0xFFFF,0xFFFF,0xFFFF,0xFFFF,0xFFFF,
0xFFFF,0xFFFF,0xFFFF,0xFFFF,0xFFFF,0xFFFF,
/* 22 */
0x0102,0x0222,0x2221,0x2101,0x0405,0x0525,
0x2524,0x2404,0xFFFF,0xFFFF,0xFFFF,0xFFFF,
0xFFFF,0xFFFF,0xFFFF,0xFFFF,0xFFFF,0xFFFF,
0xFFFF,0xFFFF,0xFFFF,0xFFFF,0xFFFF,0xFFFF,
0xFFFF,0xFFFF,0xFFFF,0xFFFF,0xFFFF,0xFFFF,
0xFFFF,0xFFFF,0xFFFF,0xFFFF,0xFFFF,0xFFFF,
/* 23 */
0x0102,0x0262,0x6261,0x6101,0x0405,0x0565,
0x6564,0x6404,0x2026,0x4046,0xFFFF,0xFFFF,
0xFFFF,0xFFFF,0xFFFF,0xFFFF,0xFFFF,0xFFFF,
0xFFFF,0xFFFF,0xFFFF,0xFFFF,0xFFFF,0xFFFF,
0xFFFF,0xFFFF,0xFFFF,0xFFFF,0xFFFF,0xFFFF,
0xFFFF,0xFFFF,0xFFFF,0xFFFF,0xFFFF,0xFFFF,
/* 24 */
0x1511,0x1120,0x2031,0x3134,0x3445,0x4554,
0x5450,0x0262,0x0363,0xFFFF,0xFFFF,0xFFFF,
0xFFFF,0xFFFF,0xFFFF,0xFFFF,0xFFFF,0xFFFF,
0xFFFF,0xFFFF,0xFFFF,0xFFFF,0xFFFF,0xFFFF,
0xFFFF,0xFFFF,0xFFFF,0xFFFF,0xFFFF,0xFFFF,
0xFFFF,0xFFFF,0xFFFF,0xFFFF,0xFFFF,0xFFFF,
/* 25 */
0x1011,0x1121,0x2120,0x2010,0x1516,0x1661,
0x6160,0x6015,0x5556,0x5666,0x6665,0x6555,
0xFFFF,0xFFFF,0xFFFF,0xFFFF,0xFFFF,0xFFFF,
0xFFFF,0xFFFF,0xFFFF,0xFFFF,0xFFFF,0xFFFF,
0xFFFF,0xFFFF,0xFFFF,0xFFFF,0xFFFF,0xFFFF,
0xFFFF,0xFFFF,0xFFFF,0xFFFF,0xFFFF,0xFFFF,
/* 26 */
0x0204,0x0415,0x1524,0x2431,0x3140,0x4050,
0x5061,0x6163,0x6336,0x0211,0x1166,0xFFFF,
0xFFFF,0xFFFF,0xFFFF,0xFFFF,0xFFFF,0xFFFF,
0xFFFF,0xFFFF,0xFFFF,0xFFFF,0xFFFF,0xFFFF,
```

```
0xFFFF,0xFFFF,0xFFFF,0xFFFF,0xFFFF,0xFFFF,
0xFFFF,0xFFFF,0xFFFF,0xFFFF,0xFFFF,0xFFFF,
/* 27 */
0x0102,0x0212,0x1221,0x2120,0x2011,0x1101,
0xFFFF,0xFFFF,0xFFFF,0xFFFF,0xFFFF,0xFFFF,
0xFFFF,0xFFFF,0xFFFF,0xFFFF,0xFFFF,0xFFFF,
0xFFFF,0xFFFF,0xFFFF,0xFFFF,0xFFFF,0xFFFF,
0xFFFF,0xFFFF,0xFFFF,0xFFFF,0xFFFF,0xFFFF,
0xFFFF,0xFFFF,0xFFFF,0xFFFF,0xFFFF,0xFFFF,
/* 28 */
0x0304,0x0422,0x2242,0x4264,0x6463,0x6341,
0x4121,0x2103,0xFFFF,0xFFFF,0xFFFF,0xFFFF,
0xFFFF,0xFFFF,0xFFFF,0xFFFF,0xFFFF,0xFFFF,
0xFFFF,0xFFFF,0xFFFF,0xFFFF,0xFFFF,0xFFFF,
0xFFFF,0xFFFF,0xFFFF,0xFFFF,0xFFFF,0xFFFF,
0xFFFF,0xFFFF,0xFFFF,0xFFFF,0xFFFF,0xFFFF,
/* 29 */
0x0102,0x0224,0x2444,0x4462,0x6261,0x6143,
0x4323,0x2301,0xFFFF,0xFFFF,0xFFFF,0xFFFF,
0xFFFF,0xFFFF,0xFFFF,0xFFFF,0xFFFF,0xFFFF,
0xFFFF,0xFFFF,0xFFFF,0xFFFF,0xFFFF,0xFFFF,
0xFFFF,0xFFFF,0xFFFF,0xFFFF,0xFFFF,0xFFFF,
0xFFFF,0xFFFF,0xFFFF,0xFFFF,0xFFFF,0xFFFF,
/* 2A */
0x1112,0x1256,0x5655,0x5511,0x1516,0x1652,
0x5251,0x5115,0x3037,0xFFFF,0xFFFF,0xFFFF,
0xFFFF,0xFFFF,0xFFFF,0xFFFF,0xFFFF,0xFFFF,
0xFFFF,0xFFFF,0xFFFF,0xFFFF,0xFFFF,0xFFFF,
0xFFFF,0xFFFF,0xFFFF,0xFFFF,0xFFFF,0xFFFF,
0xFFFF,0xFFFF,0xFFFF,0xFFFF,0xFFFF,0xFFFF,
/* 2B */
0x1213,0x1353,0x5352,0x5212,0x3032,0x3335,
0xFFFF,0xFFFF,0xFFFF,0xFFFF,0xFFFF,0xFFFF,
0xFFFF,0xFFFF,0xFFFF,0xFFFF,0xFFFF,0xFFFF,
0xFFFF,0xFFFF,0xFFFF,0xFFFF,0xFFFF,0xFFFF,
0xFFFF,0xFFFF,0xFFFF,0xFFFF,0xFFFF,0xFFFF,
0xFFFF,0xFFFF,0xFFFF,0xFFFF,0xFFFF,0xFFFF,
/* 2C */
0x5253,0x5363,0x6372,0x7271,0x7162,0x6252,
0xFFFF,0xFFFF,0xFFFF,0xFFFF,0xFFFF,0xFFFF,
0xFFFF,0xFFFF,0xFFFF,0xFFFF,0xFFFF,0xFFFF,
0xFFFF,0xFFFF,0xFFFF,0xFFFF,0xFFFF,0xFFFF,
0xFFFF,0xFFFF,0xFFFF,0xFFFF,0xFFFF,0xFFFF,
0xFFFF,0xFFFF,0xFFFF,0xFFFF,0xFFFF,0xFFFF,
/* 2D */
```

```
0x3035,0xFFFF,0xFFFF,0xFFFF,0xFFFF,0xFFFF,
0xFFFF,0xFFFF,0xFFFF,0xFFFF,0xFFFF,0xFFFF,
0xFFFF,0xFFFF,0xFFFF,0xFFFF,0xFFFF,0xFFFF,
0xFFFF,0xFFFF,0xFFFF,0xFFFF,0xFFFF,0xFFFF,
0xFFFF,0xFFFF,0xFFFF,0xFFFF,0xFFFF,0xFFFF,
0xFFFF,0xFFFF,0xFFFF,0xFFFF,0xFFFF,0xFFFF,
/* 2E */
0x5253,0x5363,0x6362,0x6252,0xFFFF,0xFFFF,
0xFFFF,0xFFFF,0xFFFF,0xFFFF,0xFFFF,0xFFFF,
0xFFFF,0xFFFF,0xFFFF,0xFFFF,0xFFFF,0xFFFF,
0xFFFF,0xFFFF,0xFFFF,0xFFFF,0xFFFF,0xFFFF,
0xFFFF,0xFFFF,0xFFFF,0xFFFF,0xFFFF,0xFFFF,
0xFFFF,0xFFFF,0xFFFF,0xFFFF,0xFFFF,0xFFFF,
/* 2F */
0x0506,0x0660,0x6050,0x5005,0xFFFF,0xFFFF,
0xFFFF,0xFFFF,0xFFFF,0xFFFF,0xFFFF,0xFFFF,
0xFFFF,0xFFFF,0xFFFF,0xFFFF,0xFFFF,0xFFFF,
0xFFFF,0xFFFF,0xFFFF,0xFFFF,0xFFFF,0xFFFF,
0xFFFF,0xFFFF,0xFFFF,0xFFFF,0xFFFF,0xFFFF,
0xFFFF,0xFFFF,0xFFFF,0xFFFF,0xFFFF,0xFFFF,
/* 30 */
0x0105,0x0516,0x1656,0x5665,0x6561,0x6150,
0x5010,0x1001,0x0161,0x0565,0x5115,0xFFFF,
0xFFFF,0xFFFF,0xFFFF,0xFFFF,0xFFFF,0xFFFF,
0xFFFF,0xFFFF,0xFFFF,0xFFFF,0xFFFF,0xFFFF,
0xFFFF,0xFFFF,0xFFFF,0xFFFF,0xFFFF,0xFFFF,
0xFFFF,0xFFFF,0xFFFF,0xFFFF,0xFFFF,0xFFFF,
/* 31 */
0x0203,0x0363,0x6065,0x0262,0x0211,0xFFFF,
0xFFFF,0xFFFF,0xFFFF,0xFFFF,0xFFFF,0xFFFF,
0xFFFF,0xFFFF,0xFFFF,0xFFFF,0xFFFF,0xFFFF,
0xFFFF,0xFFFF,0xFFFF,0xFFFF,0xFFFF,0xFFFF,
0xFFFF,0xFFFF,0xFFFF,0xFFFF,0xFFFF,0xFFFF,
0xFFFF,0xFFFF,0xFFFF,0xFFFF,0xFFFF,0xFFFF,
/* 32 */
0x1001,0x0104,0x0415,0x1525,0x2534,0x3441,
0x4150,0x5060,0x6065,0x0434,0xFFFF,0xFFFF,
0xFFFF,0xFFFF,0xFFFF,0xFFFF,0xFFFF,0xFFFF,
0xFFFF,0xFFFF,0xFFFF,0xFFFF,0xFFFF,0xFFFF,
0xFFFF,0xFFFF,0xFFFF,0xFFFF,0xFFFF,0xFFFF,
0xFFFF,0xFFFF,0xFFFF,0xFFFF,0xFFFF,0xFFFF,
/* 33 */
0x1001,0x0104,0x0415,0x1525,0x2534,0x3234,
0x3445,0x4555,0x5564,0x6461,0x6150,0x0464,
0xFFFF,0xFFFF,0xFFFF,0xFFFF,0xFFFF,0xFFFF,
```

```
0xFFFF,0xFFFF,0xFFFF,0xFFFF,0xFFFF,0xFFFF,
0xFFFF,0xFFFF,0xFFFF,0xFFFF,0xFFFF,0xFFFF,
0xFFFF,0xFFFF,0xFFFF,0xFFFF,0xFFFF,0xFFFF,
/* 34 */
0x0305,0x0565,0x0464,0x6366,0x0330,0x3040,
0x4046,0xFFFF,0xFFFF,0xFFFF,0xFFFF,0xFFFF,
0xFFFF,0xFFFF,0xFFFF,0xFFFF,0xFFFF,0xFFFF,
0xFFFF,0xFFFF,0xFFFF,0xFFFF,0xFFFF,0xFFFF,
0xFFFF,0xFFFF,0xFFFF,0xFFFF,0xFFFF,0xFFFF,
0xFFFF,0xFFFF,0xFFFF,0xFFFF,0xFFFF,0xFFFF,
/* 35 */
0x0005,0x0020,0x0121,0x2024,0x2435,0x3555,
0x5564,0x6461,0x6150,0xFFFF,0xFFFF,0xFFFF,
0xFFFF,0xFFFF,0xFFFF,0xFFFF,0xFFFF,0xFFFF,
0xFFFF,0xFFFF,0xFFFF,0xFFFF,0xFFFF,0xFFFF,
0xFFFF,0xFFFF,0xFFFF,0xFFFF,0xFFFF,0xFFFF,
0xFFFF,0xFFFF,0xFFFF,0xFFFF,0xFFFF,0xFFFF,
/* 36 */
0x0402,0x0220,0x2050,0x5061,0x6164,0x6455,
0x5545,0x4534,0x3431,0x1161,0xFFFF,0xFFFF,
0xFFFF,0xFFFF,0xFFFF,0xFFFF,0xFFFF,0xFFFF,
0xFFFF,0xFFFF,0xFFFF,0xFFFF,0xFFFF,0xFFFF,
0xFFFF,0xFFFF,0xFFFF,0xFFFF,0xFFFF,0xFFFF,
0xFFFF,0xFFFF,0xFFFF,0xFFFF,0xFFFF,0xFFFF,
/* 37 */
0x1000,0x0005,0x0525,0x2543,0x4363,0x0434,
0xFFFF,0xFFFF,0xFFFF,0xFFFF,0xFFFF,0xFFFF,
0xFFFF,0xFFFF,0xFFFF,0xFFFF,0xFFFF,0xFFFF,
0xFFFF,0xFFFF,0xFFFF,0xFFFF,0xFFFF,0xFFFF,
0xFFFF,0xFFFF,0xFFFF,0xFFFF,0xFFFF,0xFFFF,
0xFFFF,0xFFFF,0xFFFF,0xFFFF,0xFFFF,0xFFFF,
/* 38 */
0x0104,0x0415,0x1525,0x2534,0x3445,0x4555,
0x5564,0x6461,0x6150,0x5040,0x4031,0x3120,
0x2010,0x1001,0x0161,0x0464,0x3134,0xFFFF,
0xFFFF,0xFFFF,0xFFFF,0xFFFF,0xFFFF,0xFFFF,
0xFFFF,0xFFFF,0xFFFF,0xFFFF,0xFFFF,0xFFFF,
0xFFFF,0xFFFF,0xFFFF,0xFFFF,0xFFFF,0xFFFF,
/* 39 */
0x3431,0x3120,0x2010,0x1001,0x0104,0x0415,
0x1545,0x4563,0x6361,0x0454,0xFFFF,0xFFFF,
0xFFFF,0xFFFF,0xFFFF,0xFFFF,0xFFFF,0xFFFF,
0xFFFF,0xFFFF,0xFFFF,0xFFFF,0xFFFF,0xFFFF,
0xFFFF,0xFFFF,0xFFFF,0xFFFF,0xFFFF,0xFFFF,
0xFFFF,0xFFFF,0xFFFF,0xFFFF,0xFFFF,0xFFFF,
```

```
/* 3A */
0x1213,0x1323,0x2322,0x2212,0x5253,0x5363,
0x6362,0x6252,0xFFFF,0xFFFF,0xFFFF,0xFFFF,
0xFFFF,0xFFFF,0xFFFF,0xFFFF,0xFFFF,0xFFFF,
0xFFFF,0xFFFF,0xFFFF,0xFFFF,0xFFFF,0xFFFF,
0xFFFF,0xFFFF,0xFFFF,0xFFFF,0xFFFF,0xFFFF,
0xFFFF,0xFFFF,0xFFFF,0xFFFF,0xFFFF,0xFFFF,
/* 3B */
0x1213,0x1323,0x2322,0x2212,0x5253,0x5363,
0x6372,0x7271,0x7162,0x6252,0xFFFF,0xFFFF,
0xFFFF,0xFFFF,0xFFFF,0xFFFF,0xFFFF,0xFFFF,
0xFFFF,0xFFFF,0xFFFF,0xFFFF,0xFFFF,0xFFFF,
0xFFFF,0xFFFF,0xFFFF,0xFFFF,0xFFFF,0xFFFF,
0xFFFF,0xFFFF,0xFFFF,0xFFFF,0xFFFF,0xFFFF,
/* 3C */
0x0304,0x0431,0x3164,0x6463,0x6330,0x3003,
0xFFFF,0xFFFF,0xFFFF,0xFFFF,0xFFFF,0xFFFF,
0xFFFF,0xFFFF,0xFFFF,0xFFFF,0xFFFF,0xFFFF,
0xFFFF,0xFFFF,0xFFFF,0xFFFF,0xFFFF,0xFFFF,
0xFFFF,0xFFFF,0xFFFF,0xFFFF,0xFFFF,0xFFFF,
0xFFFF,0xFFFF,0xFFFF,0xFFFF,0xFFFF,0xFFFF,
/* 3D */
0x2025,0x5055,0xFFFF,0xFFFF,0xFFFF,0xFFFF,
0xFFFF,0xFFFF,0xFFFF,0xFFFF,0xFFFF,0xFFFF,
0xFFFF,0xFFFF,0xFFFF,0xFFFF,0xFFFF,0xFFFF,
0xFFFF,0xFFFF,0xFFFF,0xFFFF,0xFFFF,0xFFFF,
0xFFFF,0xFFFF,0xFFFF,0xFFFF,0xFFFF,0xFFFF,
0xFFFF,0xFFFF,0xFFFF,0xFFFF,0xFFFF,0xFFFF,
/* 3E */
0x0102,0x0235,0x3562,0x6261,0x6134,0x3401,
0xFFFF,0xFFFF,0xFFFF,0xFFFF,0xFFFF,0xFFFF,
0xFFFF,0xFFFF,0xFFFF,0xFFFF,0xFFFF,0xFFFF,
0xFFFF,0xFFFF,0xFFFF,0xFFFF,0xFFFF,0xFFFF,
0xFFFF,0xFFFF,0xFFFF,0xFFFF,0xFFFF,0xFFFF,
0xFFFF,0xFFFF,0xFFFF,0xFFFF,0xFFFF,0xFFFF,
/* 3F */
0x1001,0x0104,0x0415,0x1525,0x2534,0x3443,
0x0434,0x6263,0xFFFF,0xFFFF,0xFFFF,0xFFFF,
0xFFFF,0xFFFF,0xFFFF,0xFFFF,0xFFFF,0xFFFF,
0xFFFF,0xFFFF,0xFFFF,0xFFFF,0xFFFF,0xFFFF,
0xFFFF,0xFFFF,0xFFFF,0xFFFF,0xFFFF,0xFFFF,
0xFFFF,0xFFFF,0xFFFF,0xFFFF,0xFFFF,0xFFFF,
/* 40 */
0x6461,0x6150,0x5010,0x1001,0x0105,0x0516,
0x1646,0x4643,0x4323,0x2326,0xFFFF,0xFFFF,
```

```
0xFFFF,0xFFFF,0xFFFF,0xFFFF,0xFFFF,0xFFFF,
0xFFFF,0xFFFF,0xFFFF,0xFFFF,0xFFFF,0xFFFF,
0xFFFF,0xFFFF,0xFFFF,0xFFFF,0xFFFF,0xFFFF,
0xFFFF,0xFFFF,0xFFFF,0xFFFF,0xFFFF,0xFFFF,
/* 41 */
0x0220,0x2060,0x6061,0x6111,0x0203,0x0325,
0x2565,0x6564,0x6414,0x4144,0xFFFF,0xFFFF,
0xFFFF,0xFFFF,0xFFFF,0xFFFF,0xFFFF,0xFFFF,
0xFFFF,0xFFFF,0xFFFF,0xFFFF,0xFFFF,0xFFFF,
0xFFFF,0xFFFF,0xFFFF,0xFFFF,0xFFFF,0xFFFF,
0xFFFF,0xFFFF,0xFFFF,0xFFFF,0xFFFF,0xFFFF,
/* 42 */
0x0005,0x0516,0x1626,0x2635,0x3532,0x3546,
0x4656,0x5665,0x6560,0x0161,0x0262,0xFFFF,
0xFFFF,0xFFFF,0xFFFF,0xFFFF,0xFFFF,0xFFFF,
0xFFFF,0xFFFF,0xFFFF,0xFFFF,0xFFFF,0xFFFF,
0xFFFF,0xFFFF,0xFFFF,0xFFFF,0xFFFF,0xFFFF,
0xFFFF,0xFFFF,0xFFFF,0xFFFF,0xFFFF,0xFFFF,
/* 43 */
0x1605,0x0502,0x0220,0x2040,0x4062,0x6265,
0x6556,0x1151,0xFFFF,0xFFFF,0xFFFF,0xFFFF,
0xFFFF,0xFFFF,0xFFFF,0xFFFF,0xFFFF,0xFFFF,
0xFFFF,0xFFFF,0xFFFF,0xFFFF,0xFFFF,0xFFFF,
0xFFFF,0xFFFF,0xFFFF,0xFFFF,0xFFFF,0xFFFF,
0xFFFF,0xFFFF,0xFFFF,0xFFFF,0xFFFF,0xFFFF,
/* 44 */
0x0004,0x0426,0x2646,0x4664,0x6460,0x0161,
0x0262,0xFFFF,0xFFFF,0xFFFF,0xFFFF,0xFFFF,
0xFFFF,0xFFFF,0xFFFF,0xFFFF,0xFFFF,0xFFFF,
0xFFFF,0xFFFF,0xFFFF,0xFFFF,0xFFFF,0xFFFF,
0xFFFF,0xFFFF,0xFFFF,0xFFFF,0xFFFF,0xFFFF,
0xFFFF,0xFFFF,0xFFFF,0xFFFF,0xFFFF,0xFFFF,
/* 45 */
0x0006,0x0616,0x6066,0x6656,0x0161,0x0262,
0x3234,0x2444,0xFFFF,0xFFFF,0xFFFF,0xFFFF,
0xFFFF,0xFFFF,0xFFFF,0xFFFF,0xFFFF,0xFFFF,
0xFFFF,0xFFFF,0xFFFF,0xFFFF,0xFFFF,0xFFFF,
0xFFFF,0xFFFF,0xFFFF,0xFFFF,0xFFFF,0xFFFF,
0xFFFF,0xFFFF,0xFFFF,0xFFFF,0xFFFF,0xFFFF,
/* 46 */
0x0006,0x0616,0x0161,0x0262,0x6063,0x3234,
0x2444,0xFFFF,0xFFFF,0xFFFF,0xFFFF,0xFFFF,
0xFFFF,0xFFFF,0xFFFF,0xFFFF,0xFFFF,0xFFFF,
0xFFFF,0xFFFF,0xFFFF,0xFFFF,0xFFFF,0xFFFF,
0xFFFF,0xFFFF,0xFFFF,0xFFFF,0xFFFF,0xFFFF,
```

```
0xFFFF,0xFFFF,0xFFFF,0xFFFF,0xFFFF,0xFFFF,
/* 47 */
0x1605,0x0502,0x0220,0x2040,0x4062,0x6266,
0x6646,0x4644,0x1151,0xFFFF,0xFFFF,0xFFFF,
0xFFFF,0xFFFF,0xFFFF,0xFFFF,0xFFFF,0xFFFF,
0xFFFF,0xFFFF,0xFFFF,0xFFFF,0xFFFF,0xFFFF,
0xFFFF,0xFFFF,0xFFFF,0xFFFF,0xFFFF,0xFFFF,
0xFFFF,0xFFFF,0xFFFF,0xFFFF,0xFFFF,0xFFFF,
/* 48 */
0x0001,0x0161,0x6160,0x6000,0x0405,0x0565,
0x6564,0x6404,0x3134,0xFFFF,0xFFFF,0xFFFF,
0xFFFF,0xFFFF,0xFFFF,0xFFFF,0xFFFF,0xFFFF,
0xFFFF,0xFFFF,0xFFFF,0xFFFF,0xFFFF,0xFFFF,
0xFFFF,0xFFFF,0xFFFF,0xFFFF,0xFFFF,0xFFFF,
0xFFFF,0xFFFF,0xFFFF,0xFFFF,0xFFFF,0xFFFF,
/* 49 */
0x0104,0x6164,0x0262,0x0363,0xFFFF,0xFFFF,
0xFFFF,0xFFFF,0xFFFF,0xFFFF,0xFFFF,0xFFFF,
0xFFFF,0xFFFF,0xFFFF,0xFFFF,0xFFFF,0xFFFF,
0xFFFF,0xFFFF,0xFFFF,0xFFFF,0xFFFF,0xFFFF,
0xFFFF,0xFFFF,0xFFFF,0xFFFF,0xFFFF,0xFFFF,
0xFFFF,0xFFFF,0xFFFF,0xFFFF,0xFFFF,0xFFFF,
/* 4A */
0x0306,0x0454,0x5463,0x0555,0x5564,0x6461,
0x6150,0x5040,0xFFFF,0xFFFF,0xFFFF,0xFFFF,
0xFFFF,0xFFFF,0xFFFF,0xFFFF,0xFFFF,0xFFFF,
0xFFFF,0xFFFF,0xFFFF,0xFFFF,0xFFFF,0xFFFF,
0xFFFF,0xFFFF,0xFFFF,0xFFFF,0xFFFF,0xFFFF,
0xFFFF,0xFFFF,0xFFFF,0xFFFF,0xFFFF,0xFFFF,
/* 4B */
0x0002,0x0161,0x0262,0x6062,0x3234,0x0616,
0x1634,0x3456,0x5666,0xFFFF,0xFFFF,0xFFFF,
0xFFFF,0xFFFF,0xFFFF,0xFFFF,0xFFFF,0xFFFF,
0xFFFF,0xFFFF,0xFFFF,0xFFFF,0xFFFF,0xFFFF,
0xFFFF,0xFFFF,0xFFFF,0xFFFF,0xFFFF,0xFFFF,
0xFFFF,0xFFFF,0xFFFF,0xFFFF,0xFFFF,0xFFFF,
/* 4C */
0x0003,0x0161,0x0262,0x6066,0x6646,0xFFFF,
0xFFFF,0xFFFF,0xFFFF,0xFFFF,0xFFFF,0xFFFF,
0xFFFF,0xFFFF,0xFFFF,0xFFFF,0xFFFF,0xFFFF,
0xFFFF,0xFFFF,0xFFFF,0xFFFF,0xFFFF,0xFFFF,
0xFFFF,0xFFFF,0xFFFF,0xFFFF,0xFFFF,0xFFFF,
0xFFFF,0xFFFF,0xFFFF,0xFFFF,0xFFFF,0xFFFF,
/* 4D */
0x0001,0x0161,0x6160,0x6000,0x0506,0x0666,
```

```
0x6665,0x6505,0x1133,0x3315,0x2143,0x4325,
0xFFFF,0xFFFF,0xFFFF,0xFFFF,0xFFFF,0xFFFF,
0xFFFF,0xFFFF,0xFFFF,0xFFFF,0xFFFF,0xFFFF,
0xFFFF,0xFFFF,0xFFFF,0xFFFF,0xFFFF,0xFFFF,
0xFFFF,0xFFFF,0xFFFF,0xFFFF,0xFFFF,0xFFFF,
/* 4E */
0x0001,0x0161,0x6160,0x6000,0x0506,0x0666,
0x6665,0x6505,0x1155,0x2165,0xFFFF,0xFFFF,
0xFFFF,0xFFFF,0xFFFF,0xFFFF,0xFFFF,0xFFFF,
0xFFFF,0xFFFF,0xFFFF,0xFFFF,0xFFFF,0xFFFF,
0xFFFF,0xFFFF,0xFFFF,0xFFFF,0xFFFF,0xFFFF,
0xFFFF,0xFFFF,0xFFFF,0xFFFF,0xFFFF,0xFFFF,
/* 4F */
0x0204,0x0426,0x2646,0x4664,0x6462,0x6240,
0x4020,0x2002,0x1151,0x1555,0xFFFF,0xFFFF,
0xFFFF,0xFFFF,0xFFFF,0xFFFF,0xFFFF,0xFFFF,
0xFFFF,0xFFFF,0xFFFF,0xFFFF,0xFFFF,0xFFFF,
0xFFFF,0xFFFF,0xFFFF,0xFFFF,0xFFFF,0xFFFF,
0xFFFF,0xFFFF,0xFFFF,0xFFFF,0xFFFF,0xFFFF,
/* 50 */
0x0005,0x0516,0x1626,0x2635,0x3532,0x0161,
0x0262,0x6063,0xFFFF,0xFFFF,0xFFFF,0xFFFF,
0xFFFF,0xFFFF,0xFFFF,0xFFFF,0xFFFF,0xFFFF,
0xFFFF,0xFFFF,0xFFFF,0xFFFF,0xFFFF,0xFFFF,
0xFFFF,0xFFFF,0xFFFF,0xFFFF,0xFFFF,0xFFFF,
0xFFFF,0xFFFF,0xFFFF,0xFFFF,0xFFFF,0xFFFF,
/* 51 */
0x0104,0x0415,0x1545,0x4554,0x5451,0x5140,
0x4010,0x1001,0x0151,0x0464,0x4363,0x6365,
0xFFFF,0xFFFF,0xFFFF,0xFFFF,0xFFFF,0xFFFF,
0xFFFF,0xFFFF,0xFFFF,0xFFFF,0xFFFF,0xFFFF,
0xFFFF,0xFFFF,0xFFFF,0xFFFF,0xFFFF,0xFFFF,
0xFFFF,0xFFFF,0xFFFF,0xFFFF,0xFFFF,0xFFFF,
/* 52 */
0x0005,0x0516,0x1626,0x2635,0x3235,0x3545,
0x4556,0x5666,0x0161,0x0262,0x6062,0xFFFF,
0xFFFF,0xFFFF,0xFFFF,0xFFFF,0xFFFF,0xFFFF,
0xFFFF,0xFFFF,0xFFFF,0xFFFF,0xFFFF,0xFFFF,
0xFFFF,0xFFFF,0xFFFF,0xFFFF,0xFFFF,0xFFFF,
0xFFFF,0xFFFF,0xFFFF,0xFFFF,0xFFFF,0xFFFF,
/* 53 */
0x1504,0x0401,0x0110,0x1020,0x2055,0x1045,
0x4555,0x5564,0x6461,0x6150,0xFFFF,0xFFFF,
0xFFFF,0xFFFF,0xFFFF,0xFFFF,0xFFFF,0xFFFF,
0xFFFF,0xFFFF,0xFFFF,0xFFFF,0xFFFF,0xFFFF,
```

```
0xFFFF,0xFFFF,0xFFFF,0xFFFF,0xFFFF,0xFFFF,
0xFFFF,0xFFFF,0xFFFF,0xFFFF,0xFFFF,0xFFFF,
/* 54 */
0x1000,0x0005,0x0515,0x0262,0x0363,0x6164,
0xFFFF,0xFFFF,0xFFFF,0xFFFF,0xFFFF,0xFFFF,
0xFFFF,0xFFFF,0xFFFF,0xFFFF,0xFFFF,0xFFFF,
0xFFFF,0xFFFF,0xFFFF,0xFFFF,0xFFFF,0xFFFF,
0xFFFF,0xFFFF,0xFFFF,0xFFFF,0xFFFF,0xFFFF,
0xFFFF,0xFFFF,0xFFFF,0xFFFF,0xFFFF,0xFFFF,
/* 55 */
0x0001,0x0161,0x6160,0x6000,0x0405,0x0565,
0x6564,0x6404,0x6164,0xFFFF,0xFFFF,0xFFFF,
0xFFFF,0xFFFF,0xFFFF,0xFFFF,0xFFFF,0xFFFF,
0xFFFF,0xFFFF,0xFFFF,0xFFFF,0xFFFF,0xFFFF,
0xFFFF,0xFFFF,0xFFFF,0xFFFF,0xFFFF,0xFFFF,
0xFFFF,0xFFFF,0xFFFF,0xFFFF,0xFFFF,0xFFFF,
/* 56 */
0x0001,0x0151,0x0040,0x4062,0x6263,0x0405,
0x0545,0x4563,0x0454,0xFFFF,0xFFFF,0xFFFF,
0xFFFF,0xFFFF,0xFFFF,0xFFFF,0xFFFF,0xFFFF,
0xFFFF,0xFFFF,0xFFFF,0xFFFF,0xFFFF,0xFFFF,
0xFFFF,0xFFFF,0xFFFF,0xFFFF,0xFFFF,0xFFFF,
0xFFFF,0xFFFF,0xFFFF,0xFFFF,0xFFFF,0xFFFF,
/* 57 */
0x0001,0x0161,0x6160,0x6000,0x0506,0x0666,
0x6665,0x6505,0x5133,0x3355,0x6143,0x4365,
0xFFFF,0xFFFF,0xFFFF,0xFFFF,0xFFFF,0xFFFF,
0xFFFF,0xFFFF,0xFFFF,0xFFFF,0xFFFF,0xFFFF,
0xFFFF,0xFFFF,0xFFFF,0xFFFF,0xFFFF,0xFFFF,
0xFFFF,0xFFFF,0xFFFF,0xFFFF,0xFFFF,0xFFFF,
/* 58 */
0x0001,0x0111,0x1133,0x3315,0x1505,0x0506,
0x0616,0x1634,0x3444,0x4466,0x6665,0x6543,
0x4361,0x6160,0x6042,0x4232,0x3210,0x1000,
0xFFFF,0xFFFF,0xFFFF,0xFFFF,0xFFFF,0xFFFF,
0xFFFF,0xFFFF,0xFFFF,0xFFFF,0xFFFF,0xFFFF,
0xFFFF,0xFFFF,0xFFFF,0xFFFF,0xFFFF,0xFFFF,
/* 59 */
0x0001,0x0121,0x2132,0x3233,0x3324,0x2404,
0x0405,0x0525,0x2543,0x4363,0x6164,0x6242,
0x4220,0x2000,0xFFFF,0xFFFF,0xFFFF,0xFFFF,
0xFFFF,0xFFFF,0xFFFF,0xFFFF,0xFFFF,0xFFFF,
0xFFFF,0xFFFF,0xFFFF,0xFFFF,0xFFFF,0xFFFF,
0xFFFF,0xFFFF,0xFFFF,0xFFFF,0xFFFF,0xFFFF,
/* 5A */
```

```
0x2000,0x0006,0x0616,0x1650,0x5056,0X5060,
0x6066,0x6646,0x1016,0xFFFF,0xFFFF,0xFFFF,
0xFFFF,0xFFFF,0xFFFF,0xFFFF,0xFFFF,0xFFFF,
0xFFFF,0xFFFF,0xFFFF,0xFFFF,0xFFFF,0xFFFF,
0xFFFF,0xFFFF,0xFFFF,0xFFFF,0xFFFF,0xFFFF,
0xFFFF,0xFFFF,0xFFFF,0xFFFF,0xFFFF,0xFFFF,
/* 5B */
0x0104,0x0161,0x0262,0x6164,0xFFFF,0xFFFF,
0xFFFF,0xFFFF,0xFFFF,0xFFFF,0xFFFF,0xFFFF,
0xFFFF,0xFFFF,0xFFFF,0xFFFF,0xFFFF,0xFFFF,
0xFFFF,0xFFFF,0xFFFF,0xFFFF,0xFFFF,0xFFFF,
0xFFFF,0xFFFF,0xFFFF,0xFFFF,0xFFFF,0xFFFF,
0xFFFF,0xFFFF,0xFFFF,0xFFFF,0xFFFF,0xFFFF,
/* 5C */
0x0001,0x0156,0x5666,0x6600,0xFFFF,0xFFFF,
0xFFFF,0xFFFF,0xFFFF,0xFFFF,0xFFFF,0xFFFF,
0xFFFF,0xFFFF,0xFFFF,0xFFFF,0xFFFF,0xFFFF,
0xFFFF,0xFFFF,0xFFFF,0xFFFF,0xFFFF,0xFFFF,
0xFFFF,0xFFFF,0xFFFF,0xFFFF,0xFFFF,0xFFFF,
0xFFFF,0xFFFF,0xFFFF,0xFFFF,0xFFFF,0xFFFF,
/* 5D */
0x0104,0x0363,0x0464,0x6164,0xFFFF,0xFFFF,
0xFFFF,0xFFFF,0xFFFF,0xFFFF,0xFFFF,0xFFFF,
0xFFFF,0xFFFF,0xFFFF,0xFFFF,0xFFFF,0xFFFF,
0xFFFF,0xFFFF,0xFFFF,0xFFFF,0xFFFF,0xFFFF,
0xFFFF,0xFFFF,0xFFFF,0xFFFF,0xFFFF,0xFFFF,
0xFFFF,0xFFFF,0xFFFF,0xFFFF,0xFFFF,0xFFFF,
/* 5E */
0x0336,0x3635,0x3513,0x1331,0x3130,0x3003,
0xFFFF,0xFFFF,0xFFFF,0xFFFF,0xFFFF,0xFFFF,
0xFFFF,0xFFFF,0xFFFF,0xFFFF,0xFFFF,0xFFFF,
0xFFFF,0xFFFF,0xFFFF,0xFFFF,0xFFFF,0xFFFF,
0xFFFF,0xFFFF,0xFFFF,0xFFFF,0xFFFF,0xFFFF,
0xFFFF,0xFFFF,0xFFFF,0xFFFF,0xFFFF,0xFFFF,
/* 5F */
0x7077,0xFFFF,0xFFFF,0xFFFF,0xFFFF,0xFFFF,
0xFFFF,0xFFFF,0xFFFF,0xFFFF,0xFFFF,0xFFFF,
0xFFFF,0xFFFF,0xFFFF,0xFFFF,0xFFFF,0xFFFF,
0xFFFF,0xFFFF,0xFFFF,0xFFFF,0xFFFF,0xFFFF,
0xFFFF,0xFFFF,0xFFFF,0xFFFF,0xFFFF,0xFFFF,
0xFFFF,0xFFFF,0xFFFF,0xFFFF,0xFFFF,0xFFFF,
/* 60 */
0x0203,0x0313,0x1324,0x2423,0x2312,0x1202,
0xFFFF,0xFFFF,0xFFFF,0xFFFF,0xFFFF,0xFFFF,
0xFFFF,0xFFFF,0xFFFF,0xFFFF,0xFFFF,0xFFFF,
```

```
0xFFFF,0xFFFF,0xFFFF,0xFFFF,0xFFFF,0xFFFF,
0xFFFF,0xFFFF,0xFFFF,0xFFFF,0xFFFF,0xFFFF,
0xFFFF,0xFFFF,0xFFFF,0xFFFF,0xFFFF,0xFFFF,
/* 61 */
0x2124,0x2435,0x3565,0x6566,0x2454,0x4441,
0x4150,0x5061,0x6163,0x6354,0x5465,0x6566,
0xFFFF,0xFFFF,0xFFFF,0xFFFF,0xFFFF,0xFFFF,
0xFFFF,0xFFFF,0xFFFF,0xFFFF,0xFFFF,0xFFFF,
0xFFFF,0xFFFF,0xFFFF,0xFFFF,0xFFFF,0xFFFF,
0xFFFF,0xFFFF,0xFFFF,0xFFFF,0xFFFF,0xFFFF,
/* 62 */
0x0002,0x0161,0x6160,0x6152,0x0252,0x3235,
0x3546,0x4656,0x5665,0x6563,0x6352,0xFFFF,
0xFFFF,0xFFFF,0xFFFF,0xFFFF,0xFFFF,0xFFFF,
0xFFFF,0xFFFF,0xFFFF,0xFFFF,0xFFFF,0xFFFF,
0xFFFF,0xFFFF,0xFFFF,0xFFFF,0xFFFF,0xFFFF,
0xFFFF,0xFFFF,0xFFFF,0xFFFF,0xFFFF,0xFFFF,
/* 63 */
0x3524,0x2421,0x2130,0x3050,0x5061,0x6164,
0x6455,0x2161,0xFFFF,0xFFFF,0xFFFF,0xFFFF,
0xFFFF,0xFFFF,0xFFFF,0xFFFF,0xFFFF,0xFFFF,
0xFFFF,0xFFFF,0xFFFF,0xFFFF,0xFFFF,0xFFFF,
0xFFFF,0xFFFF,0xFFFF,0xFFFF,0xFFFF,0xFFFF,
0xFFFF,0xFFFF,0xFFFF,0xFFFF,0xFFFF,0xFFFF,
/* 64 */
0x0305,0x0454,0x5465,0x0565,0x6566,0x3431,
0x3140,0x4050,0x5061,0x6163,0x6354,0xFFFF,
0xFFFF,0xFFFF,0xFFFF,0xFFFF,0xFFFF,0xFFFF,
0xFFFF,0xFFFF,0xFFFF,0xFFFF,0xFFFF,0xFFFF,
0xFFFF,0xFFFF,0xFFFF,0xFFFF,0xFFFF,0xFFFF,
0xFFFF,0xFFFF,0xFFFF,0xFFFF,0xFFFF,0xFFFF,
/* 65 */
0x4145,0x4535,0x3524,0x2421,0x2130,0x3050,
0x5061,0x6164,0x2161,0xFFFF,0xFFFF,0xFFFF,
0xFFFF,0xFFFF,0xFFFF,0xFFFF,0xFFFF,0xFFFF,
0xFFFF,0xFFFF,0xFFFF,0xFFFF,0xFFFF,0xFFFF,
0xFFFF,0xFFFF,0xFFFF,0xFFFF,0xFFFF,0xFFFF,
0xFFFF,0xFFFF,0xFFFF,0xFFFF,0xFFFF,0xFFFF,
/* 66 */
0x1504,0x0402,0x0211,0x1161,0x6063,0x0262,
0x3031,0x3233,0xFFFF,0xFFFF,0xFFFF,0xFFFF,
0xFFFF,0xFFFF,0xFFFF,0xFFFF,0xFFFF,0xFFFF,
0xFFFF,0xFFFF,0xFFFF,0xFFFF,0xFFFF,0xFFFF,
0xFFFF,0xFFFF,0xFFFF,0xFFFF,0xFFFF,0xFFFF,
0xFFFF,0xFFFF,0xFFFF,0xFFFF,0xFFFF,0xFFFF,
```

```
/* 67 */
0x3423,0x2321,0x2130,0x3040,0x4051,0x5154,
0x3474,0x7470,0x2625,0x2534,0x2565,0x6574,
0xFFFF,0xFFFF,0xFFFF,0xFFFF,0xFFFF,0xFFFF,
0xFFFF,0xFFFF,0xFFFF,0xFFFF,0xFFFF,0xFFFF,
0xFFFF,0xFFFF,0xFFFF,0xFFFF,0xFFFF,0xFFFF,
0xFFFF,0xFFFF,0xFFFF,0xFFFF,0xFFFF,0xFFFF,
/* 68 */
0x0002,0x0161,0x0262,0x6062,0x3224,0x2425,
0x2536,0x3666,0xFFFF,0xFFFF,0xFFFF,0xFFFF,
0xFFFF,0xFFFF,0xFFFF,0xFFFF,0xFFFF,0xFFFF,
0xFFFF,0xFFFF,0xFFFF,0xFFFF,0xFFFF,0xFFFF,
0xFFFF,0xFFFF,0xFFFF,0xFFFF,0xFFFF,0xFFFF,
0xFFFF,0xFFFF,0xFFFF,0xFFFF,0xFFFF,0xFFFF,
/* 69 */
0x0203,0x0313,0x1312,0x1202,0x2223,0x2363,
0x2262,0x2123,0x6164,0xFFFF,0xFFFF,0xFFFF,
0xFFFF,0xFFFF,0xFFFF,0xFFFF,0xFFFF,0xFFFF,
0xFFFF,0xFFFF,0xFFFF,0xFFFF,0xFFFF,0xFFFF,
0xFFFF,0xFFFF,0xFFFF,0xFFFF,0xFFFF,0xFFFF,
0xFFFF,0xFFFF,0xFFFF,0xFFFF,0xFFFF,0xFFFF,
/* 6A */
0x0405,0x0515,0x1514,0x1404,0x2425,0x2464,
0x2565,0x6574,0x6473,0x7471,0x7160,0x6050,
0xFFFF,0xFFFF,0xFFFF,0xFFFF,0xFFFF,0xFFFF,
0xFFFF,0xFFFF,0xFFFF,0xFFFF,0xFFFF,0xFFFF,
0xFFFF,0xFFFF,0xFFFF,0xFFFF,0xFFFF,0xFFFF,
0xFFFF,0xFFFF,0xFFFF,0xFFFF,0xFFFF,0xFFFF,
/* 6B */
0x0002,0x0161,0x0262,0x6062,0x4244,0x2644,
0x4466,0xFFFF,0xFFFF,0xFFFF,0xFFFF,0xFFFF,
0xFFFF,0xFFFF,0xFFFF,0xFFFF,0xFFFF,0xFFFF,
0xFFFF,0xFFFF,0xFFFF,0xFFFF,0xFFFF,0xFFFF,
0xFFFF,0xFFFF,0xFFFF,0xFFFF,0xFFFF,0xFFFF,
0xFFFF,0xFFFF,0xFFFF,0xFFFF,0xFFFF,0xFFFF,
/* 6C */
0x0103,0x0262,0x0363,0x6164,0xFFFF,0xFFFF,
0xFFFF,0xFFFF,0xFFFF,0xFFFF,0xFFFF,0xFFFF,
0xFFFF,0xFFFF,0xFFFF,0xFFFF,0xFFFF,0xFFFF,
0xFFFF,0xFFFF,0xFFFF,0xFFFF,0xFFFF,0xFFFF,
0xFFFF,0xFFFF,0xFFFF,0xFFFF,0xFFFF,0xFFFF,
0xFFFF,0xFFFF,0xFFFF,0xFFFF,0xFFFF,0xFFFF,
/* 6D */
0x2022,0x2233,0x3363,0x3324,0x2425,0x2536,
0x3666,0x2060,0x6061,0x6121,0xFFFF,0xFFFF,
```

```
0xFFFF,0xFFFF,0xFFFF,0xFFFF,0xFFFF,0xFFFF,
0xFFFF,0xFFFF,0xFFFF,0xFFFF,0xFFFF,0xFFFF,
0xFFFF,0xFFFF,0xFFFF,0xFFFF,0xFFFF,0xFFFF,
0xFFFF,0xFFFF,0xFFFF,0xFFFF,0xFFFF,0xFFFF,
/* 6E */
0x2021,0x2161,0x6160,0x6020,0x3123,0x2324,
0x2435,0x3565,0xFFFF,0xFFFF,0xFFFF,0xFFFF,
0xFFFF,0xFFFF,0xFFFF,0xFFFF,0xFFFF,0xFFFF,
0xFFFF,0xFFFF,0xFFFF,0xFFFF,0xFFFF,0xFFFF,
0xFFFF,0xFFFF,0xFFFF,0xFFFF,0xFFFF,0xFFFF,
0xFFFF,0xFFFF,0xFFFF,0xFFFF,0xFFFF,0xFFFF,
/* 6F */
0x2124,0x2435,0x3555,0x5564,0x6461,0x6150,
0x5030,0x3021,0x2161,0x2464,0xFFFF,0xFFFF,
0xFFFF,0xFFFF,0xFFFF,0xFFFF,0xFFFF,0xFFFF,
0xFFFF,0xFFFF,0xFFFF,0xFFFF,0xFFFF,0xFFFF,
0xFFFF,0xFFFF,0xFFFF,0xFFFF,0xFFFF,0xFFFF,
0xFFFF,0xFFFF,0xFFFF,0xFFFF,0xFFFF,0xFFFF,
/* 70 */
0x2021,0x2132,0x3272,0x2171,0x7073,0x3223,
0x2325,0x2536,0x3646,0x4655,0x5552,0xFFFF,
0xFFFF,0xFFFF,0xFFFF,0xFFFF,0xFFFF,0xFFFF,
0xFFFF,0xFFFF,0xFFFF,0xFFFF,0xFFFF,0xFFFF,
0xFFFF,0xFFFF,0xFFFF,0xFFFF,0xFFFF,0xFFFF,
0xFFFF,0xFFFF,0xFFFF,0xFFFF,0xFFFF,0xFFFF,
/* 71 */
0x2625,0x2534,0x3474,0x2575,0x7376,0x3423,
0x2321,0x2130,0x3040,0x4051,0x5154,0xFFFF,
0xFFFF,0xFFFF,0xFFFF,0xFFFF,0xFFFF,0xFFFF,
0xFFFF,0xFFFF,0xFFFF,0xFFFF,0xFFFF,0xFFFF,
0xFFFF,0xFFFF,0xFFFF,0xFFFF,0xFFFF,0xFFFF,
0xFFFF,0xFFFF,0xFFFF,0xFFFF,0xFFFF,0xFFFF,
/* 72 */
0x2021,0x2132,0x2161,0x3262,0x6063,0x3223,
0x2325,0x2536,0x3646,0xFFFF,0xFFFF,0xFFFF,
0xFFFF,0xFFFF,0xFFFF,0xFFFF,0xFFFF,0xFFFF,
0xFFFF,0xFFFF,0xFFFF,0xFFFF,0xFFFF,0xFFFF,
0xFFFF,0xFFFF,0xFFFF,0xFFFF,0xFFFF,0xFFFF,
0xFFFF,0xFFFF,0xFFFF,0xFFFF,0xFFFF,0xFFFF,
/* 73 */
0x2521,0x2130,0x3041,0x4144,0x4455,0x5564,
0x6460,0x2141,0x4464,0xFFFF,0xFFFF,0xFFFF,
0xFFFF,0xFFFF,0xFFFF,0xFFFF,0xFFFF,0xFFFF,
0xFFFF,0xFFFF,0xFFFF,0xFFFF,0xFFFF,0xFFFF,
0xFFFF,0xFFFF,0xFFFF,0xFFFF,0xFFFF,0xFFFF,
```

```
0xFFFF,0xFFFF,0xFFFF,0xFFFF,0xFFFF,0xFFFF,
/* 74 */
0x0322,0x0363,0x2125,0x2252,0x5263,0x6364,
0x6455,0xFFFF,0xFFFF,0xFFFF,0xFFFF,0xFFFF,
0xFFFF,0xFFFF,0xFFFF,0xFFFF,0xFFFF,0xFFFF,
0xFFFF,0xFFFF,0xFFFF,0xFFFF,0xFFFF,0xFFFF,
0xFFFF,0xFFFF,0xFFFF,0xFFFF,0xFFFF,0xFFFF,
0xFFFF,0xFFFF,0xFFFF,0xFFFF,0xFFFF,0xFFFF,
/* 75 */
0x2050,0x5061,0x6163,0x6354,0x2454,0x5465,
0x6566,0x2425,0x2555,0x5566,0xFFFF,0xFFFF,
0xFFFF,0xFFFF,0xFFFF,0xFFFF,0xFFFF,0xFFFF,
0xFFFF,0xFFFF,0xFFFF,0xFFFF,0xFFFF,0xFFFF,
0xFFFF,0xFFFF,0xFFFF,0xFFFF,0xFFFF,0xFFFF,
0xFFFF,0xFFFF,0xFFFF,0xFFFF,0xFFFF,0xFFFF,
/* 76 */
0x2040,0x4062,0x6263,0x2021,0x2141,0x4162,
0x2545,0x4563,0xFFFF,0xFFFF,0xFFFF,0xFFFF,
0xFFFF,0xFFFF,0xFFFF,0xFFFF,0xFFFF,0xFFFF,
0xFFFF,0xFFFF,0xFFFF,0xFFFF,0xFFFF,0xFFFF,
0xFFFF,0xFFFF,0xFFFF,0xFFFF,0xFFFF,0xFFFF,
0xFFFF,0xFFFF,0xFFFF,0xFFFF,0xFFFF,0xFFFF,
/* 77 */
0x2021,0x2151,0x5162,0x2050,0x5061,0x6162,
0x6253,0x5333,0x5364,0x6465,0x6556,0x5626,
0xFFFF,0xFFFF,0xFFFF,0xFFFF,0xFFFF,0xFFFF,
0xFFFF,0xFFFF,0xFFFF,0xFFFF,0xFFFF,0xFFFF,
0xFFFF,0xFFFF,0xFFFF,0xFFFF,0xFFFF,0xFFFF,
0xFFFF,0xFFFF,0xFFFF,0xFFFF,0xFFFF,0xFFFF,
/* 78 */
0x2021,0x2143,0x4361,0x6160,0x6042,0x4220,
0x4344,0x2644,0x4466,0xFFFF,0xFFFF,0xFFFF,
0xFFFF,0xFFFF,0xFFFF,0xFFFF,0xFFFF,0xFFFF,
0xFFFF,0xFFFF,0xFFFF,0xFFFF,0xFFFF,0xFFFF,
0xFFFF,0xFFFF,0xFFFF,0xFFFF,0xFFFF,0xFFFF,
0xFFFF,0xFFFF,0xFFFF,0xFFFF,0xFFFF,0xFFFF,
/* 79 */
0x2040,0x4051,0x5154,0x2425,0x2565,0x6574,
0x2474,0x7470,0xFFFF,0xFFFF,0xFFFF,0xFFFF,
0xFFFF,0xFFFF,0xFFFF,0xFFFF,0xFFFF,0xFFFF,
0xFFFF,0xFFFF,0xFFFF,0xFFFF,0xFFFF,0xFFFF,
0xFFFF,0xFFFF,0xFFFF,0xFFFF,0xFFFF,0xFFFF,
0xFFFF,0xFFFF,0xFFFF,0xFFFF,0xFFFF,0xFFFF,
/* 7A */
0x3020,0x2025,0x2561,0x2460,0x6065,0x6555,
```

```
0xFFFF,0xFFFF,0xFFFF,0xFFFF,0xFFFF,0xFFFF,
0xFFFF,0xFFFF,0xFFFF,0xFFFF,0xFFFF,0xFFFF,
0xFFFF,0xFFFF,0xFFFF,0xFFFF,0xFFFF,0xFFFF,
0xFFFF,0xFFFF,0xFFFF,0xFFFF,0xFFFF,0xFFFF,
0xFFFF,0xFFFF,0xFFFF,0xFFFF,0xFFFF,0xFFFF,
/* 7B */
0x0305,0x0413,0x1323,0x2332,0x3243,0x4353,
0x5364,0x6365,0x0312,0x1222,0x2231,0x3130,
0x3142,0x4252,0x5263,0xFFFF,0xFFFF,0xFFFF,
0xFFFF,0xFFFF,0xFFFF,0xFFFF,0xFFFF,0xFFFF,
0xFFFF,0xFFFF,0xFFFF,0xFFFF,0xFFFF,0xFFFF,
0xFFFF,0xFFFF,0xFFFF,0xFFFF,0xFFFF,0xFFFF,
/* 7C */
0x0304,0x0464,0x6463,0x6303,0xFFFF,0xFFFF,
0xFFFF,0xFFFF,0xFFFF,0xFFFF,0xFFFF,0xFFFF,
0xFFFF,0xFFFF,0xFFFF,0xFFFF,0xFFFF,0xFFFF,
0xFFFF,0xFFFF,0xFFFF,0xFFFF,0xFFFF,0xFFFF,
0xFFFF,0xFFFF,0xFFFF,0xFFFF,0xFFFF,0xFFFF,
0xFFFF,0xFFFF,0xFFFF,0xFFFF,0xFFFF,0xFFFF,
/* 7D */
0x0002,0x0112,0x1222,0x2233,0x3342,0x4252,
0x5261,0x6062,0x0213,0x1323,0x2334,0x3435,
0x3443,0x4353,0x5362,0xFFFF,0xFFFF,0xFFFF,
0xFFFF,0xFFFF,0xFFFF,0xFFFF,0xFFFF,0xFFFF,
0xFFFF,0xFFFF,0xFFFF,0xFFFF,0xFFFF,0xFFFF,
0xFFFF,0xFFFF,0xFFFF,0xFFFF,0xFFFF,0xFFFF,
/* 7E */
0x0103,0x0314,0x1405,0x0506,0x0615,0x1513,
0x1302,0x0211,0x1110,0x1001,0xFFFF,0xFFFF,
0xFFFF,0xFFFF,0xFFFF,0xFFFF,0xFFFF,0xFFFF,
0xFFFF,0xFFFF,0xFFFF,0xFFFF,0xFFFF,0xFFFF,
0xFFFF,0xFFFF,0xFFFF,0xFFFF,0xFFFF,0xFFFF,
0xFFFF,0xFFFF,0xFFFF,0xFFFF,0xFFFF,0xFFFF,
/* 7F */
0x1346,0x4666,0x6660,0x6040,0x4013,0xFFFF,
0xFFFF,0xFFFF,0xFFFF,0xFFFF,0xFFFF,0xFFFF,
0xFFFF,0xFFFF,0xFFFF,0xFFFF,0xFFFF,0xFFFF,
0xFFFF,0xFFFF,0xFFFF,0xFFFF,0xFFFF,0xFFFF,
0xFFFF,0xFFFF,0xFFFF,0xFFFF,0xFFFF,0xFFFF,
0xFFFF,0xFFFF,0xFFFF,0xFFFF,0xFFFF,0xFFFF,};

/* END OF CHARACTER INITIALIZATION */


/********* End of Source Code for GRAPHIQ **********/
```

GRAPHIQ Command Syntax

The design of GRAPHIQ is discussed throughout this book. If you can read the source code, you will be able to gain a thorough understanding of the program. To use the program, however, you need to understand its command syntax.

This appendix is not by any means complete documentation for GRAPHIQ as would be required by a lay user. It is assumed that the programmer will be able to read the source code to find out about details. This summary merely provides you with the information you need to get started using GRAPHIQ. It explains how to execute the simple command set that GRAPHIQ makes available. You will probably want to add to these commands with functions of your own.

GENERAL FUNCTIONAL DESCRIPTION

GRAPHIQ enables you to draw **polylines**. A polyline is a line that can have variable color and style. You can draw lines starting at any location on a two-dimensional surface, on or off the display, and ending at any location on or off the display.

In addition to polylines, you can draw rectangular boxes, circles, filled areas, and text. You draw these entities by moving a locator crosshairs to the drawing location and activating the main menu. To activate the main menu and select from it, you press the ENTER key.

To move the locator crosshairs, you can use the arrow keys on the numeric keypad. If you have a digitizer or mouse and have created the necessary drivers, you can also move the locator using these devices.

If you use a locator device that has one or more buttons, have one button simulate pressing the ENTER key. Then you will be able to activate most functions by pressing the locator button to view and select from menus.

Function Keys

The function keys on the IBM PC are allocated in GRAPHIQ to serve specific purposes. Using the function keys F1 through F10, you can select preset grid intervals, view a help screen, change the line style and color, move to a line's starting point, and draw a line. The function keys work as follows:

Function Keys F1 Through F5   You can select from among five preset grid intervals using function keys F1 through F5. The grid intervals associated with each key are as follows:

F1   0.1 millimeter
F2   1.0 millimeter
F3   5.0 millimeters
F4   10.0 millimeters
F5   20.0 millimeters

Function Key F6   Press function key F6 to view the help menu. The menu shown in GRAPHIQ is merely a sample and can be expanded to explain more of the program's functions if you take the time to do so. If you wish, you could make function key F1 the help key. How would you do this?

Function Key F7   This key allows you to change the line style quickly. The locator crosshairs reflects the current line style. When you draw a line, it will be in the same style as the crosshairs.

Function Key F8   You can change the line color quickly by pressing function key F8. The crosshairs will change to reflect the color chosen. If you choose the color black, the crosshairs will disappear. Can you think of a way to remedy this flaw?

Function Key F9   Before you draw a line, you must specify its starting point. If you do not specify a starting point, the ending point of the last line will be assumed. To specify a starting point quickly, you can use function key F9. First locate the crosshairs at the desired starting point and then press the F9 key.

Function Key F10   To draw a line, you can use the system menu or press the F10 key. A line will be drawn from the assumed starting point (see function key F9) to the current crosshairs location using the currently defined line style and color.

You can define your own function keys if you wish. Just change the source code to do whatever you want.

The ENTER Key

The ENTER key is used extensively to view and select from menus. When in doubt, just press the ENTER key to display a menu of options. To select from the menu, use either the up and down arrows on the numeric keypad or your locator device. Once the menu cursor is positioned on the desired menu item, press the ENTER key to select it.

The Arrow Keys on the
Numeric Keypad

Only four arrow keys are used. They can be found on the numeric keypad to the right of the ENTER key. You can move the locator crosshairs or menu cursor at any time using these keys. If you have a mouse or digitizer and you have written code to incorporate it into GRAPHIQ, you can use the device interchangeably with the keypad.

Functions in the
Main Menu

The main menu for GRAPHIQ appears when you press the ENTER key. When you start the program, you will see a blue greeting message. If you then press the ENTER key, you will be able to select from the main system menu.

The main menu lists 21 functions that can almost all be executed using nothing more than the arrow keys (or locator device) and the ENTER key. You will occasionally need to type filenames or other numbers, but these cases are kept to a minimum. The functions in the main menu are as follows:

Help (F6)   The first function in the main menu is a brief help message. You can expand it if you wish. The help menu is included to show where such a menu or message should appear and how it should be implemented in a working program. Help menus can be **context sensitive**, that is, they can be made to explain things the user is doing. Context-sensitive help is worthy of a book in itself.

Grid   If you select the grid item, you will see a grid displayed in the currently selected color. The grid reveals the system grid interval, rotation angle, and origin offset.

Snap On/Off   The snap function causes the locator crosshairs to be confined in movement to grid intervals only. In other words, the locator crosshairs cannot be placed between grid points if snap is on. If snap is off (the default condition) the crosshairs can be located anywhere that the locating device can place them. If you are using the arrow keys on the numeric keypad to move the crosshairs, all movement will be confined to grid intervals regardless of whether snap is on or off. You use the snap function to draw lines that are strictly horizontal or vertical, when you do not want the full accuracy of the locator device.

Locator On/Off   The locator device can make certain drawing functions difficult because it is difficult to hold still. If you wish to confine locator activity to the arrow keys for any reason, you can turn the locator off temporarily with this function.

Style (F7)   You can choose from five possible line styles by selecting the style item. Function key F7 does the same thing without requiring you to enter the main menu. The locator crosshairs will change to reflect the line style you select.

Color (F8)   You can change the current line color by choosing the color item from the main menu. The locator crosshairs will reflect the color you have selected.

Locate (F9)   The locate function specifies a new starting point for a future line. To use this function, locate the crosshairs at the desired starting point and then activate this menu item. Any line drawn using the line function will then start at the point you have located.

Line (F10)   To draw a line, you activate the line function. Use the locate function to locate the beginning of the line before you activate this function. If you wish to use the endpoint of the last line you drew as the starting point, you do not need to use the locate function and can simply execute line repeatedly.

Box   To draw a box, you activate the box function. The program will prompt you to locate a starting corner for the box. The box will **rubber-band** as you move the locator device or press the arrow keys. Rubber-banding is the redrawing of the entire line or box each time the locator moves. When done quickly enough, this creates the appearance of "elastic" movement, hence the word "rubber-banding."

Fill   To fill an area, you select the fill function. You will be prompted to define the fill area using the box as an outline. The box will be drawn in the currently defined line style and color, which will be used for the fill.

Circle   To draw a circle, you locate its center and a point on the perimeter. The currently defined line color will be used to draw the circle. Line style for the circle is not implemented. As an exercise, why don't you try to implement it?

Text   The internal character set can be used to draw text at any size, angle, or slant. You can use the rotation function to define an angle baseline for the text string, and then use the text function to draw your text. When you activate the text function, you will be prompted first for the size of the characters to be used. To specify the size, you use the box as a rubber band to outline the area to be filled by a character cell. The program then prompts you to select the character slant using a rubber-banded line. After selecting the character size and slant, you type the string to be drawn.

Rotation   The entire coordinate system of GRAPHIQ can be rotated to any angle from 0 through 360 degrees. You specify the rotation angle by using a rubber-band line that extends from the system origin to the crosshairs location. The line defines a baseline to which the coordinate system is rotated. Experiment with this function, displaying grids in various rotations to see how it works. This feature is very powerful, but it is correspondingly difficult to understand.

Reset   You can reset the rotation angle, scale factor, and system origin to their preset values by activating the reset function. The initial rotation angle is 0 degrees. The system origin is originally 0,0 millimeters. The initial scale factor is 1.0.

Offset +X, +Y   If you select a new offset for the origin of the coordinate system, you will be prompted to locate the crosshairs at the new offset location. This will be the new location of the system origin. You would use this function to, for example, move 0,0 to the center of the display rather than the lower left-hand corner.

Scale   You can use rubber-banded boxes to define the relative scale factor to be used until changed. The first box you specify corresponds to the size of a given object under the current scale factor. The second box you specify corresponds to the new scale of that same box. All graphics you draw after changing the scale factor will be scaled to the new scale factor.

Playback   To play the entire database back, you select the playback function. You can use this function to erase the entire display and refresh it. The real reason this function was included, however, is to show how the vector database can be used. There are many more ways to use the vector database. For example, you may wish to build a sophisticated editing system that would read the database and allow you to change it dynamically.

Print   If you have an Epson dot-matrix printer, the print function will dump the display buffer to the printer. This function illustrates one way of printing hard copy. You can accommodate other printers and even plotters by changing GRAPHIQ's source code.

Picture Files   Picture files can be of two types: display and database. Display files contain the contents of the display buffer only. You can put or get a screen image using this filing system. To write the vector database to disk or get it back, you select the database file-access functions. Many features have been left out that you can add yourself. For example, you may wish to add functions here that allow the user to append data as well as replace it. This function also shows how to implement sub-menus.

Command File   You can run the GRAPHIQ system from a command file if you prepare one and use this function to activate it. Examine GRAPHIQ's source code to see how the file replaces the menu system and keyboard. You will probably want to expand the command set and capabilities of this command file function, as it is implemented only to show how such a function works.

Clear Display   You can clear the display by activating the clear display function. All pixels on the display surface will be set to black.

Quit GRAPHIQ   If you wish to leave the GRAPHIQ system and return to DOS, you can execute this item. A warning prompt will ask you to verify that you really wish to return to DOS.

Exit This Menu   This menu choice allows you to leave the main menu if you got into it by accident or you do not wish to execute any functions.

By using this command summary to get started with the software, you will quickly master GRAPHIQ's simple functions. Emphasis has been placed on showing as many ways of implementing functions as possible to create a user-friendly system. The purpose of GRAPHIQ is to show how graphics software is created, not to provide a completely functional program. If you successfully compile GRAPHIQ and link it to create an executable program, you will find that it illustrates how you can begin to achieve self-documenting software. Most functions can be accessed simply by pressing the ENTER key and using the arrow key, and each function is described as you use it.

Optimizing Using Assembler

In graphics programming it is important to realize that the machine independence of the C language must often be violated in order to get your application to run fast. C is far from being machine-independent in its implementations, and there is much doubt that it ever will be, can be, or should be. High-level languages may be adequate for non-graphics applications, but the high speed and lack of standardization of graphics programs demand compromise.

If time would permit, it would be ideal to write graphics software directly in assembler, but this usually involves too much effort. It helps to use a high-level language like C to do the work that does not require speed, and then optimize those portions of the code that can benefit from optimization. Most programming professionals like to work close to the target machine and use high-level languages as tools to enable them to work more efficiently, *not* to shield them from the necessity of knowing and using assembler.

A good compiler will give you the ability to generate assembler source for your functions. Examine assembler listings for your C code and analyze how the functions written in C are converted into machine code; do this more than once, if possible. The exercise will be thoroughly enlightening.

You can generate an assembler source listing for the Microsoft C compiler by using the /Fl, /Fa, or /Fc options. You may wish to create a batch file that contains a test version of the call to the compiler:

```
MSC %1 /F%2;
```

You could name this batch file TEST.BAT and use it to compile your program, like this:

```
test myprog c[ENTER]
```

This would create the following command line:

```
MSC myprog /Fc;
```

Let's try it. Function C-1 is a trivial program that puts a string of text into an assembler listing. It shows how the string is stored and passed to the printf( ) function.

Save this program in a file called MYPROG.C, create the batch file as discussed above, and run it. The result will be placed in a file called MYPROG.COD and is shown in its entirety in Function C-2.

If you are programming in C and do not know assembler, you should go out right now and buy several books on it and learn it. Without knowing at least the fundamentals of assembler, you will find professional graphics programming very difficult.

■ FUNCTION C-1

```
main()
{
printf("This is a test.");
}
```

You could use the C compiler to help you learn how to program in assembler. In fact, you may find that by repeating the compiler listing process you begin to understand the workings of C in a way you never imagined possible.

Line by line, the C source listing is converted to assembler before your eyes. You no longer need to spend fiendishly long hours debugging assembler code once you get a feel for the process the compiler uses. Instead you can optimize your assembler source.

Let's use another version of the /F option, /Fa, to generate assembler source that is compatible with MASM, the Microsoft MacroAssembler, using the following compiler invocation:

E:>test myprog a[ENTER]

The product of this compile is the usual .OBJ file, plus a file called MYPROG.ASM, which can be directly assembled using MASM. Function C-3 shows this listing.

■ FUNCTION C-2

myprog

```
;       Static Name Aliases
;
        TITLE    myprog

_TEXT      SEGMENT  BYTE PUBLIC 'CODE'
_TEXT      ENDS
CONST      SEGMENT  WORD PUBLIC 'CONST'
CONST      ENDS
_BSS       SEGMENT  WORD PUBLIC 'BSS'
_BSS       ENDS
_DATA      SEGMENT  WORD PUBLIC 'DATA'
_DATA      ENDS
DGROUP     GROUP    CONST,      BSS,      DATA
        ASSUME  CS: _TEXT, DS: DGROUP, SS: DGROUP, ES: DGROUP
PUBLIC  _main
_DATA      SEGMENT
EXTRN      _printf:NEAR
EXTRN      _chkstk:NEAR
_DATA      ENDS
_DATA      SEGMENT
$SG10      DB      'This is a test.', 00H
_DATA      ENDS
_TEXT      SEGMENT
;|*** main()
;|*** {
; Line 2
        PUBLIC       _main
_main      PROC NEAR
        ***  000000      55                  push    bp
        ***  000001      8b ec               mov     bp,sp
        ***  000003      33 c0               xor     ax,ax
        ***  000005      e8 00 00            call    __chkstk
;|***
;|*** printf("This is a test.");
; Line 4
        ***  000008      b8 00 00            mov     ax,OFFSET
                                                     DGROUP:$SG10
        ***  00000b      50                  push    ax

        ***  00000c      e8 00 00            call    _printf
;|*** }
; Line 5
        ***  00000f      8b e5               mov     sp,bp
        ***  000011      5d                  pop     bp
        ***  000012      c3                  ret
_main      ENDP

_TEXT      ENDS
END
```

■ FUNCTION C-3

myprog

```
;       Static Name Aliases
;
        TITLE    myprog

_TEXT      SEGMENT  BYTE PUBLIC 'CODE'
_TEXT      ENDS
CONST      SEGMENT  WORD PUBLIC 'CONST'
CONST      ENDS
_BSS       SEGMENT  WORD PUBLIC 'BSS'
_BSS       ENDS
_DATA      SEGMENT  WORD PUBLIC 'DATA'
_DATA      ENDS
DGROUP     GROUP    CONST,      BSS,      DATA
        ASSUME  CS: _TEXT, DS: DGROUP, SS: DGROUP, ES: DGROUP
PUBLIC  _main
_DATA      SEGMENT
EXTRN     _printf:NEAR
EXTRN     __chkstk:NEAR
_DATA      ENDS
_DATA      SEGMENT
$SG10     DB      'This is a test.',  00H
_DATA      ENDS
_TEXT      SEGMENT
; Line 2
     PUBLIC      _main
_main      PROC NEAR
     push      bp
     mov       bp,sp
     xor       ax,ax
     call      __chkstk
; Line 4
     mov       ax,OFFSET DGROUP:$SG10
     push      ax
     call      _printf
; Line 5
     mov       sp,bp
     pop       bp
     ret


_main      ENDP

_TEXT      ENDS
END
```

You could now do anything at all to this code, within the highly typed limits of assembly language, and it would still remain a C-callable function, yet you have control over it at the machine level for purposes of improving its performance.

Of course, if you make changes to the source in the assembler form, you must use MASM, not your C compiler, to assemble it into an object file. This process allows you to work in C and still produce code that is as efficient as if it had been tediously hacked out in assembler.

Function C-4, CONDITN.C, illustrates some of the ways in which you can use conditional testing, assignment, and passing of arguments. Compile and list this function so that you can share some observations regarding the way in which C accomplishes its tasks.

As in Function C-2, you generate the .COD file using the TEST.BAT program. The output from this process is shown in Function C-5.

Let's take this listing apart and examine the processes involved as a way of beginning to understand the results of the C expression in assembler. The program begins with the following program invocation:

```
*** 0000 0055          push      bp
*** 0000 018b ec       mov       bp,sp
*** 0000 03b8 08 00    mov       ax,8
*** 0000 06e8 00 00    call      __chkstk
```

Every C program begins with this characteristic sequence of instructions, which preserves the base pointer (bp) of the stack and makes the current stack pointer (sp) the new base pointer for the duration of the function. After the base address for the stack has been replaced, a check is made to determine whether there is room on the stack to accommodate the function (call __chkstk) with the number of bytes declared locally (8) to be found in the AX register. A compiler option allows you to omit this call to __chkstk (a built-in function of the compiler), and no

■ FUNCTION C-4

CONDITN.C

```
/* CONDITN.C produces no useful output but illustrates
** the conversion of certain code sequences into Assembler
** source.
*/

main()
{
int a, b, c, d;

b = a = 1;

if (a < b)
     return;
if (a > b || c != b)
     b = a;

test_func(a, b, c, d);

}
```

verification of the capacity of the stack will be made. This saves time but can produce disastrous results if a stack overflow should occur. The "Stack Overflow" message during runtime is generated by the __chkstk function.

So much for the beginning of the program. The first part of the function is its internal declaration:

```
;c=-2
;d=-4
;a=-6
;b=-8
;|*** int a, b, c, d;
```

■ FUNCTION C-5

conditn

```
;       Static Name Aliases
;
        TITLE    conditn

_TEXT     SEGMENT   BYTE PUBLIC 'CODE'
_TEXT     ENDS
CONST     SEGMENT   WORD PUBLIC 'CONST'
CONST     ENDS
_BSS      SEGMENT   WORD PUBLIC 'BSS'
_BSS      ENDS
_DATA     SEGMENT   WORD PUBLIC 'DATA'
_DATA     ENDS
DGROUP       GROUP     CONST,      BSS,      DATA
       ASSUME  CS: _TEXT, DS: DGROUP, SS: DGROUP, ES: DGROUP
PUBLIC   _main
_DATA     SEGMENT
EXTRN    _test_func:NEAR
EXTRN    __chkstk:NEAR
_DATA     ENDS
_TEXT        SEGMENT
; *** /* conditn.c produces no useful output but illustrates
; *** ** the conversion of certain code sequences into Assembler
; *** ** source.
; *** */
; ***
; *** main()
; *** {
; Line 7
       PUBLIC        _main
_main     PROC NEAR
       *** 000000    55              push    bp
       *** 000001    8b ec           mov     bp,sp
       *** 000003    b8 08 00        mov     ax,8
       *** 000006    e8 00 00        call    __chkstk
;      c=-2
;      d=-4
;      a=-6
;      b=-8

; *** int a, b, c, d;
; ***
; *** b = a = 1;
; Line 10
       *** 000009    b8 01 00        mov     ax,1
       *** 00000c    89 46 fa        mov     [bp-6],ax
       *** 00000f    89 46 f8        mov     [bp-8],ax
```

■ FUNCTION C-5 (continued)

conditn

```
; |***
; |***
; |*** if (a < b)
; Line 13
    *** 000012      3b c0              cmp     ax,ax
    *** 000014      7c 21              jl      $EX8
; |***       return;
; Line 14
    *** 000016      3b c0              cmp     ax,ax
    *** 000018      7f 05              jg      $L20001
    *** 00001a      39 46 fe           cmp     [bp-2],ax
    *** 00001d      74 06              je      $I14
                       $L20001:
; |***
; |*** if (a > b || c != b)
; |***       b = a;
; Line 17
    *** 00001f      8b 46 fa           mov     ax,[bp-6]
    *** 000022      89 46 f8           mov     [bp-8],ax
; |***
; |*** test_func(a, b, c, d);
; Line 19
                       $I14:
    *** 000025      ff 76 fc           push    WORD PTR [bp-4]
    *** 000028      ff 76 fe           push    WORD PTR [bp-2]
    *** 00002b      ff 76 f8           push    WORD PTR [bp-8]
    *** 00002e      ff 76 fa           push    WORD PTR [bp-6]
    *** 000031      e8 00 00           call    _test_func
    *** 000034      83 c4 08           add     sp,8
; |***
; |*** }
; Line 21
                       $EX8:
    *** 000037      8b e5              mov     sp,bp
    *** 000039      5d                 pop     bp
    *** 00003a      c3                 ret
_main     ENDP


_TEXT     ENDS
END
```

This is not a functional part of the assembler source. It is a description of the relative positions of the variables, which are all word values, on the stack. Variables defined locally are always assigned to the stack, and therefore static storage space is not required for local variables. They may come into existence on the stack at the beginning of the function, and disappear, freeing up space, at the end. This is one of the most desirable features of C.

To continue the dissection, the first assignment statement in the function follows immediately after the declarations. It sets variable "b" and variable "a" to contain the number "1":

```
;|*** b = a = 1;
; Line 10
*** 0000 09b8 01 00 mov    ax,1
*** 0000 0c89 46 fa mov    [bp-6],ax
*** 0000 0f89 46 f8 mov    [bp-8],ax
```

Look at what happens. If instead of programming in C you had decided to hack this in assembler, you would have had to

1. Move 1 into register AX (mov ax,1)

2. Move AX into the location offset −6 bytes from the base pointer BP (mov [bp−6],ax)

3. Move AX into the location offset −8 bytes from the base pointer BP (mov [bp−8],ax)

It was a lot easier to write it b = a = 1, wasn't it? Programming in C is much easier than programming in assembler, but you should always be aware of what you are doing in assembler when you are working in C. Many people think they cannot do this, or they think that C is an end in itself. No high-level language exists independent of the machine being used to implement it. The native code of that machine is, in the end, what will make your program sizzle or sink.

Note that the compiler knows that [bp−6] is where the variable "a" is located and that [bp−8] is where the variable "b" is located. Refer back to the very first part of the program, where these locations were shown to you by the compiler.

Onward to the conditional test. This one is simple. All it does is test the obvious and return from the function if the condition is true. No code should even have been generated for this obvious test, but the optimization process is far from perfect:

```
;|*** if (a < b)
; Line 13
*** 0000 123b c0 cmp ax,ax
*** 0000 147c 21 jl  $EX8
;|***       return;
```

Note that the test takes up several lines of assembler code and that the assembled version is far from clear when it is compared to the C version. The compiler already knows, at line 13, that AX contains both the contents of [bp−6] and the contents of [bp−8], because it has just assigned the value 1 to them in the previous instruction. The comparison of AX with AX is absurd (no less absurd than the test expression); it is obvious that AX will *never* be less than AX, and that the conditional jump to $EX8 (jl $EX8) will never occur. By the way, look at line 21 of Function C-5 to see the target of this jump, the end of the function.

```
; Line 14
*** 0000 163b c0 cmp     ax,ax
*** 0000 187f 05 jg      $L20001
*** 0000 1a39 46 fe      cmp[bp-2],ax
*** 0000 1d74 06 je      $I14
          $L20001:
;|***
;|*** if (a > b || c != b)
;|***       b = a;
; Line 17
*** 0000 1f8b 46 fa mov  ax,[bp-6]
*** 0000 2289 46 f8 mov  [bp-8],ax
```

Line 14 shows the sequence of operations involved in the more complex expression (a > b || c != b), an expression you might find difficult to code directly in assembler, but here it has been done for you with no effort at all. Again AX is tested against itself, a product of the same assumption the compiler made before, that is, that AX already contains both "a" and "b." This time the test is whether the value on the left is greater than the value on the right, and so the JG instruction is used. The || (OR) test is not represented at all, because the logical OR implies that either condition being true will satisfy the conditions of the expression, therefore, the instruction pointer just drops down to the next instruction.

At this point the compiler does not have a convenient register in which to look for the required test value, and so it uses an offset onto the stack corresponding to the value of the variable "c", or [bp−2], which it compares to what it knows to be the value of "b" already contained in AX. If these values are equal, a jump will be made to label $I14 (je $I14), bypassing the next couple of instructions. This produces the effect of a logical NOT, because the next two instructions are not executed if the condition is TRUE. No value was ever assigned to "c", and so the condition of this test expression depends on an arbitrary, unpredictable value that happened to be on the stack when this function was invoked!

Line 17 shows how the value of the variable "a" is assigned to "b" through the use of the trusty AX register. One of the limitations of the 8086 microprocessor is that indirect base relative moves are not possible; they always require the intervention of an intermediate register. After all, what you want to do could be accomplished in one instruction, like (mov [bp−8] ,[bp−6]) instead of two, but such an expression will not work.

```
;|*** test_func(a, b, c, d);
; Line 19
            $I14:
*** 0000 25ff 76 fc push   WORD PTR [bp-4]
*** 0000 28ff 76 fe push   WORD PTR [bp-2]
*** 0000 2bff 76 f8 push   WORD PTR [bp-8]
*** 0000 2eff 76 fa push   WORD PTR [bp-6]
*** 0000 31e8 00 00 call   _test_func
*** 0000 3483 c4 08 add    sp,8
;|***
```

Line 19 illustrates how arguments are typically passed to functions using the 86 implementation of C. You arrive at label $I14 if the expression in the previous test is false. Immediately, the words, which are already on the stack (notice that their offsets are the same as before) are again pushed onto the stack starting at the stack pointer. Each time, the stack pointer is moved down four bytes (a word), and at the end of this series of pushes a call is made to __test__func. Notice that in Microsoft C version 3, each function name is appended to an underscore character. If you write assembler functions that you wish to call from your C programs, remember to precede them with a single underscore character. Never precede them with more than one underscore; if you do, there is a danger that the compiler will think your function is one of its own internal predefined functions.

Finally, after the subsidiary function __test__func has returned control to the function, the compiler adds the number of bytes that the stack pointer was moved down due to the previous PUSH operations back to the stack, moving the pointer back up to its location before the call was made. Incidentally, the __test__func call invoked as its first duty a call to __chkstk, discussed earlier, and verified that there was room on the stack for __test__func to do its thing.

Only one more sequence of events needs to take place to return from the function back to the operating system, leaving everything neat and tidy, as though nothing had happened:

```
; | *** }
; Line 21
                $EX8:
*** 0000 378b e5    mov      sp,bp
*** 0000 395d       pop      bp
*** 0000 3ac3       ret
```

Remember the earlier reference to label $EX8? This is where that return statement would have sent us if the absurd condition created in the program could have been true. The first thing the compiler did in this function was to push BP and then move SP into BP, thus saving the old base pointer. The last thing it must do before returning from the call is reverse this process. The stack pointer that was current at the beginning of the function became the base pointer on the stack for the duration of the function, and the old base pointer was saved just above it on the stack. Now the current stack pointer is replaced by the base pointer assigned at the beginning of the function (the old stack pointer), and the old base pointer is popped off the stack to take up its rightful position. Everything is as it was. A return instruction is generated, and the effect of the original CALL is neutralized. The calling process can now take over. Because the function was entered as _main, it now returns to the operating system.

If you have followed the flow of this analysis, a great many things should now be clear to you. You should see how the C language is intimately connected in very clear and beautiful ways to machine language, even more than most high-level languages are. Many of the operations performed by C have directly analogous operations in assembler. The similarity between C and assembler is striking, both in the ways in which conditional tests are carried out (the JG, JL, JMP, and JE instructions) and in the use of data structures (such as DB, DW, and DD). Yet the functionality of C goes far beyond what is easily accomplished in assembler, even using macros. Add to this the portability of C and you can see how universal the C language can be.

Above all, do not be afraid of assembler. Many programmers start programming using high-level languages and never get deeply into assembler. If you only want to do a little graphics programming and will never sell graphics software to the public, you can get away with using C as an end in itself. Unfortunately, however, assembler is always faster than C, and in many instances you will need to optimize. Optimizing compilers are not able to read your mind.

Making Commands Accessible

You may want to run external DOS commands from any directory on your disk. If so, it is a good idea to set up a directory for all your .EXE and .COM files and define a path to it in your AUTOEXEC.BAT file. (Any .COM or .EXE file can be seen as a command.) Make a directory to hold your executable files, for example:

```
E:>md \exe
```

Drive E is used with the author's hard disk because drives C and D are reserved for use as phantom drives. To make your hard disk think it is drive E, merely set your switches or configure your PC or AT to use all four floppy drives, A, B, C, and D. Even if you do not have physical drives C and D, you can use special software to set them up as RAM drives any time you choose. Drive E then becomes the first hard disk drive.

With your DOS system files in drive B, enter the following command (it is assumed you will press the ENTER key after all commands from now on):

```
E:>copy b:*.exe \exe
```

The AUTOEXEC.BAT File

Prepare your AUTOEXEC.BAT file by using your text editor, or you can use the following method. You will probably want to include a few other commands in addition to the PATH command. Why not include MODEGA 6 while you are at it, and put MODEGA.EXE in your \EXE directory? The command to do this is as follows:

```
E:>copy con: \autoexec.bat
path \exe
modega 6
^Z
```

Now, no matter where you are on your hard disk you can run any program as though it were a DOS command. If you do not have a hard disk and you want to do some serious C programming, be advised that your compiling efforts will be increased dramatically because of the numerous libraries you will wish to create. Hard disks are nowhere near as expensive as they were years ago, so put one high on your list of hardware to acquire.

Television Graphics

One of the newest trends in graphics is the use of television technology with personal computers. Using special hardware you can capture realistic-looking images from a broadcast or home video-camera source and display them on a television monitor. AT&T's TrueVision hardware is used with the programs in this appendix to transfer images from the AT&T Image Capture Board (ICB) to the IBM EGA. Many more things can be done using this exciting technology. Images can be captured, modified, and then combined with text and printed on a laser printer. Titles can be superimposed on live images. You will see more and more emphasis on television image processing using personal computers in the future.

To illustrate the input/output techniques for this type of hardware, we will construct a simple program to transfer an image from an external display buffer (an ICB in this case) to the EGA.

The name of the program is TRANSFER.C. TRANSFER becomes a DOS command that you can use to transfer a 27-color image from the 32,768-color ICB. If you do not have an ICB, the other aspects of TRANSFER will still be of use to you. You can write the mode 16 EGA buffer to disk, and you can retrieve it again. When you begin to construct a drawing-and-painting program, you will see how a buffer-dump program such as this can be used to store and retrieve your displays. If you want to work with video capture and you have about $2000 to play with, you can do some very interesting video digitizing to create all kinds of graphics primitives. The combination is heartily recommended.

USING A VIDEO CAMERA

There are several ways to use a video camera with the EGA. You can purchase the hardware to do complete imaging. One of the most popular sources of such hardware is AT&T, which produces the ICB and TARGA boards. The ICB was used as an example for this book because it is readily available, relatively inexpensive, and can be used with a typical home video system. You can also do very elaborate manipulations with it, such as rotation, translation, scaling, enhancement, and edge detection.

You can also capture video images directly into the EGA buffer. To do this, you need to modify your hardware by adding a circuit to the expansion strip on the EGA. Unless you are an experienced electronics engineer, you should be very careful in doing this, because you could destroy your EGA in the process. The design involves the use of a digital/analog converter (DAC) to convert a properly conditioned and synchronized NTSC composite-video signal into a digital expression that is buffered and clocked into the EGA display buffer. There are already one or two sources of this hardware, and a little research into trade magazines will probably uncover one that you can work with.

THE TRANSFER ALGORITHM

The ICBEGA.C listing in Function E-1 illustrates the algorithm used to transfer a display buffer from the ICB to the EGA. This algorithm is not unique to the ICB; it is a prototype that can be modified to transfer the contents of *any* display buffer beginning at a given address to any other buffer at any other address.

The ICB Buffer

The ICB consists of a buffer that is organized in 64K of RAM, visible to the microprocessor at a starting segment location that is jumper selectable. When you purchase the board, it is set to start its buffer at 0xA000. This would conflict with the location of the new graphics buffer on the EGA, however, which also begins at 0xA000. To remedy this, set your jumpers to start ICB memory at 0xD000.

Organization of the ICB

Memory on the ICB is addressed on word boundaries, allowing, from high to low, 1 bit for overlay, 5 bits for red, 5 bits for green, and 5 bits for blue. This permits 32,767 colors per pixel on the television display. The total display memory on the ICB is proportional to the size of the display. The display is based on a 256-by-256−pixel memory map, but only 200 pixels are shown vertically. The remaining rows can be used to store interim parts of pictures, character sets, and so on, for later transfer to the visible display. If you do some arithmetic, you will discover that $256 \times 256 \times 2$ (the number of bytes in the buffer) is 131,072 bytes. This corresponds to 128K of memory, yet only 64K is visible to the microprocessor. This is possible because the ICB uses a bank-select method to switch the two halves of the display buffer into and out of control of the 8086 microprocessor.

■ FUNCTION E-1

ICBEGA.C

```c
/* ICBEGA.C dithers from ICB to EGA.
** You can use this simple program to prepare EGA menus from
** real-world images if you have an ICB and a home TV camera!
** This function assumes a properly initialized ICB.
** See your AT&T manual for details. EGA mode is 14.
** Use the /Ze option on compile to enable 'far' keyword.
** See "Exploring the EGA" in PC Magazine, August and
** September, 1986 for more detail about this technique.
** Charles Petzold describes the use of the 'far' keyword to
** rapidly move graphic data.  Also see IBM's Technical
** Reference for the Enhanced Graphics Controller Adapter. */

#include <dos.h>
#include <conio.h>

#define TRUE 0xFFFF
#define FALSE 0x0000
#define ENABLE 0x0F
#define ICBWIDTH 256L
#define EGAWIDTH 80L
#define TOTALROWS 350
#define TOTALCOLS 640
#define EGAMAXRO 199
#define ICBMAXCOL 212
#define EGAMAXCOL 79
#define INDEXREG 0x3CE
#define VALREG 0x3CF
#define ICBASE 0X3A8    /* Depends on jumper settings, */
                        /* factory default */
#define ICBMEMSEG 0xD0000000L /* Depends on jumper settings. */
                        /* Factory default is 0xA000, but */
                        /* 0xD000 avoids conflict with EGA! */
#define EGAMEMSEG 0xA0000000L /* Works for mode 14 */
#define ICBCORRECT 0x2CL /* add offset to center image */
#define OUTINDEX(index, val) {outp(INDEXREG, index); \
                                outp(VALREG, val);}

#define RED  0
#define GREEN 1
#define BLUE 2


union           /* ICB bits */
    {
    struct
        {
        unsigned blue : 5;
        unsigned green : 5;
        unsigned red : 5;
        unsigned overlay : 1;
        } colors;
```

■ FUNCTION E-1 (continued)

ICBEGA.C

```
        struct
                {
                unsigned colrs;
                } all;
} icbwd;


/*
**  This is one of many ways in which color values can be
**  set on the EGA.  Direct modification of RAM is possible,
**  as is the use of Int 10h, with varying speed and
**  complexity problems.  Transfer from other video capture
**  sources can be done by customizing this technique.
*/

icbega()
{
int icb_row;
int ega_row = 0;

/* The ICB display is read from top down. */

/* select pg 2     */
outp(ICBASE, 0xcc | 2);  /* forces display on, genlock on */

for (icb_row = 71; icb_row >= 0; --icb_row, ++ega_row)
    pr_line(icb_row, ega_row);

/* select pg 1     */
outp(ICBASE, 0xcc | 3);


for (icb_row = 127; icb_row >= 0; --icb_row, ++ega_row)
    pr_line(icb_row, ega_row);

return(0);

}



pr_line(icb_row, ega_row)
int icb_row, ega_row;
{
unsigned far *icb_dat
        = (unsigned far *)(ICBMEMSEG + ICBCORRECT
        + (long)((ICBWIDTH << 1)
        * (long)icb_row));
char far *ega_dat
        = (char far *)(EGAMEMSEG + EGAWIDTH
        * (long)ega_row);
```

■ FUNCTION E-1 (continued)

ICBEGA.C

```c
static char red[] =    "00000000001111111111112222222222";
static char green[] = "00000000001111111111112222222222";
static char blue[] =  "00000000001111111111112222222222";
unsigned char dither, color, exist_color;
unsigned char mask;
int icb_count;

/* initialize the mask */
mask = 0x80;

for (icb_count = 0; icb_count <= ICBMAXCOL; ++icb_count)
     {
     icbwd.all.colrs = *icb_dat++;

     /* red, green and blue values are extracted */

     for (dither = 0; dither <= 2; ++dither)
        {
        switch (dither)
           {
           case RED:
                switch (red[icbwd.colors.red])
                   {
                   case '0':
                        color = 0x0;
                        break;
                   case '1':
                        color = 0x4;
                        break;
                   case '2':
                        color = 0xC;
                        break;
                   }
                break;

           case GREEN:
                switch (green[icbwd.colors.green])
                   {
                   case '0':
                        color = 0x0;
                        break;
                   case '1':
                        color = 0x2;
                        break;
                   case '2':
                        color = 0xA;
                        break;
```

■ **FUNCTION E-1** (continued)

ICBEGA.C

```
                            }
                    break;

            case BLUE:
                    switch (blue[icbwd.colors.blue])
                            {
                            case '0':
                                    color = 0x0;
                                    break;
                            case '1':
                                    color = 0x1;
                                    break;
                            case '2':
                                    color = 0x9;
                                    break;
                            }
                    break;
                }

        exist_color = *ega_dat;   /* read color byte */
                                  /* into register */

        OUTINDEX(0, color);       /* set register to */
                                  /* color value */
        OUTINDEX(1, ENABLE);      /* ENABLE output from */
                                  /* register */

        OUTINDEX(8, mask);        /* set bit mask */

        *ega_dat &= TRUE;         /* force a write to EGA */

        /* rotate the mask */

        if ((mask >>= 1) == 0)
                {
                mask = 0x80;
                ++ega_dat;  /* every 8 bits (colors) the
                            ** pointer is incremented */
                }
            }
        }

OUTINDEX(0, 0);     /* reset register */
OUTINDEX(1, 0);     /* reset ENABLE */
OUTINDEX(8, TRUE);  /* reset bit mask */
}
```

Therefore, in order to work with page 2 (the upper 128 lines), you must use a designated port to select that page.

Organization of the EGA

The EGA also uses a bank-select method to restrict processor awareness of the display area. In the case of the EGA, 64K is allocated, beginning at segment 0xA000. There are four bit planes, each of which controls one color. The appropriate bit planes for read/write are selected by several elaborate methods involving the use of a graphics controller circuit. To select the color and pixel to which you wish to write, you use a combination of masking, color setting, and enabling, all controlled by writes to a specified pair of ports. You must use the display controller, byte by byte, to gain access to the bit planes on the EGA.

Executive Loop

The executive loop in ICBEGA.C consists of two parts, each of which controls one of the two 64K bank-selected buffers that make up the total display. The display origin (0,0) is at the bottom left corner. In this case the 200 lines of the display are read from the top down. The page 2 buffer is selected by setting bits 0 and 1 of ICBASE to 1. The top row for page 2 is at row 71 (remember, only 200 rows of the display are visible), and pr__ line( ) is executed for each row, having the corresponding icb__ row and ega__row passed to it. Notice that as the icb__row decreases, the ega__row increases. This is because the origin of the ICB coordinate system is in the lower left corner, whereas the origin of the EGA system is in the upper right corner. For graphics applications the ICB coordinate system is decidedly more convenient, but you can see that the inversion process can be handled quite directly and simply. The syntax of the for( ) construct greatly assists us here.

Likewise, for rows 127 through 0 on page 1, the bank is selected and the pr—line( ) function is executed until the entire display of the ICB has been transferred to the EGA. There is a lot more going on at the next level down.

The ICB display is 256 pixels wide, but only 213 of them can be used because the 640-pixel width of the EGA requires 640/3, or 213, dithered cells to represent an acceptable color range. This means that 213×3, or 639, bits will be mapped onto each EGA row. The EGA works eight bits (one byte) at a time, and so byte positions 0 through 79 will be transferred.

On the ICB 43 words will be unavailable for transfer, and so ICBEGA uses the central 213 words by offsetting $+22$ bytes when reading the ICB display. Look at the way the constant ICBCORRECT is used to accomplish this.

To dither color values into a representative range of values on the EGA, 32 states for each color (red, green, and blue) need to be allocated to 3 possible states for each color on the EGA. On the EGA two intensities of each of the primary colors are available, and so the appropriate numbers for each of these colors are used. The function pr—line( ) uses a switch with a table of values to reduce computation as much as possible. You can adjust the numbers in the table to change color contrast.

Finally, the source structure icbwd is used to split out red, green, and blue from the ICB attribute word and proportion the EGA color values. These values are rotated into the EGA display buffer through the use of a rotating mask.

Study the code for this function carefully, paying particular attention to the method used to display discrete points on the EGA display. Many alternative methods exist for reading and writing display buffers. Consider how you might use the standard Microsoft C function movedata( ) for block moves under certain circumstances. There are also alternatives to using the FAR declaration to address data.

The ICBEGA.C Flowchart

To understand what happens next, take a look at Figure E-1, ICBEGA.C. This figure illustrates the structure of ICBEGA.C, along with the display parameters and the organization of the ICB color attributes in the attribute word.

You can see the spatial coordinate ranges of the display, and how the displays are arranged. You can see how the dithering process is accomplished. The figure also depicts the layout of the ICB color attribute word. When you design your own transfer

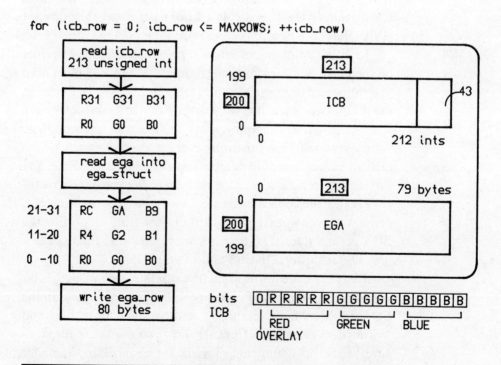

FIGURE E-1. Display buffer layouts from ICB to EGA

I/O routines, you should begin with a well-conceived diagram like this one and force yourself to work most of the details out graphically before you sit down to code.

Even if you are not using an ICB and video source as an input option for your graphics system, the design of ICBEGA.C will serve as a powerful illustration of how to transfer graphics from one memory location and data format to another. If you decide to purchase the equipment to capture and manipulate images, your investment will be very rewarding. The transfer of video-captured images is also a good way to illustrate raster input/output methods, which are necessary for the understanding of more advanced concepts (drawing and text) and to store images you have created.

The visual effect of images dithered by ICBEGA is like that of a pointillist painting. Surprising things happen when red, green, and blue combine to produce shades of white and gray. The effect is very pleasing and makes useful abstractions from familiar objects. This process can be the source of icons for your software.

RASTER OUTPUT TO DISK

No matter how you capture your images, whether you draw them on the display surface or capture them with a video camera, you will need to store them on magnetic media if they are to have any permanence and usefulness. The simplest way to do this is to store a duplicate of the display buffer. This is called a pixel dump or, more generally, a raster dump. Your graphics system, no matter what other purposes it is designed to serve, will always benefit from a raster-dump function. It enables you to create snapshots for use in slide shows, or simply to store the image and then retrieve it later to pick up where you left off.

Function E-2, PUTEGA.C, dumps the EGA raster for mode 14. Notice that the color-compare mode of the EGA graphics controller is used to select each of the six possible color-plane combinations and store the combination's bit map in binary form on the disk. Six copies of the display buffer, each having 80 × 200, or 16,000, bytes, must be stored, along with a map of the bits that are on for each color in each location. Each picture will require 96,000 bytes on disk. This is not necessarily the fastest method, but it is not the slowest, either, and it gets the job done.

To use PUTEGA.C you must pass a pointer to a string that contains the desired filename. This function will not tell you if that filename already exists, so if you wish to be protected from overwriting, you must add a routine to detect whether the file is already there and prompt for replacement if it is. You can use PUTEGA in any of your functions, or you can make it into an external DOS command. Whenever PUTEGA is invoked and mode 14 is in effect, it will take a snapshot of your display.

Background-Mode Graphics

You might want to try running PUTEGA in the background for use at any time. As a general rule, you could construct your entire graphics application to work in the background, invoked by interrupts. This method of programming is extremely difficult, and requires a thorough understanding of how DOS does (and does not) work, but such a utility could be extremely valuable for you.

An entire book could be devoted to the subject of background-mode graphics programming. You may want to experiment with it, however. It would allow you to create graphics in combination with any image on the display, no matter where it came from, and dump it into a file or output it to a hard-copy device.

■ FUNCTION E-2

PUTEGA.C

```c
/* PUTEGA.C puts the contents of the EGA buffer to disk
** given a filename.  This version works with EGA mode 14,
** but you can easily modify it.  Storage is limited to
** page 0.  Remember to use the /Ze option when you compile. */

#include <stdio.h>
#include <memory.h>
#include <dos.h>


#define TRUE 0xFFFF
#define FALSE 0x0000
#define ENABLE 0x0F
#define EGAMEMSEG 0xA0000000L /* Works for mode 14 */
#define EGAWIDTH 80L
#define EGAMAXRO 199
#define INDEXREG 0x3CE
#define VALREG 0x3CF
#define OUTINDEX(index, val) { outp(INDEXREG, index); \
                               outp(VALREG, val); }


putega(filename)
char *filename;
{
FILE *file_stream;
int ega_row;
int color;
static char table[] = { 0x01, 0x02, 0x04, 0x09, 0x0a, 0x0c };
/*                      blue  green red  l.bl  l.gr  l.rd    */

/* if any error opening file, abort with error set      */
/* Any existing file by this name will be lost!!         */
/* Test for existing files before using this function. */


if ((file_stream = fopen(filename, "wb")) == NULL)
    return(-1);

OUTINDEX(5, 0x18); /* select to color-compare */


for (color = 0; color <= 5; ++color)
    {
    OUTINDEX(2, table[color]);
```

■ FUNCTION E-2 (continued)

PUTEGA.C

```
        for (ega_row = 0; ega_row <= EGAMAXRO; ++ega_row)
             put_row(ega_row, file_stream);
        }
fcloseall();
return(0);
}


put_row(ega_row, file_stream)
int ega_row;
FILE *file_stream;
{
char buffer[80];
char far *ega_dat = (char far *)(EGAMEMSEG + EGAWIDTH
          * (long)ega_row);
int count;

        for (count = 0; count < (int)EGAWIDTH; ++count)
             buffer[count] = *ega_dat++;

        fwrite(buffer, 1, (int)EGAWIDTH, file_stream);
}
```

RASTER INPUT FROM DISK

If you can dump a graphics image from the display into a disk file, symmetry suggests that you should be able to get it back again. There are many good reasons to do this, not the least of which is that it is the only way to edit your images.

Function E-3, GETEGA.C, shows an inversion of the PUTEGA.C method. You pass getega( ) a pointer to a filename,

■ FUNCTION E-3

GETEGA.C

```
/* GETEGA.C gets the contents of the EGA buffer from disk
** given a filename.  This version works with EGA mode 14,
** but you can easily modify it.  Storage is limited to
** page 0.  Remember to use the /Ze option when you compile. */

#include <stdio.h>
#include <memory.h>
#include <dos.h>


#define TRUE 0xFFFF
#define FALSE 0x0000
#define ENABLE 0x0F
#define EGAMEMSEG 0xA0000000L /* Works for mode 14 */
#define EGAWIDTH 80L
#define EGAMAXRO 199
#define INDEXREG 0x3CE
#define VALREG 0x3CF
#define OUTINDEX(index, val) { outp(INDEXREG, index); \
                               outp(VALREG, val); }




getega(filename)
char *filename;
{
FILE *file_stream;
int ega_row;
int color;
static char table[] = { 0x01, 0x02, 0x04, 0x09, 0x0a, 0x0c };
/*                       blue  green red  l.bl  l.gr  l.rd    */
int monitor_used, mode_used;
int color_max;


/* if any error opening file, abort with error set */
if ((file_stream = fopen(filename, "rb")) == NULL)
    return(-1);

/*
** This example only uses only one monitor type, RGB.
** You could add the Enhanced Display or Monochrome monitor.
** Likewise, only two modes are used.
** You could add other modes.
** The EGA graphics spec is VERY flexible.
*/
```

■ FUNCTION E-3 (continued)

GETEGA.C

```
for (color = 0; color <= 5; ++color)
     for (ega_row = 0; ega_row <= EGAMAXRO; ++ega_row)
          get_row(ega_row, file_stream, table[color]);

fcloseall();
return(0);
}


get_row(ega_row, file_stream, color)
int ega_row;
FILE *file_stream;
char color;
{
char buffer[80];
char far *ega_dat = (char far *)(EGAMEMSEG + EGAWIDTH
          * (long)ega_row);
char exist_color;
int count;

/* read 80 characters from file */

fread(buffer, 1, (int)EGAWIDTH, file_stream);

for (count = 0; count < (int)EGAWIDTH; ++count)
     {
     exist_color = *ega_dat;  /* read existing color */

     OUTINDEX(0, color);       /* set register to color value */
     OUTINDEX(1, ENABLE);      /* enable output from register */

     OUTINDEX(8, buffer[count]);       /* set bit mask */

     *ega_dat++ = TRUE;
     }
}
```

and the binary file containing a record of the buffer contents is replaced in the display buffer. This assumes that you used the PUTEGA function to put something there to begin with.

You Must Read Before You Write

Notice that the following statement applies to both input and output functions concerned with overwriting parts of display bytes on the EGA. You *must* read each byte to load the color register before attempting to write, or the information in the other bits in the byte will be lost.

For example, if the display bits at the desired offset from 0xA000 look like this:

1 0 1 1 0 1 0 0

and you mask the byte to write only one byte using the following mask:

0 0 1 0 0 0 0 0

the result will be

0 0 1 0 0 0 0 0

This may not be what you expected. If you want to keep the remaining bits as they were before the write, you must first read the byte using any read method.

You Must Write Without Changing the Value

To write the byte from the register, you must cause a neutral write to the storage location. This amounts to choosing any fast method of causing a write that does not change the target value. The AND operator (&) in C is perfect for this. You can do this by any of a number of methods; here the value TRUE is used. If you use 0, however, the compiler will ignore the statement, since it will assume that this operation is unnecessary and a write will not occur. Therefore, if you use this method do not use 0 as the right operand.

For the most part, the getega( ) function is the mirror image of the putega( ) function. The only difference is in the settings sent to the graphics controller chip on the EGA.

THE TRANSFER.C PROGRAM

Now all you need is a program to bind icbega( ), putega( ), and getega( ) together into a meaningful command structure. An embodiment of such a command is the TRANSFER.C program, listed in Function E-4. You can run TRANSFER.C in four different ways. First, TRANSFER.C can be invoked with no arguments. In this case it will display a usage description that you could print on your line-printer for later reference. If you construct your commands so that when you enter no arguments you see an explanation of the program, you will never need to keep paper instructions around. The usage description will help you even if the program is intended only for your own use, because you forget how to use your own software from time to time.

The second way in which TRANSFER.C can be used is simply to transfer an image from the ICB to the EGA. This is accomplished using the following command line:

E:> transfer /t

This invocation of TRANSFER.C will result in the transfer of an image from the ICB (if you have installed one) and garbage if you do not have an ICB.

■ FUNCTION E-4

TRANSFER.C

```c
/* TRANSFER.C uses icbega() to dither from ICB to EGA.
** Don't forget to use the /Ze option on compile. */

/* This is a program example of a function which can be used
** independently.  In this form you can transfer display
** contents anytime you are in DOS. */


#include <string.h>
#include <ctype.h>
#include <process.h>
#include <string.h>

main(argc, argv)
int argc;
char *argv[];
{
char function[120];
char filename[120];
char far *info;
int error = 0;
int exist_mode;

exist_mode = modeget();

/* check for presence of EGA */
info = (char far *) 0x00400088L;
if ((*info & 0x0F) == 0x0F)
    {
    printf("\nEnhanced Graphics Adapter is not installed,");
    printf("\nor all dip switches on the adapter are off.\n");
    exit(-1);
    }

/* check for monochrome or color monitor */
info = (char far *) 0x00400087L;
if ((*info & 2) == 2)
    {
    printf("\nThis program only works if you have a color");
    printf("\nmonitor (RGB or Enhanced) installed.\n");
    exit(-1);
    }


/* This example works with */
/* mode 14 for color, but you could use others! */
/* Dithering patterns must be adjusted accordingly. */
```

■ **FUNCTION E-4** (continued)

TRANSFER.C

```
if (argc == 3)
    {
    strcpy(function, argv[1]);
    strcpy(filename, argv[2]);
    if (function[0] == '-' || function[0] == '/')
        switch (tolower(function[1]))
            {
            case 'g':
                modeset(14);
                error = getega(filename);
                break;
            case 'p':
                modeset(14);
                icbega();
                error = putega(filename);
                break;
            default:
                print_msg();
                exit(-1);
            }
    }
else if (argc == 2)
    {
    strcpy(function, argv[1]);
    if (function[0] == '-'
    || function[0] == '/'
    && function[1] == 't')
        {
        modeset(14);
        icbega();
        }
    }

if (argc != 2 && argc != 3)
    {
    print_msg();
    exit(0);
    }

if (!error) getch();       /* wait for a key to be pressed */

modeset(exist_mode);       /* reset EGA */

exit(0);       /* normal exit, no errors */
}
```

■ FUNCTION E-4 (continued)

TRANSFER.C

```
print_msg()
{
int counter = 0;
static char *transfer[] = {
"Usage:  transfer [[/t][[/g]|[/p] [filename]]]   ",
" ",
"           If the /t option is used, only a transfer ",
"           with no file access will be performed. ",
" ",
"           If the /p option is used, followed by at ",
"           least one space, then a legal filename,  ",
"           the named file will be put to disk. ",
" ",
"           If the /g option is used, followed by at ",
"           least one space, then a legal filename,  ",
"           the named file will be retrieved from disk. ",
" ",
"           If only the 'transfer ' command is entered ",
"           you will see this usage reminder. ",
" ",
"           After the picture is displayed a press of any ",
"           non-control key will return you to DOS.",""};

while (strlen(transfer[counter]) != 0)
     puts(transfer[counter++]);
}
```

TRANSFER.C can also be used like this:

E:>transfer /p filename

The filename is required. This invocation will first transfer the image from the ICB (if you have one) and then put (/p) the image to disk according to the filename or pathname you specify.

Finally, you can use TRANSFER.C to get (/g) the image from the disk back into the EGA buffer with the following invocation:

```
E:>transfer /g filename
```

In the case of the /t and /p functions, you must have an ICB to use TRANSFER.C. To read an image from a disk using the /g function, you need only an EGA and a color monitor.

OTHER SOURCES OF INFORMATION

A method of accessing the EGA controller is described in an article by Charles Petzold in the September 1986 issue of *PC Magazine*. You should consult this excellent article, as well as the *IBM EGA Technical Reference,* for more details regarding the functions of these complicated graphics controller registers. One of the first articles to disclose the inner workings of the EGA was "Graphic Enhancement" by Thomas V. Hoffmann in the April 1985 issue of *PC Tech Journal.* Try to find copies of these articles to learn more about the various options available to you for using the EGA.

Trademarks

Apple®	Apple Computer, Inc.
Epson®	Seiko Epson Corporation
Hewlett-Packard®	Hewlett-Packard Company
HP®	Hewlett-Packard Company
IBM®	International Business Machines Corporation
Kurta Series One™	Kurta Corporation
Macintosh™	Apple Computer, Inc.
Microsoft®	Microsoft Corporation
Mouse Systems™	Mouse Systems Corporation
PCjr™	International Business Machines Corporation
SideKick®	Borland International, Inc.
TARGA™	American Telephone and Telegraph
TrueVision®	American Telephone and Telegraph
Turbo Pascal®	Borland International, Inc.
UNIX®	American Telephone and Telegraph

Index

& operator, 655
8087 coprocessor, 115, 340
% (modulus) operator, 159
ACCESS.C, 59
Additive colors, 97
AGIC directory, 436
AGIC.LIB, 469
Algorithm
    Cohen-Sutherland, 113
    transfer, 641
Algorithms
    arc, 84
    circle, 79
    clipping, 110
    crosshatching, 94
    flood, 88
    generating code from, 121
    graphics, 63-124
    line, 71
    using, to draw lines, 165
Aliased line, 72
allocate( ), 442
ALLOCATE.C, 509
AM compiler option, 439
Analog line, 72
AND (&) operator, 655
Angular deflection, 128
Antialiasing, 78
Appearance of code, 12
Arcs
    chorded, 393
    drawing, 178
ASCII
    character set, 215
    print codes, 248
    values, 108
Aspect ratio, 108, 179
Assembler, 8
    optimizing using, 623-636
    using, to optimize transformations, 145
Asynchronous communications, 352
AT&T color graphics products, 44-45
Attributes, 57
AUTOEXEC.BAT file, 437, 638
Automatic drawing, 393
AUX, 356

Axes, horizontal and vertical, 41
Axial scaling, 134
Background mode graphics, 650
Base addresses, serial register, 356
Batch file, compiler, 438
Baud rate, 371
Baud rate divisor latch, 359
Binary pixel expression, 330
BIOS, 7, 32
    calls, 8
    characters, 222
    clearing EGA, 311
    EGA, 18
    printing text using, 218
    reading color values using, 309
    shape table, 221
Bit patterns, moving, 325
Bit planes
    reading, 159
    writing into, 161
Bitfields, 36, 260
Block moves, making, 302
Boundaries, drawing for complex fills, 196
Box function, 618
Boxes, 390
    combining, with lines, circles, and fills, 201
    drawing, 191
    filling, 194
BOXX.C, 192
boxx2( ), 442
BOXX2.C, 548
Break detection, 359
Bresenham's algorithm, 74, 79, 179
Brush, 204
Brush array, 204
brush in( ), 442
BRUSH IN.C, 205, 520
brush out( ), 442
BRUSH OUT.C, 206, 519
Brush pattern, 205
Brushes, 93
buffchr( ), 367
Buffer, acessing single pixel in EGA, 158
Buffering, intermediate, 207
Buffers, allocating, 38
Business graphics, 62

/

C compiler
 invoking, 439
 Microsoft, 434
C, review of, 33
CALL statement, 458
Calloc( ), 38
Cartesian coordinate system, 128. *See also*
 Rectangular
Cell characters, 220
Cell specification, 118
center( ), 442
CENTER.C, 86, 492
CGA. *See* Color Graphics Adapter
Character
 generators, 117
 set, hardcopy listing of, 216
Characters
 adding origin of, 239
 applying global transformations to, 239
 BIOS, 222
 border, 285
 changing height and width of, 238
 changing slant of, 239
 graphics and text, 213
 size of, 233
 stroke, 226
 varying size and angle of, 229
CHARHDLR.C, 569
Chord, 79
Chorded circles, 183, 393
Chording
 horizontal, 184
 radial, 185
Circle
 algorithm, 79, 83
 function, 618
 generator, 190
 style, 83
 three-point, 85
circle ( ), 442
CIRCLE.C, 180, 493
circle__r ( ), 442
CIRCL__R.C, 186, 515
Circles, 390
 chorded, 183, 393
 combining, with lines, boxes, and fills, 201
 drawing, 178
 other ways to draw, 190
Clear Display function, 621
Clear To Send (CTS), 361
Clearing the display, 311
clearscr( ), 312, 443
Clipping, 109
 algorithm, 111
 software, 115

Code
 generating, with algorithms, 121
 linking externally referenced, 457
Coding
 locators, 325
 style and appearance of, 12
 tranformation functions, 144
Cohen-Sutherland algorithm, 113
Color, changing line, 618
Color distribution report, 108
Color Graphics Adapter (CGA), 16, 25
Colors, additive versus subtractive, 97
com__fill( ), 443
COM__FILL.C, 197, 513
com__str( ), 443
COM__STR.ASM, 375, 532
COM#, 356
Combined tranformations, 137
Combining lines, circles, boxes, and fills, 201
Command
 entry, 389
 File function, 620
 files, 390, 413
 language, editing, 150
 line, linker, 466
 lines, 389
 syntax, GRAPHIQ, 613-622
Commands
 DOS, 637
 editing, 151
 making accessible, 637-638
Compatibility, 9, 18
Compensating
 for aspect, 179
 for center, 182
COMPILE.BAT, 438
Compiler, using, 433
Compiler references, 455
Compound three-dimensional rotation, 130
conditn function, 630
CONDITN.C, 629
Cone of vision, 173
Contrast variable, 108
Control, 40
Controller, EGA, 24. *See also* Enhanced
 Graphics Adapter
Coordinate list, dithering from, 100
Coordinate systems, 64, 139
Coordinates. *See also* Cartesian coordinates
 standard real, 163
 two-dimensional, 139
COPYAREA.C, 310
copybox( ), 443
COPYBOX.C, 210, 511
Copying, 207, 392

Count variable, 108
Counts, 7
cross__it( ), 443
Cross-reference listing, 461
Crosshairs
    locator, 127
    moving locator, 614
Crosshatching, 94
    at rotation angle, 96
Cursor, 152, 302
    functions, 295
CURSOR.H, 589
Curves, 70
Data
    Carrier Detect (DCD), 361
    Format Register, 358
    reading and moving display, 308
    Ready, 357
    register, 357
    Set Ready (DSR), 361
Database
    design, 50
    files, 408
    getting the vector, 411
    line, 123
    pointer, 404
    putting the vector, 410
    three-dimensional, 393
DEBUG
    limitations of, 28
    using, to draw lines, 25
Declarations, 37, 402
DECLARES.H, 398, 582
Definitions, 38
Deleting objects, 393
Designing applications, 2-6
Desktop publishing, 57, 244
Device coordinates, 10
Digitizer, enabling, 406
Digitizer interfacing, 370
Directionality, 84-85
disp__curs( ), 443
DISPCHAR.C, 230
Display
    areas, moving and copying, 309
    attributes, 40
    background, 294
    buffer layouts from ICB to EGA, 648
    buffers, 43
    clearing, 311
    data, reading and moving, 308
    files, 408
    locator positions, 40
    memory, location of, 23
    modes, 16, 19, 23
    pages, setting, 21

Display, *continued*
    resolution, 395
    size, compensating for, 240
display( ), 443
DISPLAY.C, 562
DISPLAY.H, 34
Distortion, 136
DITHER.C, 101
Dithering, 46, 96, 245
    matrix, 97
    practical techniques for, 258
Documentation, graphics, 417-432
DOS commands, 637
Dot-matrix protocol, 247
Double-precision arguments, 137, 163
Dragging objects, 133
draw text( ), 443
Drawing
    arcs, 84
    automatic, 393
    boxes, 191
    circles, 79
    circles and arcs, 178
    elements, 67
    lines, 26, 165, 173
    lines, Bresenham's algorithm for, 74
    pixels, 153
    points, 30, 153, 163
    text, 391
Drawings
    plotting, 261
    printing, 247
DRAWPT.C, 32
Drivers, 49
    printer and plotter, 246
    writing parallel interface, 351
Edit mode, 147-212
Editing, 41
    menus and commands used in, 149
Editing display device, GRAPHIQ, 49
Editing objects, 127
EGA, 11. *See also* Enhanced Graphics Adapter
    graphics controller, 303
    mode, preserving, 406
EGABASE, 156
Ellipse generator, 60
Enabling the controller, 161
Endpoints, 68, 168
    chord, 185
    line, 200
    locating, 173
Enhanced Graphics Adapter (EGA), 11, 16, 154, 646
    and clipping, 115
    BIOS for, 18
    controller, 24
    designing menus for, 285

Enhanced Graphics Adapter, *continued*
    organization of, 646
Enhanced graphics modes, EGA, 23
Environment, compiler, 434-435
Ergonomics, 418
Errors
    handling, 440
    link, 457, 468
EXE directory, 439
Executive loop, 406, 646
Extended character set, IBM, 318
External references, 456
Extremities, display, 157
FAR keyword, 159, 440, 457
Fast screen-write, 10
File
    headers, unions in, 53
    structure, GRAPHIQ, 52
FILE.H, 54, 126, 586
Files
    accessing, 409
    command, 413
    database, 408
    display, 408
    drawing and command, 408
    random-access, 53
    sequential, 52
    TMP, 438
Fill
    algorithm, 87, 90
    function, 618
FILLBOX.C, 194
fillbox2( ), 444
FILLBOX2.C, 559
Filling boxes, 194
Fills, 70
    combining, with lines, circles, and boxes, 201
    complex, 195, 393
    nonuniform, 93
    rectangular, 390
Filtering projections, 142
Firmware, 11
First point on or off, 169
Floating-point reals, 37
Floods, 88
Flow diagrams, 39
FONT.H, 592
Fonts, 120
    stroke, 220
Framing errors, 352
frealloc( ), 444
FREALLOC.C, 510
freopen( ), 257
Full screen locators, 332. *See also* Locators
Function keys, 152
    using, in GRAPHIQ, 614

Functions
    algorithms for graphics, 63-124
    assembler optimization, 623-636
    editing, 148
    executing, from menus, 151
    graphics controller, 304
    orchestration of, 147
    selecting graphics controller, 304
    using, for maintenance modes, 388
get__curs( ), 444
get__dig( ), 444
GET__DIG.C, 546
GET__MOUS.C, 380
get__row( ), 444
get__ser( ), 444
GET__SER.ASM, 378, 534
get__str( ), 445
GET__STR.C, 314
getdata( ), 444
GETDATA.C, 411, 565
getega( ), 444
GETEGA.C, 523, 653
Graphics
    algorithms, 63-124
    background mode, 650
    printer format, 248
    programming, introduction to, 1-14
    programming, tips for, 6
    software design, 15-46
    television, 639-660
Graphics controller, *See also* Enhanced
    Graphics Adapter
    functions, 304
    mnemonics and macros, 402
Graphics controller, EGA, 303
    enabling, 161
    using directly, 154
GRAPHICS.COM, 216
GRAPHIQ, 47-62
    command syntax for, 613-622
    functions included in, 390
    functions not included in, 392
    headers for, 580-612
    linking, 468
    locator for, 324
    printing and plotting using, 280
    source code listing of, 471-612
    suggestions for improving, 60
GRAPHIQ.C, 474-491
GRAPHIQ.H, 396, 580
GRAPHIQ.LIB, cross-reference listing of, 461
Grid
    increment, 404
    intervals, selecting, 614
    snap, 391
Grids, 391

Handshaking, 278
Hard copy, *See also* Printing
    display device, GRAPHIQ, 50
    listing of character set, 216
    text, 242
    TV, 46
Hardwire handshaking, 268
Headers, 33
    declaration, 402
    GRAPHIQ, 394, 580-612
Help, on-screen, 420
Help menu, accessing, 615
Horizontal
    chording, 184
    lines, drawing with DEBUG, 26
horline( ), 445
HORLINE.C, 496
HP-GL plotter codes, 275
I/O, redirecting, 9
IBM PC AT, using the serial port on, 270
IBM PCjr, 17
ICB, organization of, 641
ICB buffer, 641
icbega( ), 445
ICBEGA.C, 525, 642
    flowchart of, 648
Icons, 428
Identifier name, 127
Image Capture Board, 36, 45. *See also* ICB
INCLUDE directory, 436
Incremental rotation, 169
Incursions, 90
Index, 422
INDEXREG, 156
Information, other sources of, 660
inkey( ), 313, 445
INKEY.C, 531
Input status register, 361
INSTISR.C, 366, 535
Integer
    arguments, 157
    values, resolution of, 172
Intermediate buffer, copying with, 207
Internal references, 456
Interrupt enable register, 357
Interrupt Identification Register, 357
Interrupt service priorities, 357
Interrupts, 8
IRGB, 24
isr_inst( ), 445
ISR_INST.C, 542
ISRVEC structure, 365
Keyboard interaction, 312
Large memory model, 42
Laser printers, 242
LIB.EXE, 469
Libraries, compiler, 436

Library
    creating, 454
    listing contents of, 460
    managing your, 458
Light pen interfacing, 379
Line algorithm, 71
    Bresenham, 75, 165
Line-based systems, 96
Line color, 168
    changing, 615
Line function, 618
line_int( ), 445
line_it( ), 446
Line style, 169
    changing, 615
Line styles, 76
    adding, to shape tables, 121
Line width, 77
linec( ), 445
linef( ), 445
LINEF.C, 166, 507
lineloc( ), 446
linep( ), 446
LINEP.C, 176, 502
Lines, 69, 390
    aliased, 72
    analog, 72
    Bresenham's algorithm for drawing, 74
    clipping, 112
    combining, with circles, boxes, and fills, 201
    drawing, 165
    perspective, 173
    specifying starting point of, 615
Lines variable, 108
LINK.EXE, 453
Linker, using, 466
Linking the toolkit, 453
LOCALCHR.C, 215
LOCATE command, 406
Locate function, 618
locate( ), 446
Locating, 41
Locations, 68
    transforming, 125
Locator
    device, 29
    device, GRAPHIQ, 49
Locator crosshairs, 127
    moving, 614
locator( ), 446
LOCATOR.C, 328, 542
LOCATOR.H, 590
Locators, 321-340
    coding, 325
    complex, 323
    designing, 323
    full screen, 323, 332

Locators, *continued*
    rotated full screen, 336
    selecting, 152
    types of, 323
    using, in maintenance modes, 388
LONGCROS.C, 334
LPT#, 345
Macros, 170
main( ), 405, 625
Maintenance modes, 387-416
Malloc( ), 38
Manuals, software, 421
MASM, 628
Math coprocessor, 115, 340
Math errors, 144
Matrix, locator, 331
Medium memory model, 42, 405, 439
Memory
    addresses, changing values of, 27
    management, 33
    management, graphics, 15
    model, medium, 439
Memory models, 42
    referring to, 455
    using consistent, 457
MENUCURS.C, 296
Menus, 283-320
    executing functions from, 151
    exiting, 621
    selecting from, 294
    using, 389
    message( ), 446
MESSAGE.C, 566
Microsoft C compiler, 434
Mnemonics, GRAPHIQ, 394
Mnemonics and macros, EGA controller, 402
mnu__curs( ), 446
MNU__CURS.C, 573
MODE command (DOS), 19, 272, 358
MODEGA.C, 20
modeget( ), 446
MODEGET.C, 506
Modeling
    surface, 61
    three-dimensional, 61
modeset( ), 447
MODESET.C, 493
Modules
    adding, 459
    removing, 460
Modulus operator, 159, 259
Monochrome display, 16
Mouse, 29, 48
    interfacing, 376
Move, 173
movedata( ), 289

MSC directory, 436
MSC.EXE, 439
myprog function, 626
NDCXMAX, NDCYMAX, 395
NEAR, 457
Nodal connectivity, 61
Nondestructive command entry, 313
Normalized device coordinate (NDC), 10
Numeric co-processor, 115, 340
Numeric keypad, 389
OBJ extension, 459
Object identifiers, 126
Objects, 126
    deleting, 393
    dragging, 133
    editing, 127
    identifying and locating, 89
Observer, 140
Offset function, 619
Offsets, 7
    translational, 133
Operating systems, 9
Orchestration, editing, 211
Origin transfer, 82
OUTINDEX, 156
Overrun errors, 369
Page swapping, 51
PAGEGA.C, 22
Pages, display, 21
Palettes, 94
Paragraphs, system memory, 405
Parallel interfacing, 342-352
Parallel output without using DOS or BIOS, 345
Parallel port, 251
    diagram of IBM, 351
Parallel ports, 342
    receiving characters from, 347
    sending characters through, 343
Parameters, rotational, 129
Parametric
    equation, 136
    form, 184
Parity, selecting, 358
Paths, 435
Pen plotters, 261
Pen strokes, 221
Perspective, 163, 173, 178
Picture files, 392
Picture Files function, 620
Piping, 9
Pitch, 117
Pixel drawing, 153
    function, 154
Pixel fill algorithm, 92
Pixels, 69, 323
    drawing, 154

Playback function, 391, 620
playchar( ), 447
Plot
    function, 272
    loop, 273
    rotation, 275
    scale, 275
    switch, 273
    translation, 275
PLOT.C, 263
Plotter, sending strings to, 276
Plotters
    pen, 242, 261
    serial interface for, 269
Plotting, 261-282, 393
point( ), 447
Point-based systems, 96
Point-priority technique, 61
POINT.C, 31, 491
Pointer
    arguments, 145
    arrays, 285
    list, 61
Pointers, passing, 286
pointf( ), 447
POINTF.C, 155, 560
POINTG.C, 31
pointp( ), 447
POINTP.C, 164, 505
Points, 67
Points, drawing, 30, 153
    in perspective, 163
    first, 169
    projection of, 140
    translating, 132
points( ), 447
POINTS.C, 171, 501
Polar coordinates, 65
Polling, 322
Polylines, 614
pop__dbl( ), 447
Pop-up menus, 285
pr__line( ), 109, 448
PRALEL__I.C, 349
PRALEL__O.C, 346
Primitives, adding, to shape tables, 121
Print
    function, 258, 620
    wires, setting number of, 259
PRINTCHR.C, 217
Printed documentation, 420
Printer
    codes, 248
    status, monitoring, 343
Printers, 216
    dot-matrix, 247

Printers, *continued*
    laser, 242
    resetting, 108
    supported, 50
Printing, 245-282, 392. *See also* Hard copy
    and plotting functions, orchestrating, 279
    desktop, 244
    using the BIOS for, 257
printrow( ), 447
printscr( ), 448
PRINTSCR.C, 252, 575
PRN device, 347
Problem statement, 4
Professional Graphics Adapter (PGA), 43
Program
    startup and termination, 394
    termination sequence, 407
Programming. *See also* Coding
    introduction to graphics, 1-14
    tips for graphics, 6
    top-down, 3
Programs, documenting graphics, 424
Projection, 139, 163
Projection coordinate system, 139
projectr( ), 448
PROJECTR.C, 143, 506
Prototypical systems, 47
PUBLIC reference, 454
push dbl( ), 448
PUSHPOP.C, 542
put__out( ), 257, 448
PUT OUT.C, 344
putdata( ), 448
PUTDATA.C, 410, 564
putega( ), 448
PUTEGA.C, 521, 651
putrow( ), 448
Quit GRAPHIQ function, 621
Radial chording, 185
RAM, 8, 122, 161
    writing text into, 216
Random-access files, 53
Raster
    input from disk, 652
    output to disk, 649
Rasters, 51, 72
re__vid( ), 300
read__char( ), 449
read__pix2( ), 449
readbuff( ), 369, 448
READCHAR.C, 230
Reading
    address values, 159
    and writing values, 655
    stroke fonts, 229
readpt( ), 449

READPT.C, 525
Reals, floating-point, 37, 40
Received Line Signal Detect (RLSD), 361
rectangl( ), 449
RECTANGL.C, 495
Rectangular
    coordinates, 64
    figures, 191
    fills, 390
recursion( ), 467
Red, green, blue, 24
Redirection of I/O, 9
References, external and internal, 456
Registers
    functions of 3CFh, 304
    graphics controller, 304
Relative coordinates, 376
Reset
    function, 619
    printer, 108
Resetting the controller, 162
Resolution
    display, 17
    effects of aliasing on, 78
    integer values and, 172
    system and display, 395
restport( ), 449
RESTPORT.C, 542
retkey( ), 313, 449
RETKEY.C, 553
retrieve( ), 449
RETRIEVE.C, 412, 541
Reverse-video text cursors, 295
RGB, 24
    Image Capture Board, 45
Ring Indicator (RI), 361
ROM, characters stored in, 218
rotate( ), 449
ROTATE.C, 129, 500
rotate3d( ), 450
ROTATE3D.C, 131, 500
rotatec( ), 449
Rotation, 128, 169, 390
    and translation, combining, 137
    function, 619
    incremental, 169
    reversal of compound three-dimensional, 130
    state, 130
    three-dimensional, 130
rotloc( ), 336
ROTLOC.C, 337
Round-off errors, 122
SAVE__BKG.C, 293
Scale, changing, 392
Scale function, 619
scale( ), 450

SCALE.C, 135, 498
Scaling, 134, 390-391
    three-dimensional, 135
Scientific graphics, 62
Screen, printing 260
Screen dump, 51
Screen-write, fast, 10
SCREEN.H, 592
SEND__SER.ASM, 383
Sequential files, 52
Serial
    adapter base addresses, 353
    control register, 359
    interface, timing considerations with, 278
    interface for plotters, wiring diagram of, 269
    interface registers, 354-356
    interfacing, 352-385
    interfacing, polled, 374
    interrupt service, 362
    output interfacing, 382
    registers, 356
    status register, 361
Serial port, 362
    initializing, 271
Serial port mnemonics, 402
Serial ports, 352-386
SERIR.ASM, 363
SERISR.ASM, 450, 538
SET BAUD.C, 360
set__curs( ), 450
setvect( ), 450
Shape coordinate list, 119
Shape matrix, 118
Shape tables, 116, 213
    BIOS, 221
    cell specification for, 118
Shapes, rotating, translating, and scaling, 116
SHOW__BYT.C, 35
SHOWCHAR.C, 223
Small memory model, 42
Smoothing, 93
Snap, 391
Software design, graphics, 15-46
Spacing, controlling, 250
Spatial applications, 175
Stack, controlling, 467
Stack overflow, 629
    avoiding, 38
Starting point, specifying line, 615
Startup, program, 394
Status menu, 241
status( ), 257, 450
stdaux, 262
stdprn, 257
Stick parity, 359
Storage device, GRAPHIQ, 50

store( ), 450
STORE.C, 413, 547
stretch( ), 450
STRETCH.C, 136, 499
String objects, 120
Strings, moving to display, 290
Stroke character, 119, 226
Stroke fonts, 220
    BIOS, 225
    reading, 229
    sample, 242
    using, 232
Structure, program, 2
Structure flow diagrams, 39
Structures and unions, 38
Stylus, 322
Subtractive colors, 97
Surface modeling, 61
Surfaces, 321
swap( ), 451
SWAP.C, 498
Symbolic names, 455
symmetry( ), 451
SYSFILES directory, 435
System resolution, 395
System state variables, 404
TARGA board, AT&T, 46
Tasks, allocating, 418
Television, 44
    graphics, 639-660
    source, dithering from, 99
Termination, program, 394
Termination sequence, program, 407
TEST DIG.C, 372
TESTCHAR.C, 234
Text
    drawing, 391
    functions, 241, 619
    hard copy, 242
    mode, 213-244
    mode, pop-up menus in EGA, 289
    orchestration of, 240
Text background
    restoring, 290
    saving, 290
TEXTDISP.C, 291
textout( ), 451
TEXTOUT.C, 549
Three-dimensional
    line-drawing, 175
    modeling, 61
    rotation, 130
    rotation, reversal of compound, 132
    scaling, 135
    translation, 134
Three-point circle, 85
TMP files, 437

Toolkit
    graphics, 441
    linking, 453-470
Toolkit library, creating, 465
Top-down programming, 3
    misconceptions about, 5
Tranformations, combined, 137
Transcendentals, 85, 128
Transfer algorithm, 641
TRANSFER.C, 656
Transformation sequence, 137
Transformations, 125-146
    using Assembler to optimize, 145
translate( ), 451
TRANSLATE.C, 133, 499
Translation, 132, 391
    three-dimensional, 134
Translation and rotation, combining, 137
TrueVision hardware, AT&T, 639
Tutorial, 422
TV hard copy, 46
Two-dimensional attributes, 57
Typedef declaration, 33
UART, 277
UNINSTAL.C, 368, 537
uninstall( ), 451
Unions, 38, 53
unsetvec( ), 451
User units, 273
VALREG, 156
Variable names, 13
Variables, 108
    double-precision, 115
    system state, 404
    using, 58
Vector list, 95
Vectors, 51
verline( ), 451
VERLINE.C, 497
Vertical lines, drawing, with DEBUG, 27
Vertical spacing, 250
Video camera, using, 640
Video capture, 203
Video Display Adapter, 44
WIDTH, 157
Windows, clipping, 109
WRITE AR.C, 287
write__array( ), 451
write__char( ), 452
write__str( ), 452
Writing address values, 161
xform( ), 452
XFORM.C, 138, 530
XMAX, YMAX, 395
XON-XOFF protocol, 271
XOR, 294